# Data Modeling with

A practical guide to accelerating Snowflake development using universal data modeling techniques

**Serge Gershkovich**

‹packt›

BIRMINGHAM—MUMBAI

# Data Modeling with Snowflake

Copyright © 2023 Packt Publishing

*All rights reserved.* No part of this book may be reproduced, stored in a retrieval system, or transmitted in any form or by any means, without the prior written permission of the publisher, except in the case of brief quotations embedded in critical articles or reviews.

Every effort has been made in the preparation of this book to ensure the accuracy of the information presented. However, the information contained in this book is sold without warranty, either express or implied. Neither the author, nor Packt Publishing or its dealers and distributors, will be held liable for any damages caused or alleged to have been caused directly or indirectly by this book.

Packt Publishing has endeavored to provide trademark information about all of the companies and products mentioned in this book by the appropriate use of capitals. However, Packt Publishing cannot guarantee the accuracy of this information.

**Group Product Manager**: Reshma Raman
**Publishing Product Manager**: Apeksha Shetty
**Content Development Editor**: Manikandan Kurup
**Technical Editor**: Sweety Pagaria
**Copy Editor**: Safis Editing
**Project Coordinator**: Farheen Fathima
**Proofreader**: Safis Editing
**Indexer**: Hemangini Bari
**Production Designer**: Shankar Kalbhor
**Marketing Coordinator**: Nivedita Singh
**Cover Design**: Elena Kadantseva

First published: May 2023

Production reference: 2180523

Published by Packt Publishing Ltd.
Livery Place
35 Livery Street
Birmingham
B3 2PB, UK.

ISBN 978-1-83763-445-3

www.packtpub.com

*To Elena, the entity without whose relationship none of this data could have been modeled.*

*– Serge Gershkovich*

# Foreword

My first exposure to relational design and modeling concepts was in the late 1980s. I had built a few things in dBase II in the early '80s, then Dbase III a little later, but had no formal training. On a US government contract, a forward-looking manager of mine asked me if I was interested in learning something new about designing databases that he had just learned. He then walked me through the material from a class on entity-relationship modeling and normalization (taught by IBM) that he had just returned from (they were actually copies of transparencies from the class). It was amazing and made so much sense to me. That was when I learned about forms of normalization, which led me to read more in a book by Dr. CJ Date and eventually into building new databases using an early version of Oracle (version 5.1a to be exact).

Initially, I drew models on paper and whiteboards, starting with the Chen-style notation. Eventually, I did them with primitive drawing tools (such as MacDraw!) long before modern data modeling tools were available.

To say things have changed in the last few decades is an understatement.

We now have modern cloud-based, high-performance databases such as Snowflake and cloud-based data modeling and design tools such as SqlDBM. What we can do today with data and these tools is something I never dreamed of (e.g., I can now easily switch between modeling notations such as Chen, IE, and Barker on-the-fly).

For nearly a decade, during the initial era of Big Data, Hadoop, and NoSQL, it was declared far and wide, "Data modeling is dead." While many of us cringed and knew that was false, worse, we also knew that the sentiment would lead to big problems down the road (data swamps, anyone?). Unfortunately, the next generation, and other newbies, joining the industry during those times got zero exposure to data modeling of any form or the logic and theory behind it.

As the industry evolved and the cloud entered the picture, people started asking questions such as, "How will we ever get a handle on all this data?" and "How are we going to make it usable to our business users?" If only there were a way to draw a picture or map that most people could read and understand…

What a concept!

And thus, data modeling reentered the popular discussion in blogs, podcasts, webinars, and the like.

But now the question became, "Do we need to model differently for modern data and data platforms?"

Yes and no.

The fundamentals and benefits of database modeling have not changed. However, the cloud-native architecture of modern platforms such as Snowflake has redefined the rules (and costs) of how data is stored, shared, and processed. This book is an excellent start in bridging the time-tested techniques of relational database modeling with the revolutionary features and facets of Snowflake's scalable data platform. It is appropriate for those new to the concept of data modeling as well as veteran data modelers who are beginning to work with modern cloud databases.

In this book, Serge takes you from the history of data modeling and its various forms and notations to exploring the core features of Snowflake architecture to construct performant and cost-effective solutions. By learning to apply these decades-old, proven approaches to the revolutionary features of The Data Cloud, you can better leverage the data assets in your organization to remain competitive and become a 21st-century data-driven organization.

With all this in context, this book will be your guide and a launchpad into the world of modern data modeling in The Data Cloud.

Enjoy!


#LongLiveDataModeling


Kent Graziano, The Data Warrior

May 2023

# Contributors

## About the author

**Serge Gershkovich** is a seasoned data architect with decades of experience designing and maintaining enterprise-scale data warehouse platforms and reporting solutions. He is a leading subject matter expert, speaker, content creator, and Snowflake Data Superhero. Serge earned a bachelor of science degree in information systems from the **State University of New York** (**SUNY**) Stony Brook. Throughout his career, Serge has worked in model-driven development from SAP BW/HANA to dashboard design to cost-effective cloud analytics with Snowflake. He currently serves as product success lead at SqlDBM, an online database modeling tool.

*I want to thank Anna, Ed, and Ajay for recognizing the potential that even I didn't know I had. This book happened thanks to your guidance and encouragement. To my loving wife, Elena, thank you for your unwavering support throughout this process.*

## About the reviewers

**Hazal Sener** is a senior developer advocate at SqlDBM. She graduated with honors from Istanbul Technical University and earned a master's degree in geomatics engineering. Following her studies, Hazal started her career in the **geographic information system** (**GIS**) surveying industry, where, over five years ago, she discovered her passion for data. In 2019, Hazal joined the Business Intelligence team at a top-five **business-to-business** (**B2B**) bed bank as a data warehouse modeler and built warehouse models and transformational pipelines and optimized SQL queries there. Hazal's passion for data leads her to her current position as a senior developer advocate at SqlDBM. In this role, Hazal provides technical guidance and educates clients on the tool's features and capabilities.

**Oliver Cramer** is owner of data provisioning at Aquila Capital. As product manager of a data warehouse, he is responsible for guiding various teams. Creating guidelines and standards is also within his scope. His current focus is building larger teams under the heading of analytics engineering.

**Keith Belanger** is a very passionate data professional. With over 25 years of experience in data architecture and information management, he is highly experienced at assembling and directing high-performing data-focused teams and solutions. He combines a deep technical and data background with a business-oriented mindset. He enjoys working with business and IT teams on data strategies to solve everyday business problems. He is a recognized Snowflake Data Superhero, Certified Data Vault 2.0 Practitioner, Co-Chair of the Boston Snowflake User Group, and North America Data Vault User Group board member. He has worked in the data and analytics space in a wide range of verticals, including manufacturing, property and casualty insurance, life insurance, and health care.

# Table of Contents

Preface — xvii

# Part 1: Core Concepts in Data Modeling and Snowflake Architecture

## 1

## Unlocking the Power of Modeling — 3

| | | | |
|---|---|---|---|
| Technical requirements | 4 | What modeling looks like in operational systems | 12 |
| Modeling with purpose | 4 | What modeling looks like in analytical systems | 13 |
| Leveraging the modeling toolkit | 5 | | |
| The benefits of database modeling | 7 | Summary | 15 |
| Operational and analytical modeling scenarios | 10 | Further reading | 15 |
| | | References | 15 |
| A look at relational and transformational modeling | 11 | | |

## 2

## An Introduction to the Four Modeling Types — 17

| | | | |
|---|---|---|---|
| Design and process | 18 | What it is | 25 |
| Ubiquitous modeling | 18 | What it looks like | 26 |
| Conceptual | 21 | Physical modeling | 28 |
| What it is | 21 | What it is | 28 |
| What it looks like | 23 | What about views? | 29 |
| Logical | 25 | What it looks like | 29 |

| Transformational | 30 | Summary | 32 |
| --- | --- | --- | --- |
| What it is | 31 | Further reading | 33 |
| What it looks like | 31 | | |

# 3

## Mastering Snowflake's Architecture — 35

| Traditional architectures | 36 | Costs to consider | 42 |
| --- | --- | --- | --- |
| Shared-disk architecture | 37 | Storage costs | 42 |
| Shared-nothing architecture | 37 | Compute costs | 43 |
| Snowflake's solution | 38 | Service costs | 43 |
| Snowflake's three-tier architecture | 39 | Saving cash by using cache | 43 |
| Storage layer | 40 | Services layer | 44 |
| Compute layer | 40 | Metadata cache | 44 |
| Services layer | 40 | Query results cache | 44 |
| Snowflake's features | 40 | Warehouse cache | 45 |
| Zero-copy cloning | 41 | Storage layer | 45 |
| Time Travel | 41 | Summary | 45 |
| Hybrid Unistore tables | 41 | Further reading | 46 |
| Beyond structured data | 42 | | |

# 4

## Mastering Snowflake Objects — 47

| Stages | 47 | Stage metadata tables | 54 |
| --- | --- | --- | --- |
| File formats | 49 | External tables | 54 |
| Tables | 49 | Directory tables | 54 |
| Physical tables | 50 | Snowflake views | 55 |
| Permanent tables | 51 | Caching | 55 |
| Transient tables | 51 | Security | 56 |
| Temporary tables | 52 | Materialized views | 56 |
| Hybrid Unistore tables | 52 | Streams | 57 |
| Table types summary | 53 | Loading from streams | 58 |

| | | | |
|---|---|---|---|
| Change tracking | 59 | Summary | 62 |
| Tasks | 60 | References | 62 |
| Combining tasks and streams | 62 | | |

# 5

# Speaking Modeling through Snowflake Objects — 63

| | | | |
|---|---|---|---|
| **Entities as tables** | 64 | Keys taxonomy | 77 |
| How Snowflake stores data | 64 | Business key | 78 |
| Clustering | 67 | Surrogate key | 78 |
| Automatic clustering | 69 | Sequences | 78 |
| **Attributes as columns** | 70 | **Alternate keys as unique constraints** | 80 |
| Snowflake data types | 71 | **Relationships as foreign keys** | 81 |
| Storing semi-structured data | 72 | Benefits of an FK | 84 |
| **Constraints and enforcement** | 73 | Visualizing the data model | 84 |
| **Identifiers as primary keys** | 74 | Informing joins | 84 |
| Benefits of a PK | 75 | Automating functionality in BI tools | 85 |
| | | Enforcing referential integrity (Hybrid Unistore) | 85 |
| Determining granularity | 75 | | |
| Ensuring correct join results | 76 | **Mandatory columns as NOT NULL constraints** | 86 |
| Avoiding duplicate values (Hybrid Unistore) | 76 | | |
| Specifying a PK | 77 | **Summary** | 87 |

# 6

# Seeing Snowflake's Architecture through Modeling Notation — 89

| | | | |
|---|---|---|---|
| **A history of relational modeling** | 90 | Adding conceptual context to Snowflake architecture | 98 |
| **RM versus entity-relationship diagram** | 91 | Many-to-many | 98 |
| **Visual modeling conventions** | 93 | Representing subtypes and supertypes | 99 |
| Depicting entities | 94 | **The benefit of synchronized modeling** | 101 |
| Depicting relationships | 95 | | |
| Crow's foot | 95 | **Summary** | 102 |
| IDEF1X | 97 | | |

# Part 2: Applied Modeling from Idea to Deployment

## 7

## Putting Conceptual Modeling into Practice — 105

| | | | |
|---|---|---|---|
| **Embarking on conceptual design** | **106** | Identify the facts | 111 |
| Dimensional modeling | 106 | From bus matrix to a conceptual model | 112 |
| Understanding dimensional modeling | 106 | **Modeling in reverse** | **113** |
| Setting the record straight on dimensional modeling | 106 | Identify the facts and dimensions | 114 |
| Starting a conceptual model in four easy steps | 107 | Establish the relationships | 115 |
| Define the business process | 109 | Propose and validate the business processes | 117 |
| Determine the grain | 110 | **Summary** | **117** |
| Determine the dimensions | 110 | **Further reading** | **118** |

## 8

## Putting Logical Modeling into Practice — 119

| | | | |
|---|---|---|---|
| **Expanding from conceptual to logical modeling** | **120** | Many-to-many relationships | 123 |
| | | Weak entities | 126 |
| **Adding attributes** | **120** | Inheritance | 128 |
| **Cementing the relationships** | **122** | **Summary** | **131** |

## 9

## Database Normalization — 133

| | | | |
|---|---|---|---|
| **An overview of database normalization** | **134** | **Database normalization through examples** | **138** |
| **Data anomalies** | **135** | 1NF | 138 |
| Update anomaly | 135 | 2NF | 139 |
| Insertion anomaly | 136 | 3NF | 140 |
| Deletion anomaly | 137 | BCNF | 141 |
| Domain anomaly | 137 | 4NF | 143 |

| | | | |
|---|---|---|---|
| 5NF | 144 | Data models on a spectrum of normalization | 149 |
| DKNF | 146 | | |
| 6NF | 147 | Summary | 150 |

# 10
# Database Naming and Structure 151

| | | | |
|---|---|---|---|
| **Naming conventions** | 152 | Managed schemas | 157 |
| Case | 152 | OLTP versus OLAP database structures | 158 |
| Object naming | 153 | Source layer | 158 |
| Tables | 153 | Staging layer | 159 |
| Primary key columns | 154 | Normalized self-service analytics | 160 |
| Foreign key constraints | 155 | Denormalized reporting analytics | 160 |
| Suggested conventions | 156 | Departmental data | 161 |
| **Organizing a Snowflake database** | 157 | Database environments | 161 |
| Organization of databases and schemas | 157 | **Summary** | 163 |

# 11
# Putting Physical Modeling into Practice 165

| | | | |
|---|---|---|---|
| **Technical requirements** | 166 | Physicalizing the logical objects | 169 |
| **Considerations before starting the implementation** | 166 | Defining the tables | 171 |
| | | Naming | 171 |
| Performance | 166 | Table properties | 171 |
| Cost | 166 | Declaring constraints | 172 |
| Data quality and integrity | 167 | **Deploying a physical model** | 174 |
| Data security | 167 | **Creating an ERD from a physical model** | 174 |
| Non-considerations | 168 | | |
| **Expanding from logical to physical modeling** | 168 | **Summary** | 176 |

# Part 3: Solving Real-World Problems with Transformational Modeling

## 12
## Putting Transformational Modeling into Practice — 179

| | | | |
|---|---|---|---|
| Technical requirements | 180 | Performance considerations and monitoring | 189 |
| Separating the model from the object | 180 | Common query problems | 190 |
| Shaping transformations through relationships | 180 | Additional query considerations | 192 |
| Join elimination using constraints | 183 | Putting transformational modeling into practice | 193 |
| When to use RELY for join elimination | 184 | Gathering the business requirements | 193 |
| When to be careful using RELY | 185 | Reviewing the relational model | 194 |
| Joins and set operators | 187 | Building the transformational model | 195 |
| | | Summary | 197 |

## 13
## Modeling Slowly Changing Dimensions — 199

| | | | |
|---|---|---|---|
| Technical requirements | 200 | Type 7 – complete as-at flexibility | 207 |
| Dimensions overview | 200 | Overview of SCD types | 208 |
| SCD types | 200 | Recipes for maintaining SCDs in Snowflake | 209 |
| Example scenario | 200 | Setting the stage | 209 |
| Type 0 – maintain original | 201 | Type 1 – merge | 210 |
| Type 1 – overwrite | 201 | Type 2 – Type 1-like performance using streams | 212 |
| Type 2 – add a new row | 202 | | |
| Type 3 – add a new column | 202 | Type 3 – one-time update | 215 |
| Type 4 – add a mini dimension | 203 | Summary | 216 |
| Type 5 – Type 4 mini dimension + Type 1 | 204 | | |
| Type 6 – the Type 1,2,3 hybrid | 206 | | |

# 14

## Modeling Facts for Rapid Analysis 217

| | | | |
|---|---|---|---|
| Technical requirements | 218 | Maintaining fact tables using | |
| Fact table types | 218 | Snowflake features | 226 |
| Fact table measures | 219 | Building a reverse balance fact table with Streams | 227 |
| Getting the facts straight | 220 | Recovering deleted records with leading load dates | 230 |
| The world's most versatile transactional fact table | 220 | Handling time intervals in a Type 2 fact table | 233 |
| The leading method for recovering deleted records | 222 | Summary | 236 |
| Type 2 slowly changing facts | 224 | | |

# 15

## Modeling Semi-Structured Data 237

| | | | |
|---|---|---|---|
| Technical requirements | 238 | Schema-on-read != schema-no-need | 242 |
| The benefits of semi-structured data in Snowflake | 238 | Converting semi-structured data into relational data | 245 |
| Getting hands-on with semi-structured data | 239 | Summary | 251 |

# 16

## Modeling Hierarchies 253

| | | | |
|---|---|---|---|
| Technical requirements | 254 | Maintaining hierarchies in Snowflake | 258 |
| Understanding and distinguishing between hierarchies | 254 | Recursively navigating a ragged hierarchy | 258 |
| A fixed-depth hierarchy | 254 | Handling changes | 261 |
| A slightly ragged hierarchy | 255 | Summary | 261 |
| A ragged hierarchy | 256 | | |

# 17

## Scaling Data Models through Modern Techniques — 263

| | | | |
|---|---|---|---|
| Technical requirements | 264 | Star schema | 274 |
| Demystifying Data Vault 2.0 | 264 | Snowflake schema | 274 |
| Building the Raw Vault | 266 | **Discovering Data Mesh** | **275** |
| Hubs | 267 | Start with the business | 276 |
| Links | 268 | Adopt governance guidelines | 277 |
| Satellites | 269 | Emphasize data quality | 277 |
| Reference tables | 270 | Encourage a culture of data sharing | 277 |
| Loading with multi-table inserts | 271 | **Summary** | **278** |
| Modeling the data marts | 273 | | |

# 18

## Appendix — 281

| | | | |
|---|---|---|---|
| Technical requirements | 281 | Read the functional manual (RTFM) | 282 |
| The exceptional time traveler | 281 | Summary | 283 |
| The secret column type Snowflake refuses to document | 282 | | |

## Index — 285

## Other Books You May Enjoy — 296

# Preface

Snowflake is one of the leading cloud data platforms and is gaining popularity among organizations looking to migrate their data to the cloud. With its game-changing features, Snowflake is unlocking new possibilities for self-service analytics and collaboration. However, Snowflake's scalable consumption-based pricing model demands that users fully understand its revolutionary three-tier cloud architecture and pair it with universal modeling principles to ensure they are unlocking value and not letting money vaporize into the cloud.

Data modeling is essential for building scalable and cost-effective designs in data warehousing. Effective modeling techniques not only help businesses build efficient data models but also enable them to better understand their business. Though modeling is largely database-agnostic, pairing modeling techniques with game-changing Snowflake features can help build Snowflake's most performant and cost-effective solutions.

This book combines the best practices in data modeling with Snowflake's powerful features to offer you the most efficient and effective approach to data modeling in Snowflake. Using these techniques, you can optimize your data warehousing processes, improve your organization's data-driven decision-making capabilities, and save valuable time and resources.

## Who this book is for

Database modeling is a simple, yet foundational tool for enhancing communication and decision-making within enterprise teams and streamlining development. By pairing modeling-first principles with the specifics of Snowflake architecture, this book will serve as an effective tool for data engineers looking to build cost-effective Snowflake systems for business users looking for an easy way to understand them.

The three main personas who are the target audience of this content are as follows:

- **Data engineers**: This book takes a Snowflake-centered approach to designing data models. It pairs universal modeling principles with unique architectural facets of the data cloud to help build performant and cost-effective solutions.
- **Data architects**: While familiar with modeling concepts, many architects may be new to the Snowflake platform and are eager to learn and incorporate its best features into their designs for improved efficiency and maintenance.
- **Business analysts**: Many analysts transition from business or functional roles and are cast into the world of data without a formal introduction to database best practices and modeling conventions. This book will give them the tools to navigate their data landscape and confidently create their own models and analyses.

# What this book covers

*Chapter 1*, *Unlocking the Power of Modeling*, explores the role that models play in simplifying and guiding our everyday experience. This chapter unpacks the concept of modeling into its constituents: natural language, technical, and visual semantics. This chapter also gives you a glimpse into how modeling differs across various types of databases.

*Chapter 2*, *An Introduction to the Four Modeling Types*, looks at the four types of modeling covered in this book: conceptual, logical, physical, and transformational. This chapter gives an overview of where and how each type of modeling is used and what it looks like. This foundation gives you a taste of where the upcoming chapters will lead.

*Chapter 3*, *Mastering Snowflake's Architecture*, provides a history of the evolution of database architectures and highlights the advances that make the data cloud a game changer in scalable computing. Understanding the underlying architecture will inform how Snowflake's three-tier architecture unlocks unique capabilities in the models we design in later chapters.

*Chapter 4*, *Mastering Snowflake Objects*, explores the various Snowflake objects we will use in our modeling exercises throughout the book. This chapter looks at the memory footprints of the different table types, change tracking through streams, and the use of tasks to automate data transformations, among many other topics.

*Chapter 5*, *Speaking Modeling through Snowflake Objects*, bridges universal modeling concepts such as entities and relationships with accompanying Snowflake architecture, storage, and handling. This chapter breaks down the fundamentals of Snowflake data storage, detailing micro partitions and clustering so that you can make informed and cost-effective design decisions.

*Chapter 6*, *Seeing Snowflake's Architecture through Modeling Notation*, explores why there are so many competing and overlapping visual notations in modeling and how to use the ones that work. This chapter zeroes in on the most concise and intuitive notations you can use to plan and design database models and make them accessible to business users simultaneously.

*Chapter 7*, *Putting Conceptual Modeling into Practice*, starts the journey of creating a conceptual model by engaging with domain experts from the business and understanding the elements of the underlying business. This chapter uses Kimball's dimensional modeling method to identify the facts and dimensions, establish the bus matrix, and launch the design process. We also explore how to work backward using the same technique to align a physical model to a business model.

*Chapter 8*, *Putting Logical Modeling into Practice*, continues the modeling journey by expanding the conceptual model with attributes and business nuance. This chapter explores how to resolve many-to-many relationships, expand weak entities, and tackle inheritance in modeling entities.

*Chapter 9*, *Database Normalization*, demonstrates that *normal* doesn't necessarily mean *better*—there are trade-offs. While most database models fall within the first to third normal forms, this chapter takes you all the way to the sixth, with detailed examples to illustrate the differences. This chapter also explores the various data anomalies that normalization aims to mitigate.

*Chapter 10*, *Database Naming and Structure*, takes the ambiguity out of database object naming and proposes a clear and consistent standard. This chapter focuses on the conventions that will enable you to scale and adjust your model and avoid breaking downstream processes. By considering how Snowflake handles cases and uniqueness, you can make confident and consistent design decisions for your physical objects.

*Chapter 11*, *Putting Physical Modeling into Practice*, translates the logical model from the previous chapter into a fully deployable physical model. In this process, we handle the security and governance concerns accompanying a physical model and its deployment. This chapter also explores physicalizing logical inheritance and demonstrates how to go from DDL to generating a visual diagram.

*Chapter 12*, *Putting Transformational Modeling into Practice*, demonstrates how to use the physical model to drive transformational design and improve performance gains through join elimination in Snowflake. The chapter discusses the types of joins and set operators available in Snowflake and provides guidance on monitoring Snowflake queries to identify common issues. Using these techniques, you will practice creating transformational designs from business requirements.

*Chapter 13*, *Modeling Slowly Changing Dimensions*, delves into the concept of **slowly changing dimensions (SCDs)** and provides you with recipes for maintaining SCDs efficiently using Snowflake features. You will learn about the challenges of keeping record counts in dimension tables in check and how mini dimensions can help address this issue. The chapter also discusses creating multifunctional surrogate keys and compares them with hashing techniques.

*Chapter 14*, *Modeling Facts for Rapid Analysis*, focuses on fact tables and explains the different types of fact tables and measures. You will discover versatile reporting structures such as the reverse balance and range-based factless facts and learn how to recover deleted records. This chapter also provides related Snowflake recipes for building and maintaining all the operations mentioned.

*Chapter 15*, *Modeling Semi-Structured Data*, explores techniques required to use and model semi-structured data in Snowflake. This chapter demonstrates that while Snowflake makes querying semi-structured data easy, there is effort involved in transforming it into a relational format that users can understand. We explore the benefits of converting semi-structured data to a relational schema and review a rule-based method for doing so.

*Chapter 16*, *Modeling Hierarchies*, provides you with an understanding of the different types of hierarchies and their uses in data warehouses. The chapter distinguishes between hierarchy types and discusses modeling techniques for maintaining each of them. You will also learn about Snowflake features for traversing a recursive tree structure and techniques for handling changes in hierarchy dimensions.

*Chapter 17*, *Scaling Data Models through Modern Frameworks*, discusses the utility of Data Vault methodology in modern data platforms and how it addresses the challenges of managing large, complex, and rapidly changing data environments. This chapter also discusses the efficient loading of the Data Vault with multi-table inserts and creating Star and Snowflake schema models for reporting information marts. Additionally, you will be introduced to Data Mesh and its application in managing data in large, complex organizations. Finally, the chapter reviews modeling best practices mentioned throughout the book.

*Chapter 18*, *Appendix*, collects all the fun and practical Snowflake recipes that couldn't fit into the structure of the main chapters. This chapter showcases useful techniques such as the exceptional time traveler, exposes the (secret) virtual column type, and more!

## To get the most out of this book

This book will rely heavily on the design and use of visual modeling diagrams. While a diagram can be drawn by hand, maintained in Excel, or constructed in PowerPoint, a modeling tool with dedicated layouts and functions is recommended. As the exercises in this book will take you from conceptual database-agnostic diagrams to deployable and runnable Snowflake code, a tool that supports Snowflake syntax and can generate deployable DDL is recommended.

This book uses visual examples from SqlDBM, an online database modeling tool that supports Snowflake. A free trial is available on their website here: https://sqldbm.com/Home/.

Another popular online diagramming solution is LucidChart (https://www.lucidchart.com/pages/). Although LucidChart does not support Snowflake as of this writing, it also offers a free tier for designing ER diagrams as well as other models such as **Unified Modeling Language** (**UML**) and network diagrams.

| Software/hardware covered in the book | Operating system requirements |
| --- | --- |
| Snowflake Data Cloud | Windows, macOS, or Linux |
| SQL | Windows, macOS, or Linux |

**If you are using the digital version of this book, we advise you to type the code yourself or access the code from the book's GitHub repository (a link is available in the next section). Doing so will help you avoid any potential errors related to the copying and pasting of code.**

## Download the example code files

You can download the example code files for this book from GitHub at https://github.com/PacktPublishing/Data-Modeling-with-Snowflake. If there's an update to the code, it will be updated in the GitHub repository.

We also have other code bundles from our rich catalog of books and videos available at https://github.com/PacktPublishing/. Check them out!

## Conventions used

There are a number of text conventions used throughout this book.

`Code in text`: Indicates code words in text, database table names, folder names, filenames, file extensions, pathnames, dummy URLs, user input, and Twitter handles. Here is an example: "Adding a discriminator between the CUSTOMER supertype and the LOYALTY_CUSTOMER subtype adds context that would otherwise be lost at the database level."

A block of code is set as follows:

```
-- Query the change tracking metadata to observe
-- only inserts from the timestamp till now
select * from myTable
changes(information => append_only)
at(timestamp => $cDts);
```

**Bold**: Indicates a new term, an important word, or words that you see onscreen. For instance, words in menus or dialog boxes appear in **bold**. Here is an example: "**Subtypes** share common characteristics with a **supertype** entity but have additional attributes that make them distinct."

> **Tips or important notes**
> Appear like this.

## Get in touch

Feedback from our readers is always welcome.

**General feedback**: If you have questions about any aspect of this book, email us at `customercare@packtpub.com` and mention the book title in the subject of your message.

**Errata**: Although we have taken every care to ensure the accuracy of our content, mistakes do happen. If you have found a mistake in this book, we would be grateful if you would report this to us. Please visit `www.packtpub.com/support/errata` and fill in the form.

**Piracy**: If you come across any illegal copies of our works in any form on the internet, we would be grateful if you would provide us with the location address or website name. Please contact us at `copyright@packt.com` with a link to the material.

**If you are interested in becoming an author**: If there is a topic that you have expertise in and you are interested in either writing or contributing to a book, please visit `authors.packtpub.com`.

## Share Your Thoughts

Once you've read *Data Modeling with Snowflake*, we'd love to hear your thoughts! Scan the QR code below to go straight to the Amazon review page for this book and share your feedback.

https://packt.link/r/1-837-63445-9

Your review is important to us and the tech community and will help us make sure we're delivering excellent quality content.

## Download a free PDF copy of this book

Thanks for purchasing this book!

Do you like to read on the go but are unable to carry your print books everywhere? Is your eBook purchase not compatible with the device of your choice?

Don't worry, now with every Packt book you get a DRM-free PDF version of that book at no cost.

Read anywhere, any place, on any device. Search, copy, and paste code from your favorite technical books directly into your application.

The perks don't stop there, you can get exclusive access to discounts, newsletters, and great free content in your inbox daily

Follow these simple steps to get the benefits:

1. Scan the QR code or visit the link below

https://packt.link/free-ebook/9781837634453

2. Submit your proof of purchase
3. That's it! We'll send your free PDF and other benefits to your email directly

# Part 1: Core Concepts in Data Modeling and Snowflake Architecture

This part provides you with a comprehensive overview of the power and potential of data modeling within the Snowflake cloud data platform. You will be introduced to the fundamental concepts and techniques that underpin effective modeling, including the importance of understanding data relationships and the role of modeling in driving better business outcomes. This part also includes a detailed examination of the four different types of modeling, highlighting their benefits and use cases. Finally, we focus specifically on Snowflake architecture and objects, exploring how to master this powerful platform and optimize it for maximum performance and value. Through a combination of theoretical insights and practical examples, you will gain a deep understanding of how to use modeling to unlock the full potential of Snowflake and transform your approach to data management and analysis.

This part has the following chapters:

- *Chapter 1, Unlocking the Power of Modeling*
- *Chapter 2, An Introduction to the Four Modeling Types*
- *Chapter 3, Mastering Snowflake's Architecture*
- *Chapter 4, Mastering Snowflake Objects*
- *Chapter 5, Speaking Modeling through Snowflake Objects*
- *Chapter 6, Seeing Snowflake's Architecture through Modeling Notation*

# 1
# Unlocking the Power of Modeling

The word *modeling* has come to mean very different things in the half a century that it has been practiced in database systems. This opening chapter prefaces the book's overall aim to demystify modeling, along with its applications, methodologies, and benefits. Throughout this journey, the concept of modeling will unfold into a set of methods and terms that help organizations design and manage data and, more importantly, help them understand themselves.

In its broadest interpretation, modeling is a selective simplification that aids in navigating or designing something more complex. Any system can be broken down into smaller, more manageable pieces. Manipulating any piece individually may be straightforward, but doing so without regard to an overall strategy is a tenuous proposal that is sure to encumber scalability and maintenance down the line.

While modeling is generally considered database-agnostic, modern cloud data platforms, such as Snowflake, present their users with many unique features thanks to their innovative architecture and consumption-based pricing. A clear and forward-looking design that takes advantage of the native features of the platform that supports it is the key to building cost-effective solutions capable of meeting and anticipating business needs.

As the analytical requirements of a data-driven organization are notoriously complex and constantly evolving, modeling must keep pace and accompany data teams from idea to execution. To achieve this, modeling must go beyond the structure and relationships of database tables and embrace the transformational logic that moves and shapes the underlying data. Only by leaning into the specifics of Snowflake features and architecture can a model be built efficiently from beginning to end.

In this chapter, we're going to cover the following main topics:

- Recognizing the utility of models in our daily lives
- Getting a glimpse of modeling conventions in action
- Getting acquainted with the tools in the modeling toolkit

- Uncovering the benefits of modeling for enterprise teams
- Incorporating modeling into strategic planning
- Understanding modeling applications for transactional and analytical systems

## Technical requirements

This book focuses on data modeling specifically for the Snowflake Data Cloud. While modeling includes many system-agnostic terms and conventions, this book will leverage unique features of Snowflake architecture, data types, and functions when building physical models and **Structured Query Language** (**SQL**) transformations.

To follow along with the exercises in the following chapters, you will need a Snowflake account with access to a sandbox area for creating schemas, objects, and loading data.

You can sign up for a 30-day free trial of Snowflake (`https://signup.snowflake.com/`) if you do not already have access.

This book will frequently use visual modeling diagrams as part of the modeling process. While a diagram can be drawn by hand and constructed in PowerPoint or Lucidchart, a tool that supports common database modeling features is recommended. The exercises in this book will take the reader from conceptual database-agnostic diagrams to deployable and runnable Snowflake code. For this reason, a tool that supports various modeling types and can forward engineer Snowflake syntax is recommended.

The diagrams in this book were generated using the SqlDBM online database modeling tool (`https://sqldbm.com/Home/`), which supports the previously mentioned features and offers a 2-week free trial.

## Modeling with purpose

Models are used to simplify complex systems. Take a modern city as an example, and you will see that it consists of intricately linked systems such as highways, electrical grids, and transit systems. While these systems operate in the same physical territory, they require very different models to help us understand them. For example, a subway system snakes and curves below a city's varied terrain, but our model of it—a subway map—uses straight lines and places stations at nearly equidistant intervals. The subway map is not the city—it is a selective simplification of the city that makes it easier for passengers to visualize their journey. The transit map is a model so ubiquitous that it's hard to imagine doing it any other way—yet it took time to evolve.

The subway map, as we know it today, was invented by Harry Beck in 1931 while re-designing the map used by the London Underground. The old design was confusing to riders because it focused on the wrong goal—geographical exactness. Here's what it looked like before Beck:

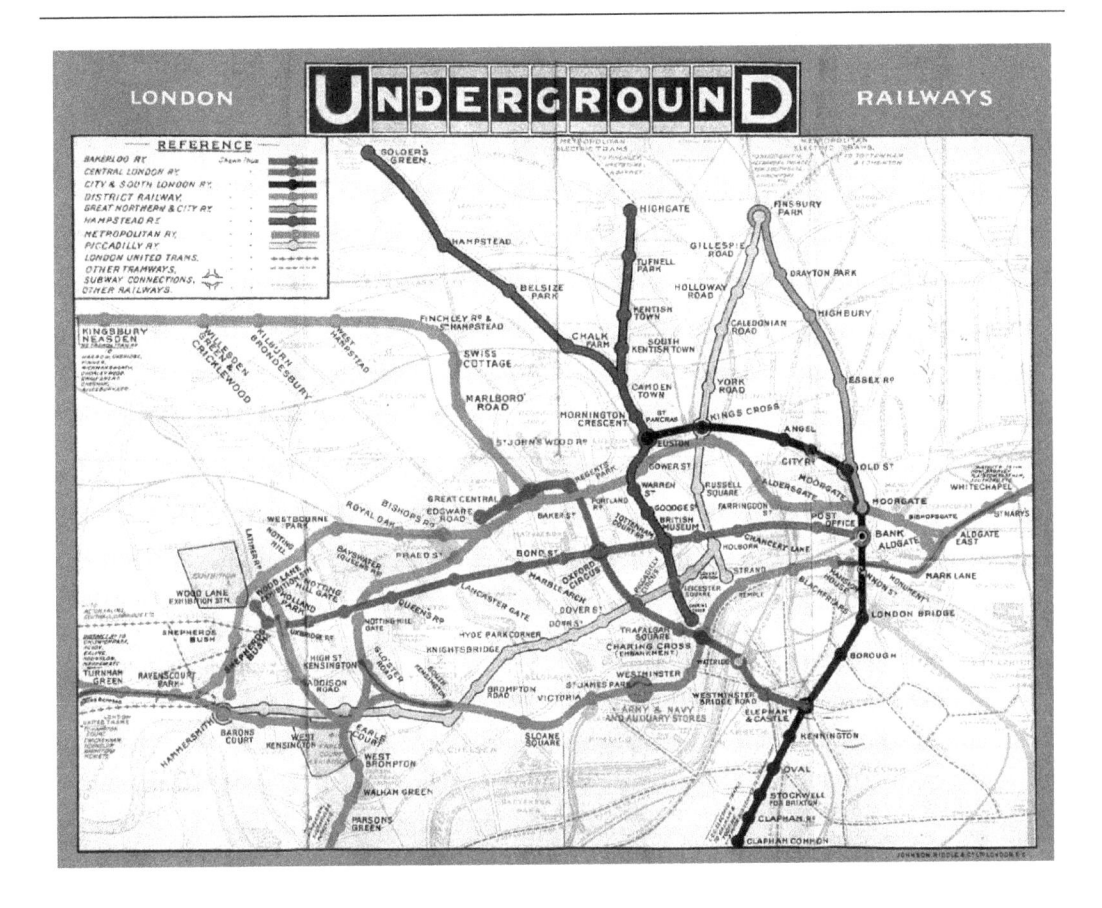

Figure 1.1 – London tube map, before Beck (Legacy Tube map)

Thankfully, Beck was not a cartographer—he was an engineer. By sacrificing topographical detail, Beck's design allowed passengers to quickly count the number of stops required for their journey while retaining their overall sense of direction. This story reminds us (quite literally) of the refrain, *the map is not the territory*.

As with maps, various kinds of modeling exist to help teams within an organization make sense of the many layers that make up its operational landscape. Also, like maps, models help organizations prepare for the journey ahead. But how does one use a model to navigate a database, let alone plan its future?

# Leveraging the modeling toolkit

Before we continue, we need to formally delineate three distinct concepts often used together in the service of modeling to make it simpler to refer to a specific tool in the modeling toolkit in later sections. By understanding where each piece fits in the broader domain of database design and management, diving into deeper technical concepts later in the book will become more meaningful and easier to digest.

The three components are listed here:

- Natural language semantics—words
- Technical semantics—SQL
- Visual semantics—diagrams

Let's discuss each of these in detail, as follows:

- **Natural language semantics**: Terminology employed in communicating details of a model between people. These are agreed-upon words that employ pre-defined conventions to encapsulate more complex concepts in simpler terms. For example, when both parties involved in a verbal exchange understand the concept of a *surrogate key*, it saves them from having to explain that it is a unique identifier for a table record that holds no intrinsic business meaning, such as an integer sequence or a hash value.

  To ensure effective technical conversations, it helps to be fluent in the semantics of modeling. Not only does it save time by succinctly communicating a complex concept, but it also saves even more time by not miscommunicating it. A waiter would return different foods when ordering *chips* in London rather than in Los Angeles. A properly modeled database would never return different records for the same surrogate key.

- **Technical semantics**: SQL is a domain-specific language used to manage data in a **Relational Database Management System (RDBMS)**. Unlike a general-purpose language (for example, YAML or Python), domain-specific languages have a much smaller application but offer much richer nuance and precision. While it can't format a website or send an email, SQL allows us to create the structure of our database and manipulate its contents.

  SQL bridges modeling concepts (expressed in words or images) and what is physically defined in the database. Snowflake uses an **American National Standards Institute (ANSI)**-compliant SQL syntax, meaning its basic commands (such as SELECT, UPDATE, DELETE, INSERT, and WHERE) are compatible with other database vendors who use this standard. Snowflake also offers many extra functions, clauses, and conventions that go beyond ANSI-standard SQL and give users added flexibility to manage the database.

  Unfortunately, due to its domain-specific nature, SQL presents a significant limitation: it can only express what the database explicitly understands. While SQL can define table structure and precisely manipulate data, it is too detailed to easily articulate the underlying business requirements.

- **Visual semantics**: Through their simplicity, images can convey a density of information that other forms of language simply cannot. In modeling, diagrams combine the domain-specific precision of SQL with the nuance of natural language. This gives diagrams a lot to work with to capture a data model's business meaning and technical specifics.

To start, diagrams vary in the level of detail they present—giving the observer exactly what they're looking for without overwhelming (or underwhelming) them with information. Most importantly, the semantic conventions used in diagrams are universal and can be understood by people besides data analysts and engineers. Yes—modeling diagrams are considered technical drawings; they represent strict technical concepts through agreed-upon visual conventions. However, in their simplest form, models can be understood almost intuitively with no prior knowledge. Even at the more advanced levels, such as logical and physical, learning to read a model is much simpler than learning SQL.

When all these semantics come together and are understood by the entire organization, they form a *ubiquitous language*, a concept first described by Eric Evans in *Domain-Driven Design*. Modeling then forms a part of the vocabulary that is understood universally throughout the organization to describe its business and store the data assets that support it. But that is just one of the many benefits that modeling provides.

## The benefits of database modeling

*Tactics without strategy is the noise before defeat. (Sun Tzu)*

For many people, database modeling brings to mind stale diagrams, arcane symbols, or extra work at the end of a project. Only a decade ago, fueled by the rise of distributed computing in the early 2000s—which popularized the concept of big data—the notion that *modeling is dead* gained notoriety. More precisely, it was thought that cheap and near-limitless computing power had made planning and designing a thing of the past. It was said that flexible semi-structured data formats and the ability to parse them on the fly—known as **schema-on-read**—had made modeling obsolete.

Eventually, operating and maintenance costs caught up with reality and revealed two great shortcomings of the schema-on-read approach. One is that no matter how data is structured, it must be functionally bound to the business that it helps support. In other words, semi-structured formats are neither a panacea nor an excuse to forgo the process of business validation. The second—and most important—is that a model is not simply the shape that data takes once uploaded to a database, but rather, the blueprint for business operations, without which it is impossible to build sustainable architectures.

Sustainable solutions require a long-term strategy to ensure their design matches the underlying business model. Without this, schema-on-read (discussed in *Chapter 15, Modeling Semi-Structured Data*), star schema (discussed in *Chapter 17, Scaling Data Models through Modern Techniques*), or any other schema are narrow-sighted tactics that lead nowhere. But done right, modeling makes developing database architectures more agile and helps the project evolve from the idea phase to implementation. At every stage of development, the model serves as a guide for supporting the conversations necessary to propel the design into the next phase and provide additional business context. Once implemented, the model becomes a living document that helps users understand, navigate, and evolve the system it helped create.

While every organization models in the *technical* sense—creating tables and transforming data—not everyone models *strategically*, end to end, in the broad sense of the word—thereby foregoing the long-term benefits. Some of these benefits include the following:

- Consensus and visibility of the broader business model
- More productive conversations with business teams
- Better quality of requirements
- Higher signal, lower noise in technical conversations
- Cross-platform, cross-domain, and widely understood conventions
- Big-picture visual overview of the business and its database footprint
- Preliminary designs become implementation blueprints
- Accelerating onboarding of new team members
- Making data more accessible and unlocking self-service within organizations
- Keeping the database landscape manageable at scale
- Getting a handle on complex data pipelines

To demonstrate the difficulties of working without formal modeling, we can take a simple schema based on Snowflake's shared TPC-H dataset (available in the shared database called SNOWFLAKE_SAMPLE_DATA), which, at first glance, looks like this:

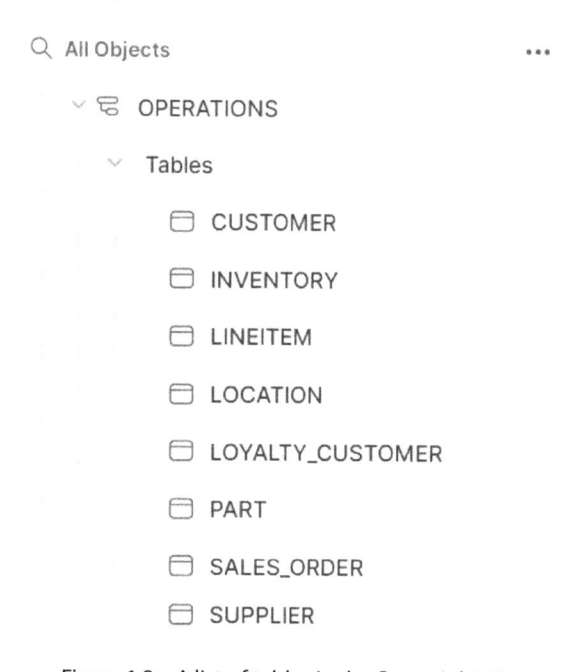

```
Q All Objects                          ...
    ∨ ⊟ OPERATIONS
        ∨ Tables
            ⊟ CUSTOMER
            ⊟ INVENTORY
            ⊟ LINEITEM
            ⊟ LOCATION
            ⊟ LOYALTY_CUSTOMER
            ⊟ PART
            ⊟ SALES_ORDER
            ⊟ SUPPLIER
```

Figure 1.2 – A list of tables in the Snowsight UI

While these tables have been modeled in the strict sense of the word and even contain data, we get very little information on what that data represents, how it relates to data in other tables, or where it fits in the broad context of business operations.

Intuition suggests that SALES_ORDER and CUSTOMER share a relationship, but this assertion needs to be tested. Even in this trivial example of only eight tables, it will take considerable time to thoroughly sift through the data to understand its context.

The irony is that many of the details we're looking for are already baked into the design of the physical tables, having been modeled at some point in the past. We just can't see them. Without a map, the terrain is lost from view.

Here is the same set of tables visualized through a modeling convention called an **Entity-Relationship Diagram (ERD)**:

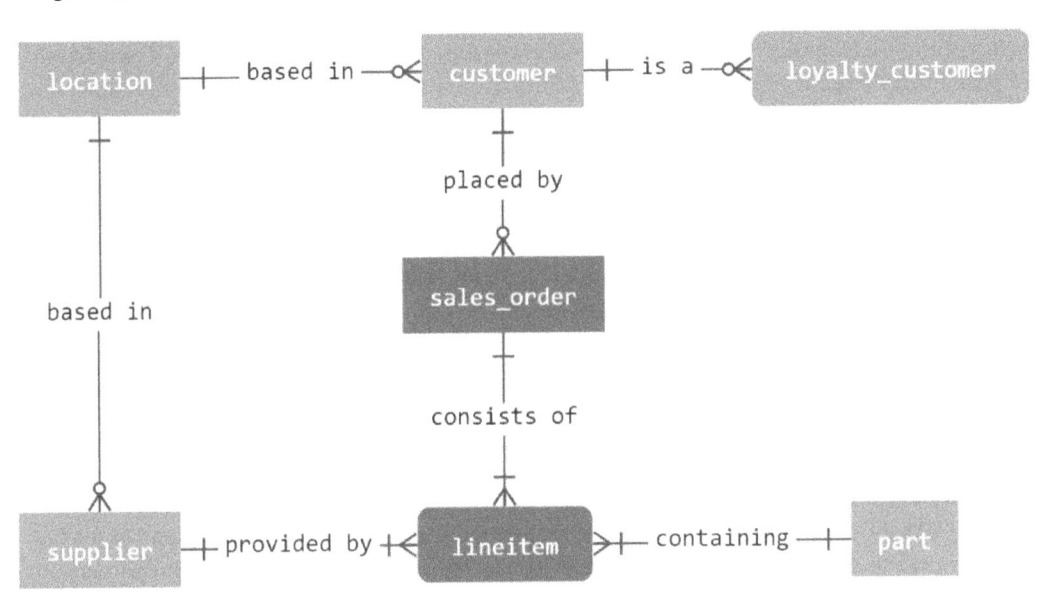

Figure 1.3 – A conceptual model using crow's foot notation

At a glance, the big picture comes into focus. Diagrams such as this one allow us to understand the business concepts behind the data and ensure they are aligned. Having a visual model also lets us zoom out from individual tables and understand the semantics of our business: What are the individual pieces involved and how do they interact? This global perspective gives everyone in the organization a means of finding and making sense of data assets without requiring a technical background—thus, business analysts or new hires can unlock the value of the information without any help from the data team.

As the organization grows, expanding in personnel and data assets, it will inevitably become too big for any person, or even a team of people, to coordinate. Here, organizations that have embraced data modeling will stand out from those that did not. Modeling can be the thing that helps organizations scale their data landscape, or it can be the technical debt that holds them back.

Yet, for all its benefits, modeling is not a cookie-cutter solution that guarantees success. There are many approaches to modeling and various modeling methodologies that are suited for different workloads. Throughout this book, we will tackle the fundamentals of modeling that will allow you to understand these differences and apply the best solution using a first-principles approach. First, we will begin by breaking down the two main database use cases and observing the role modeling plays in each of them.

## Operational and analytical modeling scenarios

The relational database as we know it today emerged in the 1970s—allowing organizations to store their data in a centralized repository instead of on individual tapes. Later that decade, **Online Transaction Processing** (**OLTP**) emerged, enabling faster access to data and unlocking new uses for databases such as booking and bank teller systems. This was a paradigm shift for databases, which evolved from data archives to operational systems.

Due to limited resources, data analysis could not be performed on the same database that ran operational processes. The need to analyze operational data gave rise, in the 1980s, to **Management Information Systems** (**MIS**), or **Decision Support Systems** (**DSS**) as they later became known. Data would be extracted from the operational database to the DSS, where it could be analyzed according to business needs. OLTP architecture is not best suited for the latter case, so **Online Analytical Processing** (**OLAP**) emerged to enable users to analyze multidimensional data from multiple perspectives using complex queries. This is the same paradigm used today by modern data platforms such as Snowflake.

The approach to storing and managing data in OLAP systems fundamentally differs from the operational or transactional database. Data in OLAP systems is generally stored in **data warehouses** (also known as **DWs** or **DWHs**)—centralized repositories that store structured data from various sources for the purpose of analysis and decision-making. While the transactional system keeps the up-to-date version of the truth and is generally concerned with individual records, the data warehouse snapshots many historical versions and aggregates volumes of data to satisfy various analytical needs.

Data originates in the transactional database when daily business operations (for example, bookings, sales, withdrawals) are recorded. In contrast, the warehouse does not create but rather loads extracted information from one or various source systems. The functional differences between transactional databases and warehouses present different modeling challenges.

A transactional system must be modeled to fit the nature of the data it is expected to process. This means knowing the format, relationships, and attributes required for a transaction.

*The main concern of a transactional database model is the structure and relationships between its tables.*

By contrast, the data warehouse loads existing data from the source system. A data warehouse isn't concerned with defining a single transaction but with analyzing multitudes of transactions across various dimensions to answer business questions. To do this, a data warehouse must transform the source data to satisfy multiple business analyses, which often means creating copies with varying granularity and detail.

*Modeling in a data warehouse builds upon the relational models of its source systems by conforming common elements and transforming the data using logic.*

Wait—if transformational logic is a core concept in data warehouse modeling, why is it so consistently absent from modeling discussions? Because in order to do transformational modeling justice, one must forgo the universality of general modeling principles and venture into the realm of platform specifics (that is, syntax, storage, and memory utilization). This book, in contrast, will embrace Snowflake specifics and go beyond physical modeling by diving into the transformation logic behind the physical tables. This approach provides a fuller understanding of the underlying modeling concepts and equips the reader with the required SQL recipes to not only build models but to load and automate them in the most efficient way possible. As we'll see in later chapters, this is where Snowflake truly shines and confers performance and cost-saving benefits.

> **Is Snowflake limited to OLAP?**
>
> Snowflake's primary use case is that of a data warehouse—with all the OLAP properties to enable multidimensional analysis at scale over massive datasets. However, at the 2022 *Snowflake Summit*, the company announced a new table type called **Hybrid Unistore**, which features both an OLTP-storage table and an OLAP analysis table under one semantic object. This announcement means Snowflake users can now design transactional OLTP database schemas while leveraging the analytical performance that Snowflake is known for. Hybrid Unistore tables are discussed in more detail in later chapters.

Although OLAP and OLTP systems are optimized for different kinds of database operations, they are still databases at heart and operate on the same set of objects (such as tables, constraints, and views) using SQL. However, each use case requires very different approaches to modeling the data within. The following section demonstrates what modeling will typically look like in each scenario.

# A look at relational and transformational modeling

The previous section describes how modeling varies between operational and data warehouse scenarios. Before exploring the modeling process in detail, it's helpful to understand the look and feel of relational and transformational modeling and what we're working toward. Before proceeding, it would help to summarize the main differences between transactional databases and data warehouses. You can see what these are in the following table:

| Transactional Database | Data Warehouse |
|---|---|
| Supports daily operations | Provides operational insight |
| Operates on single records | Summarizes many records |
| Accurate as of the present instant | Historical snapshots over time |
| **Single source of truth** (**SSOT**), non-redundant | Redundant to support different analyses |
| Data models defined by business operations | Data models generated by business questions |
| Static and structured data model | Inherited structure and dynamically transformed data model |
| Single-application data | Multiple sources of converging data |

Figure 1.4 – Common differences between transactional databases and warehouses

Given these differences, the following sections demonstrate what modeling looks like in each system and what it aims to achieve.

## What modeling looks like in operational systems

Completely ignoring the modeling workflow that got us here, which will be covered in later chapters, we can observe an example of the type of modeling most commonly seen in transactional systems. The physical diagram in *Figure 1.5* serves both as a blueprint for declaring the required tables and a guide to understanding their business context.

Following modeling conventions (don't worry if they are still unfamiliar—they will be covered thoroughly in the coming chapters), we can infer a lot of information from this simple diagram. For example, a person is uniquely identified by an eight-digit identifier (the primary key) and must have a **Social Security number** (**SSN**), driver's license, name, and birth date.

The one-to-many relationship between the two tables establishes that while a person does not necessarily need to have an account created, an account must belong to just one person:

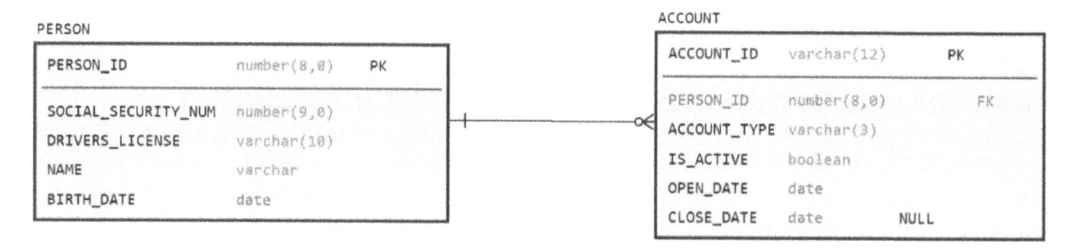

```
PERSON                                          ACCOUNT
┌─────────────────────────────────────┐         ┌─────────────────────────────────────┐
│ PERSON_ID          number(8,0)  PK  │         │ ACCOUNT_ID     varchar(12)      PK  │
├─────────────────────────────────────┤         ├─────────────────────────────────────┤
│ SOCIAL_SECURITY_NUM number(9,0)     │         │ PERSON_ID      number(8,0)      FK  │
│ DRIVERS_LICENSE    varchar(10)      │────────<│ ACCOUNT_TYPE   varchar(3)           │
│ NAME               varchar          │         │ IS_ACTIVE      boolean              │
│ BIRTH_DATE         date             │         │ OPEN_DATE      date                 │
└─────────────────────────────────────┘         │ CLOSE_DATE     date         NULL    │
                                                └─────────────────────────────────────┘
```

Figure 1.5 – A physical model using crow's foot notation

These details, combined with the list of attributes, data types, and constraints, not only dictate what kinds of data can be written to these tables but also provide an idea of how the business operates. So, how does this differ in analytical databases?

## What modeling looks like in analytical systems

In a data warehouse scenario, the PERSON and ACCOUNT tables would not be defined from scratch—they would be extracted from the source in which they exist and loaded—bringing both structure and data into the process. Then, the analytical transformations begin in answer to the organization's business questions. This is a process known as **Extract Transform Load** (ETL). (Although ELT has become the preferred processing order, the original term stuck.)

Suppose the management team wanted to analyze which age groups (by decade) were opening which account types and they wanted to store the result in a separate table for an independent analysis.

The following diagram shows the resulting relational model of an object obtained through transformational analysis but provides no business context:

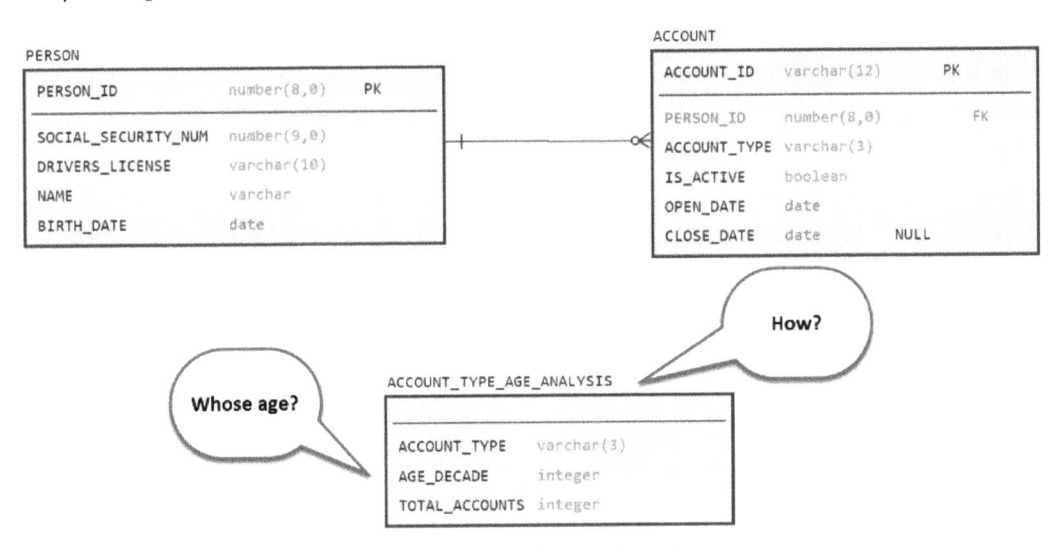

Figure 1.6 – A relational model of a transformational requirement

Although physical modeling could describe such a table (as seen in *Figure 1.6*)—containing the account type with age and count of accounts as integers—such a model would fail to communicate the most relevant details, presented here:

- The logic used to perform the analysis
- The relationship between the source tables and the output

The business requirement for ACCOUNT_TYPE_AGE_ANALYSIS in this example purposely excludes the source key fields from the target table, preventing the possibility of establishing any relational links. However, the relational model still serves a vital role: it tells us how the sources are related and how to join them correctly to produce the required analysis.

## Unlocking the Power of Modeling

The logic could then be constructed by joining PERSON and ACCOUNT, as shown here:

```
CREATE TABLE account_types_age_analysis AS
SELECT
    a.account_type,
    ROUND(DATEDIFF(years, p.birth_date, CURRENT_DATE()), -1
    ) AS age_decade,
    COUNT(a.account_id) AS total_accounts
    FROM account AS   a
      INNER JOIN person AS p
      ON a.person_id = p.person_id
GROUP BY    1, 2;
```

Although there is no relational connection between ACCOUNT_TYPE_AGE_ANALYSIS and its sources, there is still a clear dependency on them and their columns. Instead of using ERDs, which convey entities and relationships, transformational pipelines are visualized through a lineage diagram. This type of diagram gives a column-level mapping from source to target, including all intermediate steps, as shown here:

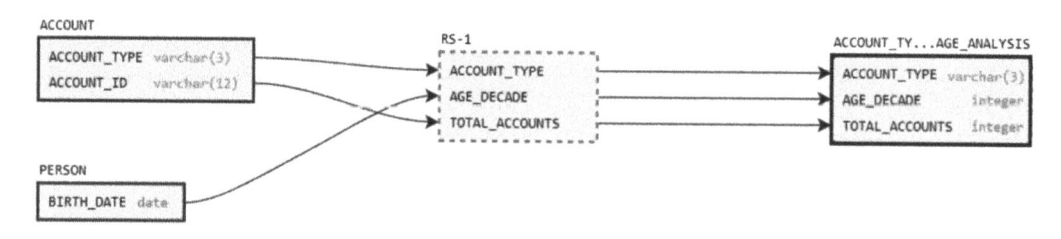

Figure 1.7 – Transformational modeling seen visually

Paired with the SQL logic used to construct it, the lineage graph gives a complete picture of the transformational relationship between sources and targets in an analytical/warehousing scenario.

Having witnessed both relational and analytical approaches to modeling, it is clear that both play a vital role in navigating the complex dynamic environments that one is liable to encounter in an enterprise-scale Snowflake environment.

Although we have only skimmed the surface of what modeling entails and the unique features of the Snowflake platform that can be leveraged to this end, this chapter has hopefully given you an idea of the vital role that modeling plays in building, maintaining, and documenting database systems. Before diving into the specifics of verbal, technical, and visual modeling semantics of modeling in the chapters to come, let's review what we learned.

# Summary

There is no escaping modeling. We use it in our everyday lives to plan and navigate the complexities of the world around us—databases are no exception. For some readers, the modeling styles presented in this chapter may be a new way of conceptualizing their database landscape, while others may be getting reacquainted with its notation and use cases. Whether thinking about a company business model or sharing a finalized design with team members, we all engage in modeling to varying degrees.

Embracing database modeling and learning to speak in a commonly understood language unlocks many time-saving and collaborative benefits for the entire organization. Thinking long-term and modeling strategically, as opposed to reacting tactically, aligns database designs to the business that they underpin, ensuring their viability. Having seen the advantages that modeling uncovers and where it can be implemented, we can begin to analyze its components to understand precisely where they should be used and how they form a natural design progression.

In the next chapter, we will explore the four modeling types used in database design and discuss where they excel and how they build on one another to help take an idea and evolve it into a technical system design while generating living project artifacts to navigate and maintain the final product.

# Further reading

Eric Evans' book, mentioned earlier in this chapter, explores how to create effective models by going beyond the surface and getting to the intention of the system itself. It is a recommended read for those wishing to go deeper into the realm of effective communication through models, unrestricted by specific technical domains, methods, or conventions:

*Evans, Eric. Domain-Driven Design: Tackling Complexity in the Heart of Software. Addison-Wesley Professional, 2004.*

# References

- Legacy Tube map *Wikimedia Commons*, `https://commons.wikimedia.org/wiki/File:Tube_map_1908-2.jpg`. Accessed October 2, 2022.

# 2
# An Introduction to the Four Modeling Types

The previous chapter introduced the concept of a model as a selective simplification of reality. Like Harry Beck's Tube map, designed expressly to navigate London's subway system, other map variants—such as street and topographical—exist to describe different aspects of geography. The same applies to databases and the organizations that rely on them to enable their business operations and analytics.

Many people think of modeling as simply documenting a database—diagramming. But modeling goes way beyond tables and databases by not only helping the developers understand the business but also helping the business understand itself.

Organizations use different models and modeling styles from org charts to network diagrams to navigate their many complexities. None of these provide a perfect map, but some serve as the right map for the right job. This chapter will explore the modeling types used to map and navigate the business and its data assets at various levels of detail.

While each of these modeling types has a dedicated chapter—the intention here is to understand where and why each process is used before proceeding to further detail.

In this chapter, we will cover the following main topics:

- Breaking modeling down to a flow
- How to use modeling elements to find a common language for communicating with business teams
- Aligning the business model to the data model with conceptual modeling
- Expanding on business concepts beyond database objects with logical modeling
- Creating the blueprint for database design by translating a logical model into a physical one
- Creating and managing **extract, load, and transform** (ELT) pipelines using **transformational modeling**

## Design and process

Over the years, many books have been written about modeling and designing database systems. However, many of these books fail to make the connection between technicality and practicality—which are inextricably linked. Often, modeling books prioritize completeness—such as describing four different notations to express a relationship—and ignore usability (e.g., which notation would be most accessible to business users?).

The most significant complexity of a database system is not technical. It is the business model itself—the interactions within a business and the rules that govern them. If the business model is not aligned with the data model, the database will be repeatedly forced to adjust (while losing organizational trust and resources in the process.)

What is needed is a business-readable language that developers use to build and document the database landscape.

## Ubiquitous modeling

Before defining data structures, we need to understand the business model that generates them. Such a model will make it possible to build a database system aligned with business processes and able to anticipate change. Like seeing a forest for the trees, ubiquitous modeling allows us to see the business for the data.

A business has many layers: from a mission statement that defines a company ethos, to the sales transactions, to the logistics that support them, to the data, metadata, analysis, and more. However, when most people think of a model, they tend to focus only on the data layer—forgetting that, in isolation, the data only tells part of the story.

In reality, the modeling process involves teams across the entire organization, including management, business departments, data teams, and analysts. Everyone in the organization, no matter their technical background or domain expertise, will work with modeling in some capacity (even if it is in the role of a viewer). Never lose sight of the variance in skillsets when modeling—ensuring they are kept as simple as possible while including all the necessary information for the task at hand.

The following diagram depicts what is commonly thought of as data modeling within the broader business context:

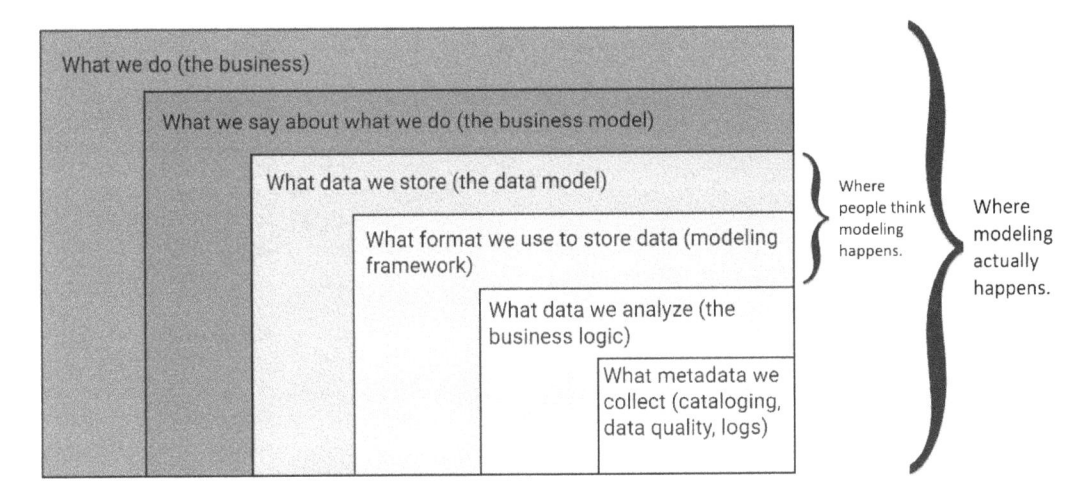

Figure 2.1 – Business layers where modeling actually happens

> **Relying exclusively on the data, a cautionary tale**
>
> The management team asks you to build a model that handles all business data. Providing sample data {0,3,6,9}, they say they can work with you to ensure you understand what you're building—ask any (yes/no) questions you like.
>
> Q. Is 12 in the set? Yes.
>
> Q. Is 21 in the set? Yes.
>
> Great, you understand the numbers and build a model to handle *multiples of three*.
>
> The next day, a -1 arrives and breaks your model because the business set is *the set of all integers*.

Starting in the late 1960s and evolving to the present day, modeling, and modeling notation, have changed often: beginning with the first eponymous designs by Peter Chen, Charles Bachman, and Richard Barker, national standards such as Merise, and industry standards such as IDEF1X, **Information Engineering** (**IE**), **Unified Modeling Language** (**UML**), and others. Many notations, no clear winner, and no standard governing body to arbitrate—no wonder so many people are confused.

Here is a collage of data models using various standards:

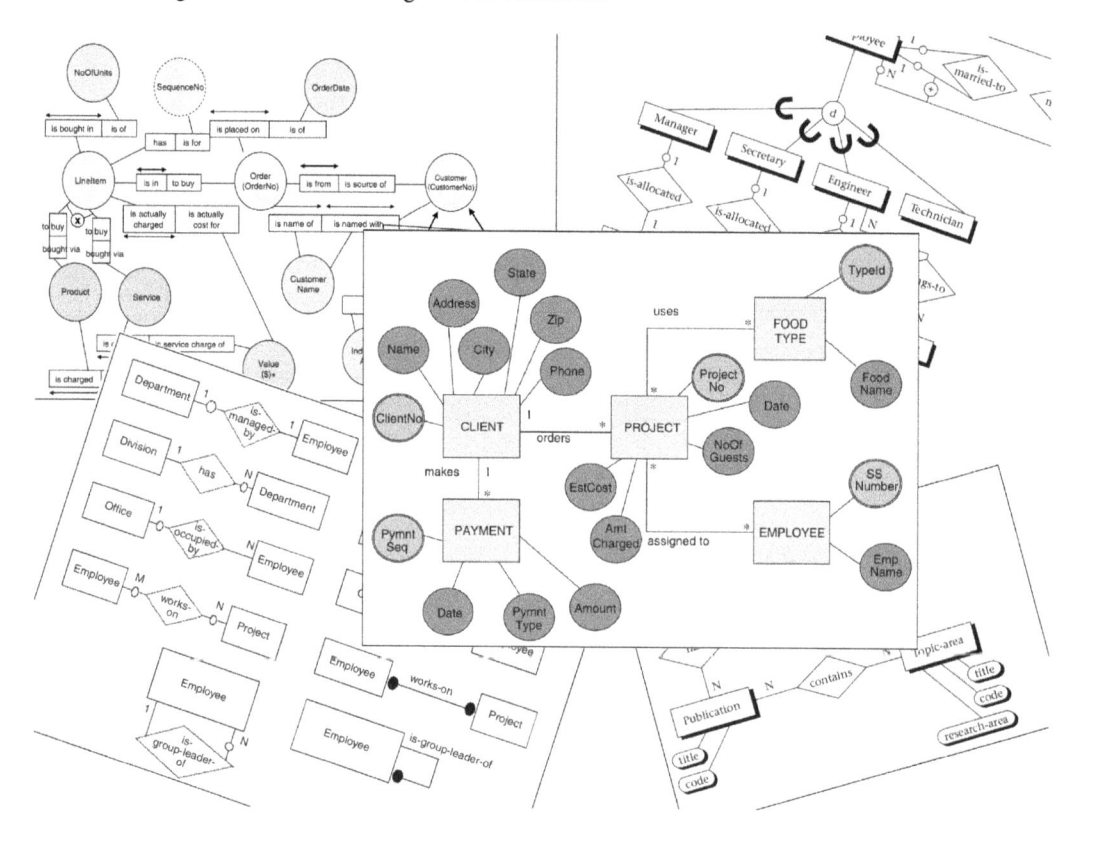

Figure 2.2 – Examples of modeling notations

This book is not intended as an encyclopedia of modeling. It is meant to be a practical guide for applying modeling concepts in Snowflake to ensure efficiency, consistency, and scalability. This, and future chapters, will employ the most understandable and concise notation that makes modeling accessible to data engineers, developers, analysts, and business users alike by adhering to the following principles:

- **Keep it simple stupid (KISS)**: In modeling (as in life), the simplest approach is often the best approach
- **Be concise**
- **Be unambiguous**: Never give two meanings to the same convention
- **Embrace industry standards**: When they facilitate understanding
- **Break industry standards**: Be flexible and eschew dogmatism in favor of usability

With these principles in mind, let's take a high-level look at the kinds of modeling that exist and where they are used. The following is meant to be an introduction to the concept of modeling and its implementation, so do not worry about the specifics or terminology. All of this will be covered in detail in later chapters.

# Conceptual

Modeling begins long before databases—or even data—enter the picture; it starts with the business itself. A conceptual diagram should be as valid for describing the organization's operating model as it would be for laying the foundations of its database landscape.

## What it is

**Conceptual modeling** is a process of identifying and visually mapping the moving pieces, or entities, of a business operation. Before going further, let's establish what an entity is.

**Entity**: A person, object, place, event, or concept relevant to the business for which an organization wants to maintain information. Examples of entities common to many companies include employee, customer, sale, and item. Entities are typically referenced in the singular and represent the class or type of an object (more on this and the singular versus plural naming debate in *Chapter 10, Database Naming and Structure*). **Entity instances** are occurrences of such a class or type:

- `Superman` is an instance within the `SUPERHERO` entity

Conceptual modeling is a collaborative process of discovery between the business and the data teams that produces visual project artifacts. Before data about entities can be collected and stored, the entities themselves must be uncovered and agreed upon. The goal of conceptual modeling is the synthesis of business and technical understanding between operational and data teams—the diagram is the by-product. The conversations that take place in the conceptual modeling service move the organization forward and add value in further stages of design and analysis.

Because business teams are unlikely to be familiar with model design, it is possible that working with the data team forces them to think in such terms for the first time. It is possible that when preliminary conceptual designs are initially drafted, business teams may be confronted with a reality that is not universally shared—and this is a good thing. When business processes are first set down in concrete, unambiguous diagrams, they bring to light the misalignments that individuals unknowingly carry, allowing them to converge on the truth.

For instance, are we in the business of serving meals to people in restaurants or selling ingredients wholesale to restaurant kitchens? If so, by phone, web, mobile sales force, or all the above? The data team, in isolation, is unlikely to know for sure.

Once the domain experts have established the entities, the analysis broadens to uncover their properties and relationships. Properties, or **attributes**, are descriptive pieces of information related to an entity:

- The `Superhero` entity has a `Birthplace` attribute with the value `Krypton` for the `Superman` instance

A customer might have a name, address, height, and driver's license—but which of these are relevant to our restaurant business? Are there other pertinent properties that were not included? The business teams can confirm this information.

Finally, there is the interaction between entities called a **relationship**. Relationships are expressed as verb phrases such as *is*, *has*, or *attends*. Relationship names are labeled in the diagram on the relationship line:

- SUPERHERO *has* a SUPER_POWER

Comic geeks know there are four types of superhero classes: alien savior, tech soldier, science-accident survivor, and vigilante. Superman, born under the red sun of Krypton, is of the first variety—an alien savior. So far, we have two entities (SUPERHERO and SUPERHERO_TYPE) and a relationship (SUPERHERO has a SUPERHERO_TYPE). The business teams must now confirm the granularity of both the entities and the relationship they share:

- **Entity granularity**: This is what a single instance of an entity represents.
  - The SUPERHERO entity is maintained at the grain of an individual hero. A single row in SUPERHERO represents one unique hero and their attributes.
  - The SUPERHERO_POWER entity is maintained at the grain of the hero superpowers. A single row in SUPERHERO_POWER represents just one of the many powers that a superhero can have.
- **Relationship granularity**: This is the granularity between entities. This consists of two parts: cardinality and optionality:
- **Cardinality**: This is the maximum number of instances that two entities can share. This is either *one* or *many*:
  - A SUPERHERO has one SUPERHERO_TYPE
  - A SUPERHERO can have more than one SUPERHERO_POWER
- **Optionality**: This signifies whether the relationship is *mandatory* or *optional* (e.g., *must*, *may*, or *can*). The word *zero* is often used as a synonym for *optional* in this context (e.g., *zero to many* instead of *optional many to many*) but should not be confused with cardinality. More details on the related nomenclature and notation are provided in *Chapter 6, Seeing Snowflake's Architecture through Modeling Notation*:
  - A SUPERHERO must have a SUPERHERO_TYPE
  - A SUPERHERO may or may not have a SUPERHERO_POWER

When describing the granularity, all this information is condensed into one term. Suppose the business teams confirm that superheroes must be classified into one of the four earlier types and can have many or no superpowers. In that case, we can describe the relationship between the entities as follows:

- A SUPERHERO must have one and only one SUPERHERO_TYPE
- A SUPERHERO can have zero or one or more SUPERHERO_POWER

Even in this primitive example, the word salad is becoming hard to swallow. But if we are to create tables in Snowflake to accurately store this information, we must be able to systematically capture these nuances, and a diagram is an ideal way to do so.

## What it looks like

It is easier to define a conceptual model by what it is not expected to contain than by what it does. Unlike a physical model, which must have strict database-specific precision to be deployable, conceptual models include as much or as little detail as needed to view and understand the details of the model at a high level.

At a minimum, a conceptual model must depict entities and their relationships. Beyond that, details such as attributes, granularity, and even some logical features may be included. Below are two examples of the superhero model we covered in the previous section.

Even at the highest level of abstraction, conceptual modeling is flexible in its details and presentation to fit the needs of the use case. Here, we see the model at its lowest resolution—as it might appear during the discovery phase of a development process—showing only entities and relationships:

SUPERHERO ----can have---● HERO_SUPER_POWER ●----------- SUPER_POWER

SUPERHERO_TYPE

Figure 2.3 – Conceptual entity-relationship (ER) modeling

The same design can be augmented with descriptions to give additional context to an audience who is not familiar with the domain in question:

## An Introduction to the Four Modeling Types

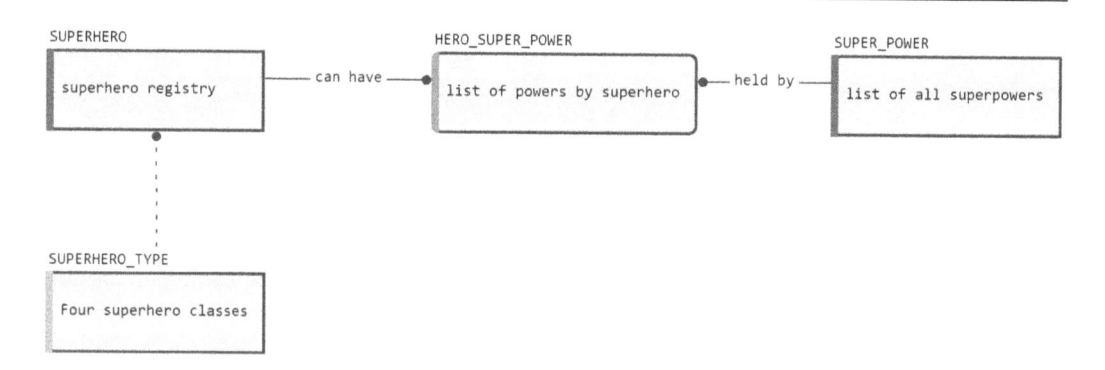

```
SUPERHERO                          HERO_SUPER_POWER                    SUPER_POWER
┌─────────────────────┐            ┌─────────────────────────┐         ┌─────────────────────────┐
│ superhero registry  │── can have─│ list of powers by       │─held by─│ list of all superpowers │
│                     │            │ superhero               │         │                         │
└─────────────────────┘            └─────────────────────────┘         └─────────────────────────┘
         ┆
         ┆
SUPERHERO_TYPE
┌─────────────────────┐
│ Four superhero classes │
└─────────────────────┘
```

Figure 2.4 – Conceptual ER modeling with descriptions

In this early stage, details such as data types or granular attributes are not required. For example, listing an `address` attribute and unpacking later into constituent parts, such as street, city, and postal code may suffice:

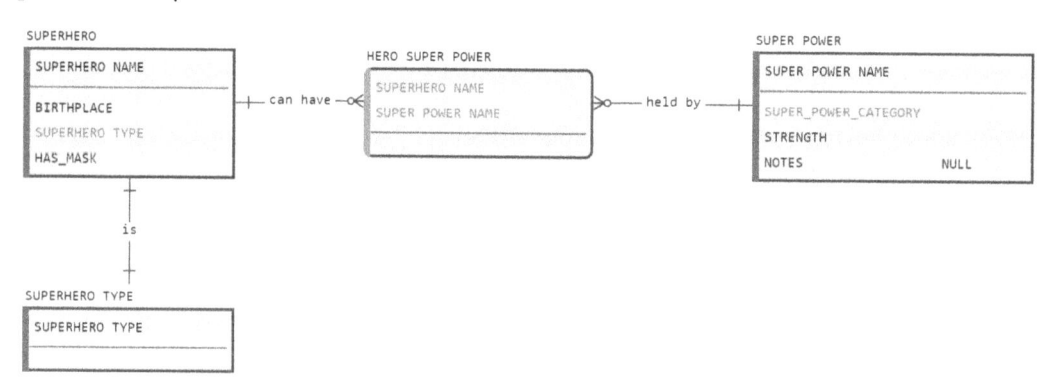

```
SUPERHERO                          HERO SUPER POWER                    SUPER POWER
┌─────────────────────┐            ┌─────────────────────────┐         ┌─────────────────────────┐
│ SUPERHERO NAME      │            │ SUPERHERO NAME          │         │ SUPER POWER NAME        │
├─────────────────────┤── can have─┤                         │─held by─├─────────────────────────┤
│ BIRTHPLACE          │            │ SUPER POWER NAME        │         │ SUPER_POWER_CATEGORY    │
│ SUPERHERO TYPE      │            │                         │         │ STRENGTH                │
│ HAS_MASK            │            └─────────────────────────┘         │ NOTES            NULL   │
└─────────────────────┘                                                └─────────────────────────┘
         │
         is
         │
SUPERHERO TYPE
┌─────────────────────┐
│ SUPERHERO TYPE      │
└─────────────────────┘
```

Figure 2.5 – Conceptual ER modeling with attributes and cardinality

Conceptual models remain useful well after deployment. New employees might use a conceptual model to acquaint themselves quickly with the business model. A business user can likewise rely on the simplicity of the conceptual model to explore an adjacent domain to understand how it interacts with the one they are familiar with.

Conceptual modeling is also used to create mock-ups for planning new designs. Like a whiteboard, conceptual models capture early-stage ideas and allow them to evolve as changes and details are introduced. Unlike a whiteboard, a conceptual model is easy to modify and share with team members when maintained online in a collaborative modeling tool.

Now that we understand how conceptual models are used and what they look like, it's time to move on to the next phase of modeling: logical.

# Logical

Once the building blocks of the business model have been identified through conceptual modeling (entities, attributes, and relationships), logical modeling begins. However, there is no strict distinction between the elements used in logical and conceptual designs. In fact, many database design textbooks do not differentiate between the two, combining them into a single style and tackling them in a single step.

This book takes a different approach—distinguishing between conceptual and logical modeling, not due to the elements or their notation but due to the natural flow of the design process. Because database textbooks are geared towards a technical audience, many lose sight of the less technical participants of database modeling: the business users.

Although a logical model can express everything that a conceptual one can, it also includes a great deal of technical detail, which may alienate those team members who lack the foundation to make sense of it. In the initial stages, domain knowledge is more important than technical details, so it may help to pivot between the two modeling styles, depending on the audience.

Unlike paper or a whiteboard, a modeling tool will allow you to switch between different modeling styles and notations seamlessly without affecting the underlying objects, allowing you to choose the appropriate level of abstraction, depending on the audience.

Let's try and understand what this means in practice.

## What it is

**Logical modeling** is the bridge between the business's conceptual operating model and the physical structure of the database. Logical modeling uses conventions that give context to the nature of the data beyond what conceptual or physical models can express.

Logical modeling augments the conceptual by adding notation describing relationship metadata and incorporates elements of physical database design, such as data types and keys. Logical concepts such as subtypes and supertypes may already be familiar to those with a programming background but may appear arcane to business users.

In the logical modeling phase, technical details required for database implementation, such as data types and keys, are also introduced, albeit in a simplified form. What separates logical modeling from the physical is that the technical details are not specific to any database type.

Sitting between the physical and conceptual realms allows logical modeling to bridge both worlds and express nuance that would otherwise be lost in the rigidity of pure database objects.

In short, logical modeling helps teams ascertain business nuance on top of a model that closely resembles their existing (or soon-to-be) physical landscape.

Let's take a look at some of the logical-only elements that we can expect to find on such a diagram.

## What it looks like

The logical modeling phase includes details such as data types, unique identifiers, and relationships. Contextual notation for subtypes and supertypes, as well as many-to-many relationships, are also included.

Subtypes are used on logical diagrams to represent inheritance. In the superhero example, the SUPERHERO_TYPE can be used to create subtype tables based on the SUPERHERO supertype. This way, common attributes such as SUPERHERO_NAME can be shared, while attributes unique to each subtype can be maintained in the respective subtype tables (such as the IS_HUMANOID indicator for alien savior-type heroes).

Here's what it looks like for a subtype relationship that is both complete (double parallel lines) and exclusive (letter **X** in the center):

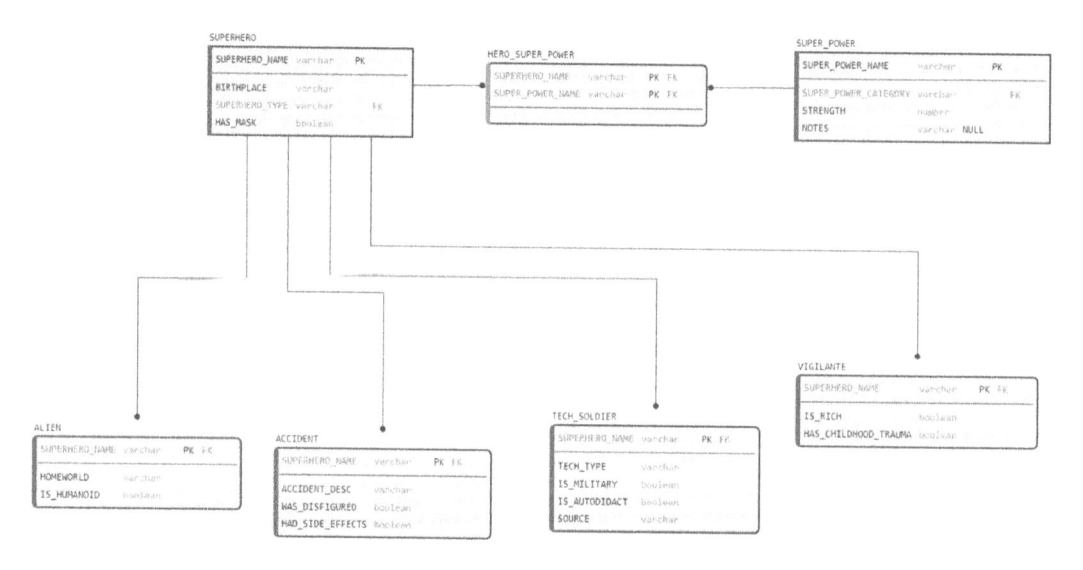

Figure 2.6 – A logical subtype/supertype relationship

**Many-to-many relationships** (M:M) present a unique challenge for logical models. In our superhero example, we established that a superhero might have many powers (or, like Batman, none). Also, a superpower—let's say, flight—can be shared by many superheroes (or none if the power is *turning one's ears invisible*). In short, many superheroes with many superpowers. The problem is that in a physical database, there is no way to store this information without duplicating the data in both tables:

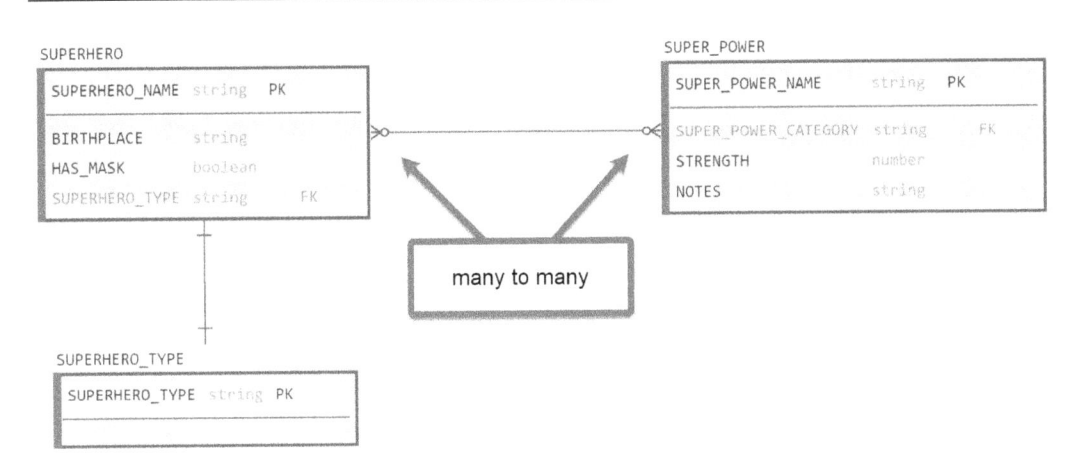

Figure 2.7 – A logical M:M relationship between two tables

To represent an M:M relationship in a physical database, an intermediate associative table is required. Although M:M relationships between tables are allowed in logical designs, they violate the first two modeling principles outlined earlier in this chapter by using two tables to signify the existence of three.

To avoid such confusion, we borrow the diamond from the Chen notation to label the associative table in an M:M relationship:

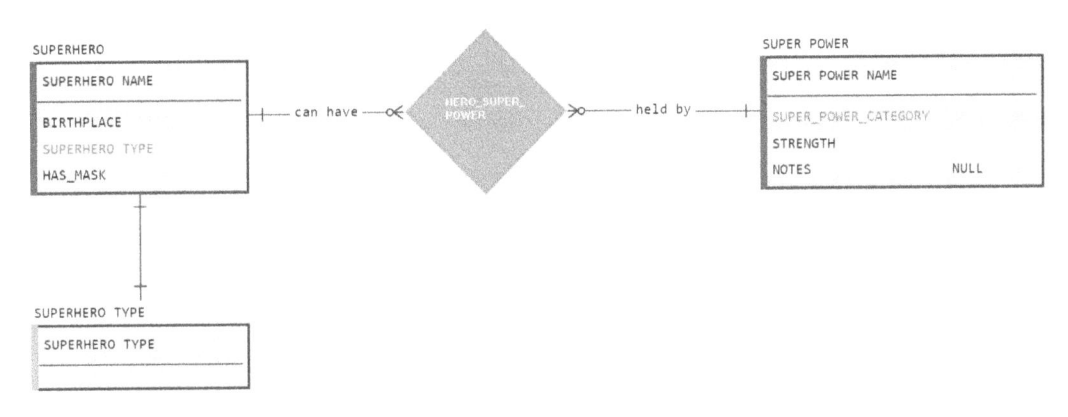

Figure 2.8 – A logical M:M relationship as an associative table in Chen diamond notation

Here, it is clear to the observers that an M:M relationship exists and that a third table will be required (containing its own independent attributes) to capture the required information.

Once the logical context has been defined, work on the physical Snowflake model can begin.

## Physical modeling

*Chapter 1, Unlocking the Power of Modeling* separated the many meanings and applications of the word *model*, noting how it is used for the physical structure of database tables and the accompanying visual diagram. A **physical model** contains all the information necessary to construct and deploy the design to a specific database (e.g., Snowflake).

This also works in the opposite direction; many modeling tools and SQL **integrated development environments (IDEs)** can reverse engineer diagrams directly from the database **data definition language (DDL)**. **Reverse engineering** lets users generate visual representations of the underlying schema on the fly to help them explore relationships.

How exactly does this conversion work?

### What it is

The physical model is a blueprint for deploying a database to Snowflake and the map that holds the technical and operational links that help users navigate it.

The transition from logical to physical modeling is largely systematic (relationships become constraints, data types are converted to database equivalents, and database properties are defined), but some design decisions may still be required (e.g., rollups for subtypes, discussed in *Chapter 11, Putting Physical Modeling into Practice*). Such decisions will depend on business factors and future data consumption patterns.

Some modeling tools separate logical and physical models into different projects. Others, such as SqlDBM, keep conceptual, logical, and physical models in sync, allowing users to view a model at any level of detail without conversion.

> Logical data types and Snowflake conversion
>
> To facilitate migrations from other database platforms, Snowflake offers various compatible data types as synonyms for its own. For example, defining a column as either `STRING` or `TEXT` is allowed but would result in the column being created as a Snowflake standard `VARCHAR(16777216)`. This means that generic data types often used in logical models, such as `STRING` or `INTEGER`, can be used and automatically generate Snowflake equivalents upon deployment. More info can be found at `https://docs.snowflake.com/en/sql-reference/intro-summary-data-types.html`.

Physical modeling is the final step before Snowflake deployment. While the diagram displays data types and constraints, much more detail is embedded within the objects as part of this phase. Clustering keys, table types, and identity properties are set where required and supporting objects such as sequences and file formats are also created and assigned. All this happens during a new development, but physical modeling is also used for existing schemas.

For organizations whose databases lack a formal model document, physical modeling—through reverse engineering—is the most direct way to create one. Many modeling tools can even suggest relationships in schemas where constraints have not been defined by detecting naming patterns. Although this lacks the metacontext of a logical model, it is a significant improvement over having no diagram at all.

## *What about views?*

So far, we have been exploring database modeling in parallel with the business model–capturing and storing business-critical information as entities, attributes, and relationships. Views, however, do not store any data, as they are the `SELECT` statements stored as database objects. While it may be impossible to construct the `CUSTOMER` entity in a transactional database as a view without an underlying `CUSTOMER` table, data warehouses may use a view to logically unify several `CUSTOMER` sources into one dimension. In such a scenario, is the view not part of the `CUSTOMER` model? Of course, it is and should be visible in the physical model.

However, the *model* used by such a view is transformational, not physical, and will be covered in the corresponding sections. It's unfortunate that the word *logical* has already been taken by a class of modeling and can't be used to express logic-based transformations such as views and **CREATE TABLE AS SELECT (CTAS)** tables. Alas, we must adhere to the principle of unambiguity, which states *never give two meanings to the same convention*, so that's that.

So, how does a physical model differ visually from those discussed previously?

## What it looks like

Physical diagrams look remarkably like their logical counterparts. However, they pack in much more information. Although the presentation options are configurable in most modeling tools, essential elements such as a complete column list, data types, and constraints must be defined. However, a physical model has many more details than can be displayed at a given time. Each element in the diagram (relationships, tables, and columns) holds its own set of physical attributes, which can be edited separately.

This is an example of the superhero database seen as a physical model:

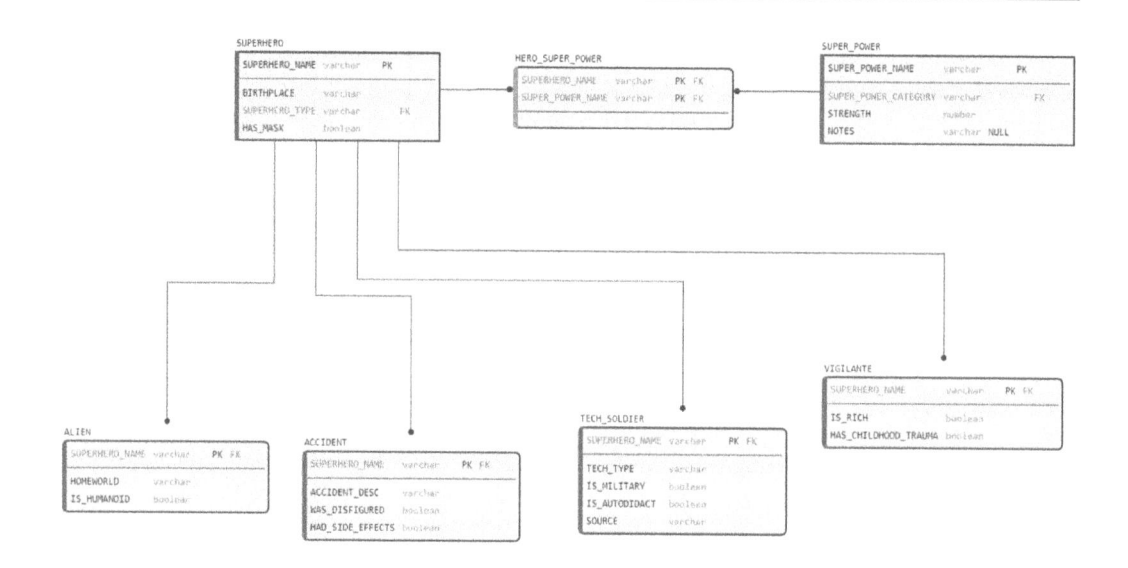

Figure 2.9 – A physical model of the superhero database

A physical model, therefore, presents the viewer with only those properties that can be translated directly to the database. The relationships, as previously discussed, are as much a technical asset as they are clues to the operational nature of a business. Even in a data warehouse, where much of the landscape is defined through transformational modeling, the relationships outlined in the relational model help inform the connections and the joins that are made to make the transformations work.

## Transformational

It all begins with `SELECT`. Modeling through transformational logic is a powerful and highly maneuverable method for modeling data that comes with one serious drawback: it needs existing data to `SELECT` from. Transformational modeling is rarely done in transactional databases because, in such systems, data is created and modified through the company's operational processes (e.g., purchases and profile updates)—with which expensive transformational processes should not compete for critical system resources. However, in data warehouses, where conformed datasets are extracted and duplicated with fresh timestamps for each load, transformational modeling becomes a necessity.

Because transformational modeling selects from existing structured data, the result set is already structured. Selecting the `SUPERHERO_NAME` and `HAS_MASK` columns and creating a table will preserve their structure (`VARCHAR` and `BOOLEAN`, respectively). However, as with all modeling, transformations must also be duly documented to allow database users to make sense of the complex data landscape that results.

## What it is

Transformational modeling, unlike relational, isn't concerned with the structure of the data it is meant to hold because it uses existing data as part of the creation process. Instead, Transformational modeling creates new objects by selecting data from existing sources. This is done through views using the **CREATE TABLE AS SELECT (CTAS)** command, or other DML statements.

But there is more to transformational modeling; it is also the MERGE and the bulk INSERT used to keep data in such tables up to date. When it comes to data, **online transactional processing** (**OLTP**) databases generally hold just one source of truth (the latest). But **online analytical processing** (**OLAP**) systems, by design, are disconnected from the latest data and must be loaded and synchronized on a schedule. The transformational approach is used to display the latest changes.

OLTP databases are generally used in operational use cases (such as sales, reservations, or application data) and operate on the **create, read, update, delete** (**CRUD**) of individual records. In contrast, warehouses rely on transformational modeling to unify data from disparate sources and create versions of the conformed data at various levels of detail and aggregation.

Transformational logic is also used by **business intelligence** (**BI**) and dashboarding tools when building visualizations and summarizing information. Such tools automate the work of writing queries by performing the required joins and aggregations when data is pulled onto the screen in the form of tables and charts.

Since transformations are expressed as code, what can we visualize with transformational modeling?

## What it looks like

The best abstraction for the complexity of database logic is the SQL that produced it. At its core, transformational logic is SQL. It is the CTAS statement that creates and populates a table, but it is also the INSERT or MERGE statements that may be used to update it or the VIEW that these statements may call to do so.

However, just as reverse engineering DDL can produce ER diagrams from DDL, it can also generate lineage diagrams from transformational SQL logic. Unlike relational diagrams, lineage graphs are low-res depictions of data flow from source to target in a SELECT statement. Without the accompanying SQL, the details that led to the creation of the table are lost:

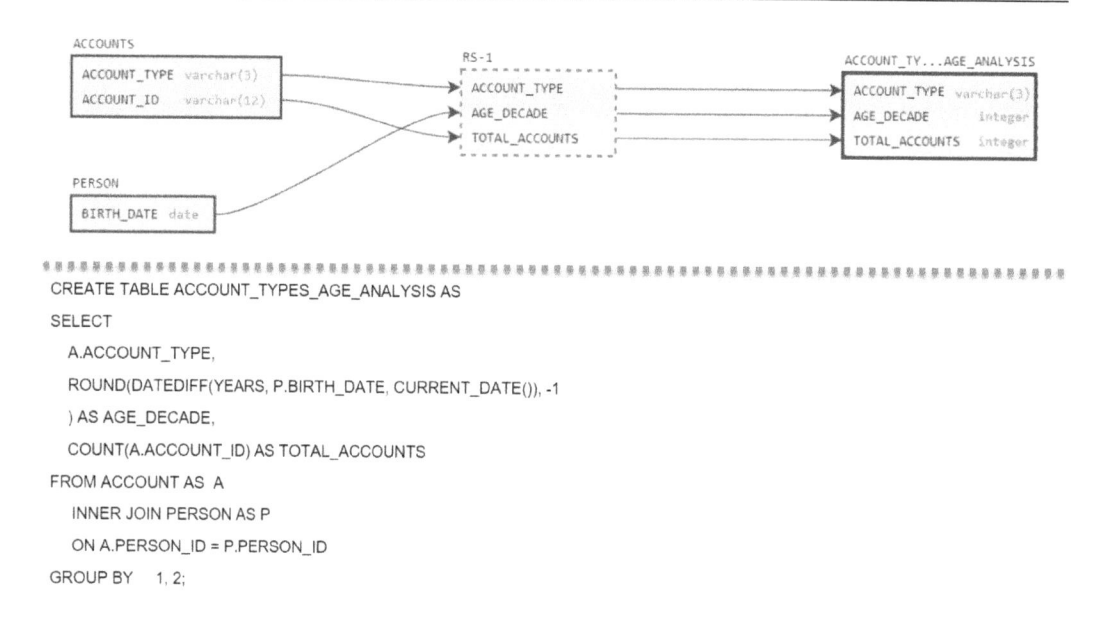

```
                                                                    ACCOUNT_TY...AGE_ANALYSIS
ACCOUNTS                            RS-1
ACCOUNT_TYPE  varchar(3)            ACCOUNT_TYPE                    ACCOUNT_TYPE  varchar(3)
ACCOUNT_ID    varchar(12)           AGE_DECADE                      AGE_DECADE    integer
                                    TOTAL_ACCOUNTS                  TOTAL_ACCOUNTS integer

PERSON
BIRTH_DATE  date
```

```sql
CREATE TABLE ACCOUNT_TYPES_AGE_ANALYSIS AS
SELECT
    A.ACCOUNT_TYPE,
    ROUND(DATEDIFF(YEARS, P.BIRTH_DATE, CURRENT_DATE()), -1
    ) AS AGE_DECADE,
    COUNT(A.ACCOUNT_ID) AS TOTAL_ACCOUNTS
FROM ACCOUNT AS A
    INNER JOIN PERSON AS P
    ON A.PERSON_ID = P.PERSON_ID
GROUP BY   1, 2;
```

Figure 2.10 – Transformational modeling expressed as code and on a lineage diagram

Unlike the other modeling diagrams—where pictures tell a clearer story than DDL—transformational modeling benefits from having code visible alongside the lineage graph. This allows users to acquaint themselves with the inputs and outputs of the transformation at a high level before diving into the details of the logic if they so choose.

After covering four different modeling styles with overviews, examples, and use cases, let's review what we've learned.

## Summary

As we have seen throughout this chapter, modeling is a process used to agree, plan, and develop a database design and a means to navigate and explore it to gain greater insight into the underlying business context. Every new project must pass through the four modeling stages, whether formally recognized or not. But even for existing databases that have not been adequately documented, reverse engineering is an effective mechanism to work backward from a database to uncover its business meaning.

The design journey starts with conceptual modeling—a collaborative process that involves business and data teams working together to understand the core elements that underpin business operations and how they interact. Conceptual models favor simplicity over detail—making them accessible to team members of all backgrounds and helping steer conversations to converge at a shared understanding of the business model.

After conceptual modeling, the data team can add further business context to the diagram using logical modeling elements. Logical models resemble physical designs but offer business nuances, such as many-to-many relationships, subtype classes, and relationship names—none of which can be represented in the database. This also makes logical models an ideal bridge for transitioning to physical modeling.

Physical modeling is concerned with database-specific details to ensure that the business rules are captured correctly and with the proper parameters to ensure efficient performance. Since the entities, attributes, and relationships have already been nailed down through conceptual and logical collaborations, the focus can turn to physical database details, where database-specific properties are defined.

Transformational modeling can begin by using the physical model as an orientative map—reshaping data into the format (or formats) best suited to answer business questions and drive decision-making. Although transformational modeling is performed purely through SQL logic, accompanying visuals (as in all types of modeling) can help accelerate the understanding and maintenance of complex logic.

Now that you have seen the types of modeling that exist and where they are used, the next step is learning to apply them. However, before getting to that, we must make sure we understand the revolutionary cloud architecture of Snowflake that we'll be using as our canvas. In the next chapter, we will familiarize ourselves with the unique features that make Snowflake the fastest-growing cloud database platform on the market and how to use them to optimize costs and performance.

## Further reading

Effective communication between technical and business teams is notoriously challenging. In *The Rosedata Stone*, Steve Hoberman presents a guide for creating a precise diagram of business terms within your projects. The business terms model is a simple yet powerful communication tool to help bridge the technical knowledge gap and meet business teams on their own *terms*.

- Hoberman, Steve. *The Rosedata Stone: Achieving a Common Business Language Using the Business Terms Model*. Technics Publications, 2020.

# 3
# Mastering Snowflake's Architecture

For as long as databases have existed, they have faced recurring challenges in managing concurrency and scalability in the face of growing data volume and processing demands. Many innovative designs have been attempted over the years and have been met with varying degrees of success. However, that success often came with fresh drawbacks.

The Snowflake team saw that overcoming the age-old challenges of handling independent consumption demands of data storage and analysis required a radically new approach. The team decided to design a database that could operate natively on top of cloud computing platforms and thereby offer near-limitless scalability. Their efforts resulted in the creation of what Snowflake calls the Data Cloud—a platform that enables real-time data sharing and on-demand workload sizing through the separation of storage and compute.

In this chapter, we will cover the following topics:

- Explore how databases have tried to achieve database scalability in the past
- Discover how Snowflake built a scalable database to run natively in the cloud
- See the unique features made possible by Snowflake's innovative architecture
- Understand the costs associated with Snowflake's variable spend mode
- Learn how to utilize various forms of cache to save on costs and improve performance

To truly appreciate what Snowflake has achieved, it is worth remembering the various traditional architectures that came before it and the limitations they tried to overcome.

## Traditional architectures

To appreciate the innovation of the **Snowflake Data Cloud**, we have to take a step back and recall the designs and related limitations associated with its predecessors. Long before the advent of the cloud, databases started as physical on-premises appliances and, since their inception, have all faced the same challenge: scalability.

In the past, databases were confined to a physical server on which they relied for storage and processing power. As usage increased, memory would fill up, and CPU demand would reach the available limit, forcing the user to add more resources to the server or buy a new one altogether. As either response involved maintenance and downtime, hardware purchases had to be forward-looking, anticipating database growth several years into the future.

The following figure outlines the structure and key pieces of a traditional database. Although processing power, memory, and disk space were all customizable to a degree, they came packaged in a physical machine that could not scale.

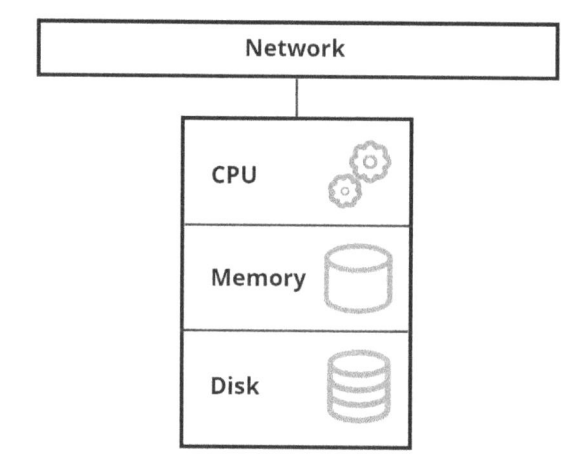

Figure 3.1 – A diagram of a typical on-premises database server

Before cloud architecture unlocked the **software as a service** (**SaaS**) model and introduced variable spend pricing, hardware purchases required considerable **capital expenditure** (**CapEx**). Thus, hardware sizing—estimating current and future computing needs—requires careful planning. A conservative estimate resulted in a sooner-than-expected upgrade, while overshooting meant paying top dollar for cutting-edge tech and not using it to its full potential for years to come. While data volume and CPU demands tended to grow synchronously with the business, unpredicted usage spikes in storage or compute were also common and led to similar headaches. That is when new architectures such as shared-disk and shared-nothing emerged to address the limits of scaling physical machines.

First, let us understand what changes shared-disk architecture introduced over traditional designs and the advantages that it offered.

## Shared-disk architecture

The **shared-disk** approach uses a central storage location and makes it available to various compute clusters in a network. It is a simple design that, unfortunately, suffers from physical implementation issues when locking and accessing the data concurrently.

The following figure illustrates how shared-disk architecture externalized data storage away from individual machines and made it accessible to all computing clusters on the network.

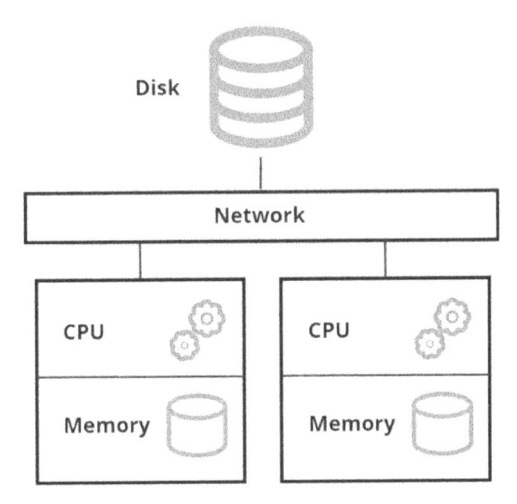

Figure 3.2 – A diagram of a shared-disk architecture

The shared-disk design made it possible to add compute clusters of varying sizes to accommodate different workloads within the organization. However, this led to an inevitable bottleneck. The more clusters that are added to the network in a shared-disk architecture, the worse the contention for the central disk becomes. This design failed to deliver on the promise of scalability because it suffered from bottlenecks on the most important resource of a database: the data.

Where shared-disk failed, shared-nothing nearly succeeded.

## Shared-nothing architecture

**Shared-nothing** architectures, like the ones used by AWS Redshift and Greenplum, avoided the issues of shared-disk by isolating it and making it part of the compute cluster. This design also addressed the varying consumption needs of teams across the organization, allowing database clusters to be sized based on demand. However, as we learn in grade school, sharing nothing is not the best strategy for collaboration.

The following figure shows how shared-nothing architecture allows self-sufficient but isolated database clusters.

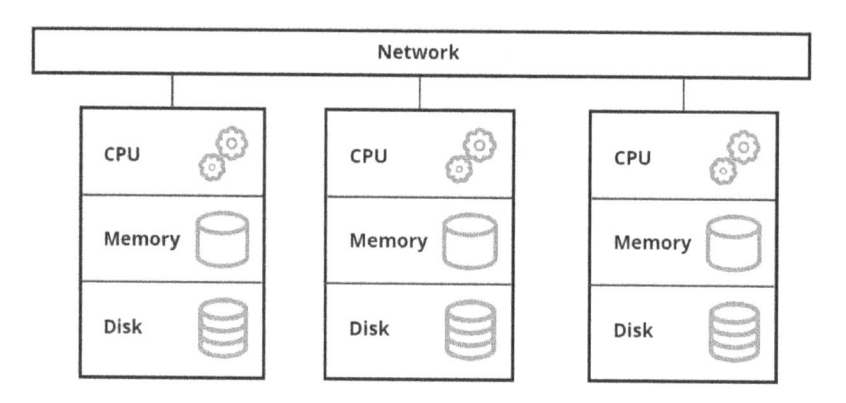

Figure 3.3 – Components of a shared-nothing architecture

Creating database clusters in a shared-nothing architecture, especially one that runs on virtual cloud resources, solves the issue of investing up front in physical hardware. However, nodes in a shared-nothing architecture require data transfer to share information, which penalizes performance.

Tying the disk to the overall cluster also means striking the right balance between storage and processing patterns, which can vary independently. A heavy data science workload might require lots of compute to be directed at a relatively small dataset, while an ETL bulk-loading process might need the opposite. However, shared-nothing platforms did not offer many options for tuning each resource individually, nor were they simple to maintain and administer.

While shared-nothing architecture did not quite live up to the promise of seamless and easily managed scalability, it did pave the way for platforms such as Snowflake to tackle cloud computing challenges with cloud-native designs.

## Snowflake's solution

To address the scalability issue that has plagued databases since inception, the Snowflake team decided to formulate a new approach that would not be tied down by the limitations of past designs. They developed a modern platform built natively for the cloud that uses its unique features to enable concurrency, scalability, and real-time collaboration.

Snowflake's innovative cloud architecture still relies on physical disks, but it integrates them logically to make centralized storage available to its computing clusters without concurrency bottlenecks or data replication overhead. Finally, the best of what shared-disk and shared-nothing promised: separating the data from compute workloads, which can be independently provisioned and resized.

Snowflake runs entirely on virtually provisioned resources from cloud platforms (Amazon, Microsoft, and Google Cloud). Snowflake handles all interactions with the cloud provider transparently, abstracting the underlying virtual resources and letting the customer manage their data through a unified three-layer architecture.

# Snowflake's three-tier architecture

Snowflake architecture consists of three layers: storage, compute, and cloud services. Snowflake manages all three layers so that interactions with the underlying cloud architecture are transparent to the users.

The following is an illustration of how Snowflake's architecture runs on top of cloud data platforms and separates disk from virtual compute clusters while managing a separate operational services layer (so you, the user, don't have to).

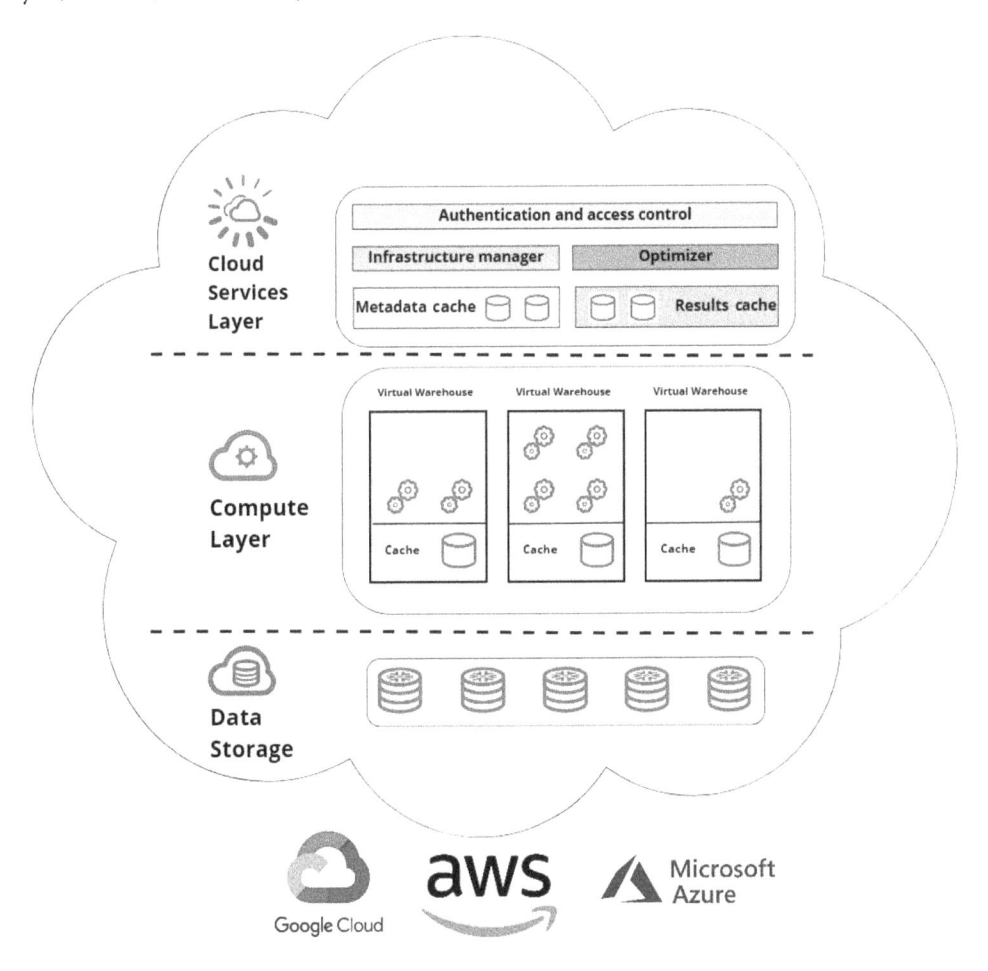

Figure 3.4 – Snowflake hybrid cloud architecture

Now, let us get to know each of the three layers before explaining how they combine to enable Snowflake's innovative features, such as zero-copy cloning and Time Travel.

## Storage layer

The **storage layer** physically stores data on disks in the cloud provider hosting the Snowflake account. As data is loaded into Snowflake, it is compressed, encrypted, and logically organized into tables, schemas, and databases. The users define the logical hierarchy of the database and its objects, while Snowflake takes care of the underlying partitioning and storage. The customer is billed only for the data they store, with no provisioning or sizing required.

Later chapters go into more detail on how Snowflake manages and optimizes data storage and the types of backup and redundancy options it offers. For now, let us understand how compute and virtual warehouse clusters work in Snowflake.

## Compute layer

The **compute layer**, also known as the processing or virtual warehouse layer, provides a cluster of virtually provisioned CPU and temporary memory resources for executing queries. These clusters are called *warehouses* and are provisioned in t-shirt sizes—from XS to 6XL benchmarks. Through warehouses, Snowflake simplifies the consumption of virtual cloud resources using a simple formula. Each increase in warehouse size doubles the number of virtual servers in the cluster while also doubling the cost.

The packetization of virtual compute clusters into warehouses, with simple t-shirt sizes, abstracts the underlying cloud architecture and ensures simple and consistent utilization no matter the platform on which the Snowflake account is hosted. This way, warehouses can scale in a way that's simple to track. Scaling up, or resizing a warehouse to the next size in the t-shirt size, doubles the number of servers in the cluster, and scaling out adds warehouses of the same size to a compute cluster for increased concurrency (think of scaling up or out as compute *times two* or *plus one*, respectively).

## Services layer

Snowflake's **services layer** coordinates all account activity in this hybrid-layer model and manages everything from security to encryption to metadata. The services layer handles operations such as query parsing and optimization, data sharing, and caching. From login, the services layer is there for the user through every operation they perform in the warehouse. The amount of time-saving work and automation that the services layer provides is reflected in Snowflake's marketing language: promising the user *near-zero maintenance* along with low cost and exceptional performance.

Now, let us see how Snowflake's three-tier architecture comes together to unlock unprecedented possibilities for its users.

# Snowflake's features

With its revolutionary cloud architecture, Snowflake continues to innovate and (pleasantly) surprise its users with game-changing performance enhancements beyond those that made it famous from

## Zero-copy cloning

**Zero-copy cloning** allows Snowflake users to clone data without physically duplicating it. Not having to move data means cloning happens instantly—whether cloning a table or an entire database. Cloned objects are virtual copies of their source, so they do not incur storage costs. Once data changes occur in the clone or its source, the clone becomes a physical object and begins consuming storage resources.

Cloning is an ideal way to create system backups and testing environments—achieving in seconds what used to take days. At the object level, cloning is a convenient way to bring data across environments when developing or debugging.

Another enhancement made possible through innovative columnar storage techniques (which are explained in later chapters) is Time Travel.

## Time Travel

Imagine the ability to go back in time, to a better moment like before you dropped that table in PROD, thinking it was TEST. Snowflake Time Travel makes that possible.

With **Time Travel**, users can query or clone data from a previous point in time, allowing them to recover from mistakes or compare changes from the present state. Time Travel is a built-in backup feature for Snowflake objects and, as such, uses extra storage and comes with the associated storage costs compared to objects that have this feature disabled. Later chapters will describe how to configure Time Travel to balance cost and flexibility.

Now, instead of table backups, let us turn our attention to an entirely different way of working with tables through one of Snowflake's latest innovations.

## Hybrid Unistore tables

Data warehouses run **online analytical processing** (**OLAP**) architectures to enable them to efficiently perform the massive aggregations and calculations that analytic workloads require. However, use cases that depend on single-row operations or indexes perform better in **online transactional processing** (**OLTP**) databases. At Snowflake Summit 2022, a new kind of table was announced to give users the best of both worlds: Hybrid Unistore.

**Hybrid Unistore** tables are really two tables in one—an analytical and a transactional table working together under the hood to provide users with a unified solution that offers the best of both worlds. Like all Snowflake objects, Hybrid Tables live up to the promise of near-zero maintenance by having the services layer automatically route workloads to the underlying table best suited for the task.

Hybrid Unistore tables are discussed in later chapters, so let us now go beyond structured data and discuss another of Snowflake's strong points.

## Beyond structured data

Snowflake is known for its benchmark-setting performance abilities with relational tables and agility in working with semi-structured data. Even unstructured files are supported through external tables. Users can work with any of these file formats from a single place in a way that is as familiar and performant as querying a table.

Semi-structured files, such as logs and hierarchies, stored in JSON or similar formats can be loaded into Snowflake and queried like regular tables with almost no impact on performance. Snowflake provides an extensive library of functions that allow users to work with semi-structured records or flatten them into structured columns. Techniques for doing so are discussed in later chapters.

Unstructured data is also supported, and (its metadata) can be queried through external tables—metadata objects created on top of external stages. External tables are read-only but do support constraints for relational modeling. Additional information for working with external tables can be found in the Snowflake documentation here: `https://docs.snowflake.com/en/user-guide/tables-external-intro.html`.

All these great features and the agility of the cloud are bound to cost a fortune, right? Actually, with no upfront costs, competitive pricing, and the ability to size warehouses to user needs or suspend them entirely, users can often spend less on Snowflake than they did for legacy on-premises hardware. The caveat is that to do so, users must understand how Snowflake pricing works and how to manage it effectively.

## Costs to consider

Unlike on-premises databases, which are purchased upfront and used for the duration of their life cycle, Snowflake employs a consumption-based model known as **variable spend** (commonly referred to as *pay-as-you-go*). Variable spend enables teams to do rapid prototyping or experiment with proofs of concept without any upfront investment and to control their costs by monitoring and adjusting usage patterns. Here, we will break down the types of costs associated with using the Snowflake platform so that we can make informed design decisions later on.

Let us begin with the cost of storing data in the cloud.

### Storage costs

Snowflake bills its customers based on the daily average of the data stored in the platform. Since Snowflake's services layer automatically compresses data for optimal storage, customers enjoy lower storage costs without sacrificing performance. However, it is not just the raw data that counts toward storage quotas. Time Travel and fail-safe backups (discussed in detail in the next chapter) must also be considered.

Now, let us talk about the cost of processing data.

## Compute costs

Snowflake consumption is billed based on the number of virtual warehouses used, how long they run, and their size. An active warehouse is billed per second (with a 60-second minimum). Snowflake uses standard units called credits to simplify the math around warehouse pricing.

The exact cost of a credit varies based on factors such as the cloud provider, hosting region, and Snowflake edition (i.e., Standard, Enterprise, Business Critical, or VPS). Once these variables are fixed, *a credit equates to one XS warehouse running for one hour*. An important consideration is that warehouses consume credits for as long as they are active, regardless of whether they are running queries. An effective cost strategy should consider when warehouses are instantiated and shut down (auto-resume and auto-suspend options are available) and the size required for a given workload.

Finally, there is the cost of running and managing the platform.

## Service costs

The services layer manages essential operations such as access control and query optimization. However, it also performs automated serverless tasks, such as automatic (re)clustering, loading streaming data (Snowpipe), and replication. Many user-generated actions, such as querying table metadata (e.g., count, sum, or max), creating objects, and retrieving object metadata through commands such as show and describe are handled by the services layer and do not require an active warehouse.

The cost of the services layer is included in the warehouse credits as long as it does not exceed 10% of the daily warehouse consumption. When the services layer consumption does exceed 10% of warehouse spend, its operation is billed at standard credit rates (i.e., one credit per hour of XS or equivalent).

Having covered the costs associated with each of the three layers of Snowflake's architecture, we should also discuss how we can save on these costs by learning to use Snowflake's various caches.

# Saving cash by using cache

With on-premises databases, inefficient operations resulted in longer execution times. In Snowflake's variable spend model, that extra time is coupled with monetary penalties. Besides writing efficient SQL, Snowflake users should also understand the various caches associated with the service and virtual compute layers to understand where they can take advantage of pre-calculated results. A firm grasp of Snowflake caching will also inform decisions when modeling and building data pipelines.

Let us start with the services layer and familiarize ourselves with the caches it manages and offers its users.

## Services layer

The services layer handles two types of cache: metadata and query results cache.

### Metadata cache

The services layer manages object metadata, such as structure, row counts, and distinct values by column. Reviewing this metadata through related SQL functions or the Snowflake UI will not require a running warehouse and does not consume credits.

Snowflake stores metadata at the table level (e.g., size in bytes and date created) and keeps statistics (e.g., count, min/max, and null count) for columns in every micro-partition in the table.

> **Micro-partitions**
> Micro-partitions are groups of rows within tables organized in a columnar fashion. Micro-partitions allow for the granular pruning of large tables, which can comprise millions of micro-partitions. The Snowflake services layer automatically creates and manages micro-partitions as DML operations are performed in tables. Micro-partitions and caching are explained in detail in a later chapter, but for more information, see *Micro-partitions & Data Clustering* in the Snowflake documentation: `https://docs.snowflake.com/en/user-guide/tables-clustering-micropartitions.html`.

The services layer also stores metadata for object definitions and structure. This includes the DDL for database objects and details such as the column list, data types (even for views), and constraints. DDL details can be retrieved through SQL functions such as `describe` and `get_ddl` or by querying `INFORMATION_SCHEMA` directly. The latter will require an active warehouse and consume credits, while the services layer handles the former automatically.

The other cache type managed by the services layer is the query results cache.

### Query results cache

All query results in a Snowflake account are persisted for 24 hours by the services layer and can be reused by other users. Referencing a cached result resets the 24-hour clock for a maximum duration of 31 days, after which the result is purged. Aside from access privileges, there are other considerations to ensure that cached results can be reused. These include the following:

- The query must be syntactically equivalent
- Dynamic functions such as `current_date()` are not used
- The data in the underlying tables has not changed
- Users have the required permissions to access the underlying sources

Obtaining a result from the query cache is infinitely preferable to recalculating it because the operation happens instantly and consumes no compute credits. Unlike legacy databases, where the cache could be sacrificed to meet memory demands or lost altogether if the cluster was suspended, Snowflake's result cache is maintained until purged under the conditions previously mentioned.

Understanding the results cache is crucial for efficiently using Snowflake resources and making design decisions. However, that is not the only cache that users can take advantage of.

## Warehouse cache

When a virtual warehouse accesses data from the central storage layer (referred to as *remote disk* in underlying cloud storage such as AWS S3 buckets, Azure containers, or Google storage containers), the data is read into the warehouse cache (implemented using SSD storage). The amount of SSD storage depends on the warehouse size.

Reading from SSD storage is faster than reading from a remote disk, and the query optimizer (i.e., the services layer) will attempt to use the cache before defaulting to remote storage. However, unlike the services layer caches, warehouse cache comes with two significant differences: the cache is specific to a given warehouse, and suspending the warehouse purges its cache.

With this in mind, users accessing the same data sources would benefit from sharing the same warehouse. However, trade-offs must be considered between the credits required to keep a warehouse active to preserve the cache and the I/O required to read the data from scratch from remote storage.

When a query is unable to hit any of the previously mentioned caches, Snowflake must access the storage layer to perform the operation.

## Storage layer

Snowflake stores data on remote disks in the underlying cloud platform filesystem where the account is hosted. Reading data from a remote disk is less efficient than doing so from the warehouse cache (stored on SSD drives) and much less efficient than fetching a pre-calculated result. The storage layer has no cache to speak of. It is the last resort when no cache exists.

Let's summarize what've learned in this chapter.

## Summary

Snowflake's hybrid cloud-native design, built for the cloud from the ground up, enables real-time data sharing and on-demand workload sizing that gives its users unparalleled flexibility—overcoming many scalability limitations of previous database architectures. Snowflake's architecture allows secure data sharing between organizations across regions and cloud providers as quickly as it does between databases in the same account.

By understanding each of the layers that make up Snowflake's cloud architecture (storage, compute, and services), we gained insight into how they enable powerful features such as zero-copy cloning, Time Travel, Hybrid Unistore, and **hybrid transactional/analytical processing** (**HTAP**) tables and open the gates to interacting with semi-structured and unstructured data.

This chapter also outlined the costs of each of the three architecture layers and how to keep them in check. Furthermore, we discussed how various caching mechanisms across Snowflake's architecture could work together to save costs and boost performance.

With so many revolutionary features, Snowflake does not think of itself as just a database but a *Data Cloud*. When considering everything its features make possible—services such as a data and app marketplace—it is easy to see why new terminology was needed.

Now that we have had a glimpse of how Snowflake operates under the hood, it is time to dive deeper to understand the internal workings of its database objects. In the next chapter, we will look at Snowflake tables and explore their various types and parameters, as well as other object types that can be used as data sources and modeled as part of a database design. Understanding these objects and their unique features will allow you to model scalable and efficient database designs that take advantage of all the tools available in Snowflake's arsenal.

## Further reading

For the definitive guide (says so right there in the title!) on all of Snowflake's features and object types, beyond the modeling-related content covered in this book, consider Joyce Avila's excellent and complete reference:

- Avila, Joyce. *Snowflake: The Definitive Guide: Architecting, Designing, and Deploying on the Snowflake Data Cloud*. O'Reilly Media, 2022.

# 4
# Mastering Snowflake Objects

The previous chapter introduced the innovative architecture that powers the Data Cloud and unlocks possibilities that have never been possible in other databases. In this chapter, we will explore the database objects that Snowflake customers will use in their modeling journey. Objects such as tables and views will undoubtedly be familiar to most people who have previously worked with SQL. Still, even here, Snowflake's unique features unlock potential efficiencies in designing physical models, so users should be well acquainted with them.

Due to its variable spend pricing, Snowflake data modeling requires users to be well acquainted with the cost/performance trade-offs of its supported objects and their parameters. For those who have never worked with Snowflake, exclusive features such as streams and external tables may still be unfamiliar. But making good design decisions demands that users have a firm grasp and a thorough understanding of Snowflake's complete modeling toolset.

In this chapter, we're going to cover the following main topics:

- Stages and file format objects used for loading data into Snowflake
- The various physical table types used to store data
- Metadata tables for reviewing staged files
- Views and associated cost and performance benefits
- Materialized views and when to use them
- Streams for data change tracking
- Tasks for automating continuous ETL pipelines

## Stages

Before data can make its way into tables, it must be loaded into Snowflake using a stage. **Stages** are logical objects that abstract cloud filesystems so they can be used in a standard manner to load data into Snowflake. There are two types of stages that can be defined: **external** and **internal**. External stages can be created on top of a cloud location (for the supported cloud storage services) outside Snowflake and are used to load data from external source systems. Internal stages are created within the Snowflake account and therefore use the storage type of the hosting provider. Internal stages are used to stage files that originate from within the Snowflake account and can not be used to load external data.

Supported cloud storage services for external stages are as follows:

- Amazon S3 buckets
- Google Cloud Storage buckets
- Microsoft Azure containers

The following figure shows the layout of external stages in relation to internal stage types.

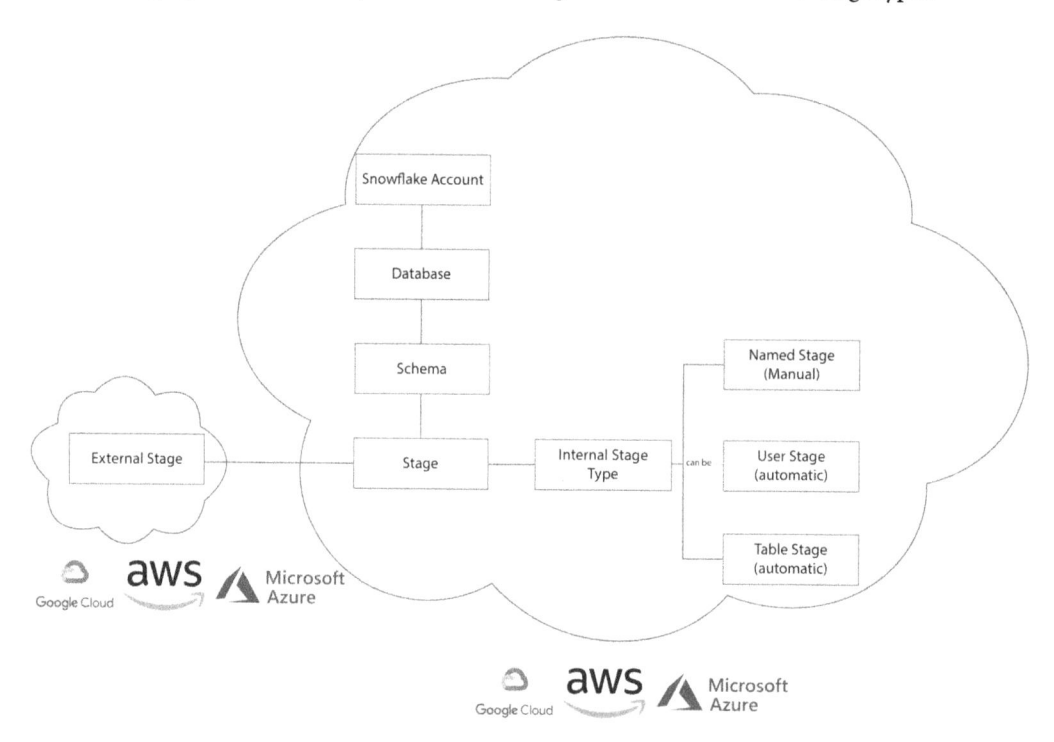

Figure 4.1 – External and internal stages in Snowflake

Unlike the data stored in tables, which is micro-partitioned and uses an internal columnar format, stages can store any type of file. Although only certain structured and semi-structured file types are supported for loading data into Snowflake, the visibility of unstructured files in a stage is an important consideration when paired with external and directory tables (discussed later in this chapter).

Stages can store any variety of files and file types. However, a file format must be specified when accessing data from a stage for subsequent loading into a Snowflake table.

## File formats

**File formats** can be thought of as templates describing the file types for reading or writing data to a file. A file format defines properties such as the delimiter type (e.g., comma, tab, or other), date/time formats, and encoding (for example, **Hex Base64**, and **UTF-8**).

Snowflake provides several structured and semi-structured file formats, such as **CSV**, **JSON**, and **Parquet**, with commonly used defaults. However, users are free to create their own named file formats when loading or unloading files of a specified type. File format properties may also be specified at runtime when using the `COPY INTO` command.

A description of supported file types and file formats for data loading is available in the Snowflake documentation: `https://docs.snowflake.com/en/user-guide/data-load-prepare.html`.

For a complete overview of data loading of all kinds, including streaming, see the guide on the Snowflake website: `https://docs.snowflake.com/en/user-guide-data-load.html`.

Having seen how data is loaded from stages into Snowflake using file formats, let's get to know the tables that will be used to store it.

## Tables

Data in Snowflake is stored in tables, which, as discussed, are one of the fundamental components of data modeling. However, before exploring them in a modeling context, we should understand the various table types that exist in Snowflake and their costs.

The previous chapter described Snowflake's **Time Travel**, a feature that allows restoring dropped objects or querying data at a prior point in time. However, Time Travel comes with associated storage costs, and the number of available Time Travel days—known as the retention period—depends on the table type, as we'll shortly review in detail.

Snowflake also offers a managed type of Time Travel, known as **Fail-safe**. All permanent tables have a Fail-safe period of seven days. Unlike Time Travel, which the user can access, Fail-safe is managed by and accessible only to Snowflake to protect user data from disasters such as system failures and data breaches. To recover data stored in Fail-safe, users need to contact Snowflake directly.

For tables that offer Time Travel and Fail-safe, the seven-day Fail-safe period begins immediately after the Time Travel period ends. The following figure illustrates the types and duration of data protection that Snowflake tables offer:

## Continuous Data Protection Lifecycle

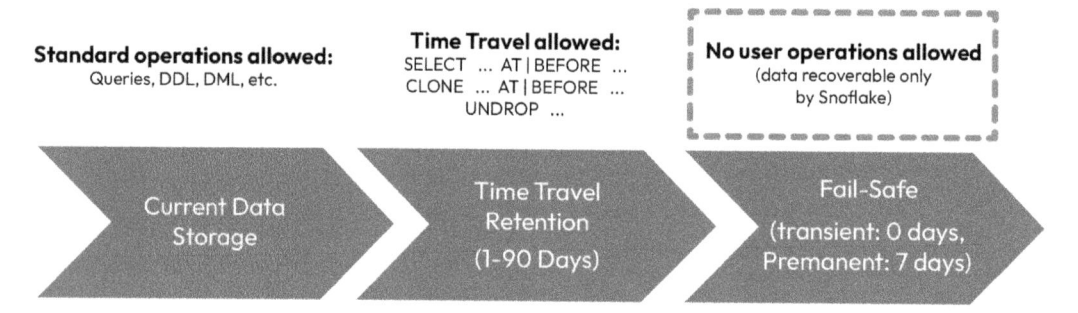

**Standard operations allowed:**
Queries, DDL, DML, etc.

**Time Travel allowed:**
SELECT ... AT | BEFORE ...
CLONE ... AT | BEFORE ...
UNDROP ...

**No user operations allowed**
(data recoverable only by Snoflake)

Current Data Storage → Time Travel Retention (1-90 Days) → Fail-Safe (transient: 0 days, Premanent: 7 days)

Figure 4.2 – Continuous Data Protection Lifecycle

Different use cases call for different backup strategies. Transactional data may require days of history, while a staging table may be needed only temporarily. Snowflake offers several physical table types with varying retention (and associated cost) options. These include the following:

- **Permanent**
- **Transient**
- **Temporary**
- **Hybrid Unistore tables**

Snowflake also provides several metadata table constructs for stage contents. These are semantic objects that exist on top of stages to allow users to query file contents and metadata (such as filenames) just like they would a regular table. These objects are read-only and are offered in the following formats:

- **External tables**
- **Directory tables**

The following sections detail the unique properties of each table type.

## Physical tables

In Snowflake, data is stored in physical tables logically grouped by schemas. Tables consist of columns with names, data types, and optional constraints and properties (for example, nullability, default value, and primary key).

The DDL command for creating a table is `CREATE TABLE` and is used in the relational modeling scenario to instantiate an empty table with a given structure.

Other variants of the CREATE TABLE command are used in the transformational context to create, pattern, or clone tables from existing objects with corresponding data, where applicable. These operations are referred to as *transformational* because they require a relational model/schema to exist beforehand (for example, creating a table by cloning an existing table). The supported variants are as follows:

- CREATE TABLE AS SELECT: Commonly referred to as **CTAS**, creates a table containing the data returned from a query (and using the implied data types).
- CREATE TABLE USING TEMPLATE: Creates an empty table using column definitions derived from semi-structured files (currently supported for **Parquet**, **Avro**, and **ORC** formats).
- CREATE TABLE LIKE: Creates an empty table using the column definitions of an existing table. Column properties, defaults, and constraints are also copied.
- CREATE TABLE CLONE: Does the same as LIKE but uses zero-copy cloning to also include all the data from the source table (without actually copying it). The CLONE variant can be used with Time Travel to clone the data at a specific point in the past. Cloned tables do not consume storage until the structure or contents are modified in the clone or source objects.

Let's look at the different physical tables offered by Snowflake.

## Permanent tables

Snowflake's default table type is a permanent table. This is a slight misnomer since all Snowflake tables except for **temporary** tables persist until explicitly dropped. Permanent tables come with built-in backup features. They include a Fail-safe period of seven days that cannot be modified or disabled, and a default of one day of Time Travel. The Time Travel period for permanent tables can be disabled or extended on Snowflake's Enterprise plan to upward of 90 days.

Their extensive recoverability makes permanent tables an ideal candidate for storing business-critical information that would be costly or impossible to regenerate in the event of a catastrophe.

We can use the following command to create a permanent table:

```
CREATE TABLE <table_name>
```

However, not all tables require backups or extended Time Travel periods. In such cases, transient tables should be considered instead.

## Transient tables

Unlike permanent tables, transient tables have no Fail-safe period but do come with one day of Time Travel by default. Users can turn off Time Travel by setting it to 0 but can not extend it beyond 1, even on Enterprise plans.

Transient tables are a good choice when backup and recovery are not a high priority—as in the case of staging tables. The same is true for development and test environments where transient defaults can be set at the schema and database level (described later in this chapter).

The command for creating a transient table is as follows:

```
CREATE TRANSIENT TABLE <table_name>
```

While transient tables are ideal for staging data and development environments, Snowflake also offers a temporary table type that persists only for the duration of a user session.

## Temporary tables

The data retention properties of temporary tables are identical to those of transient tables, aside from one critical difference: temporary tables are dropped at the end of the user session. A session can be thought of as an active login. Although multiple sessions (such as when using multiple worksheets) can run in parallel, they all terminate along with the connection or login.

Due to their impermanent nature, temporary tables are meant to hold intermediate results for processes during the same session. Temporary tables can also be used for throw-away tests in development environments, saving the user the labor of dropping them explicitly.

The command for creating a temporary table is as follows:

```
CREATE TEMPORARY TABLE <table_name>
```

> **Note on temporary table naming**
>
> Although temporary tables must be assigned to a schema like all database objects, their session-based persistence exempts them from uniqueness collisions with other table types. A temporary table can have the same name as a non-temporary table and will take precedence over it for the remainder of the session (thereby hiding the non-temporary table).

There is one more physical table offered by Snowflake. Its properties have less to do with retention times than being a total game changer for the types of workloads that Snowflake is able to support. We are talking about the Hybrid Unistore table.

## Hybrid Unistore tables

Snowflake announced Hybrid Unistore tables at Summit 2022 and is currently offering private preview for access. As they will likely be released to GA in 2023, they are included here in anticipation of the game-changing possibilities they are poised to unlock.

Hybrid Tables in Snowflake are two tables that are transparently managed under a single semantic object. A Hybrid Table consists of a standard (permanent) OLAP table and an OLTP table that the Snowflake services layer manages synchronously and transparently. The combination of OLAP and OLTP is known as **hybrid transactional and analytical processing** (**HTAP**) and offers the best of both worlds.

The OLAP table will use the standard columnar format of the permanent tables described previously and provide all the analytical performance features that Snowflake is known for. The OLTP table offers exclusive features that are not found in OLAP tables. These features, which are covered in more detail in the next chapter, include the following:

- Constraint enforcement
- Support for indexes
- Row-level locking for changes and updates

Snowflake synchronously updates the OLAP and OLTP tables when data is loaded into a Hybrid Table. The query optimizer then redirects DML or DQL queries to the table best suited to the required operation.

Although the complete documentation for Hybrid Tables is not publicly available, the `CREATE` command has been shared and uses the existing syntax for declaring constraints, as shown here:

```
CREATE HYBRID TABLE <table_name>
```

When it comes to flexibility in selecting the right backup and workload for a table, Snowflake gives its users plenty to choose from. Let us recap the physical table types and their properties.

## Table types summary

Snowflake offers its users many choices when it comes to tables and retention periods. Now that we are acquainted with the three physical OLAP-style tables and the newly announced Hybrid HTAP table, it is worth summarizing their properties in a single chart.

| Type | Persistance | Fail-safe Period (Days) | Time Travel Period (Days) | Workload |
|---|---|---|---|---|
| Temporary | Remainder of session | 0 | 0 or 1 (default is 1) | OLAP |
| Transient | Until explicitly dropped | 0 | 0 or 1 (default is 1) | OLAP |
| Permanent | Until explicitly dropped | 7 | 0 or 1 (default is 1) Standard Ed. - or - 0 to 90 (default is configurable) Enterprise Ed. | OLAP |
| Hybrid | Until explicitly dropped | tbd* | tbd* | OLAP + OLTP |

Figure 4.3 – Retention periods for permanent tables

We have gone into detail on Time Travel and recovery, but it is worth mentioning that another type of history can also be enabled for physical tables: change history. Unlike Time Travel, which allows users to access a historical snapshot of a table, change history records individual table changes and enables **change data capture** (CDC). This functionality is covered in greater detail later in this chapter.

Physical tables are what Snowflake users most often interact with for storing and manipulating information, but other table types can be defined. External and directory tables—metadata tables over stage objects—can be created and modeled relationally. Let's explore these metadata objects in more detail.

## Stage metadata tables

External and directory tables exist in Snowflake to allow users to access data in staged files as though selecting from regular tables. External tables are mentioned in this section as they allow primary and foreign keys and can be modeled in a standard relational context. Directory tables are similar to external tables but do not allow the creation of columns or constraints and are included for completeness.

### *External tables*

External tables are metadata objects created on top of stages that allow users to query the data in externally staged files as if it were inside the database. The same file formats supported by a stage are supported for accessing the data through external tables. The following columns are included for all external tables:

- VALUE : A VARIANT-type column representing a single row in the external file
- METADATA$FILENAME: Identifies the name of each staged data file in the external table, including its path in the stage
- METADATA$FILE_ROW_NUMBER: Shows the row number for each record in a staged data file

Although read-only, external tables allow users to create virtual columns as expressions over the VALUE or METADATA column. Querying data through external tables will likely be slower than native tables. It should be used to *peek* at file contents or metadata rather than relying on them as data sources.

The following command is used to create an external table:

```
CREATE EXTERNAL TABLE <table_name>
```

External tables enable users to access staged file contents as if they were stored in regular tables. However, when only the file directory information is needed, directory tables can be used.

### *Directory tables*

Conceptually, directory tables resemble external tables; however, there are several notable differences. As opposed to external tables, directory tables have the following differences:

- Are not separate database objects but can be enabled as part of a stage
- Provide file metadata such as path, size, and URL but not file contents
- Do not allow the creation of virtual columns (or constraints)
- Can be created on both internal and external stages

External tables permit users to access data stored in external cloud storage using the same conventions as regular physical tables, but directory tables only show file metadata. Directory tables are more like the LIST function—which returns a list of files from a stage—than an actual table. Using a directory table instead of the LIST function allows users to use familiar SELECT syntax to access the information.

The following command displays how to create a directory table:

```
CREATE STAGE <stage_name>
...
DIRECTORY = (ENABLE = TRUE);
```

Now that we have covered Snowflake tables in all their incarnations, let's look at views.

## Snowflake views

Snowflake views behave like most relational databases; they store a `SELECT` statement over physical objects as an object in a schema. Storing a `SELECT` statement as a shareable database object offers several advantages to users of the system:

- The `SELECT` statement does not need to be written from scratch each time it is required. This provides time savings and maintainability benefits through reusable modular code for data pipelines and analytics.
- Consistency in filters and business logic for everyone with access to the view.
- Views are separate database objects to the data sources they reference and can therefore have different permissions that do not expose all the underlying data.
- Can select data from multiple sources at once.
- Always shows the latest data from source tables without having to refresh it (as opposed to materializing the results as a physical table).
- Zero storage cost as data is not physically copied but read in real time when the view is called.

To create a view, use the following command:

```
CREATE VIEW <view_name>
```

These benefits come at the expense of a single trade-off: performance. Each time a view is called, the data must be read from the underlying tables, and all the logic and formulas in the view are calculated using compute resources and consume credits. However, this is not as alarming as it sounds when we consider that Snowflake caching features, described in the previous chapter, also work for views.

### Caching

Views attempt to take advantage of Snowflake's various caches to mitigate performance and cost issues when executing a user query.

The results cache, managed by the services layer, holds all query results in the system, including queries executed on views. As long as the underlying data has not changed, subsequent queries will return the results instantly from the cache if they are syntactically equivalent without using compute credits.

If the results cache cannot be used, Snowflake will attempt to take advantage of the warehouse cache when referencing table data through a view. Table data read from cloud storage will be available in memory through the warehouse cache for as long as the warehouse remains active—reducing the data retrieval times for the views that access it.

## Security

As mentioned earlier, views can be used to enforce data security as they are standalone securable database objects. Tables containing sensitive data—at either the row or column level—can be restricted from public access through views. Views can limit what columns are selected and what filters are applied and have separate access roles assigned to them.

Snowflake users have access to an added level of security by using **secure views**. A secure view—declared like a regular view, but with the word `secure` in the `CREATE` statement—functions like a non-secure (regular) view except that the view definition (DDL) is not visible to the consumers, but only to the role that owns the view. Some internal optimizations are disabled for secure views to not expose the underlying data, but performance is generally comparable to non-secure views.

The following command creates a secure view:

```
CREATE SECURE VIEW <view_name>
```

Now that we understand tables and views, let's get to know materialized views—a Snowflake object that offers benefits from both of these object types.

## Materialized views

Not exactly views, yet not quite tables, materialized views sit at the intersection of these two object types and offer interesting benefits with one important caveat.

As the name suggests, materialized views are actually physical tables that store the results of a view. When the underlying data changes, the result is re-materialized automatically. This means that materialized views offer the performance of a table combined with a cached query result while offering all the security benefits of a regular view.

The only trade-off is the cost. Since materialized views store query results in physical tables, they incur related storage costs. Additionally, materialized views will use credits when refreshing the data.

Materialized views have certain limitations in the logic they permit in the `SELECT` statement compared to regular views. Chief among them is that materialized views can only be built over a single data source (stages are allowed), so they cannot use joins. This limitation reduces the use case of materialized views to that of precalculated table results or aggregates. On the plus side, the Snowflake optimizer is smart enough to automatically redirect table queries to materialized views whenever possible.

Snowflake users should consider materialized views if *all* of the following conditions are met but discount them if *any* are not:

- The query results do not change often
- The view results are used significantly more frequently than data changes occur
- The query consumes a lot of compute resources

To create a materialized view, use the following command:

```
CREATE MATERIALIZED VIEW <view_name>
```

Having covered Snowflake's various data source options, let us focus on detecting their data changes and automating transformational pipelines between them.

## Streams

Streams are logical objects that capture data changes in underlying sources, including the previously mentioned objects (physical tables, views, and external and directory tables). Whenever a DML operation occurs in the source object, a stream tracks the changes (inserts, deletions, and the before/after images of updates). Streams achieve this through an *offset storage* technique—logically taking an initial snapshot of data and then tracking changes through metadata columns. Although a stream can be queried like a table, it is not a separate object and does not contain table data.

When a stream is created, metadata columns are tacked onto the source object and begin tracking changes. The following table describes the metadata fields and their contents:

| Column | Allowed Values | Description |
| --- | --- | --- |
| METADATA$ACTION | INSERT, DELETE | Denotes the action performed on the row. New rows are marked as INSERT, while updates are separated into an INSERT row with new values and DELETE the row with old values. |
| METADATA$ISUPDATE | TRUE, FALSE | A value of TRUE indicates that the INSERT and DELETE actions are the results of an update. Deleted (not updated) rows have a value of FALSE. |
| METADATA$ROW_ID | 40-character hash value | Snowflake assigns a unique ID to every table record, which can be seen here. |

Figure 4.4 – Stream metadata columns

The following command creates a stream on a table:

```
CREATE STREAM <stream_name> ON TABLE <table_name>
```

For every subsequent DML operation, the stream holds the before and after images of the changed records and, by pairing them with the relevant metadata that identifies the type of DML operation (insert, update, or delete), enables accurate CDC to downstream objects.

## Loading from streams

Snowflake keeps streams manageable and prevents them from growing excessively through an elegant method of consumption. Consuming—or using stream contents to (successfully) load or update downstream sources—empties the stream, readying it to absorb future DML changes without requiring manual periodic pruning. Selects and failed consumption attempts will not clear the stream.

In the following diagram, let's look at how this works in practice across various DML operations. This example assumes that the stream is consumed (emptied) after each change to the source table.

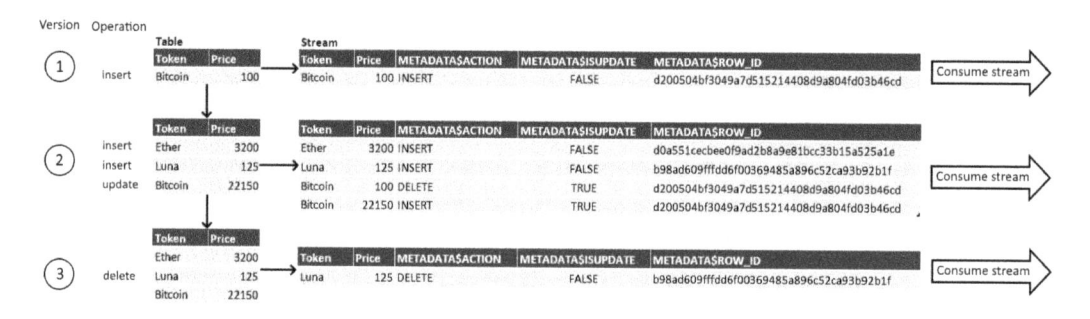

Figure 4.5 – Consuming data from a stream after table changes

Depending on the nature of the data being tracked, streams are available in two varieties:

- **Standard** (or delta): Records inserts, deletes, and updates. This type of stream is supported for tables, directory tables, and views.

- **Append/insert-only**: Only tracks inserted records and ignores any updates or deletions. This stream type is supported for physical tables, directory tables, and views as *append-only* and, for external tables, as *insert-only*.

Being able to track changes without any processing overhead associated with manually tracking and comparing versions simplifies downstream DML operations by anticipating the type of change that needs to be updated. Due to this, streams are frequently used when modeling fact tables and **slowly changing dimensions** (**SCDs**) and keeping them up to date (these objects and the techniques used to maintain them are covered in later chapters).

Streams are intended to be consumed regularly. The default retention period for changes in a stream is 14 days. Although this can be extended, Snowflake cannot guarantee stream freshness beyond that period. However, there is a less volatile alternative, one that doesn't disappear when consumed.

The following section describes change tracking and how it can be used in conjunction with or as an alternative to streams for CDC.

## Change tracking

While a stream is created as a standalone object in a schema, change tracking is enabled directly on tables, allowing Snowflake users to query CDC metadata. Change tracking uses the same metadata fields found in streams but appends them directly to a table. Unlike streams, the changes are not eliminated if they are used to update downstream objects; instead, the change tracking persists for the data retention time of the table.

Here is an example of how change tracking is enabled and queried for a table. In this example, three records are inserted into a change tracking-enabled table. Subsequently, one record is updated and another is deleted:

```
create or replace table myTable (
   myTable_id varchar(10),
   my_date date
);

-- Enable change tracking
alter table myTable set change_tracking = true;

-- Initialize a session variable for the current

--create timestamps
set cDts  = (select current_timestamp());
set cDate = (select current_date());

--perform DML
insert into myTable (myTable_id,my_date)   values
('yesterday', $cDate-1 ),
('today'    , $cDate+0 ),
('tomorrow' , $cDate+1 );

delete from myTable where myTable_id = 'yesterday';

update myTable set my_date = '1970-01-01'
where myTable_id = 'today';

-- Query the change tracking metadata to observe the delta
-- from the timestamp till now
select * from myTable
changes(information => default)
at(timestamp => $cDts);
```

The result returned from querying the table's change log shows the cumulative effect (latest version) of the record. Note that the `yesterday` and `today` records are absent from the result as they did not exist before the timestamp was set.

| | MYTABLEID | MYVALUE | METADATA$ACTION | METADATA$ISUPDATE | METADATA$ROW_ID |
|---|---|---|---|---|---|
| 1 | 2023-04-13 | good day | INSERT | FALSE | 133fa6ef17ae2a64e8aa7330ef17fa3528e1b5c4 |
| 2 | 2023-04-14 | tomorrow | INSERT | FALSE | b9bc59f1f41fc0f6380d2ff08131ec465acec9ac |

Figure 4.6 – Query results from default table change tracking

But watch what happens when the same change log is queried in append-only mode:

```
-- Query the change tracking metadata to observe
-- only inserts from the timestamp till now
select * from myTable
changes(information => append_only)
at(timestamp => $cDts);
```

The result only returns records that were inserted into the table, regardless of subsequent deletions or updates. Notice that both the `today` and `tomorrow` records have returned while `good day`, which was an update, is absent.

| | MYTABLEID | MYVALUE | METADATA$ACTION | METADATA$ISUPDATE | METADATA$ROW_ID |
|---|---|---|---|---|---|
| 1 | 2023-04-12 | yesterday | INSERT | FALSE | c2f7a8407f8a2f76dbd94ef153787617ad85035f |
| 2 | 2023-04-13 | today | INSERT | FALSE | 133fa6ef17ae2a64e8aa7330ef17fa3528e1b5c4 |
| 3 | 2023-04-14 | tomorrow | INSERT | FALSE | b9bc59f1f41fc0f6380d2ff08131ec465acec9ac |

Figure 4.7 – Query results from table change tracking in append-only mode

Barring some limitations, change tracking can even be enabled for views as long as the underlying tables have it enabled as well. Since change tracking metadata persists for the entire data retention period of a table and cannot be cleared when consumed, it is not suited for automated CDC pipelines but for analyzing the changes themselves.

Speaking of automated data pipelines, the final object that we will tackle in this chapter is designed to handle this crucial task and plays very nicely with streams and CDC detection.

## Tasks

Snowflake uses tasks to schedule and automate data loading and transformation. Although data movement is not tracked in relational modeling, it is an integral part of transformational modeling and is covered here for completeness.

Tasks automate data pipelines by executing SQL in serial or parallel steps. Tasks can be combined with streams for continuous ELT workflows to process recently changed table rows. This can be done serverlessly (using auto-scalable Snowflake-managed compute clusters that do not require an active warehouse) or using a dedicated user-defined warehouse.

The code for creating a task is as follows:

```
CREATE TASK <task_name>
...
[ AFTER <parent_task_1> [ , <parent_task_2> , ... ] ]
[ WHEN <boolean_expr> ]
AS <sql>
```

Tasks are simple to understand—they run a SQL command (or execute a stored procedure) on a schedule or when called as part of a parent task. The following figure shows how tasks can be chained serially and in parallel to form dependencies for data pipelines.

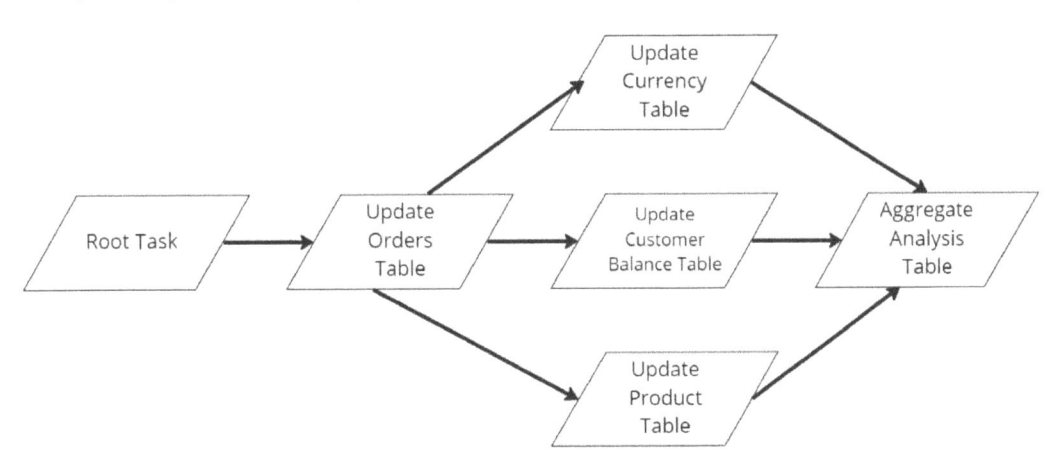

Figure 4.8 – A task tree with serial and parallel dependencies

> **Stored procedures and scripting**
>
> Stored procedures and Snowflake scripting allow you to write procedural code using looping and branching constructs and fall outside the context of this book. For information on working with procedural logic, refer to the Snowflake documentation on stored procedures (https://docs.snowflake.com/en/sql-reference/stored-procedures.html) and Snowflake Scripting (https://docs.snowflake.com/en/developer-guide/snowflake-scripting/index.html).

Now that we understand how tasks can be chained to form data pipelines within Snowflake, we can take them even further by combining them with streams.

### Combining tasks and streams

Tasks pair nicely with streams and allow users to check for changes before executing. As part of their definition, tasks have a WHEN <boolean_expr> clause, which sets a logical condition that needs to be met before it can execute. The condition must return a Boolean value but can run any function or sub-select that the user wishes. Fittingly, streams come with a system function that returns a value of TRUE whenever there are CDC records present and, otherwise, FALSE. The function can be called, referencing the stream name as follows:

```
SYSTEM$STREAM_HAS_DATA('<stream_name>')
```

Setting this condition at the start of a task means that it can be scheduled to run as frequently as changes are expected but will only be executed when there are records to process.

Let's summarize what we've learned in this chapter.

## Summary

In this chapter, we demonstrated that Snowflake objects pack a lot of features, even behind familiar ones like tables and views. A table in Snowflake can store more than just the data—depending on its settings, it can also hold months of historical and disaster recovery backups and offer offset change tracking for CDC. Views, likewise, exceed expectations by providing change tracking and automated re-materialization.

We saw how stages mark the entry point for data to make its way from external sources to Snowflake tables. Stages also provide helpful features, such as external table access for reading file contents without copying them to a table beforehand.

Finally, to coordinate incoming data, establish automated ELT pipelines, and streamline CDC, Snowflake pairs tasks with streams to give its users full serverless or managed control—tying stages, tables, views, and all the connective transformational logic together.

Having understood the strengths and capabilities of each object, we will open the next chapter by discussing the building blocks of data modeling and tying them to their Snowflake object counterparts: columns, tables, constraints, and others. These fundamentals will lay the groundwork to explore each of the four modeling types in detail later in the book.

## References

You can refer to the following resources for additional information:

- *Understanding & Using Time Travel* (Snowflake documentation): https://docs.snowflake.com/en/user-guide/data-time-travel.html. Accessed 16 November 2022.

# 5
# Speaking Modeling through Snowflake Objects

In its purest form, relational modeling (normalized tables with strictly enforced physical constraints) is most often found in **online transaction processing** (**OLTP**) databases. Transactional databases store the latest (as-is) version of business information, unlike data warehouses, which store historical snapshots and track changes in the information over time, allowing for additional (as-at) analysis across a temporal dimension.

However, this does not mean that relational modeling concepts do not apply in an **online analytical processing** (**OLAP**) database—quite the contrary. A data warehouse not only replicates existing entities and relations from transactional systems but also needs to manage the added task of conforming dimensions from other sources and joining them together in downstream transformations and analyses.

Another reason to master the common language of modeling is the Hybrid Unistore tables described in the previous chapter, which are poised to blur the line between a transactional system and warehouse and unlock use cases that have never before been possible in other architectures (such as real-time, no-ELT-required analytical access to transactional data from the same platform that functions as both the operational system and warehouse).

In this chapter, we're going to cover the following main topics:

- Ensuring efficient designs by understanding how entities are represented as tables and how Snowflake manages the underlying storage
- Exploring the benefits of proper data typing for attributes
- Understanding database constraints and managing them in Snowflake
- Learning how to reap the benefits of identifiers and primary keys
- Using alternate keys when multiple primary key candidates exist
- Tying the model together through foreign key relationships
- Specifying and checking for mandatory columns

Let us start by revisiting the foundational modeling concepts covered in the previous chapters while tying them to their corresponding Snowflake objects.

## Entities as tables

Before delving into database details, let's recall the concept of an entity at the business level: *a person, object, place, event, or concept relevant to the business for which an organization wants to maintain information*. In other words, an entity is a business-relevant concept with common properties. A rule of thumb for identifying and naming entities is that they conform to singular English nouns, for example, customer, item, and reservation.

The obvious candidate for storing and maintaining information in Snowflake is a table. Through SQL, tables give users a standard and familiar way to access and manipulate entity details. As we saw in the last chapter, Snowflake tables come in several flavors, offering different backup and recovery options. Besides selecting a table type that provides adequate Time Travel and Fail-safe, Snowflake tables live up to the company's claim of near-zero maintenance—there are no indexes, tablespaces, or partitions to maintain by hand.

The only two facets of storage over which users have control are the micro-partitions that Snowflake uses to store data in its internal columnar format and how they are clustered. Let's look at the two facets in more detail.

### How Snowflake stores data

Data in Snowflake tables is stored in a columnar format using continuous storage units called **micro-partitions**. Typically, databases divide large tables into physical partitions to improve performance and scalability. However, physical partitions require maintenance and result in data skew (some partitions growing larger than others).

Snowflake escapes these limitations by keeping the micro-partitions small (around 50-500 MB uncompressed) and managing them transparently through the services layer. Micro-partitions are immutable, so **data manipulation language** (DML) operations are more efficient and always create new partitions. Due to their small size, granular statistics can be kept for individual columns within a micro-partition, and each one compresses optimally based on its data type. Unlike traditional partitioning, micro-partitions can overlap in their value ranges (but a single record can never be split across multiple partitions).

Micro-partitions are created by the natural ordering of data as it is loaded into a table. For example, if new transactions are loaded daily into a `SALES` table, `transaction_date` would form the natural partition of the table. If, on the other hand, the table was sorted by `client` instead, then partitions by `client` would be formed, and `transaction_date` values would overlap.

Entities as tables | 65

The main benefit of micro-partitions is that their metadata (ranges of values, distinct counts, and others) allows the Snowflake optimizer to prune user queries. Pruning avoids searching through micro-partitions where filter values are known not to exist. For example, even if the `SALES` table from the previous example were to grow to millions of records and span thousands of micro-partitions, query results could still be returned in milliseconds by pruning unnecessary partitions and only scanning those whose value ranges match the query filter conditions.

Using a simplified conceptual example, let us see micro-partitions in action. The following table contains data about superheroes and their creators. This is how it would appear to the user:

| Superhero | Date Debuted | Creator | First Appearance |
|---|---|---|---|
| Dick Tracy | 1931-10-04 | Chester Gould | Dick Tracy |
| Conan the Barbarian | 1932-12-01 | Robert E. Howard | The Phoenix on the Sword Weird Tales |
| Flash Gordon | 1934-01-07 | Alex Raymond | Newspaper Comic |
| The Phantom | 1936-02-17 | Lee Falk | The Phantom |
| Sheena, Queen of the Jungle | 1938-01-01 | Will Eisner and S.M. "Jerry" Iger | Wags #46 |
| Superman (Clark Kent) | 1938-06-01 | Jerry Siegel, Joe Shuster | Action Comics #1 |
| Arrow | 1938-09-01 | Paul Gustavson | Funny Pages vol. 2 #10 |
| Batman (Bruce Wayne) | 1939-05-01 | Bob Kane, Bill Finger | Detective Comics #27 |
| The Spirit | 1940-06-02 | Will Eisner | The Spirit |
| Spider-Man (Peter Parker) | 1962-08-01 | Stan Lee, Steve Ditko | Amazing Fantasy #15 |

Figure 5.1 – The logical view of Snowflake table data

Internally, two micro-partitions are created, and the data is compressed using a columnar format.

**Micro Partition 1**

| | | | | | | Value Ranges (Example of Partition Metadata) |
|---|---|---|---|---|---|---|
| Superhero | Dick Tracy | Conan the Barbarian | Flash Gordon | The Phantom | Sheena, Queen of the Jungle | Dick Tracy / Sheena, Queen of the Jungle |
| Date Debuted | 1931-10-04 | 1932-12-01 | 1934-01-07 | 1936-02-17 | 1938-01-01 | 1931-10-04 / 1938-01-01 |
| Creator | Chester Gould | Robert E. Howard | Alex Raymond | Lee Falk | Will Eisner and S.M. "Jerry" Iger | Alex Raymond / Will Eisner and S.M. "Jerry" Iger |
| First Appearance | Dick Tracy | The Phoenix on the Sword Weird Tales | Newspaper Comic | The Phantom | Wags #46 | Dick Tracy / Wags #46 |

**Micro Partition 2**

| | | | | | | |
|---|---|---|---|---|---|---|
| Superhero | Superman (Clark Kent) | Arrow | Batman (Bruce Wayne) | The Spirit | Spider-Man (Peter Parker) | Arrow / The Spirit |
| Date Debuted | 1938-06-01 | 1938-09-01 | 1939-05-01 | 1940-06-02 | 1962-08-01 | 1938-06-01 / 1962-08-01 |
| Creator | Jerry Siegel, Joe Shuster | Paul Gustavson | Bob Kane, Bill Finger | Will Eisner | Stan Lee, Steve Ditko | Bob Kane, Bill Finger / Will Eisner |
| First Appearance | Action Comics #1 | Funny Pages vol. 2 #10 | Detective Comics #27 | The Spirit | Amazing Fantasy #15 | Action Comics #1 / The Spirit |

Figure 5.2 – A Snowflake table divided into two micro-partitions

Since the table is ordered by `Date Debuted`, when the services layer breaks the table up into micro-partitions, this column will have a natural clustering of values. While this example uses only two, Snowflake tables can be composed of millions of micro-partitions depending on their size.

Using the partition metadata, only some of which is shown in *Figure 5.2* (column value ranges), Snowflake's query optimizer can prune or ignore partitions depending on the query filters.

In the following example, the optimizer can safely skip reading *partition 1* because its value range (known from the metadata) does not correspond to the filter condition.

| Micro Partition 1 | Partition Ignored | | | | | Value Ranges (Example Metadata) |
|---|---|---|---|---|---|---|
| Superhero | Dick Tracy | Conan the Barbarian | Flash Gordon | The Phantom | Sheena, Queen of the Jungle | Dick Tracy / Sheena, Queen of the Jungle |
| Date_Debuted | 1931-10-04 | 1932-12-01 | 1934-01-07 | 1936-02-17 | 1938-01-01 | 1931-10-04 / 1938-01-01 |
| Creator | Chester Gould | Robert E. Howard | Alex Raymond | Lee Falk | Will Eisner and S.M. "Jerry" Iger | Alex Raymond / Will Eisner and S.M. "Jerry" Iger |
| First Appearance | Dick Tracy | "The Phoenix on the Sword" Weird Tales | Newspaper Comic | The Phantom | Wags #46 | Dick Tracy / Wags #46 |

| Micro Partition 2 | Partition Read | | | | | |
|---|---|---|---|---|---|---|
| Superhero | Superman (Clark Kent) | Arrow | Batman (Bruce Wayne) | The Spirit | Spider-Man (Peter Parker) | Arrow / The Spirit |
| Date_Debuted | 1938-06-01 | 1938-09-01 | 1939-05-01 | 1940-06-02 | 1962-08-01 | 1938-06-01 / 1962-08-01 |
| Creator | Jerry Siegel, Joe Shuster | Paul Gustavson | Bob Kane, Bill Finger | Will Eisner | Stan Lee, Steve Ditko | Bob Kane, Bill Finger / Will Eisner |
| First Appearance | Action Comics #1 | Funny Pages vol. 2 #10 | Detective Comics #27 | The Spirit | Amazing Fantasy #15 | Action Comics #1 / The Spirit |

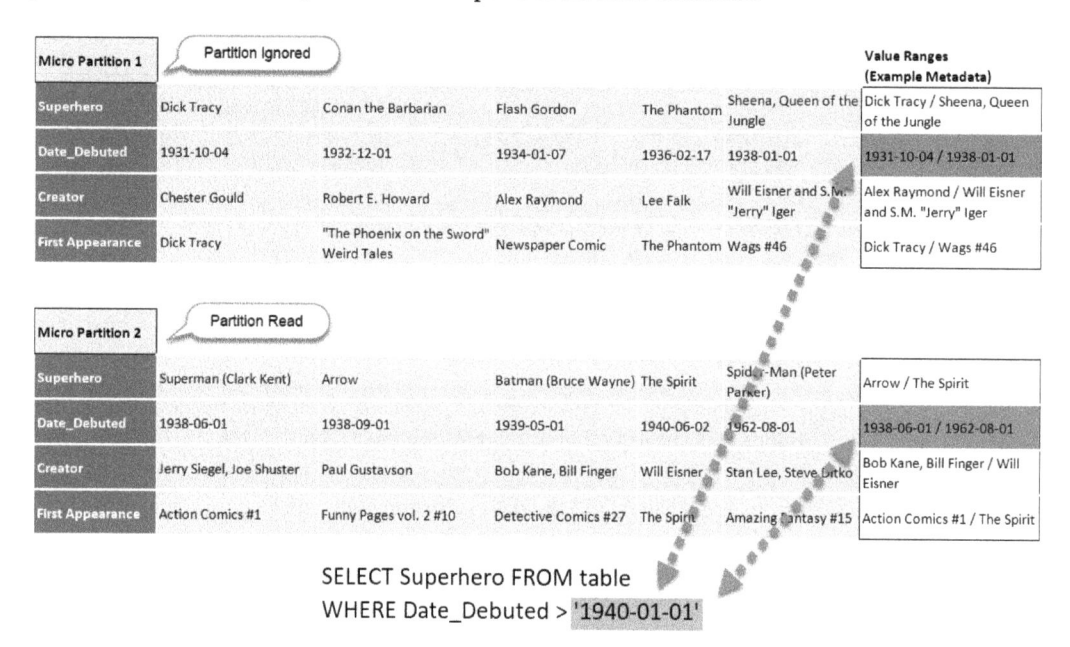

```
SELECT Superhero FROM table
WHERE Date_Debuted > '1940-01-01'
```

Figure 5.3 – Successful query pruning

If the optimizer cannot eliminate any micro-partitions based on their value ranges, then all the partitions and their contents need to be read to find matching records.

In the following example, query pruning cannot be performed because both partitions match the search condition based on their value range, even though the creator *Paul Gustavson* only exists in *partition 2*:

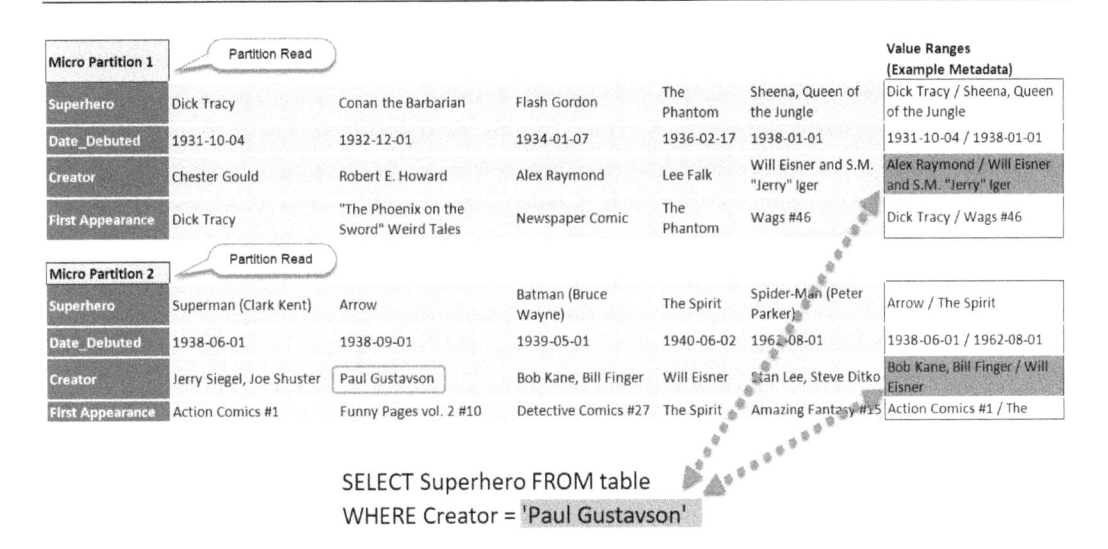

Figure 5.4 – Query pruning cannot be performed with a given filter

How Snowflake manages micro-partitions depends on the order in which data is loaded into a table. Data can be ordered explicitly upon insertion using the ORDER BY clause or implicitly by the natural load pattern (for example, by CREATED_DATE or LOAD_DATE). When partitioning matches search filters, query performance is improved through pruning. For example, in a table with millions of rows, where data is loaded by LOAD_DATE and queried for LOAD_DATE = CURRENT_DATE, performance will be identical to a table that only held data for CURRENT_DATE. However, discounting this filter or searching for any other attribute would likely not benefit from query pruning.

As shown in the preceding examples, micro-partitioning creates multiple data segments with varying degrees of overlapping column values. This data segmentation, known as clustering, can be used strategically to organize the table structure and improve query performance. Let's understand how to use it to our advantage.

## Clustering

As table data is broken up into micro-partitions, column values naturally group themselves into data segments. The degree of variance of column values and their overlap across micro-partitions is known as **clustering**. The less overlap is encountered between partitions, the higher the degree of query and column pruning that the optimizer can provide.

In addition to column metadata for micro-partitions, the Snowflake services layer also stores clustering statistics such as the following:

- The total number of micro-partitions in each table
- The number of micro-partitions containing values that overlap with each other (in a specified subset of table columns)
- The depth of the overlapping micro-partitions

The following (simplified) example shows how three micro-partitions can overlap in their clustering range. An actual table could have many more partitions and columns, and achieving a perfect separation is neither likely nor required for improving query performance.

## Clustering Depth

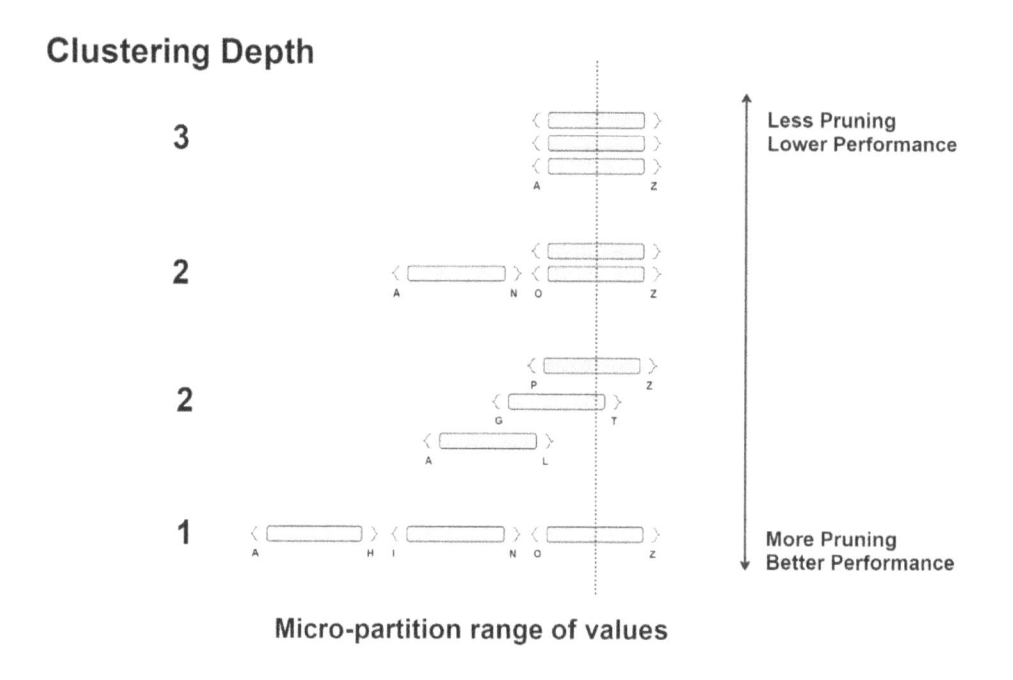

Figure 5.5 – Partition overlap and clustering depth

When considering how data is loaded and queried from a table, the clustering depth or degree of overlap (less is better for pruning and performance) should be considered as tables reach a considerable size. Although ordering a table across one or multiple dimensions might improve query performance through pruning, the cost of the sorting operation may offset those gains.

Generally, even tables with several million rows would provide adequate performance without any sorting or ordering applied to the rows. However, query performance may degrade after a certain table size if the load pattern does not match the search pattern (for example, data is loaded by TRANSACTION_DATE but queried by CLIENT).

Users can assess query pruning information using Snowflake's visual query profiler. The total number of micro-partitions is displayed on the screen alongside the number of partitions accessed during a query.

The following screenshot shows that the number of scanned partitions equals the total—meaning the optimizer could not perform any pruning.

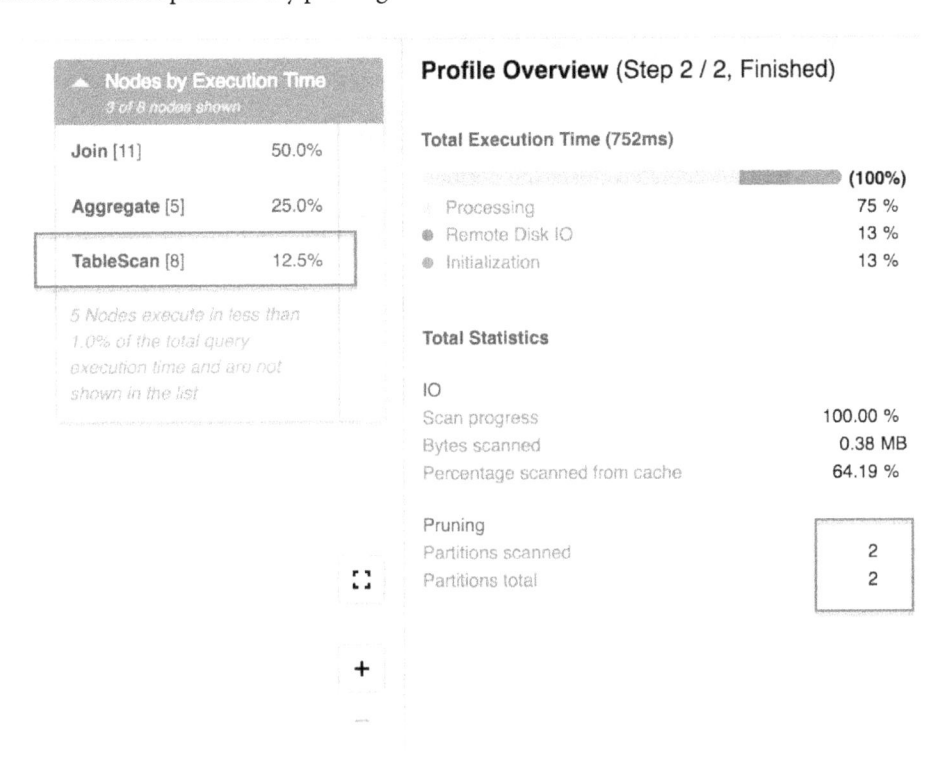

Figure 5.6 – Evaluating pruning using the query plan

As stated earlier, a lack of pruning alone is not an indicator of poor query performance. Query duration is subjective due to factors such as caching, query complexity, and data volume. However, when query performance fails to meet expectations, factors such as a high table scan percentage, as shown in *Figure 5.6*, relative to other query operations and a lack of pruning, may indicate a need to recluster the table.

Reclustering can be performed manually by recreating the table while applying the required sorting or can be handled automatically by Snowflake.

## Automatic clustering

Snowflake automatically handles clustering through the natural loading pattern of the incoming data. However, on large tables (multi-terabyte and above), DML operations may degrade the clustering quality on desired columns and impact query performance.

Due to the large table size, manual re-sorting of the table would be costly, so Snowflake provides the option of automated reclustering of a table through a specified clustering key. A **clustering key** is one or more columns (or an expression) that Snowflake uses to automatically sort the data in a given table and transparently re-sort it when necessary.

The benefits of defining a clustering key include the following:

- Improved query performance through pruning by skipping data that does not match query filters
- Better column compression and reduced storage costs
- Maintenance-free automated reclustering performed by Snowflake

However, remember that automated reclustering operations incur the same processing costs as those performed manually. Therefore, only consider setting a clustering key if performance is prioritized over cost or the clustering performance offsets the credits required to maintain it. The following considerations help determine when the latter is likely to occur:

- The table contains multiple **terabytes** (**TB**) of data and many micro-partitions.
- The queries can take advantage of clustering. Typically, this means that one or both of the following are true:
  - The queries need to read only a small percentage of rows in the table
  - The queries sort the data (for example, using an ORDER BY clause)
- A high percentage of queries can benefit from the same clustering key by selecting or sorting on the same few columns.

Further information on clustering depth can be found in the Snowflake documentation (https://docs.snowflake.com/en/user-guide/tables-clustering-micropartitions.html).

Entities are the main elements of a relational model. In this section, we saw how to translate an entity into a physical table in Snowflake and the design considerations to contemplate for optimal performance and storage. We will expand on the entity in the next section by adding properties.

## Attributes as columns

Recall from the previous section that an entity is a business-relevant concept for which an organization wishes to maintain information. Recall that attributes—defined with the business team during conceptual modeling or loaded from existing source data during the ETL process—are properties that describe the entity and are stored as columns. Attributes can be descriptive (such as NAME, ADDRESS, and QUANTITY) or metadata (such as ETL_SOURCE and LOAD_DATE).

The nature of the attribute—whether numeric, string, date, or other—is an essential detail for understanding the business requirement at the conceptual level and selecting the right data type at the physical level. Snowflake offers basic data types found in other databases (such as `VARCHAR`, `DATE`, and `INTEGER`) and less-common ones (such as `VARIANT` and `GEOGRAPHY`), which offer exciting possibilities for modeling and working with table contents.

Let us get to know Snowflake data types and their unique properties so that we can adequately assign them to entity attributes.

## Snowflake data types

Snowflake is an ANSI-compliant database and supports the common SQL data types for storing strings, dates, and numbers. In addition, Snowflake provides more advanced types for storing semi-structured and geospatial data. When we discussed micro-partitions, column compression (based on data type) was mentioned as a critical factor in performance and cost management. However, using data types correctly can also yield usability benefits when querying table contents.

Before continuing, please review the list of Snowflake data types in the documentation (https://docs.snowflake.com/en/sql-reference/intro-summary-data-types.html) unless you're already familiar with them.

Some data types offer properties that can be applied during table creation, such as collation and autoincrement. Collation lets the user set options such as case, accent sensitivity, and space-trimming for string comparisons. For numeric data types, identity and autoincrement options generate unique sequences that come in handy for surrogate keys (described in a later section).

Besides storage and compression, adequate typing of attribute columns offers advantages from a usability perspective by ensuring consistent formatting during data loading (for example, no stray characters in numeric columns or improper date formats in date). Beyond that, proper typing unlocks all relevant data type functions that Snowflake supports, such as `DATEDIFF` (calculates the difference between two dates) for dates and `STRTOK` (tokenizes a given string and returns the requested part) for strings. The complete SQL function reference can be found in the Snowflake documentation (https://docs.snowflake.com/en/sql-reference-functions.html).

> **Storing strings in Snowflake**
>
> Snowflake uses the `VARCHAR` data type to store string values. The maximum length of a `VARCHAR` column is 16 MB, or 16,777,216 characters/bytes. How much data fits in 16 MB? How about the contents of Tolstoy's *War and Peace* (587,287 words) four times over? Interestingly, the 16 MB length is also the default. But do not panic. Snowflake efficiently compresses column contents to their exact lengths and does not bill for the 16 MB maximum. However, sometimes it makes sense to explicitly limit a column to a fixed set of characters to inform database users that its contents are not meant to exceed the specified setting (for example, setting a column containing ISO currency codes to `VARCHAR(3)`).

Now, let us turn from structured columns to semi-structured data types.

## Storing semi-structured data

Snowflake is widely recognized for its ease and agility in handling semi-structured data. There are three dedicated data types available for storing semi-structured information (VARIANT, ARRAY, and OBJECT), and aside from unique functions available to each (to be discussed shortly), they allow users to query their semi-structured contents using native SQL and without having to convert or flatten the data beforehand. Querying semi-structured data is discussed in later chapters and explained in the Snowflake documentation (https://docs.snowflake.com/en/user-guide/querying-semistructured.html).

Snowflake tables can consist of structured and semi-structured data types, which can be queried natively in the same SELECT statement. However, there are some differences between the three semi-structured data types and how they are used, so let us understand what they are:

- VARIANT: This is the recommended data type for hierarchical semi-structured data that allows users to load and query JSON, Avro, ORC, and Parquet data without converting or explicitly describing their structure. VARIANT has a maximum length of 16 MB and can store a value of any other data type (except VARIANT). Common uses of the VARIANT data type include email logs, web activity, and event data.

- OBJECT: A Snowflake OBJECT is analogous to a JSON object or dictionary, hash, or map, as it is known in other programming languages. An OBJECT is a key-value pair, where the key is VARCHAR text that identifies the value and the VARIANT-type value itself. An OBJECT is used when the keys (names) convey meaningful information (for example, a list of countries by ISO currency code used). An OBJECT has a maximum size of 16 MB and can store a value of any other data type, including OBJECT.

- ARRAY: A Snowflake ARRAY is similar to arrays in other programming languages. An array contains zero or more (the length is dynamic and not set explicitly) elements and references to their positions. Unlike an OBJECT, whose elements are accessed by (key) name, ARRAY elements are referenced by their positions. This makes an ARRAY data type suitable for looping or processing data in natural/chronological order. An OBJECT has a maximum length of 16 MB and can store a value of any other data type, including ARRAY. However, ARRAY positions contribute to the 16 MB limit, so their effective size is smaller.

We have only briefly touched on the available options and functions surrounding Snowflake's various structured and semi-structured data types. For further reading on Snowflake data types, the following documentation provides a sectioned reference for each of them: https://docs.snowflake.com/en/sql-reference/data-types.html.

Having understood data types for defining attribute columns, we can move on to learning about the various constraints that can be defined on them. However, before we can explore constraints in detail, we need to highlight one crucial factor regarding Snowflake's management of them.

## Constraints and enforcement

The remainder of this chapter deals with table constraints, so it is necessary to understand what they are and to mention several important details regarding their use in Snowflake. In the ANSI-SQL standard, constraints define integrity and consistency rules for data stored in tables. Snowflake supports four constraint types:

- PRIMARY KEY
- UNIQUE
- FOREIGN KEY
- NOT NULL

Since the function of each of these constraints is covered later in this chapter, this section will be limited to their enforcement.

Enforcement, on the part of the database, means actively monitoring the integrity rules of a given constraint when DML operations are performed on a table. By enforcing a constraint, a database ensures that an error is raised when the constraint is violated, and the offending DML operation is not allowed to complete.

For example, a NOT NULL constraint on a column indicates that this column cannot contain NULL values. By enforcing this constraint, Snowflake raises an error if an operation tries to insert or update a NULL value in that column.

The NOT NULL example was chosen strategically because out of the four existing constraints, this is the only one that is enforced. The other three constraints are orientative, meaning that while they are not enforced (can be violated without resulting in an error), they inform database users of some valuable metadata details (discussed later in this chapter). At least, this was the case before Hybrid Unistore tables were announced.

Hybrid Unistore tables (described in the previous chapter) have a completely different HTAP architecture, allowing Snowflake to enforce all four constraints.

With this in mind, let us look at the PRIMARY KEY constraint so we can understand what function this constraint serves both with and without enforcement.

## Identifiers as primary keys

Tables store information for business entities using attributes of relevant data types. A row in the CUSTOMER table holds information for a given customer, and a row in the ORDERS table represents an order—or does it? Perhaps in this example, orders can contain multiple products and span just as many rows. To determine a unique instance of an entity, an **identifier**—or **primary key** (**PK**), if referring to a physical database—is used.

A PK is a column or set of columns whose values uniquely determine an instance of an entity. Only one PK can be defined per table. From a business perspective, a PK represents a single entity instance. To return to the previous example—is an order a single row containing one product, or does our organization allow multiple products per order? PKs inform database users of what that reality looks like at the table level.

The following figure shows some sample data from a fictitious ORDERS table.

| | O_ORDERSKEY | O_ORDERKEY | O_PRODKEY | O_ORDERSTATUS | O_TOTALPRICE | O_ORDERDATE | O_ORDERPRIORITY |
|---|---|---|---|---|---|---|---|
| 31 | 30 | 3,639,712 | 143,420 | F | 239,880.58 | 1993-07-18 | 3-MEDIUM |
| 32 | 31 | 2,533,890 | 142,628 | O | 160,918.7 | 1998-06-26 | 1-URGENT |
| 33 | 32 | 3,909,985 | 12,454 | F | 140,327.59 | 1993-06-07 | 3-MEDIUM |
| 34 | 33 | 2,895,783 | 74,347 | F | 181,920.99 | 1993-08-30 | 2-HIGH |
| 35 | 34 | 2,445,186 | 139,993 | O | 194,939.31 | 1997-09-02 | 2-HIGH |
| 36 | 35 | 520,964 | 54,752 | O | 159,309.83 | 1997-05-26 | 5-LOW |
| 37 | 36 | 419,684 | 11,422 | F | 112,659.1 | 1992-06-03 | 3-MEDIUM |
| 38 | 37 | 1,644,164 | 21,691 | O | 247,340.72 | 1996-04-26 | 5-LOW |
| 39 | 38 | 61,382 | 37,204 | F | 162,991.79 | 1992-05-11 | 4-NOT SPECIFIED |

Figure 5.7 – Sample data from an ORDERS table

There appear to be no duplicate values for the O_ORDERKEY column, but this is a small sample from a table with millions of records. It is impossible to tell by looking at the data whether an order is uniquely identified by O_ORDERKEY only, O_ORDERKEY in conjunction with O_PRODKEY, or some other combination of columns (when a PK consists of multiple columns, it is called a **composite** or **compound key**).

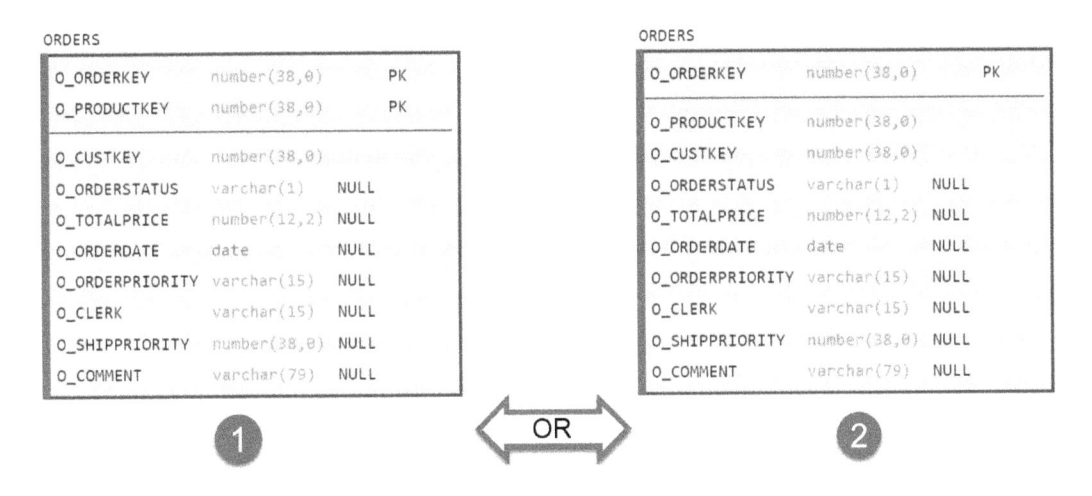

Figure 5.8 – Single or compound PK defined on the ORDERS table

Even reviewing every record in the table and finding no duplicates does not guarantee that one won't arrive later if the business model and the corresponding data model are configured as per scenario 2 in *Figure 5.8*. Only by establishing a conceptual identifier and defining it physically in the corresponding Snowflake table can users definitively know how to isolate a unique entity instance within it.

Having understood how a PK is used to identify a unique record, let us discuss the practical advantages of using it.

## Benefits of a PK

The most compelling argument in favor of PKs comes not from a textbook but from *Too Many Daves*, a children's poem by Dr. Seuss. The poem tells of Mrs. McCave and her poor lifestyle choices, such as having twenty-three children and naming all of them Dave. Henceforth, without a unique identifier, Mrs. McCave is unable to isolate a singular instance of Dave—an all-too-familiar problem for many database users (`https://allpoetry.com/poem/11575842-Too-Many-Daves-by-Theodor-Seuss-Geisel`).

Besides isolating the Dave you are looking for, there are other compelling reasons to define PKs.

### Determining granularity

Once data has been populated in a table, the need to query individual entities or aggregate entity statistics immediately follows. However, how can the users tell how many rows constitute a single record? Is an order stored in a single line, or does it generate one line per product that it contains? In other words, what is the lowest level of detail?

The PK answers this question by defining the granularity of the table and telling the users the lowest level of data it contains and how to uniquely identify an entity instance.

Knowing the PK of a table allows database users to query the data precisely on the required column(s) and values and eliminate ambiguity (of having multiple Daves, for example).

The precision of isolating a unique entity also applies to aggregating table data for counting and summarizing its **metrics** (**numerical attributes**). Snowflake offers various aggregating functions to summarize table data—such as COUNT, SUM, and MAX—but they require the user to specify the entity's unique identifier (or other grouping dimensions) in the GROUP BY statement. Incorrectly specifying (or assuming) a valid identifier of a table will result in queries that return erroneous counts and aggregates.

### *Ensuring correct join results*

Queries often require data from one table to be joined and enriched by information from another. While there are many types of joins (LEFT, INNER, and FULL), users tend to avoid the Cartesian or cross join, which multiplies the rows from one table by the number of matching rows in another. Cartesian joins most often occur due to the inability to correctly identify a unique record in one or both tables involved in a join.

In the Dr. Seuss example, the ambiguity results in 23 rows instead of 1. In a database, where queries may operate on millions of records, unexpected record explosions could result in billions of extra rows and a meaningless final result. Such queries can run exponentially longer than expected under correct join conditions. In any database, this would be a total waste of time, but in Snowflake, this would also come with a hefty credit spend.

### *Avoiding duplicate values (Hybrid Unistore)*

A PK uniquely identifies an entity. Therefore, duplicate values in PK columns would violate this constraint and should be disallowed. However, only Hybrid Unistore tables can enforce this rule. They can do so through an index that allows Snowflake to efficiently scan for existing values when performing a DML operation.

If using regular Snowflake tables, ad-hoc validation can be performed before or after a DML operation to test for duplicates.

Dr. Seuss takes the poem to its logical conclusion that Mrs. McCave would have avoided much hardship by uniquely naming her children, saying, *But she didn't do it. And now it's too late*. But unlike naming children, it is never too late to assign a PK to a table. Let us look at the three methods Snowflake provides for doing so.

## Specifying a PK

A PK can be specified when creating a Snowflake table in one of two ways—inline, next to the corresponding column(s) in the `CREATE TABLE` statement, or out of line, at its end:

- **New table inline**: A PK can be declared directly next to a corresponding column when creating a table. This method is only valid for single-column PKs and cannot be used to define composite keys:

    ```
    CREATE TABLE ORDERS
    (
        O_ORDERKEY number(38,0) CONSTRAINT my_pk_name PRIMARY KEY,
        O_PRODUCTKEY number(38,0) NOT NULL,
        O_CUSTKEY number(38,0) NOT NULL,
        -- < rest of columns>
        O_COMMENT varchar(200) COMMENT 'Order details'
    );
    ```

- **New table out of line**: This method allows Snowflake users to specify a PK at the end of the `CREATE` statement and include multiple columns as part of the definition:

    ```
    CREATE TABLE ORDERS
    (
        O_ORDERKEY number(38,0),
        O_PRODUCTKEY number(38,0),
        O_CUSTKEY number(38,0) NOT NULL,
        -- < rest of columns>
        O_COMMENT varchar(200) COMMENT 'Order details',
        CONSTRAINT my_pk_name PRIMARY KEY ( O_ORDERKEY, O_PRODUCTKEY )
    );
    ```

- **Existing table out of line**: A PK can still be defined for existing tables by performing an `ALTER TABLE` statement and specifying it like an out-of-line constraint:

    ```
    ALTER TABLE ORDERS
    ADD CONSTRAINT my_pk_name PRIMARY KEY (O_ORDERKEY,
    O_PRODUCTKEY);
    ```

Now that we have seen how to define a PK, let us discuss the different types of keys that exist and how they are used in modeling.

## Keys taxonomy

Having seen the vital role that PKs play in defining and querying database tables, it is time to drill down into the various kinds of keys that exist to understand their taxonomy and the roles they play when designing tables.

Although the function of a PK remains unchanged—to uniquely identify a record in a table—the language of modeling allows for distinctions based on the nature of the key columns. Let us see what that looks like in practice, starting with the most common type: the business key.

### Business key

A **business key** is a PK whose values hold meaning or significance within the organization. Any random group of characters can serve to identify an entity instance as long as they are unique. What sets the business key apart is that its values are significant in themselves.

All the examples from this chapter have been business keys. In the example in *Figure 5.7*, the values in O_ORDERKEY and O_PRODKEY are understood within the organization in operational teams and their systems, and the same codes are referenced, for example, in the CRM system and in other tables where they exist. If used as PKs, a Social Security number or an ISO country code would also qualify as business keys because of their broader significance in the outside world.

When modeling columns that contain business keys, a prefix or suffix of BKEY is often used to designate the distinction.

However, a key need not have business significance to be useful in table design. Meet the surrogate key.

### Surrogate key

Unlike a business key—which holds business significance—a **surrogate key** is a PK whose value holds no special meaning. Surrogate keys are typically created using random characters, column hashes, or sequential integers. They satisfy the condition of uniqueness, but their values carry no intrinsic meaning.

Tables often have compound PKs with numerous member columns, which makes them tedious to type when, for example, needing to join one table to another. Surrogate keys get around this inconvenience because, by nature, they are single-column and have a standard value format (for example, column hash or sequence). Some data models—such as Data Vault 2.0, discussed in a later chapter—rely on surrogate keys to ensure strict naming and value patterns to make table design repeatable and consistent.

When modeling columns that contain surrogate keys, a prefix or suffix of SKEY is often used to designate the distinction.

## Sequences

When creating a sequential surrogate key, Snowflake provides a mechanism for generating it called a sequence. A **sequence** is an independent database object that generates sequential (but not necessarily gap-less) integers, ensuring unique column values. A start number and increment can be specified when creating a sequence.

As independent objects, a single sequence can be shared by multiple tables or manipulated through function calls.

Sequences can be used as surrogate keys by assigning them as the default column value when creating a table. To do so, use a sequence's `nextval` function as the column default like so:

```
create or replace sequence seq1;
create or replace table foo (k number default seq1.nextval, v number);
```

The following example demonstrates how new records would behave under various conditions of the `nextval` function:

```
-- insert rows with unique keys (generated by seq1) and explicit values
insert into foo (v) values (100);
insert into foo values (default, 101);

-- insert rows with unique keys (generated by seq1) and reused values.
-- new keys are distinct from preexisting keys.
insert into foo (v) select v from foo;

-- insert row with explicit values for both columns
insert into foo values (200, 202);

select * from foo;

+------+------+
|   K  |   V  |
|------+------|
|    1 |  100 |
|    2 |  101 |
|    3 |  100 |
|    4 |  101 |
|  200 |  202 |
+------+------+
```

Alternatively, Snowflake can create and manage the sequence object transparently for a given table by using the `AUTOINCREMENT` or `IDENTITY` keywords when creating a column:

```
CREATE TABLE FOO
(
    k number DEFAULT seq1.nextval,
    v number
);

CREATE TABLE BAR
(
    k number NOT NULL AUTOINCREMENT START 10 INCREMENT 5,
    v number NOT NULL
);
```

For more information on using sequences, consult Snowflake's documentation: https://docs.snowflake.com/en/user-guide/querying-sequences.

We now understand the PK taxonomy and can distinguish a business key, which has business significance, from a surrogate key, which is not meaningful in itself and whose sole purpose is to provide a unique value. However, recall that a table can only have one PK defined. So, what happens when there are multiple columns that can uniquely identify an entity instance?

## Alternate keys as unique constraints

Suppose we were modeling an EMPLOYEE table that contains an EMPLOYEE_ID column—a unique business identifier—and Social Security numbers—government-issued personal identifiers. Either column would satisfy the PK requirement of uniquely identifying a record in the EMPLOYEE table, but recall that a table may only be assigned one PK. To let database users know that another column (or columns) satisfies the conditions for a PK when a PK already exists, **alternate keys** (**AKs**) or UNIQUE constraints can also be defined.

In the previous example, the EMPLOYEE table had two valid PK candidates: EMPLOYEE_ID and SOCIAL_SECURITY_ID. In OLTP databases, the column or columns that act as the organizational business key should be made the primary. In a data warehouse, where business keys from multiple source systems may be loaded, a surrogate key would be used instead. By this convention, the EMPLOYEE table should be modeled with EMPLOYEE_ID as the PK and SOCIAL_SECURITY_ID as the AK (UNIQUE).

The following example shows what that would look like:

```
CREATE TABLE EMPLOYEE
(
    EMPLOYEE_ID varchar(10),
    SOCIAL_SECURITY_ID number(9),
    -- < rest of columns>
    NAME varchar,
    CONSTRAINT pk_employee PRIMARY KEY ( EMPLOYEE_ID ),
    CONSTRAINT ak_employee UNIQUE (SOCIAL_SECURITY_ID)
);
```

Unlike a PK, a table can have as many AKs as necessary. AKs give database users insight into the granularity of a table and its various columns and carry the same functional benefits as PKs. Like PKs, UNIQUE constraints are only enforced in Hybrid Unistore tables and are merely orientative for standard ones.

So far, the chapter has focused on individual tables and their constraints, but modeling is concerned with defining entire database landscapes, which represent the interrelated nature of the many business entities. The following section will explain how to form relationships between entities and why this is a crucial detail in a database model.

# Relationships as foreign keys

Any business can be broken down into a set of entities and their interactions. For example, customers place orders for items provided by suppliers while applying promotion codes from an active marketing campaign—which is still a very narrow slice of what goes on in a typical organization. So far, this chapter has focused on the entities themselves: orders, items, and suppliers, for example. Now it is time to focus on the interactions—or relationships, as they are called in modeling parlance—such as placing orders, providing items, and applying promotions.

When business entities are related, their corresponding tables must have a way to capture the details of the interaction. When a customer orders an item, the order details must capture who the customer is and what items they ordered. Remember, PKs identify a unique record in a table. Therefore, when two tables share a **relationship**, the PKs of one must be included in the other to store the details of the interaction. In a database, this relationship is established through a table constraint called a **foreign key** (**FK**).

When PK columns from one table (known as the parent) are included in another (known as the child), an FK constraint can be declared in the child table to formalize the relationship. The FK constraint tells the database and its users that it is no coincidence that the two tables have some columns in common but that they share a relationship through some business context.

An FK is represented on a diagram by a line connecting the parent table to the child. Recall the example of PERSON and ACCOUNT from *Chapter 1, Unlocking the Power of Modeling*, where it was established that an account must be assigned to a person, and a person can open zero or many accounts. If it is established that PERSON_ID uniquely identifies a PERSON (its PK), this column must be included in the ACCOUNT table and declared an FK constraint. When creating the ACCOUNT table (a child table), the PK and the FK constraints must be defined.

The following code snippet shows the creation of the PERSON and ACCOUNT tables:

```
CREATE TABLE PERSON
(
    PERSON_ID number(8,0) NOT NULL,
    SOCIAL_SERCURITY_NUM number(9,0) NOT NULL,
    DRIVERS_LICENSE varchar(10) NOT NULL,
    NAME varchar NOT NULL,
    BIRTH_DATE date NOT NULL,
    CONSTRAINT PK_1 PRIMARY KEY ( PERSON_ID )
);

CREATE TABLE ACCOUNT
(
    PERSON_ID number(8,0) NOT NULL,
    ACCOUNT_ID varchar(12) NOT NULL,
    ACCOUNT_TYPE varchar(3) NOT NULL,
```

```
        IS_ACTIVE boolean NOT NULL,
        OPEN_DATE date NOT NULL,
        CLOSE_DATE date,
        CONSTRAINT PK_2 PRIMARY KEY ( PERSON_ID, ACCOUNT_ID ),
        CONSTRAINT FK_1 FOREIGN KEY ( PERSON_ID ) REFERENCES PERSON (
        PERSON_ID )
);
```

The resulting diagram, which makes this relationship much easier for a human to perceive, is the one initially shown in *Chapter 1, Unlocking the Power of Modeling*:

| PERSON | | |
|---|---|---|
| PERSON_ID | number(8,0) | PK |
| SOCIAL_SERCURITY_NUM | number(9,0) | |
| DRIVERS_LICENSE | varchar(10) | |
| NAME | varchar | |
| BIRTH_DATE | date | |

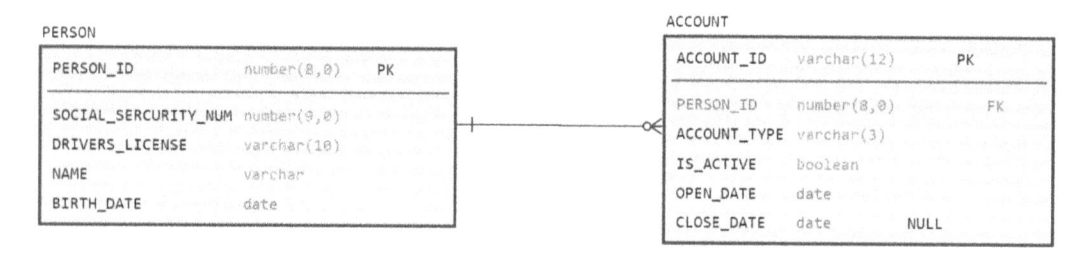

| ACCOUNT | | | |
|---|---|---|---|
| ACCOUNT_ID | varchar(12) | | PK |
| PERSON_ID | number(8,0) | | FK |
| ACCOUNT_TYPE | varchar(3) | | |
| IS_ACTIVE | boolean | | |
| OPEN_DATE | date | | |
| CLOSE_DATE | date | NULL | |

Figure 5.9 – Two tables that share a relationship

The PKs and FKs defined in the preceding DDL and expressed in *Figure 5.10* ensure that the business rules regarding account opening are baked into the database design.

Sample values for the resulting tables are presented in the following diagram to illustrate the data such a model might contain.

**PERSON**

| (PK) | (AK) | (AK) | | |
|---|---|---|---|---|
| PERSON_ID | SOCIAL_SERCURITY_NUM | DRIVERS_LICENSE | NAME | BIRTH_DATE |
| 1 | 123,456,789 | A12345BC67 | Joe Person | 2000-01-01 |
| 2 | 359,437,832 | Z12345DE34 | Jane Person | 2002-02-02 |

**ACCOUNT**

| (FK) | (PK) | | | | |
|---|---|---|---|---|---|
| PERSON_ID | ACCOUNT_ID | ACCOUNT_TYPE | IS_ACTIVE | OPEN_DATE | CLOSE_DATE |
| 1 | eav4a4tasrgr | SAV | TRUE | 2022-04-04 | null |
| 1 | afm402mf03r3 | CHK | TRUE | 2022-03-03 | null |

Figure 5.10 – Sample values for PERSON and ACCOUNT tables

In databases, FK-to-PK references are the most common form of relationship, but they are not the only form. An FK may also reference an AK. Often, a table might have a surrogate key as the PK and various business keys declared as AKs. Since the surrogate key is a technical artifact with no business value, related tables will instead refer to the alternate business key, as shown in the following example:

# Relationships as foreign keys

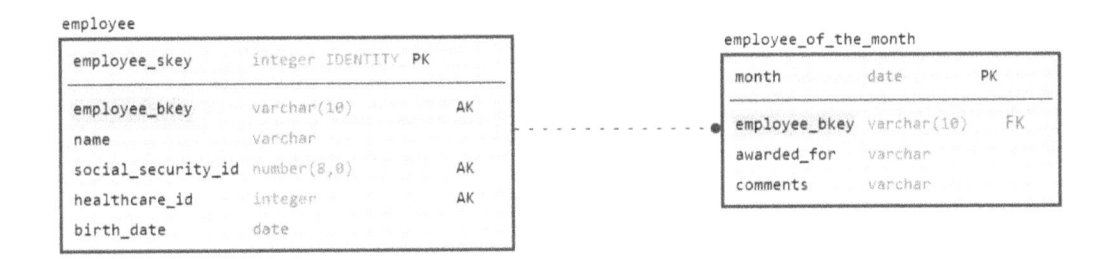

Figure 5.11 – An FK referencing an AK

As you can see in the accompanying code, the syntax for referencing an AK for an FK is identical to that used to reference a PK:

```
CREATE OR REPLACE TABLE employee
(
    employee_skey       integer NOT NULL AUTOINCREMENT START 1
    INCREMENT 1,
    employee_bkey       varchar(10) NOT NULL,
    name                varchar NOT NULL,
    social_security_id  number(8,0) NOT NULL,
    healthcare_id       integer NOT NULL,
    birth_date          date NOT NULL,

    CONSTRAINT pk_employee_skey PRIMARY KEY ( employee_skey ),
    CONSTRAINT ak_employee_bkey UNIQUE ( employee_bkey ),
    CONSTRAINT ak_healthcare_id UNIQUE ( healthcare_id ),
    CONSTRAINT ak_ss_id         UNIQUE ( social_security_id )
);

CREATE OR REPLACE TABLE employee_of_the_month
(
    month          date NOT NULL,
    employee_bkey  varchar(10) NOT NULL,
    awarded_for    varchar NOT NULL,
    comments       varchar NOT NULL,
    CONSTRAINT pk_employee_of_the_month_month PRIMARY KEY ( month ),
    CONSTRAINT fk_ref_employee FOREIGN KEY ( employee_bkey )
    REFERENCES employee ( employee_bkey )
);
```

Having understood what FKs are, let us get to know their benefits.

## Benefits of an FK

Declaring an FK formalizes the functional relationship between two tables. This metadata now becomes part of the data model and is available for reference to anyone using the database. Here are some of the advantages this brings.

### Visualizing the data model

Humans use visualizations to enhance cognition. The previous section demonstrated how a simple diagram could communicate the same information stored in code faster and in more detail. Now imagine going from two tables to an entire database schema. Without visual guidelines to help map out the entities and relationships, it would be challenging to make sense of all the tables and their contents without prior knowledge.

The following figure shows what going from 2 tables to 20 would look like on a diagram. Considering that data models in enterprise systems can span hundreds if not thousands of tables, the aid of a diagram becomes invaluable in navigating the business/data landscape.

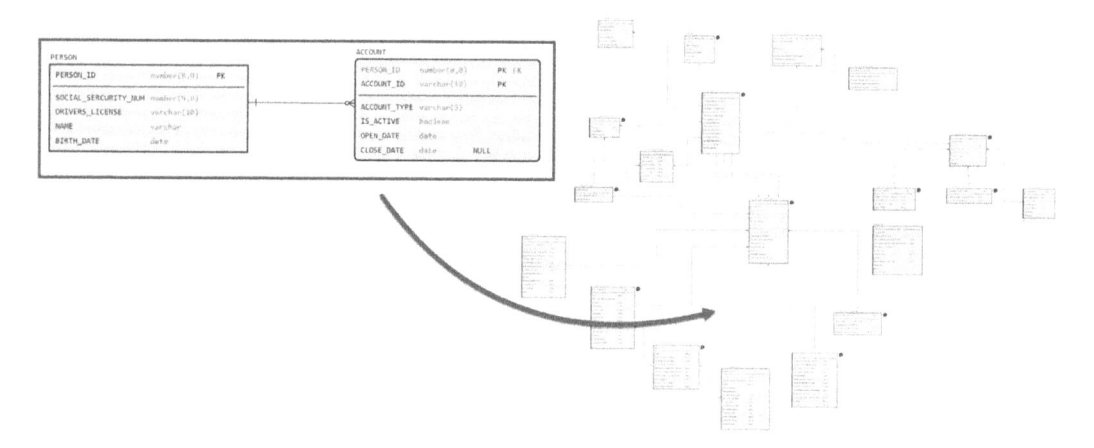

Figure 5.12 – Going from two tables to an entire schema

However, relationships between tables are not just visual aids—they serve a practical purpose for writing queries.

### Informing joins

Defining an FK requires the user to specify the reference between the parent PK column(s) and those in the corresponding child table. This means that the link between the two tables is now baked into the data model and can be referenced by users wishing to join the table data for analysis or transformation.

The following figure shows how the FK relationship highlights the common column (PERSON_ID) between the two tables.

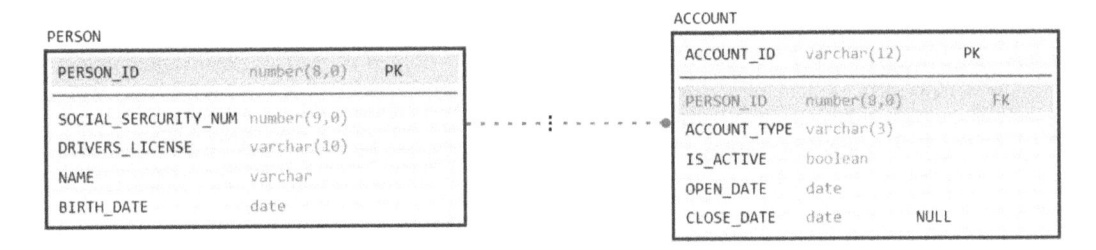

```
PERSON                                          ACCOUNT
┌─────────────────────────────────────┐        ┌─────────────────────────────────────────┐
│ PERSON_ID          number(8,0)   PK │        │ ACCOUNT_ID     varchar(12)          PK  │
├─────────────────────────────────────┤        ├─────────────────────────────────────────┤
│ SOCIAL_SERCURITY_NUM number(9,0)    │        │ PERSON_ID      number(8,0)          FK  │
│ DRIVERS_LICENSE    varchar(10)      │ - - -: │ ACCOUNT_TYPE   varchar(3)               │
│ NAME               varchar          │        │ IS_ACTIVE      boolean                  │
│ BIRTH_DATE         date             │        │ OPEN_DATE      date                     │
└─────────────────────────────────────┘        │ CLOSE_DATE     date              NULL   │
                                                └─────────────────────────────────────────┘
```

Figure 5.13 – Highlighting FK columns to infer join conditions

Now, users can leverage this metadata to write queries that retrieve PERSON and ACCOUNT data by joining the two tables using PERSON_ID.

However, FKs are not just helpful to people—**business intelligence** (**BI**) tools also leverage them.

More importantly, Snowflake can leverage these details to avoid performing the join and improve performance when it is not required (more on this and the RELY property in *Chapter 12, Putting Transformational Modeling into Practice*).

## *Automating functionality in BI tools*

Many BI tools use FKs to enhance usability and save time for their users. For example, dashboarding and analytics tools such as Tableau and Power BI detect FKs to use them to automatically create joins between tables without explicit help from the users.

Modeling tools and some SQL IDEs can generate an ER diagram by reading database DDL. While every database object carries a corresponding CREATE statement, the ER diagram will only be meaningful if the objects represented by the CREATE statement are also related through FKs.

The next benefit we'll discuss is only possible through enforcing the FK constraint and is therefore reserved for Hybrid Unistore tables. However, it unlocks powerful new possibilities in the Snowflake platform that users should be aware of.

## *Enforcing referential integrity (Hybrid Unistore)*

As we discussed, an FK relationship is not purely orientative—it formalizes business rules through database conventions. Recall the earlier example where it was stipulated that an ACCOUNT can not be opened without a PERSON_ID. So, when a new account is created, how can a database ensure that a PERSON_ID is provided and, more importantly, that it corresponds to a valid record in the PERSON table? By enforcing the FK constraint.

When a database enforces an FK constraint, it checks to ensure that the unique identifiers used in the child table exist in the parent—a condition known as **referential integrity**. Referential integrity ensures that the FK values in the child table correspond to valid records in the parent. Just as it would not make sense to open an account for a person who does not exist in the database, referential integrity checks ensure that DML operations do not result in erroneous and anomalous data.

Just like enforcing the PK constraint, FK enforcement relies on the existence of an index to perform the referential integrity check quickly and is, therefore, only possible in Hybrid Unistore tables(unless manually performed).

Whether enforced or not, there are many compelling reasons to use FKs. The last constraint we will cover is the only one enforced on all Snowflake tables, not only Hybrid Unistore, so let us learn how it works.

## Mandatory columns as NOT NULL constraints

When defining attributes for an entity, the question of which ones are mandatory and which are optional inevitably arises. As with most modeling decisions, the answer depends on the business context more than any technical database property. The same attribute, for example, the email address for CUSTOMER, may be mandatory for an online store but optional for a brick-and-mortar retailer. In the latter case, not having an email address means missing sales announcements, while in the former, it may mean being unable to access the website.

When moving from a conceptual model to a physical Snowflake design, mandatory columns can be defined through the NOT NULL constraint. The NOT NULL constraint is declared inline next to the corresponding column and does not need to be given a name. Due to this, it is not possible to declare NOT NULL constraints out of line.

The format for adding a NOT NULL constraint to a column is as follows:

```
<col1_name> <col1_type> [ NOT NULL ]
```

Previous examples, such as the ACCOUNT table, have demonstrated instances of NOT NULL constraints. Here, we can see that CLOSE_DATE is the only column in the ACCOUNT table that is not mandatory and is allowed to have a NULL value:

```
CREATE TABLE ACCOUNT
(
    PERSON_ID number(8,0) NOT NULL,
    ACCOUNT_ID varchar(12) NOT NULL,
    ACCOUNT_TYPE varchar(3) NOT NULL,
    IS_ACTIVE boolean NOT NULL,
    OPEN_DATE date NOT NULL,
    CLOSE_DATE date,
    CONSTRAINT PK_2 PRIMARY KEY ( PERSON_ID, ACCOUNT_ID ),
    CONSTRAINT FK_1 FOREIGN KEY ( PERSON_ID ) REFERENCES PERSON (
PERSON_ID )
);
```

Unlike the other constraints, enforcing NOT NULL does not require lookups or references to other tables—it can be done directly on the individual rows by checking for values in the designated columns. For this reason, NOT NULL is enforced for all Snowflake tables and does not incur any performance overhead during DML operations.

## Summary

This chapter discussed how to transition from logical modeling concepts to physical Snowflake objects. During this process, we learned how Snowflake handles tables of near-infinite size by breaking them down into manageable micro-partitions and how these partitions can be clustered to optimize query and DML performance.

After that, we learned how to define attributes by understanding Snowflake's data types and their properties. Snowflake offers a variety of functions to make working with data types easier and more performant, to say nothing of the powerful options it offers for semi-structured data.

Before diving into individual constraint types, we understood what database constraints are and how Snowflake organizes and enforces them depending on the type of table where they are applied.

We saw why unique identifiers are vital for defining tables and how Snowflake manages this through the PK constraint. PKs help make life easier for database users by helping identify the minimum level of detail in a table and ensuring accurate searches and joins. We also saw that sometimes, when multiple candidates exist for a PK, AKs can be defined through UNIQUE constraints and offer the same benefits.

Then, we saw how relationships are formalized in a physical database by defining FK constraints. FKs make visualizing and navigating complex data landscapes possible by capturing the functional relationships between tables—information that human users of the database and BI tools frequently leverage.

Finally, we learned how to declare mandatory columns and enforce the rule using the NOT NULL constraint to ensure data quality.

This chapter and others have frequently relied on relational diagrams to clarify examples and explain abstract concepts. However, there has been no formal explanation of the modeling notation or an overview of the various elements in the visual modeling toolkit. Now that we understand the core elements of a data model at a logical and physical level, the next chapter will focus on modeling notation for designing or visualizing data models at any scale.

# 6
# Seeing Snowflake's Architecture through Modeling Notation

Throughout this book, relational diagrams have been used to support examples and illustrate ideas in ways that words could not. Although various modeling styles and notations have been introduced, a thorough overview of the visual semantics of modeling and the various elements and their properties has not been covered.

In this chapter, we will run through the complete visual toolkit that will enable users to accelerate the design and understanding of a physical Snowflake database and add functional context through conceptual conventions. Using a simplified and pragmatic approach, users of any background can view and explore a database schema at the level of detail that best suits their needs.

In this chapter, we're going to cover the following main topics:

- Recall the history of modeling styles and notations
- Understand the connection between the relational model and its visual depictions
- Learn how to depict the various types of entities
- Explore how to represent relationships at the physical and conceptual levels
- Understand how to add functional context to go beyond physical tables
- Discover how to simplify various modeling conventions to arrive at a synchronized modeling practice
- Do it all in a manner that is accessible to technical and business users alike

# A history of relational modeling

The diagrams and examples throughout this book rely on relational modeling to illustrate database concepts and constructs. Learning how to parse and communicate through relational diagrams provides a dual-faceted benefit to database users by allowing them to rapidly visualize and bring to life complex database landscapes and design them from scratch using visual cognitive aids. Yet, despite these benefits, many database users consider modeling an arcane practice without relevance in the modern warehouse and mistake it for a chore instead of the time-saving boon it really is.

The practice of data modeling and its associated notations have passed through many changes and diverging trends without a final standard ever emerging, encumbering universal adoption. The conceptual data model dates back to the 1960s when Charles Bachman first used rectangles to denote record types and arrows to form relationships between them. Toward the end of the decade, Edgar F. Codd formalized the **relational model** (**RM**), which gave rise to the relational database as we know it today. Using the RM, Codd managed to tie mathematical theory, consistent with the structure and language of first-order predicate logic, to database systems. Unfortunately, Codd was less concerned with the visual aspect of the model and offered no diagramming guidelines.

In the 70s, computer scientists such as Peter Chen and Richard Barker expanded Bachman's simplistic modeling conventions to include more context for the underlying entities and relationships.

However, none of these designs were convincing enough to warrant widespread adoption. While singular elements of these designs gained prevalence—such as the use of crow's foot notation to describe cardinality—wholesale adherence to any one diagramming style proved too restrictive for widespread adoption by failing to strike a balance between readability and technical detail. Some, including Chen's original ER format, arguably, achieve neither.

The following diagram in Chen notation attempts to describe a simple RM consisting of four entities and their attributes. Yet, it fails to do so effectively due to an overwhelming number of visual elements.

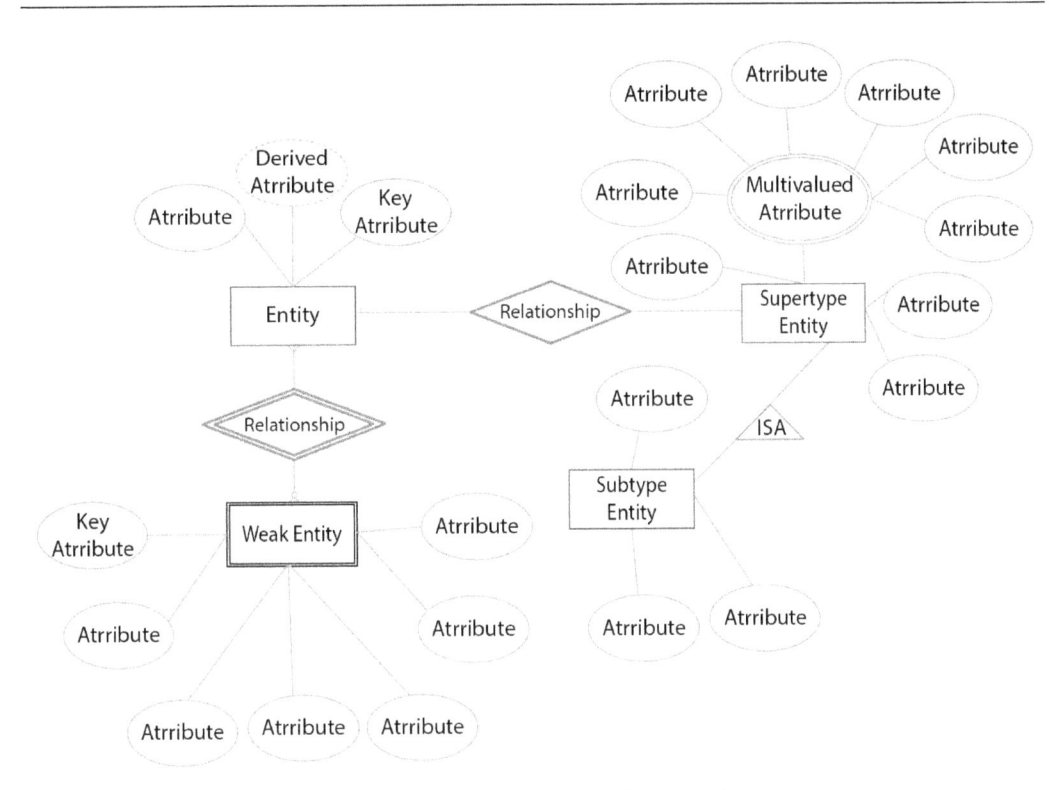

Figure 6.1 – An ER diagram in Chen notation

To effectively use visual diagrams, it is essential to separate the model (structure) from its presentation (diagram). A data model's visual representation may vary depending on the level of abstraction, but the elements it represents correspond to real-world business entities that are not subject to reinterpretation.

## RM versus entity-relationship diagram

Recall that an RM can be identified from business-relevant concepts and mapped onto a database schema that includes their attributes, identifiers, and relationships. An **entity-relationship diagram** (**ERD**) is a visual rendering of the RM using simple, easy-to-understand semantics.

In the following examples, we will revisit a set of relational entities from *Chapter 1, Unlocking the Power of Modeling*. In the RM, each of the three entities corresponds to a table identified by a primary key and related to other entities through foreign keys. Just observing the table names or even a data preview does not make it easy to determine these relationships, as can be seen in the following RM:

```
SUPERHERO
---------
SUPERHERO_NAME|BIRTHPLACE     |SUPERHERO_TYPE|HAS_MASK|
--------------+---------------+--------------+--------+
Ratman        |Gotham Gutter  |Accident      |true    |
Razor Tooth   |Amazonia       |Accident      |false   |
Galactoid     |Krab Nebula    |Alien         |true    |

SUPERHERO_TYPE
--------------
SUPERHERO_TYPE|
--------------+
Accident      |
Tech Soldier  |
Vigilante     |
Alien         |

COMIC_BOOK
----------
COMIC_BOOK_NAME                |ISSUE_DATE|
-------------------------------+----------+
BC Comics v4                   |1978-04-03|
Tales from the Underground v3  |1985-12-23|
Tales from the Underground v24 |1995-07-15|
BC Comics v103                 |2015-06-19|

APPEARED_IN
-----------
COMIC_BOOK_NAME                |SUPERHERO_NAME|
-------------------------------+--------------+
BC Comics v4                   |Razor Tooth   |
Tales from the Underground v3  |Ratman        |
Tales from the Underground v24 |Ratman        |
Tales from the Underground v24 |Razor Tooth   |
BC Comics v103                 |Galactoid     |
```

However, an ERD brings the associative context of the tables into rapid focus by highlighting the entities and relationships behind the data being presented.

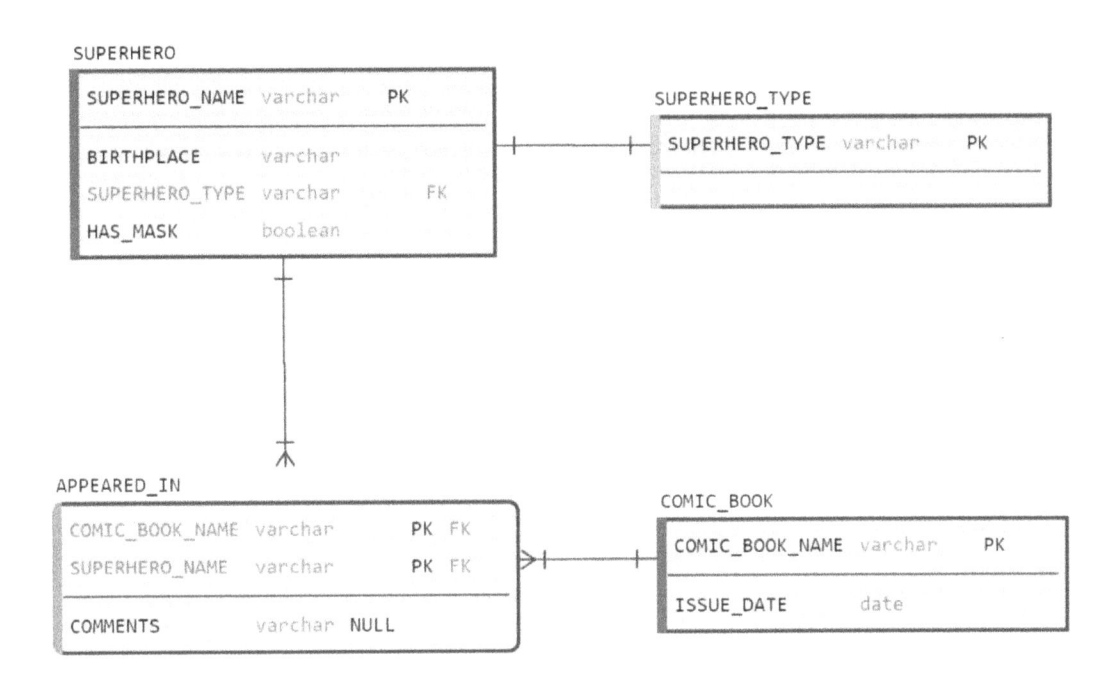

Figure 6.2 – A physical model using crow's foot relationship notation

Thanks to the visual clues of the ERD in *Figure 6.2*, the context behind the data, such as the **many-to-many (M:M)** relationship between COMIC_BOOK and SUPERHERO, instantly comes into focus—that is, if the viewer is familiar with the visual semantics that the ERD is using. So, let us review these elements in detail and demonstrate how we can represent a wide array of technical and conceptual modeling conventions using a few visual conventions.

## Visual modeling conventions

This chapter will highlight all the semantic elements that will be used throughout the rest of the book. As described earlier, no fixed and universally prescribed standard for drawing modeling diagrams exists. The conventions used here, along with their accompanying visual semantics, are the author's attempt at simplifying the broad spectrum of modeling concepts and notations into a core set of elements, using the most widely used symbols to represent them. The visual semantics in this book do not conform to any single modeling notation but borrow freely from several leading industry standards. The aim is to provide a modeling language that is both precise enough to accurately reflect technical database details and simple enough for business users to understand the business context that lies beyond the technical specifications.

Unlike those textbooks that separate conceptual, logical, and physical models and force users to convert and adapt one to the other, this book will use conventions that make it possible to keep all three in sync throughout the modeling process. This approach minimizes the effort involved in maintaining the models consistently as development unfolds and offers a consistent view at various levels of abstraction.

With that in mind, let us begin with the notation used to describe the central element of the data model: the entity.

## Depicting entities

Since the early days of modeling, entities have been depicted using rectangles. Whether they are displayed on a conceptual diagram with no additional detail besides the entity name or on a physical diagram containing a list of attributes, data types, and other information, entities are always represented as rectangles.

However, modeling semantics do distinguish between strong and weak entities. When we think of an entity, we generally think of a **strong entity**—identified by its primary key. However, **weak entities** cannot stand independently and depend on attributes from another table to help identify them. Weak entities must use a foreign key as part of their primary key because the information they contain does not make sense in isolation. This dynamic can be observed in the SIDEKICK weak entity table in *Figure 6.3*, which can only exist in relation to the strong entity, SUPERHERO.

The following diagram shows the strong entity, SUPERHERO, alongside a weak entity, APPEARED_IN:

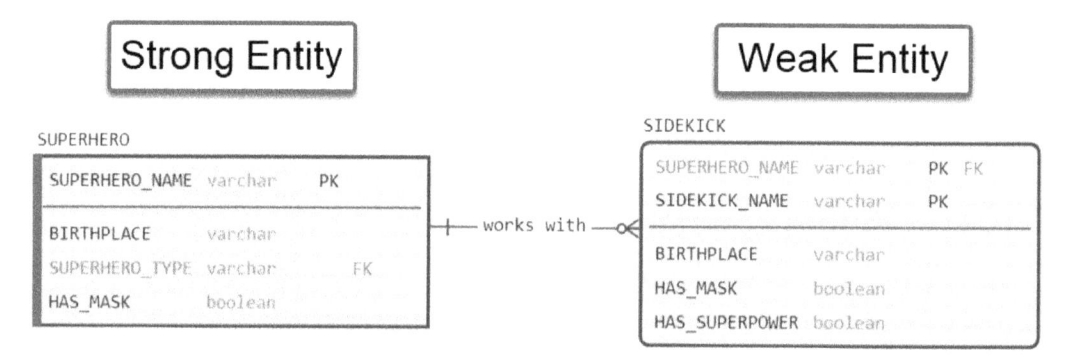

Figure 6.3 – Strong and weak entity types in a diagram

On a diagram, entities are depicted as rectangles, with their corners depicting their strong or weak nature. Strong entities are shown with straight, perpendicular corners, while weak entities use rounded corners.

Now, let's zoom in on the details inside the entity. In logical and physical modeling, entities include details about their attributes, constraints, and data types. The following figure explains what the details inside the entity represent.

Visual modeling conventions | 95

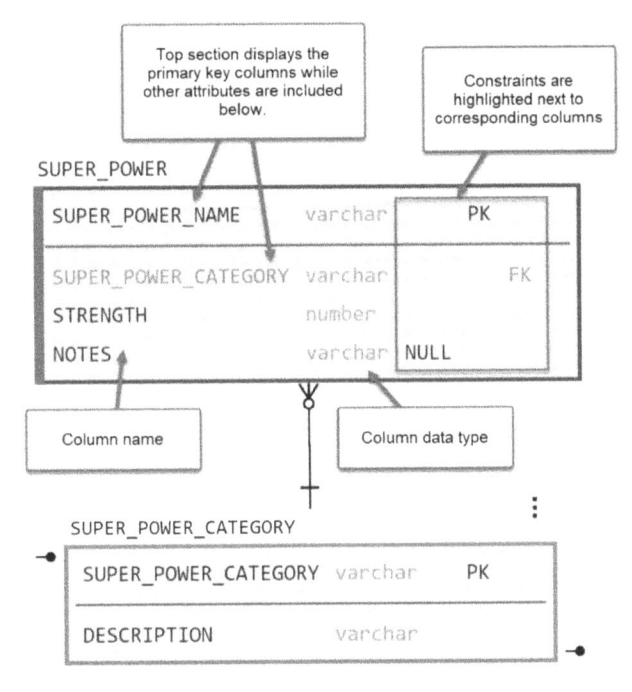

[Figure 6.4 diagram showing SUPER_POWER entity with SUPER_POWER_NAME (varchar, PK), SUPER_POWER_CATEGORY (varchar, FK), STRENGTH (number), NOTES (varchar, NULL); related to SUPER_POWER_CATEGORY entity with SUPER_POWER_CATEGORY (varchar, PK) and DESCRIPTION (varchar). Annotations: "Top section displays the primary key columns while other attributes are included below.", "Constraints are highlighted next to corresponding columns", "Column name", "Column data type".]

Figure 6.4 – Entity details illustrated

Now that we know how to draw entities, let us learn how to represent their relationships.

## Depicting relationships

Relationships between entities are represented as connecting lines. However, a relationship can convey more context than a solid line can capture. Relationship lines can also relay information about cardinality and dependency between the associated entities. Some of these details map perfectly onto the physical database, while others are conceptual and orientative. This book uses two notations to represent relationships depending on the context. To understand them, let us start with crow's foot, the more common of the two, and discover how it depicts granularity.

### Crow's foot

Crow's foot notation derives its name from the three-pronged *many* symbol that resembles a crow's foot. Each side of a crow's foot connector displays information about the cardinality and optionality of the relationship.

There are two cardinality options (one or many) and two optionality indicators (required or optional). This gives us four possible combinations, as described in the following figure:

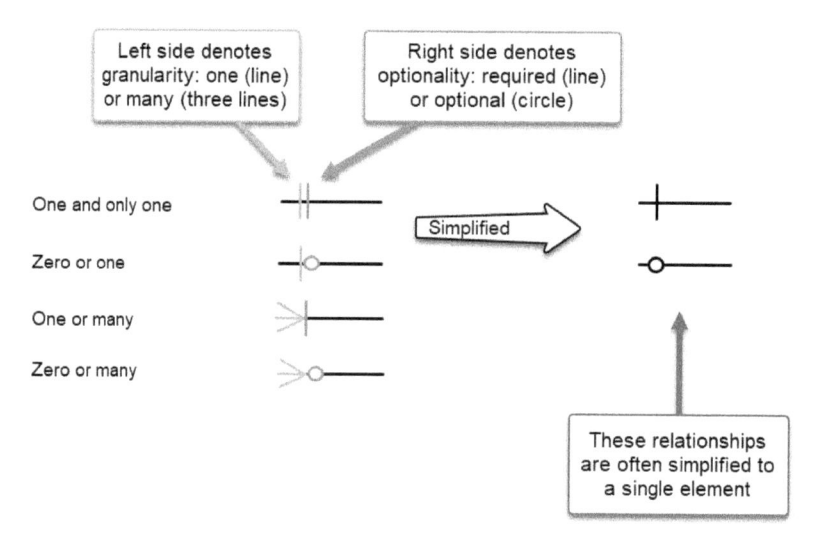

Figure 6.5 – Crow's foot relationship types

In logical/conceptual modeling, a relationship name (also known as a role name) can be specified to add context. When specifying cardinality, remember that it applies to both edges of the relationship—meaning, a relationship can be read in either direction, as shown in the following example:

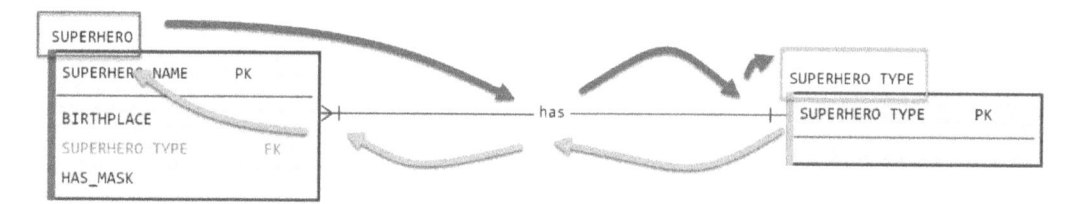

Figure 6.6 – Reading a crow's foot relationship

The diagram is read from the entity to the role name, to the connector on its far side, to the other entity. Take the following example:

- A superhero has one and only one superhero type
- A superhero type is had by one or many superheroes

Using crow's foot notation, database modelers can capture functional details of the minimum and maximum granularities in entity relationships. However, crow's foot cardinalities do not map one to one onto physical designs. When technical precision is needed for physical models, IDEF1X notation is preferred.

## IDEF1X

**IDEF1X** (correctly pronounced *eye-def-one-ex* but often shortened to *eye-dee-fix*) notation was invented in the 1970s by the US Air Force. The appeal of IDEF1X is how closely it maps onto physical database structures. The entities and relationships defined in IDEF1X notation can be unambiguously translated into SQL and vice versa.

> **Note**
> While the IDEF1X standard does include a specific connection relationship syntax (e.g., P, Z, n, n-m), this syntax is not easily readable and is not widely used.

Instead of cardinality, IDEF1X notation focuses on the strong or weak entity nature of the relationship. Strong entity relationships are depicted by dotted lines and are referred to as **non-identifying**. Relationships to weak entities use a solid line and are called **identifying** because they require a primary key from a strong entity to identify a unique instance.

Because IDEF1X notation is tied to physical database properties, it is limited to optionality options directly supported by the database. When a non-identifying FK is nullable in a child entity, the parent edge of the connector is displayed as a diamond instead of a circle.

In the following diagram, the weak entity, APPEARED_IN—displayed with corresponding rounded corners—connects to strong entities using solid lines. For demonstration, the SUPERHERO_TYPE FK in SUPERHERO has been changed to accept nulls and therefore causes the SUPERHERO_TYPE edge to take a diamond symbol.

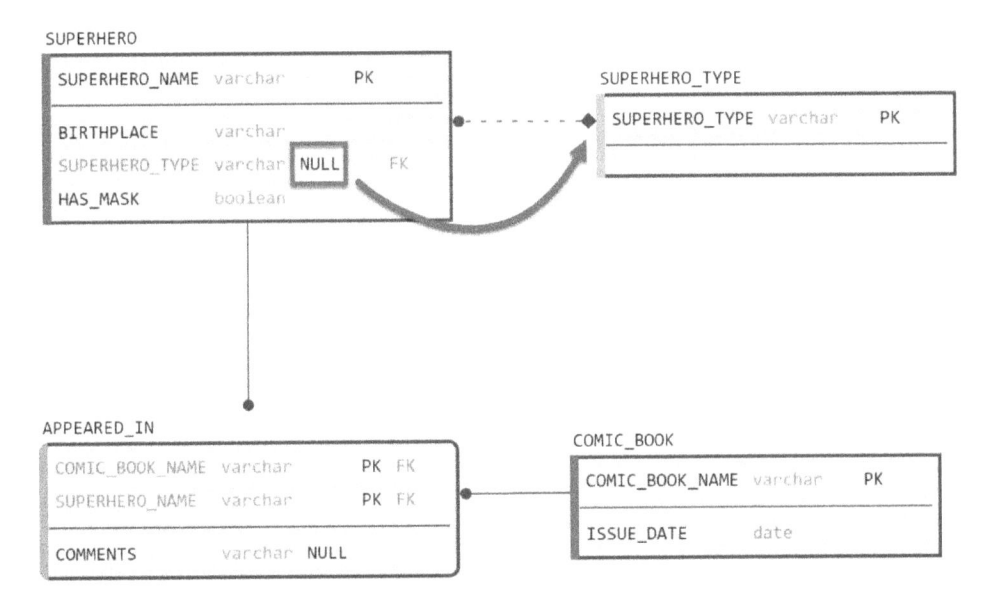

Figure 6.7 – A physical model using IDEF1X notation

Having covered entities and relationships, let us expand on the possible context displayed on a diagram, such as M:M relationships and subtypes.

## Adding conceptual context to Snowflake architecture

In the overview of logical modeling in *Chapter 2, An Introduction to the Four Modeling Types*, we were introduced to concepts such as the M:M relationship and subtypes. M:M relationships are peculiar because they cannot be created in a physical database without an intermediary associative table. Subtypes also hold a special significance beyond mere child tables as they embody the principles of inheritance in entity classes. To ensure that this context is not lost in a physical database, logical modeling conventions exist to describe them.

Let us expand on these concepts and understand the options available for displaying them, starting with the M:M relationship.

### *Many-to-many*

Although crow's foot notation allows for M:M relationships in theory, in practice, the approach suffers from one significant limitation: it prevents modelers from keeping their conceptual/logical model in sync with their physical model.

Recall that the following relationship is impossible to create in a physical database without using an associative table.

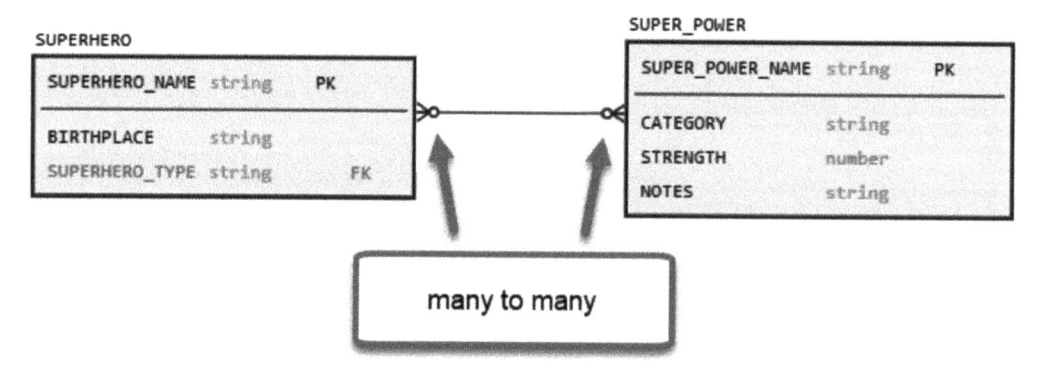

Figure 6.8 – An M:M relationship between two tables

However, by coopting the relationship diamond from Chen notation to represent the associative table, we can keep the physical and conceptual models in sync while keeping the necessary context within the model.

The following figure shows the same M:M relationship in both physical and logical models.

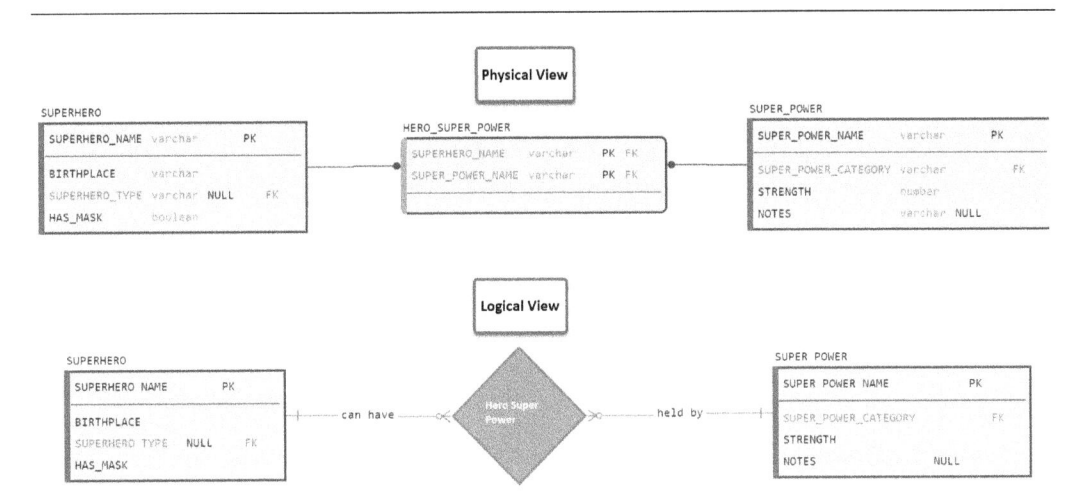

Figure 6.9 – An M:M relationship synchronized between physical and logical models

Now that we know how to retain the context of an M:M relationship and keep it in sync across logical and physical models, let's break down the notation for subtypes.

## Representing subtypes and supertypes

In *Chapter 2, An Introduction to the Four Modeling Types*, we saw how subtypes were used on logical diagrams to represent inheritance. Recall the example in the following figure showing how a SUPERHERO entity can have four subtypes.

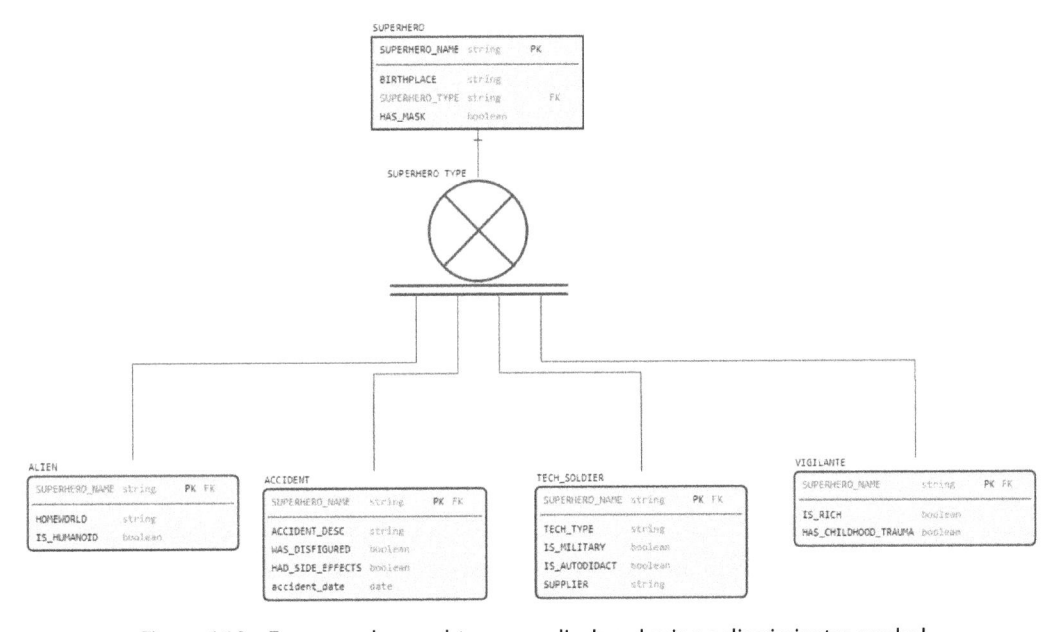

Figure 6.10 – Four superhero subtypes are displayed using a discriminator symbol

The figure not only identifies the four tables as subtypes of SUPERHERO but also gives us context into the nature of the subtype—that it is both complete (double parallel lines) and exclusive (letter *X* in the center). Let's understand these properties and how to denote them.

Subtype relationships have two binary properties to describe their nature:

- **Complete/incomplete**: Indicates whether all the subtypes are known or whether more can be added in the future, respectively. The previous diagram is an example of a complete relationship, as all four superhero types are present.
- **Inclusive/exclusive**: Indicates whether the supertype can exist as multiple subtypes. Since a superhero can only belong to one of the four subtypes, the relationship is exclusive.

These properties can be displayed using a mix of IE and IDEF1X notation. The central discriminator icon can be displayed as a circle or the letter D rotated 90 degrees counterclockwise. The defining elements are the letter *X* through the middle to denote an exclusive relationship and single or double lines at the bottom to describe complete and incomplete, respectively. The four configurations can be seen in the following figure:

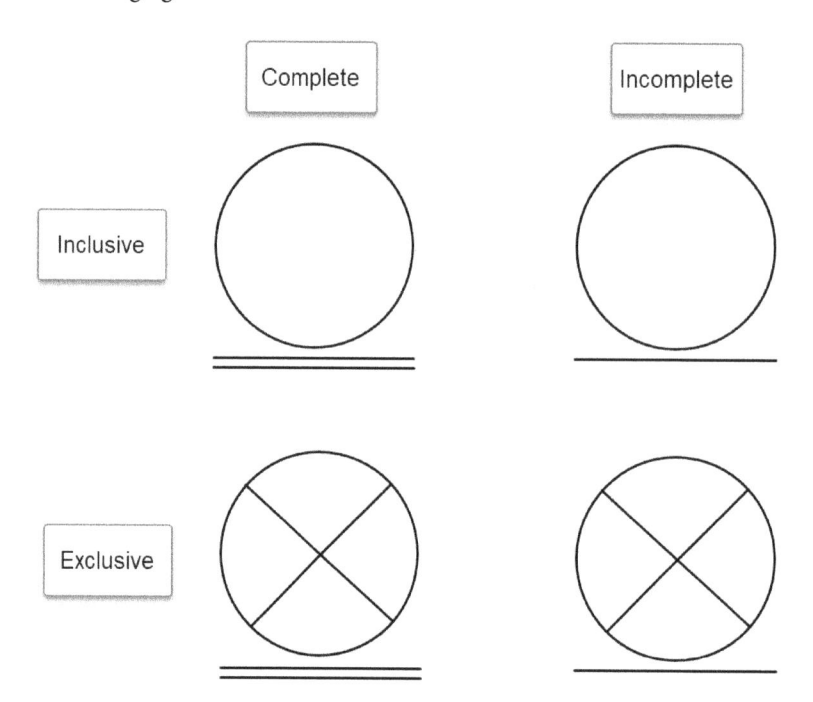

Figure 6.11 – Four possible configurations of a discriminator symbol

Now that we have covered how to depict the physical database on a diagram and extend the visual context beyond what the physical database is capable of storing, let's consider how we can take advantage of the primary challenge we laid out at the start of the chapter: keeping the models in sync.

# The benefit of synchronized modeling

Throughout this chapter, we have seen examples of diagrams describing data models and capturing details that may not have a strict corollary in SQL. By simplifying modeling to its core components—many of which are likely to be understood even by people without a formal background in database design—we ensure that modeling is not confined solely to the database team. As you recall, a model describes not only the database but also the business itself.

Keeping the physical and conceptual models in sync provides another benefit: the model can be viewed at any time at various levels of abstraction because the underlying physical elements remain the same. Users can view the model at a physical level when more detail is needed and flip to a conceptual view if they wish to see it more abstractly.

To illustrate this, the various diagrams in *Figure 6.2* are displayed side by side, demonstrating how physical and conceptual elements can be mixed and matched as necessary to perform an analysis.

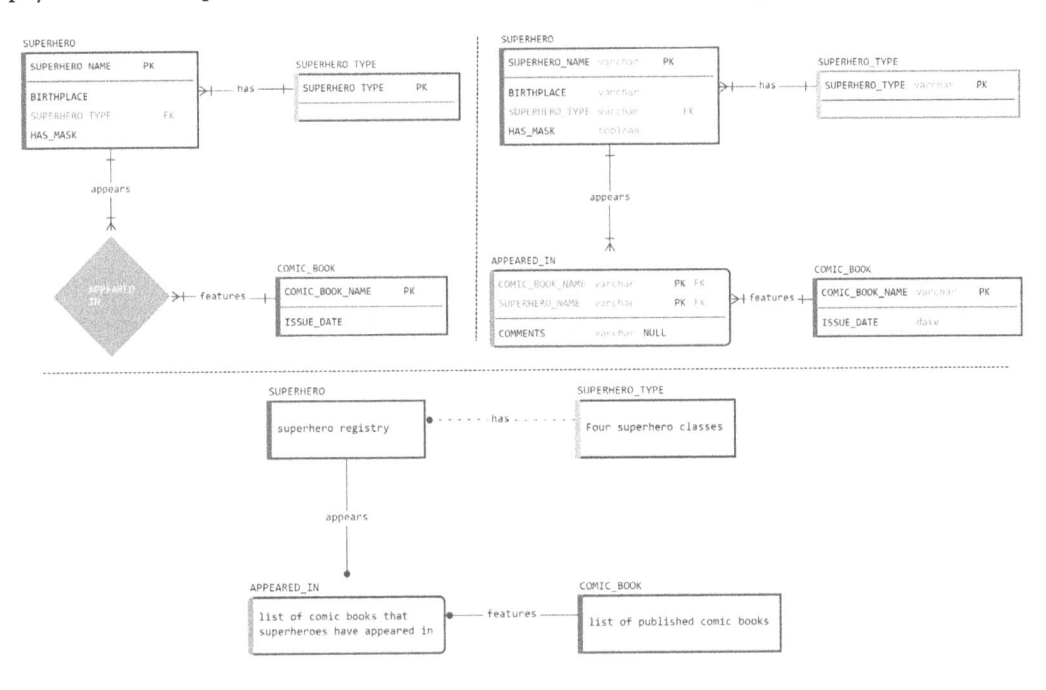

Figure 6.12 – Elements from conceptual, logical, and physical models displayed side by side

Keeping the entities consistent across models carries an additional benefit in that no other maintenance is required to keep the models consistent. By changing the detail level, no conversion or rework is needed to adapt one style to the other.

Now that we've seen how modeling notation has evolved and how to harness its most relevant and valuable elements in a simple-to-use and simple-to-read style, let's review the practical takeaways of this chapter.

## Summary

In this chapter, we looked back at the history of relational modeling and the various notation styles that have been used to help visualize the designs. Focusing on the most straightforward and practical semantics of these modeling styles, we could zero in on a pragmatic approach that preserves technical precision while being simple enough to be understood even by people without a formal background in database design. The modeling technique proposed in this book keeps the number of entities synchronized across conceptual, logical, and physical models, thus saving manual effort and ensuring that anyone at any level of detail can view the same model.

Using the consolidated list of modeling conventions, we looked at how to display an entity on a relational diagram in the simplest way possible. Next, we covered relationship notation and the additional context that can be conveyed beyond a simple line using two of the most popular conventions in database modeling: crow's foot and IDEF1X. The former is ideal for communicating granularity details between entities, and the latter uses a simplified style that maps exactly into the physical model.

We also learned how to go beyond what the physical model can display and added functional context through conceptual/logical modeling conventions such as subtypes and M:M relationships.

Having learned how to use the semantic elements in the modeling toolkit and mastered Snowflake architecture and objects in previous chapters, we are ready to begin the modeling journey in earnest, starting from conceptual modeling. The next chapter will break down the conceptual modeling process into simple, repeatable steps that bridge the gap between functional and technical teams, allowing them to communicate effectively to identify and translate business processes into database designs.

# Part 2: Applied Modeling from Idea to Deployment

This part focuses on the practical application of data modeling techniques across different stages of the database design process. You will learn how to put conceptual modeling into practice by gaining a solid understanding of the data entities, relationships, and business rules that define the underlying data structure. You will also learn how to enrich these details and add nuance using a logical model that cannot be captured in a physical database. This part also delves into the critical concept of database normalization, essential for minimizing data redundancy and ensuring accurate and consistent data storage. After covering database naming and structure and exploring the best practices for creating intuitive, meaningful, and scalable database schemas, you will learn how to put physical modeling into practice while optimizing database performance.

This part has the following chapters:

- Chapter 7, *Putting Conceptual Modeling into Practice*
- Chapter 8, *Putting Logical Modeling into Practice*
- Chapter 9, *Database Normalization*
- Chapter 10, *Database Naming and Structure*
- Chapter 11, *Putting Physical Modeling into Practice*

# 7
# Putting Conceptual Modeling into Practice

Conceptual database modeling is a high-level approach to designing a database that focuses on capturing business entities and their relationships. This approach allows designers to develop a deeper understanding of the data, making it easier to identify potential issues or inconsistencies in the design. It can also make the database more flexible and adaptable to future changes and make it easier to understand and use for people who are unfamiliar with it. As a result, conceptual database modeling can help make a database more effective and efficient at supporting the needs of an organization.

In this chapter, we will generate a conceptual model from scratch using Kimball's **dimensional modeling** (**DM**) technique. This approach brings the data team together with business experts to ensure that database designs reflect the reality of business processes from inception, thereby saving costly rework down the line.

However, conceptual models are not solely used in initiating new designs—they carry all the same benefits for existing physical schemas. This chapter will also explain a simple method for adapting a physical design to a conceptual model and generating an easy-to-read diagram that can be used by business and technical teams alike.

In this chapter, we will cover the following main topics:

- Discovering DM and its applications
- Constructing a bus matrix using Kimball's four-step method
- Creating a conceptual model using the bus matrix
- Reverse engineering a conceptual model from a physical schema

# Embarking on conceptual design

Out of all the modeling types, conceptual captures and displays the least amount of detail. This makes conceptual modeling ideal for getting acquainted with a database landscape at a high level and for designing one from scratch. Designing data models is an art honed over many iterations, but where do you begin if you are new to modeling?

## Dimensional modeling

In the early 2000s, Ralph Kimball and Margy Ross published the groundbreaking book *The Data Warehouse Toolkit*, which has persisted for decades as the authoritative blueprint for constructing database designs. Many of the terms, concepts, and techniques described in later chapters of this book trace their origins to *The Data Warehouse Toolkit*—whose latest edition fittingly carries the subtitle, *The definitive guide to dimensional modeling*.

To be clear, Kimball's approach is not the only way to go about creating a conceptual model. The agile-based **Business Event Analysis and Modeling** (**BEAM**) method (see the *Further reading* section at the end of this chapter) and other techniques are also worth exploring. However, Kimball methodology is widely used and universally recognized and will serve as a springboard for our modeling journey.

## Understanding dimensional modeling

DM is a longstanding technique for making databases simple by aligning them to business processes—a theme that should now be familiar to you. As simple as that sounds, DM covers many wide-ranging topics, from business requirement workshops to types of fact and dimension tables, to industry-specific modeling best practices.

This chapter will focus on the early stages of DM and discuss how data teams can engage with business experts to uncover the dimensions and business processes that lay the groundwork for a conceptual model. However, one point needs to be addressed before getting started.

## Setting the record straight on dimensional modeling

Critics of DM have argued that platforms such as Snowflake, which provides cheap and easily scalable computing resources, have made the effort and rigor involved in DM obsolete. Nonsense. A variable spend platform such as Snowflake can get very expensive if left unchecked. Grounding designs in time-tested frameworks is a good way to keep costs under control.

Another frequent argument is that analytics engineering through tools such as dbt has quickened development to such a pace that allows you to build and fix a design, if need be, in less time than what DM calls for. While analytics engineering does accelerate the delivery cycle, not having a solid grounding in the fundamentals only enables you to make mistakes faster. For example, dbt *snapshots* use Kimball's **Type-2 slowly changing dimensions** (**SCD**) under the hood and require a good understanding of their fundamentals to use them effectively.

The third criticism of the Kimball methodology goes something like this: *Kimball is no longer relevant because* **Data Vault** *or <some other modeling> is easier to scale*. Ensemble methodologies, such as Data Vault 2.0 (covered in *Chapter 17, Scaling Data Models through Modern Techniques* of this book) are indeed highly scalable and effective modeling frameworks. However, they do not suit all scenarios and still require knowing and implementing DM concepts (a satellite is also a Type-2 SCD).

Finally, despite having debunked the main arguments against DM, it remains to be said that this book is not advocating for DM to be used as the principal framework for database or warehouse design. Rather, since DM objects and language permeate database design, it is essential to know the rules and fundamentals and to understand when and where to deviate.

With this in mind, let's dive in and see how we can use DM principles to kick-start a conceptual model or validate an existing physical design through the same means.

## Starting a conceptual model in four easy steps

This section will review the four-step DM method for creating a conceptual model by identifying the business processes and dimensions involved. Recall that the aim of conceptual modeling and database modeling as a whole is to align as closely as possible to the reality of the business operations. For this reason, this stage of the modeling process will require the most collaboration from the business teams to identify the conceptual building blocks for future technical developments.

To witness this process in action, we will use the tables in the `SNOWFLAKE_SAMPLE_DATA.TPCH_SF1` schema to represent a real-world retail organization. So that you understand what we are working toward, you can explore the sample tables in the Snowflake **user interface** (**UI**) or see the following diagram resulting from this exercise.

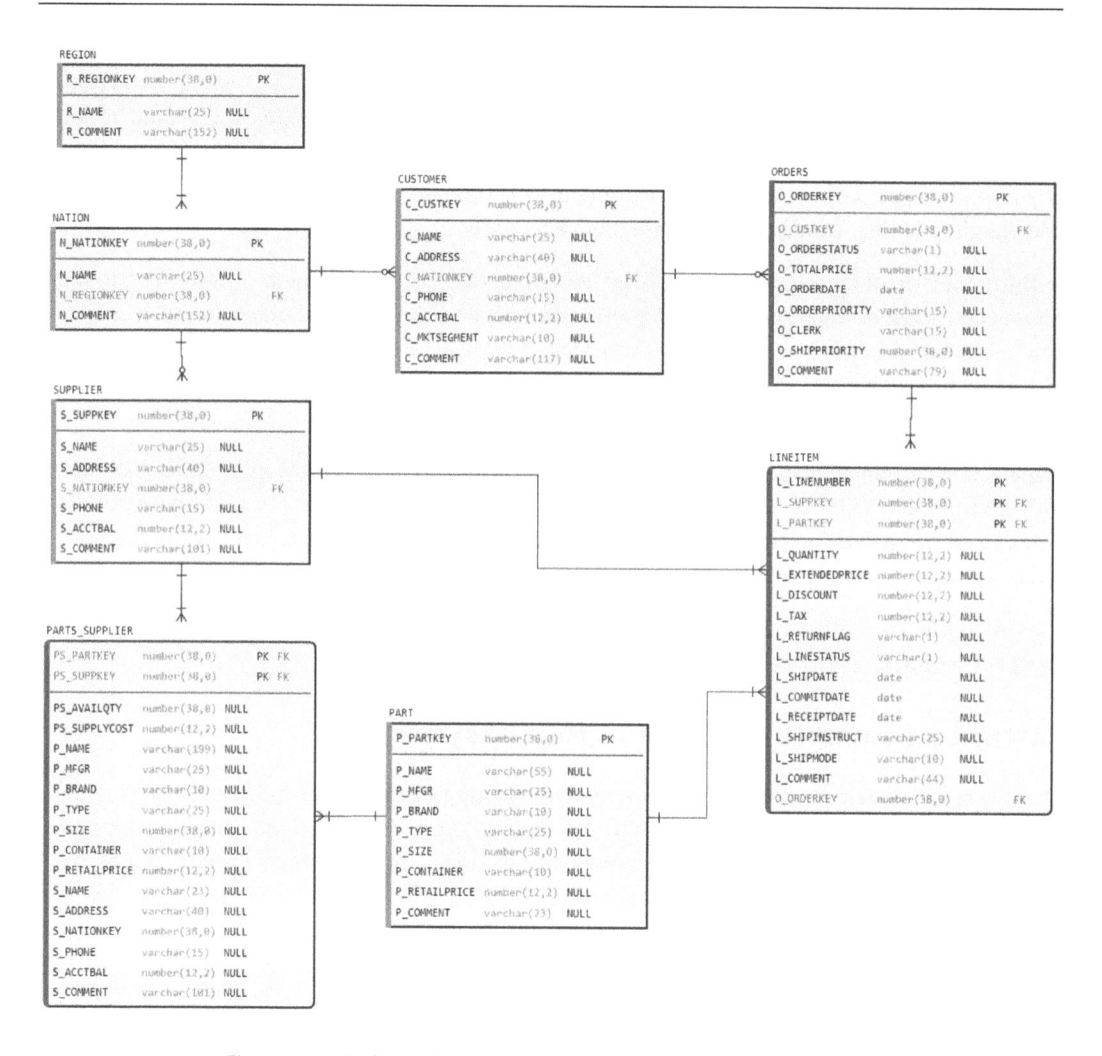

Figure 7.1 – A physical model of Snowflake's sample TPC-H schema

Before reviewing each step individually, here are the four steps that Kimball suggests for starting DM at a conceptual level:

- Define the business process
- Declare the grain
- Identify the dimensions
- Identify the facts

Modeling begins by organizing workshops with business domain experts and department stakeholders to determine the answers to these four points. This is where the reality of the business is discussed, formally defined, and agreed upon by the stakeholders so that its relevant data can be modeled and captured. Everyone must understand that although the concepts are being discussed at a high level, they will later be used to determine design decisions regarding database details, business rules, and their governing logic—details that can be extremely difficult to alter in later stages of development.

The outcomes and decisions established during the collaborative workshops should be considered binding contracts between the business and technical teams, who will later carry them forward to implementation.

Before making its way to an **entity-relationship** (**ER**) diagram, the information captured during these discovery sessions is captured in what Kimball calls the bus matrix. In a bus matrix, each row represents a business process or subject area, and each column represents a dimension or fact table—their intersections form the relationships or transactions within an organization.

As we work through each of the four steps, we will see how the bus matrix unfolds and helps guide the development of the model. As the first step in the process, let us begin by working with the domain experts to identify the existing business processes in the TPC-H organization.

## Define the business process

As the consultants in the film *Office Space* famously inquired: *what would you say you do here?* While the answer for a given organization might sound simple, such as *selling merchandise* or *taking reservations*, the reality is usually much more complex when additional activities, such as procurement, inventory, promotions, and cancelations, are considered.

Recall that the primary goal of modeling is to capture the relevant metrics and properties we want to track, measure, and analyze. Think of business processes as the transactions that occur naturally as the business operates. In DM, transactions are referred to as **facts**, and tables that record them and (nearly always) pair them with metrics are called **fact tables** (more on fact tables in a bit).

Starting with the company's primary function, such as selling, registering, or manufacturing, extend the discussion to the supporting functions, such as sourcing inventory, stocking warehouses, and contracting with suppliers, until every department has been heard from and has relevant operational processes cataloged.

The resulting list generated from these meetings will form the left side of the bus matrix. In the TPC-H example, the list may look something like this:

| Purchase Parts |
| Track Inventory |
| Sell Parts |
| Customer Returns |
| Supplier Returns |

Figure 7.2 – The business processes that will later form the bus matrix

Once the business processes have been identified, it's time to go into more detail and determine their lowest grain of analysis.

## Determine the grain

In the previous step, we listed the operational transactions that make up our business processes. These transactions will become fact tables in the database that we are designing. But what does a row for each transaction represent? For example, the primary function of our business may be to sell parts, but do we record and analyze such a transaction at the part or customer level? Or can it be both or either, depending on the business unit?

The answer to this question, we must now determine the **grain**—the lowest level of detail required for meaningful analysis of each business process. Generally, the recommended grain is the lowest level of detail captured by the business processes themselves—this is referred to as the **atomic grain**. Grounding our design at the atomic grain ensures that it can accommodate any subsequent rollups and aggregations to higher levels of analysis. With this approach, changes in business requirements will not require changing the model because the model already contains the maximum granularity recorded by the business processes.

When selecting the grain, we must also ensure that different grains are not mixed in the same fact table. For example, a sales fact table maintained at the grain of daily transactions must not include monthly or yearly totals. Doing so would result in costly and inefficient database update operations on the table every time a transaction was recorded.

Conversations about grain will naturally bring to light the entities involved in the operational functions: customers, suppliers, and parts. This information will help us determine the other half of the bus matrix.

## Determine the dimensions

The entities that came to light during the conversations surrounding business processes help give context to the nature of our business. Entities help answer questions such as *who*, *what*, and *where* and will often contain attributes that offer further descriptive context.

In our example, the conversation may have started with sales and moved through the logical paces of the part being sold, the supplier who provided the part, and the warehouse used to store the inventory of available parts until all the relevant entities were identified. These entities, which often correspond to singular nouns in spoken language, will become dimension tables in the database we are building and contain attributes that need to be defined and modeled.

Having identified several key dimensions, such as customer, order, and part, we can draw the other axis of the bus matrix. The following screenshot shows the resulting grid when business processes are placed next to their component dimensions:

| Business Processes (facts) | Entities (dimensions) |||||||
|---|---|---|---|---|---|---|---|
| | Date | Order | Customer | Location | Supplier | Part | Inventory |
| Purchase Parts | | | | | | | |
| Track Inventory | | | | | | | |
| Sell Parts | | | | | | | |
| Customer Returns | | | | | | | |
| Supplier Returns | | | | | | | |

Figure 7.3 – The bus matrix with business processes and dimensions

Notice that the date dimension is the first one named. Facts, such as sales, streams, and logins, have at least one relevant time dimension that needs to be recorded (although factless fact tables also exist and are covered in later chapters).

When all dimensions have been identified, it's time to finalize the bus matrix by nailing down the facts.

## Identify the facts

DM defines facts as tables containing transactions among business dimensions paired with relevant metrics. The metrics record information is pertinent to the grain of the fact table, which comprises relevant dimensions. This relationship can be mapped directly in the bus matrix by putting an X at the intersection of business processes and their required dimensions.

In our example, the finished bus matrix may look something like this:

| Business Processes (facts) | Entities (dimensions) |||||||
|---|---|---|---|---|---|---|---|
| | Date | Order | Customer | Location | Supplier | Part | Inventory |
| Purchase Parts | X | | | X | X | X | X |
| Track Inventory | X | | | | X | X | X |
| Sell Parts | X | X | X | | X | X | |
| Customer Returns | X | X | X | | X | X | X |
| Supplier Returns | X | | | X | X | X | X |

Figure 7.4 – The bus matrix that maps business processes to the dimensions involved

Using the resulting matrix, we can revisit the earlier question of sales grain and see whether we've answered it correctly. While the problem may seem technical, the answer is always business driven. Perhaps the atomic grain of a sale consists of its date and time, the details of the customer and product being purchased, and the metrics surrounding the transaction, such as price, quantity, and discount. Our business teams may want to track total sales and cancelations at the customer level while reviewing product margins and discounts at the part level. We can construct tables to accommodate business needs by capturing this atomic grain in the design.

## 112 Putting Conceptual Modeling into Practice

Performance and maintenance decisions at further stages of the modeling process may result in multiple rollup tables being created from the granular atomic facts. Still, the analysis at the conceptual level is sufficient to accommodate any such decisions.

Having laid the groundwork for uncovering the facts and dimensions, let's visualize the bus matrix in a conceptual model.

## From bus matrix to a conceptual model

Now that we have a bus matrix worked out and agreed upon with the business teams, we can begin to transfer the details onto a conceptual diagram. The first step in the process is to create the dimensions as entities. Usually, the most relevant attributes would have also been identified as part of the business workshops and could also be included in the model. But, to split the exercise into cleanly separated steps, this will be done in the next chapter, where we discuss logical modeling.

Here is what the diagram would look like with only the dimensions included:

LOCATION
location assigned to customer or supplier

—— located in ——

CUSTOMER
Registered cusotmers

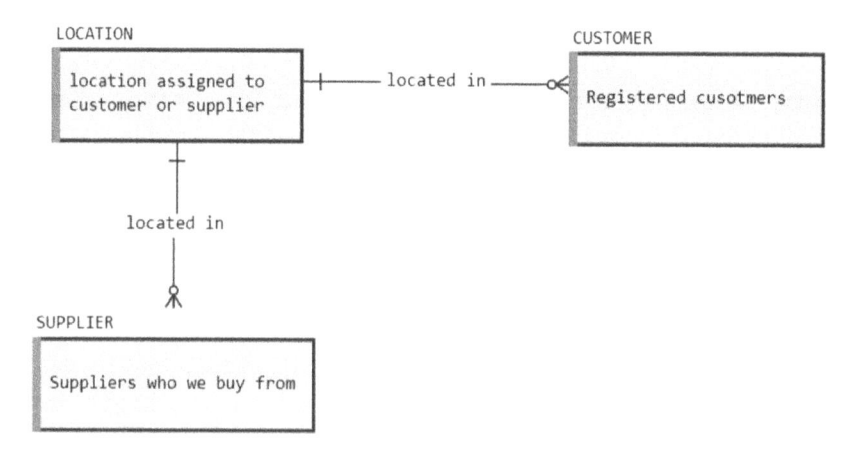

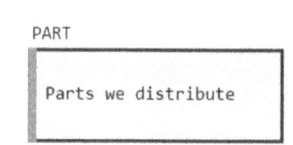

located in

SUPPLIER
Suppliers who we buy from

PART
Parts we distribute

Figure 7.5 – A conceptual model showing only dimensions

With the entities in place, we can now create the fact tables and connect them using the relationships and business rules defined in the workshops. The model now contains all the facts and dimensions listed in the bus matrix, as shown in the following diagram:

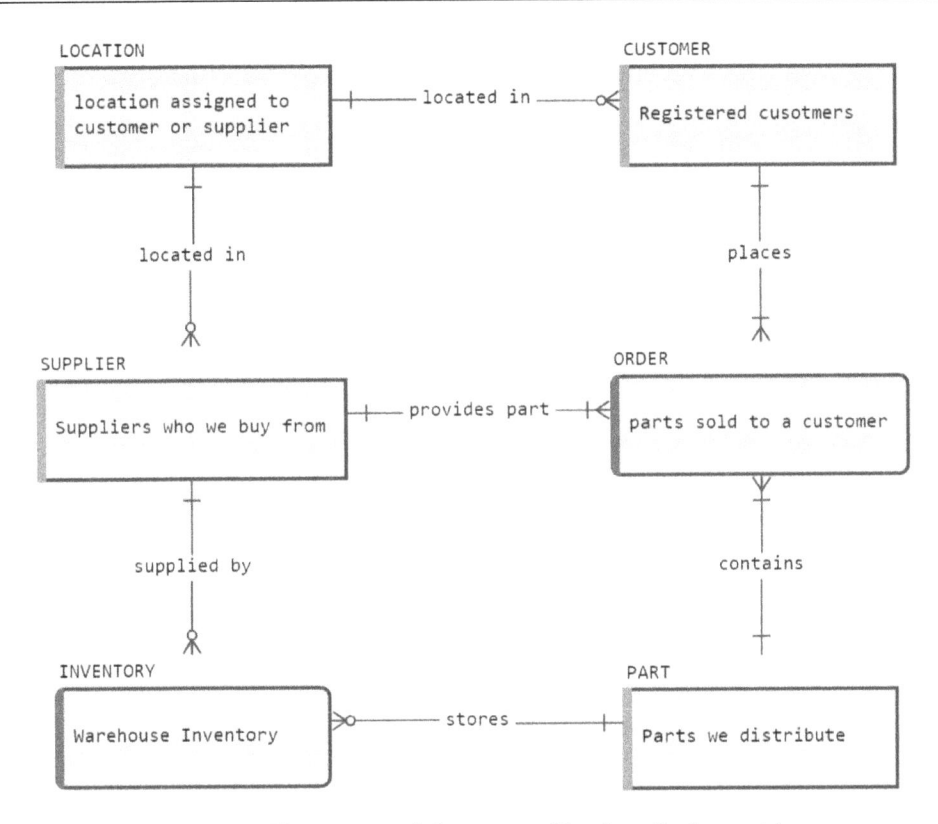

Figure 7.6 – The conceptual diagram resulting from the bus matrix

Notice that while five business processes are listed in the matrix, only two fact tables have been modeled in the diagram. Often, the same fact table can include enough details to cover multiple business processes—for example, customer sales and returns, because they occur at the same grain.

By asking a few business-oriented questions, we have seen how to determine the grain of the various operations of our company and identify the related facts and dimensions, putting it all together into the bus matrix. A conceptual diagram can be easily generated and used as a foundation for later steps in the modeling process using the information in the bus matrix. But just as a conceptual model can be used to initiate database design by formalizing existing business processes, it can also work in reverse to help sense-check existing physical designs.

## Modeling in reverse

Real-world enterprise operational systems and data warehouses can reach heights of great complexity, especially if they have evolved over many years and absorbed untold numbers of dubious design decisions. Even the standing members of the data team may not be able to explain every detail, let alone a new hire or a business analyst. Fortunately, conceptual modeling can help simplify and visualize existing database landscapes as quickly as it does when starting new ones.

Database modeling tools allow users to take schema definitions as DDL and ingest them to generate a corresponding diagram—a process known as **reverse engineering**. Since all the table structures and constraints are already defined in the database, generating an ER diagram and visualizing the database landscape can be done in seconds. Because reverse engineering uses Snowflake object DDL, it produces physical models. As physical models contain the highest level of detail of all modeling types, they can be easily abstracted into conceptual. While modeling tools can automate most of the steps of going from physical to conceptual, the task can also be performed by hand without much effort by following the four-step method in reverse.

We are embarking on an exercise of going from *what is* to *what ought to be*. The latter part cannot be known from the database but verified with the business teams through workshops and discussions. This exercise aims to generate a best-guess conceptual model from *what is* so that it can facilitate those discussions. Let's begin by labeling the existing tables.

## Identify the facts and dimensions

Start by taking the existing tables in the physical schema and classifying them into facts and dimensions using previously discussed rules of thumb. Dimension tables will typically be named using singular nouns and contain descriptive attributes but not quantitative measurements. Facts are usually named using transitive verbs, including measures that quantify each transaction.

In our example, the result of this exercise would look something like the following diagram:

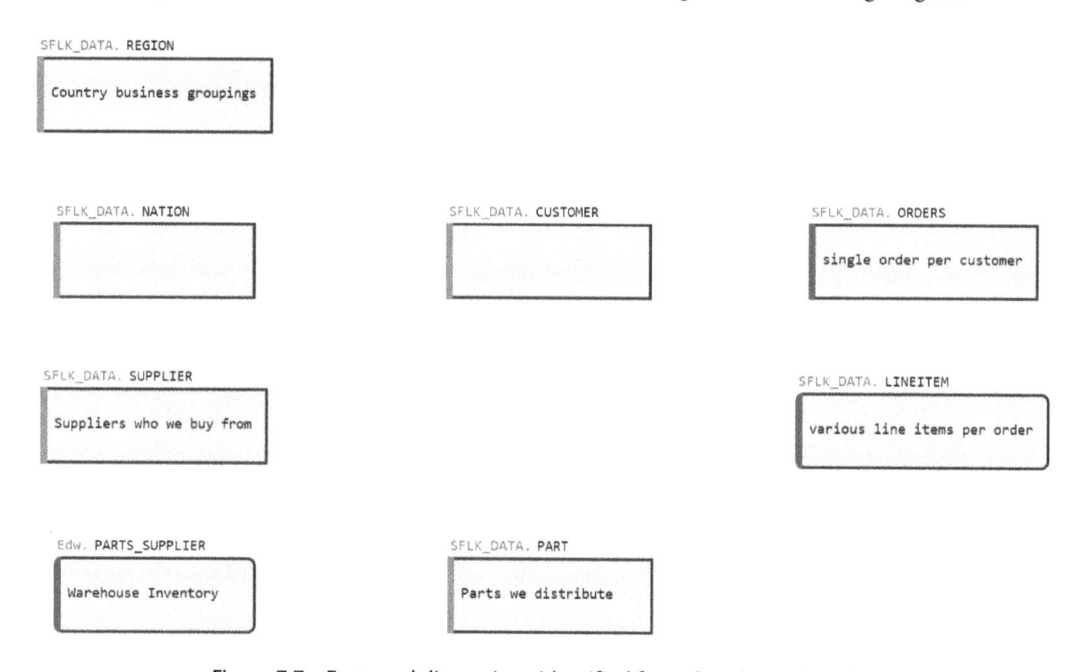

SFLK_DATA. REGION
| Country business groupings |

SFLK_DATA. NATION

SFLK_DATA. CUSTOMER

SFLK_DATA. ORDERS
| single order per customer |

SFLK_DATA. SUPPLIER
| Suppliers who we buy from |

SFLK_DATA. LINEITEM
| various line items per order |

Edw. PARTS_SUPPLIER
| Warehouse Inventory |

SFLK_DATA. PART
| Parts we distribute |

Figure 7.7 – Facts and dimensions identified from the physical model

Now that the entities have been mapped, we must identify the relationships.

## Establish the relationships

Identifying the relationships between tables can be swift or arduous depending on whether standards and best practices have been observed in the physical schema. For example, if primary and **foreign keys** (**FKs**) have been declared, modeling tools will use this information to automatically establish and visualize all the relationships in the schema.

Absent these constraints, we can rely on column naming conventions to intuit the relationships. Starting with the dimensions, look for columns that resemble the table name and include something that hints at their being a **primary key** (**PK**) (keywords such as *id*, *key*, or *code*). For example, the NATION dimension contains a column called N_NATIONKEY and is, therefore, likely to be the PK. Test the assertion with GROUP BY HAVING, which should return no values greater than one if the column is a PK, and the underlying data is clean.

The following query should return no results if N_NATIONKEY is the PK for NATION:

```
SELECT N_NATIONKEY , COUNT(*) AS CNT FROM NATION
GROUP BY 1
HAVING CNT > 1
```

Remember that even the data cannot conclusively prove what the PK should be—it can only point to a highly likely candidate. Only the business users can conclusively confirm the grain of a business dimension.

Once PK candidates have been proposed for dimensions, look for instances of the PK columns in facts and other dimension tables. In DM, columns with the same structure and meaning across multiple tables are known as **conformed dimensions**. For example, an ID column in the CUSTOMER table is a conformed dimension of CUSTOMER_ID in SALES if both columns share the same data type and values. When individual attributes within a dimension are consistent across multiple tables, they are considered **conformed attributes**. For example, STAR_RATING may be a conformed attribute in both PRODUCT and SUPPORT_SURVEY. Consistent naming of columns across tables is immensely helpful in this type of analysis. Modeling tools rely on the naming of conformed attributes to automatically propose FK relationships.

Once the relationships have been identified, attempt to establish their cardinality and optionality details. While the table constraints give some clues about the nature of the relationship, only the business teams can confirm the reality (although the data can be an indicator). In the following example, the physical constraints can have multiple conceptual interpretations:

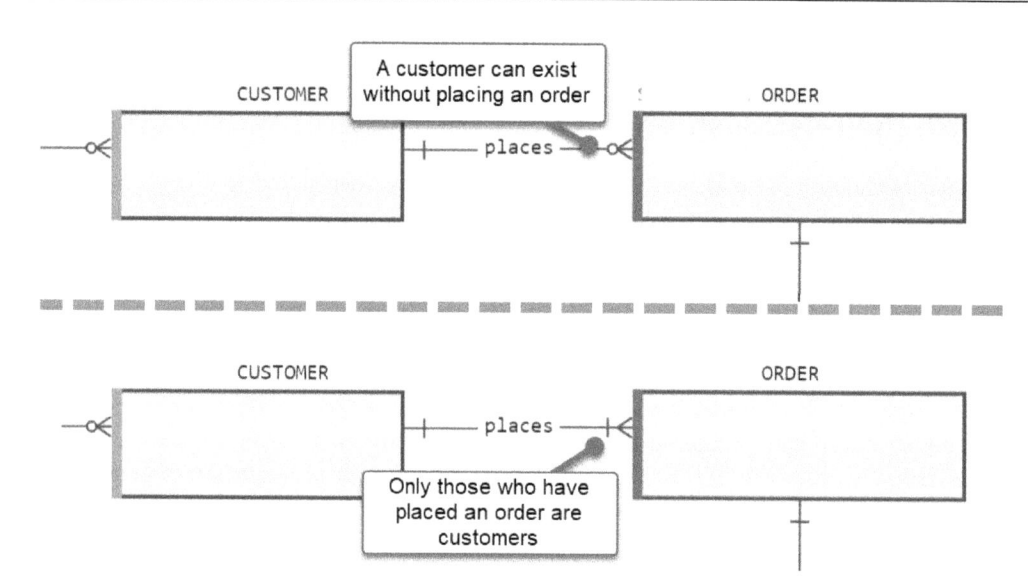

## 116 Putting Conceptual Modeling into Practice

Figure 7.8 – Multiple conceptual representations of a physical relationship

Once we have established all the entities and relationships and made an informed guess as to their cardinality, we have completed the draft of a conceptual model, which might look something like the following diagram:

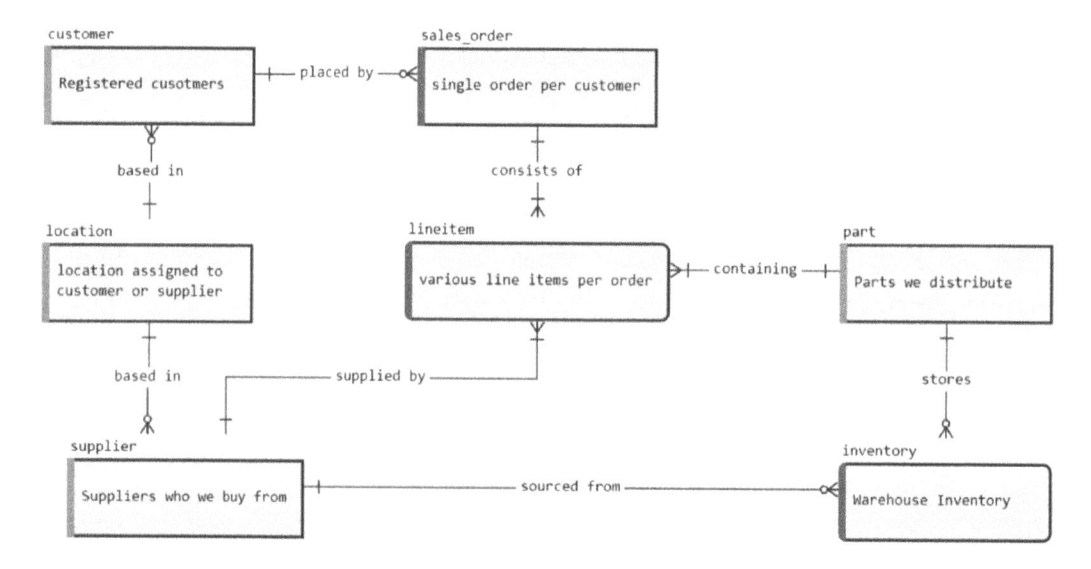

Figure 7.9 – A conceptual model of a physical schema

Using the conceptual model, which provides a clear visual representation of the existing database design, we can open the dialogue with the various domain teams responsible for each business process and their respective dimensions to validate what has been built.

## Propose and validate the business processes

Even though we are working with a relatively small schema, classifying and identifying the tables and relationships has not been easy. We have generated a simplified vision of the business model using a conceptual diagram that must now be validated with the business teams and product owners. Recall that the same fact table can capture multiple business processes and identifying them cannot be done without input from the business teams.

Based on the input of business owners and domain experts, the conceptual model can be adjusted and refined to reflect the true reality of business operations. The conceptual review may even result in changes to the physical model if the business and database models have deviated over time.

Whatever the scenario, we now have a clear and accurate conceptual database model that fully aligns with the business it supports. The conceptual model can help analysts and new hires quickly get acquainted with the business. After having put in the work to validate it, the conceptual model should be maintained going forward by repeating the process described in this chapter.

Now that we have seen how to generate a conceptual model using Kimball's methods as well as working backward from a physical database, let's review what we've learned.

# Summary

In this chapter, we have seen how a conceptual model and its accompanying diagram make it easy to visualize an organizational business model and validate it with domain experts against the intended business operations that it is meant to support.

To get started in conceptual modeling, we used Kimball's DM methodology, which has been used for decades to guide the design of database and warehouse architectures. Kimball uses a four-step method to initiate discussions between the data team and business teams, and domain experts to identify the business processes that an organization engages in.

Once business processes have been identified, we determine their grain or lowest level of detail pertinent to our business. Describing the grain will also help us discover the core dimensions of our business. Plotting dimensions and business processes on a chart, known as the bus matrix, produces an elegant cross-section of our business and lets us transfer its details easily to a conceptual diagram.

It is not only new designs that benefit from the aid of conceptual models. A conceptual model can also be used to visualize and validate a physical database. Modeling tools can automatically generate physical diagrams from existing DDL through reverse engineering. Otherwise, modelers can reverse the four-step Kimball method to arrive at a conceptual model starting from a physical database.

Depending on its initial design or changes that have occurred over time, a physical database may deviate from the actual business model of the organization. Conceptual diagrams are an important tool in opening the conversation with business teams to align the physical and business models by giving non-technical users a simple way to understand what has been built.

However, the collaboration between the data and business teams does not stop at the conceptual model. In the next chapter, we will expand on what we have built by adding functional details and preparing our model for physical deployment.

## Further reading

Kimball and company popularized and significantly contributed to DM and data warehousing. Their books are still relevant today and offer great overviews of concepts and fundamental terminology. For an agile alternative to Kimball, you should look at the BEAM method, described in *Agile Data Warehouse Design*:

- Kimball, Ralph, and Margy Ross. *The Data Warehouse Toolkit: The Definitive Guide to Dimensional Modeling*. John Wiley and Sons, 2013.

- Kimball, Ralph, et al. *The Kimball Group Reader: Relentlessly Practical Tools for Data Warehousing and Business Intelligence Remastered Collection*. John Wiley and Sons, 2015.

- Corr, Lawrence, and Jim Stagnitto. *Agile Data Warehouse Design: Collaborative Dimensional Modeling, From Whiteboard to Star Schema*. DecisionOne Consulting, 2011.

# 8
# Putting Logical Modeling into Practice

In the previous chapter, we observed data teams working with business teams to create a high-level conceptual model representing an organization's main entities and relationships. While a conceptual model helps to understand the overall structure and requirements of the data without going into excessive detail, the next stage in the modeling process requires us to go further and develop a detailed model to be used as a blueprint for moving to a physical database design.

To complete the logical model, the data team will have to collaborate with domain experts from the business once again to expand the list of entities, attributes, and relationships that will be used in the database, as well as the data types and constraints for each element. Just as the conceptual model held bidirectional benefits in both developing a fresh design and simplifying an existing one, a logical model is not merely a stepping stone in the modeling process.

Logical models are much more detailed and granular than conceptual ones. Although they lack the database-specific information of a physical model, they make up for it by providing contextual information that physical databases cannot capture. Once developed, a logical model provides a basis for taking a design forward and adapting it for deployment on a specific database.

In this chapter, we will cover the following main topics:

- Identifying and adding attributes and data types
- Adding structural and technical details to entity relationships
- Resolving many-to-many relationships
- Expanding weak entities
- Understanding inheritance in database models

Let's continue where we left off with the conceptual model developed in the previous chapter and evolve it into a logical one.

## Expanding from conceptual to logical modeling

In the previous chapter, we used Kimball's four-step methodology to develop a bus matrix and create a conceptual model based on the recorded information. Details that informed the bus matrix were gathered through workshops and discussions between the data team and experts on the business side, who could elucidate the business's operational model and create a functional artifact—the conceptual diagram.

The following diagram shows the conceptual model as it looked at the end of the exercise:

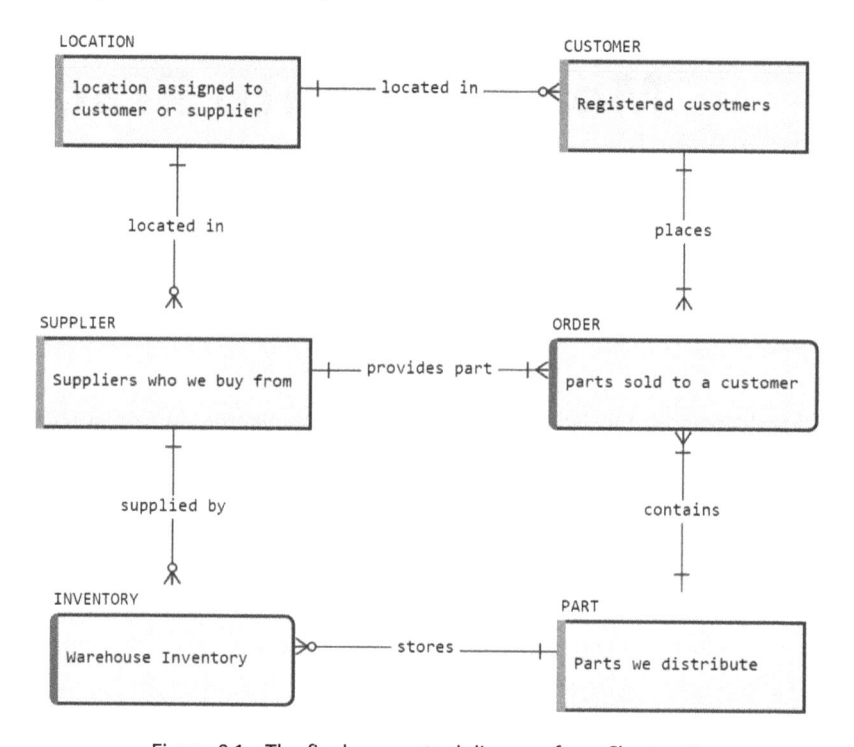

Figure 8.1 – The final conceptual diagram from Chapter 7

Despite the obvious deficiencies, such as missing attributes and Snowflake-specific object properties, the conceptual diagram did not attempt to add any contextual detail on the functional relationships between the entities, such as subtypes and many-to-many associations.

To uncover the relevant fields that should be added to our model's entities, we should again engage business experts specializing in the related business domains.

## Adding attributes

The most important detail in a dimension is its unique identifier. This determines what constitutes a unique instance of each entity in our business. Examples of unique identifiers include things such as serial numbers for parts and employee IDs for a company's human capital. Domain experts from each business area can confirm these and other necessary details. We will use the CUSTOMER dimension as an example to identify the relevant details and incorporate them into the model.

Suppose we sat down with the head of the sales team to learn about how our organization identifies customers and their relevant attributes. The domain expert explains that besides typical customer attributes such as name and address, our organization is also interested in tracking the account balance and identifying its market segment. The sales team also explains how customers are grouped into regions based on their NATION attribute, maintained in a separate LOCATION dimension. Besides identifying the attributes and their data types, we also learn that all of them are required (cannot be NULL) besides the optional comments field.

> **ANSI compliance in Snowflake data types**
>
> Snowflake supports most basic SQL data types in table columns and semi-structured and geo-spacial data types. For compliance with the **American National Standards Institute (ANSI)** SQL standard, Snowflake also supports synonyms for many common data types found in other databases and logical modeling. For example, although Snowflake stores string data as VARCHAR, a column could be modeled as STRING or CHAR, and upon deployment, such a column would be created as VARCHAR. For a summary of supported data types and aliases, refer to the following documentation: https://docs.snowflake.com/en/sql-reference/intro-summary-data-types.html.

With the feedback from the sales team, we now have a logical model of the customer dimension, complete with details about its **primary key (PK)**, **foreign key (FK)**, data types, and their mandatory or optional nature. The transition from conceptual to a logical level of detail is shown in the following image:

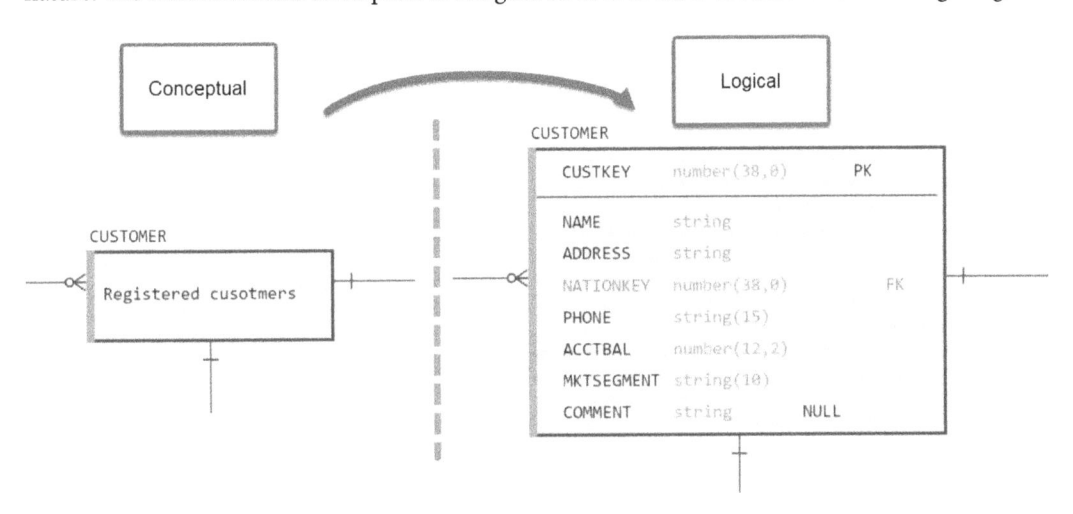

Figure 8.2 – Going from conceptual to logical modeling

After completing the exercise for all existing dimensions, we focus on how they come together to record the facts.

## Cementing the relationships

With attributes and PK and FK relationships established in the dimensions, we again turn to the business experts to help flesh out the fact tables and determine their grain.

Building from the conceptual model, we ensure that all relationships have a defined granularity and optionality and that the data teams understand their business context. Mistakes made in the fact table definition are the costliest to reconcile and could result in costly readjustment, so extra care should be taken. Work with domain experts to ensure that the fact tables capture the true atomic grain of the information recorded by business operations and that the optionality is correctly understood.

In the following example, the logistics team confirms that our warehouse separates parts by the supplier to facilitate returns and inventory tracking. In short, the warehouse can store many parts from many suppliers. Role names are also verified and documented at this point for non-obvious relationships. The resulting logical model now looks like this:

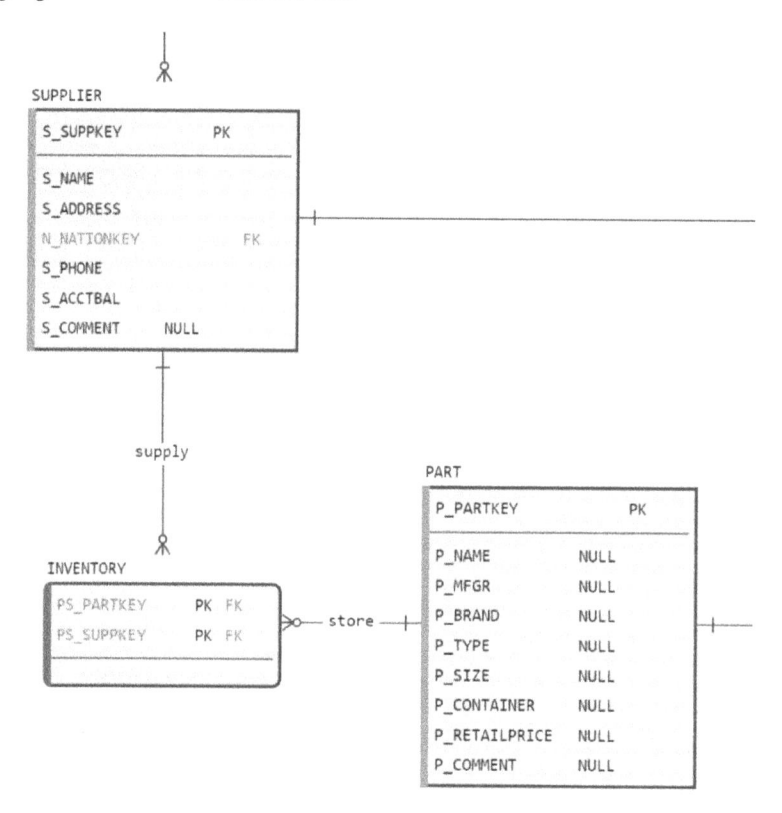

Figure 8.3 – Determining the fact table grain

However, we have yet to define the measures describing the facts stored in the table. For warehouse inventory, this can be as simple as the quantity of the parts on hand and the cost for which each part was obtained (since this can fluctuate by supplier).

The following diagram shows the final state of the `INVENTORY` table, complete with cardinality, granularity, role names, and required measures:

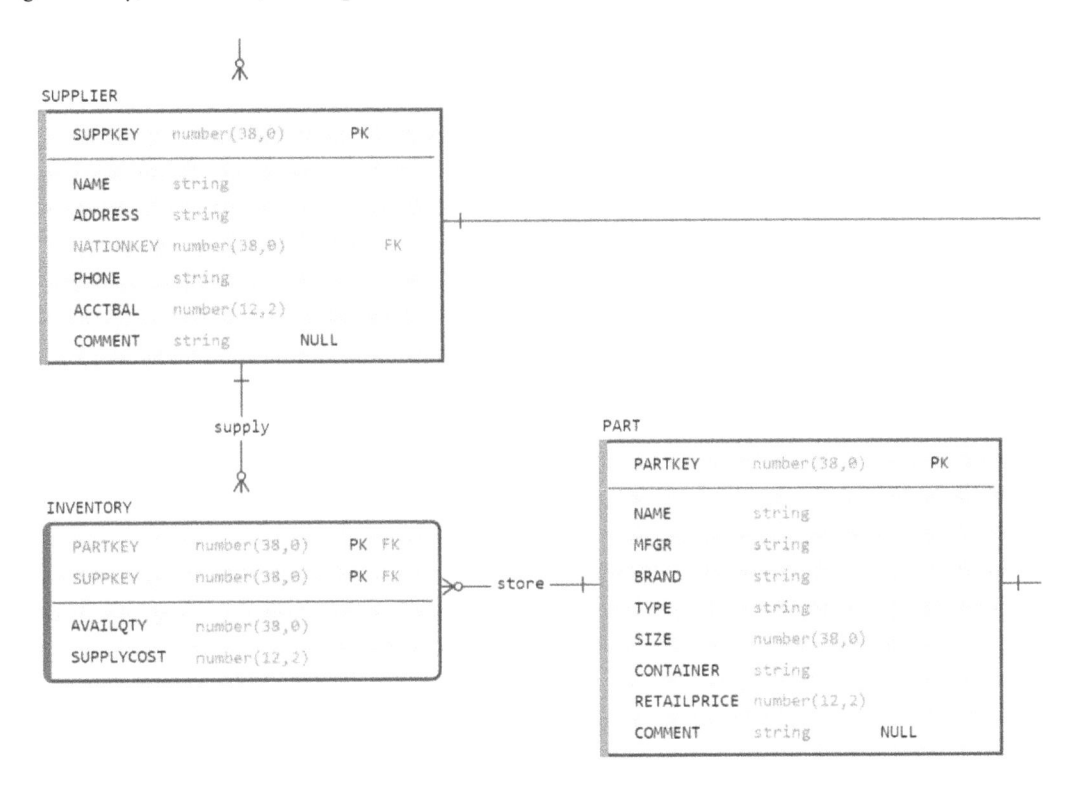

Figure 8.4 – Fact table with grain and measures

Repeating the exercise for all the facts in our model gives us a complete vision for proceeding to subsequent design phases. The next step is to identify the many-to-many relationships.

## Many-to-many relationships

A **many-to-many** (**M:M**) relationship exists between two entities when each can have many instances of the other. For example, in our organization, suppliers can supply many parts, and parts can be supplied by many different suppliers. Therefore, a third entity (inventory), called an **associative** or **junction entity**, is required to store and track which part came from which supplier.

## 124 Putting Logical Modeling into Practice

Recall the example from *Chapter 2, An Introduction to the Four Modeling Types*, where a list of all available superpowers required an associative table to represent the possible superpowers of a superhero:

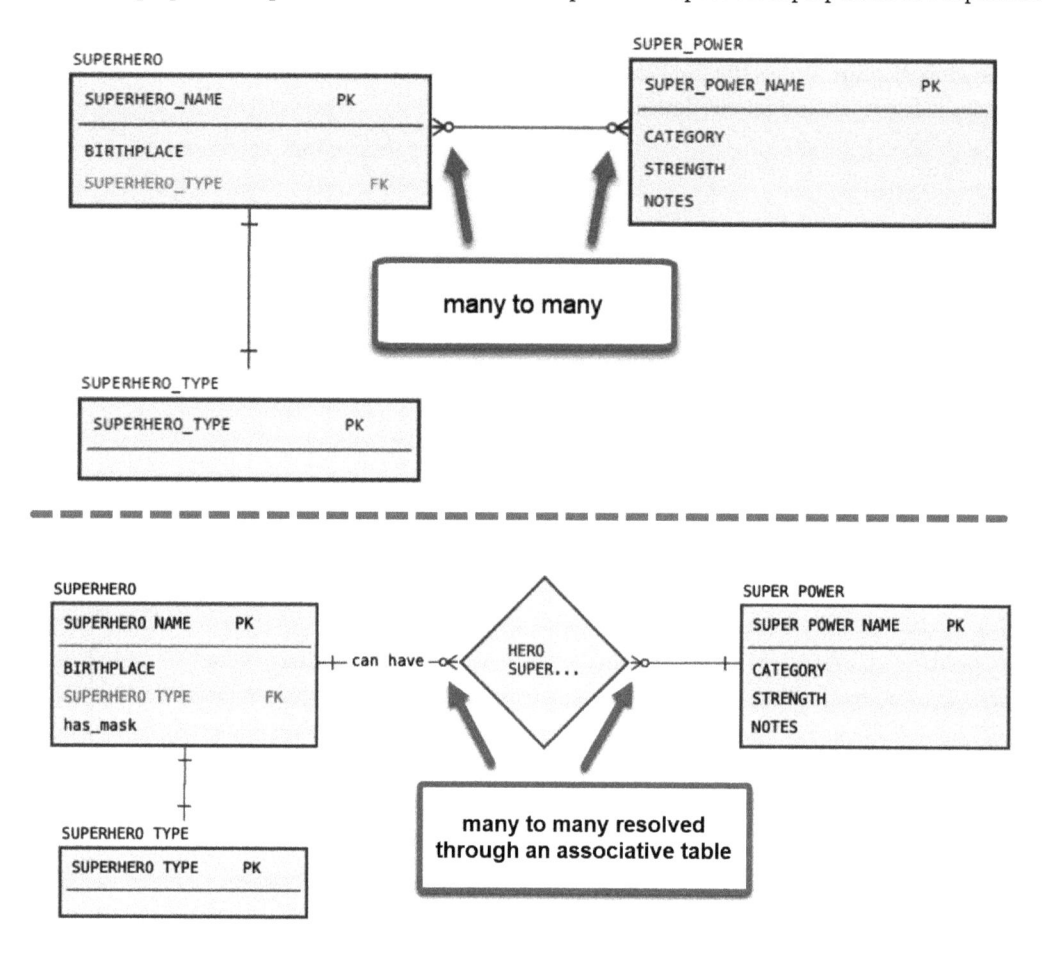

Figure 8.5 – Resolving an M:M relationship through an associative table

In the current example, there are no unresolved M:M relationships because the real-world operation of our business necessitates a physical entity (the warehouse) to store an inventory of many parts provided by many suppliers. However, by using the diamond notation to capture the business context of this relationship, we communicate beyond the database level the idea that inventory cannot exist on its own. Rather, it only exists due to an interaction (procurement) of a part from a supplier:

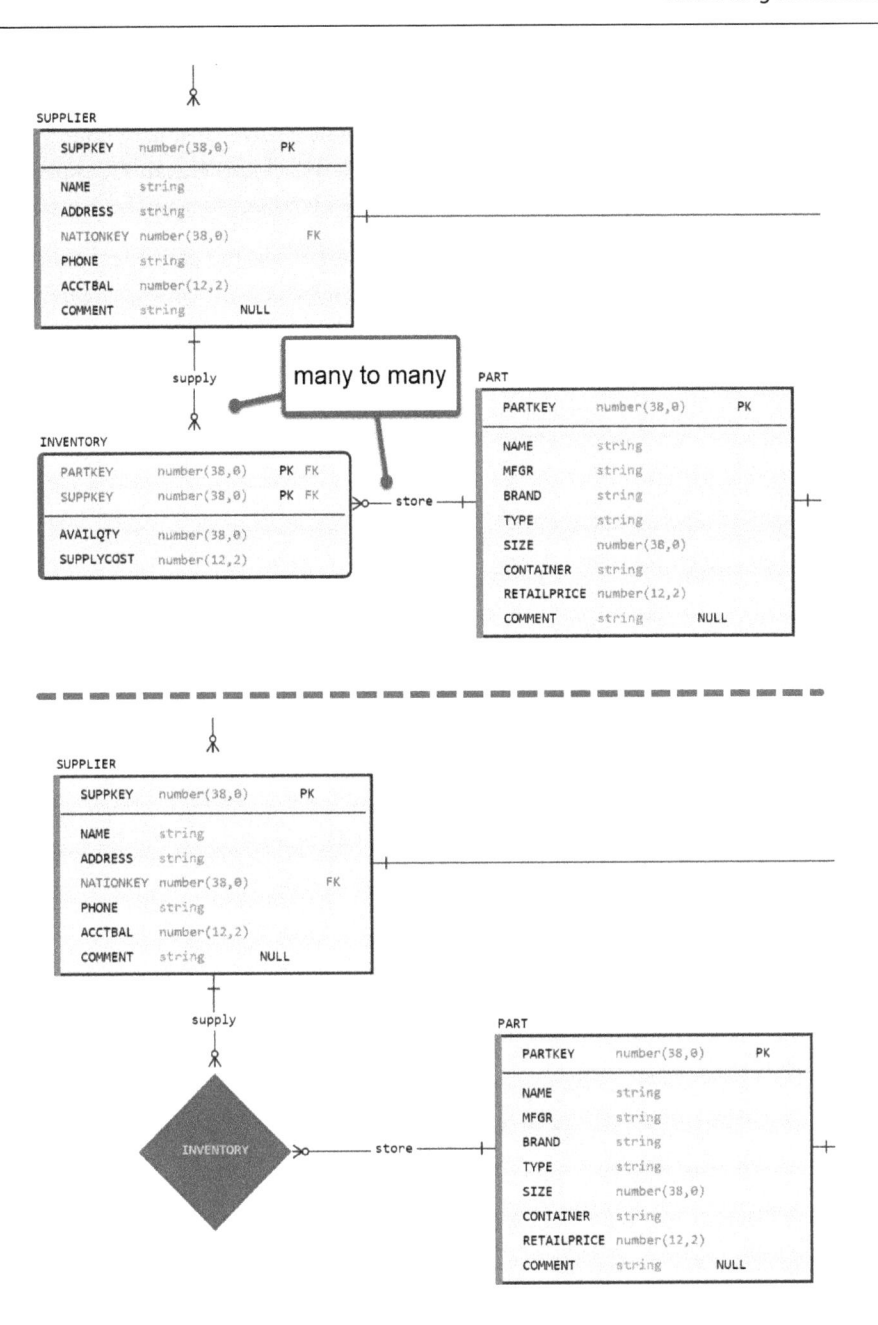

Figure 8.6 – Highlighting an existing M:M relationship on a logical diagram

An M:M relationship is one example of an entity that cannot exist in isolation—weak entities are another.

## Weak entities

A **weak entity** is an entity that cannot be uniquely identified by its own attributes; it must use an FK in conjunction with its own to create a PK. In other words, a weak entity has an FK as part of its PK instead of a strong entity that depends entirely on its unique identifier.

On a diagram, weak entities are identified by their rounded corners instead of the perpendicular edges of strong entities. However, their implications extend beyond semantics and impact how the model handles changes in the data. Let's look at an example using the ORDERS table.

At first glance, ORDERS has multiple crow's feet connectors, which make it seem like an associative M:M table. Notice the similarities between ORDERS and INVENTORY in the following diagram:

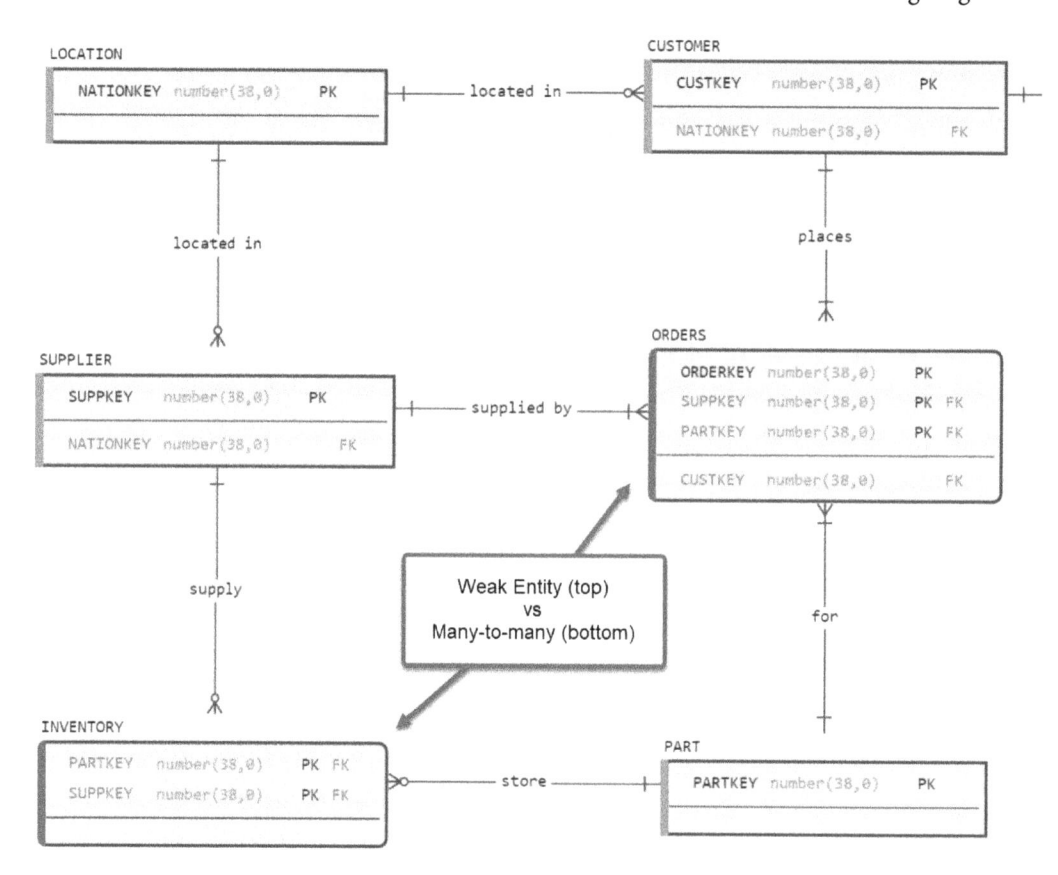

Figure 8.7 – Weak entities distinguished from M:M by their PKs

Orders are business entities with unique codes that must be tracked and audited. On the other hand, INVENTORY has no unique identifier, nor does it make business sense to give it one—recording the PKs of the part, supplier, and quantity on hand is sufficient.

After speaking to the sales team, we learn that an order is viewed differently depending on the business context. An order is a single transaction between a customer and the company viewed from a sales perspective. However, from a logistics perspective, an order consists of many records to reflect individual items purchased, returned, or discounted. Our business teams need to reference and analyze individual orders, but keeping everything in one table makes that difficult.

The solution is to separate orders into a strong entity (ORDERS) and a weak entity (LINEITEM), thereby facilitating storage, analysis, and maintenance. This means using the order identifier (ORDERKEY) as the PK of the ORDERS entity and creating a weak entity called LINEITEM, with its own unique identifier and previously existing FK columns as part of the PK and ORDERKEY as a non-PK, FK attribute.

The transition from a weak entity to separate strong and weak entities can be seen in the following diagram:

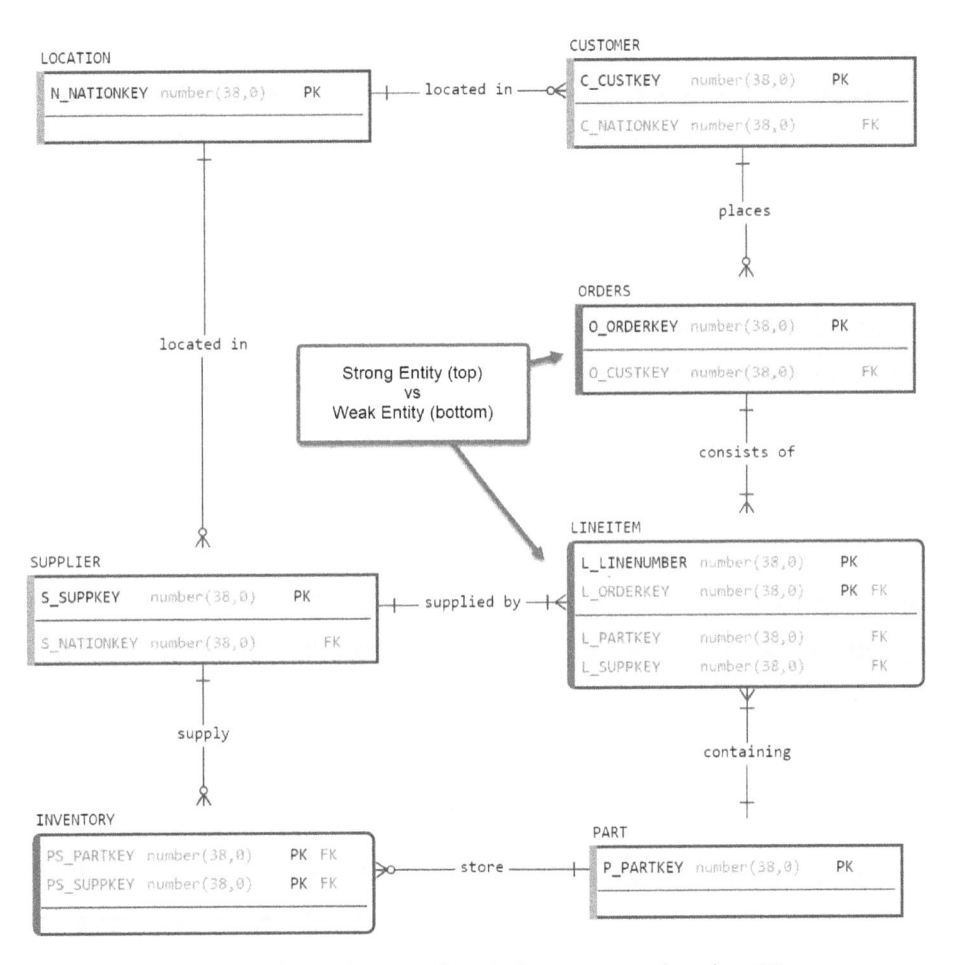

Figure 8.8 – Separating a weak entity into strong and weak entities

In this scenario, orders can be quickly reviewed and counted because each is stored in one individual record, and line items can be changed and updated in a separate table.

While weak entities rely on strong entities to identify them, they are inherently different elements. Let's explore what happens when we want to model entities that are similar in nature and share common characteristics.

## Inheritance

Those with a background in object-oriented programming will be familiar with inheritance—the passing of properties from a parent to a child class. The same is true in data modeling, except that parent and child classes are called supertype and subtype, respectively. **Subtypes** share common characteristics with a **supertype** entity but have additional attributes that make them distinct.

Suppose that our sales team maintains a particular category of loyal customers based on the volume of their repeat business. A loyal customer has the same attributes as a regular customer, even sharing the same identifier, and contains attributes that describe their loyalty level and reward points.

At the physical level, the resulting table, LOYALTY_CUSTOMER, may appear as an ordinary child table or weak entity when viewed on a diagram:

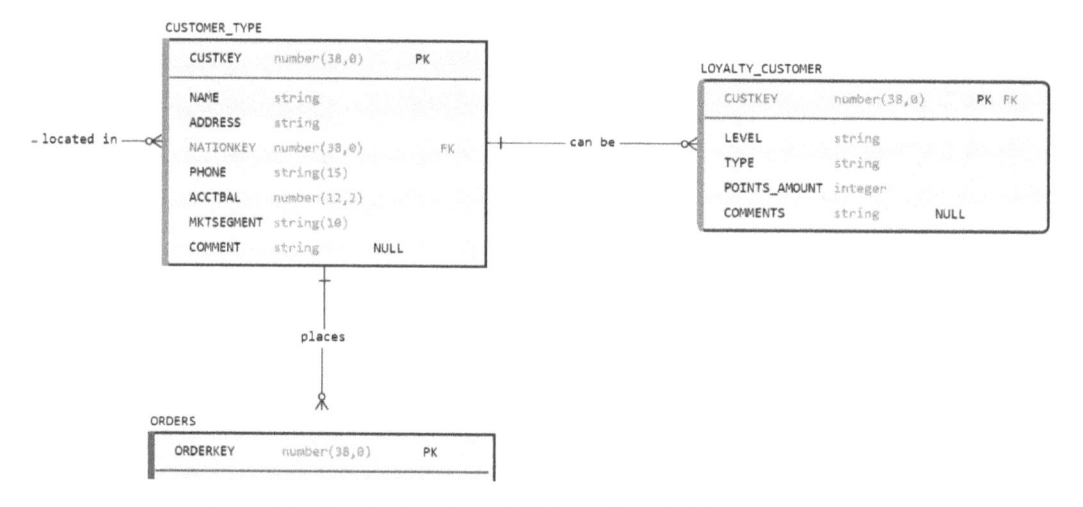

Figure 8.9 – The physical view of CUSTOMER and LOYALTY_CUSTOMER

However, this would not capture the true nature of its relationship to CUSTOMER as subtype notation would. Adding a discriminator between the CUSTOMER supertype and the LOYALTY_CUSTOMER subtype adds context that would otherwise be lost at the database level:

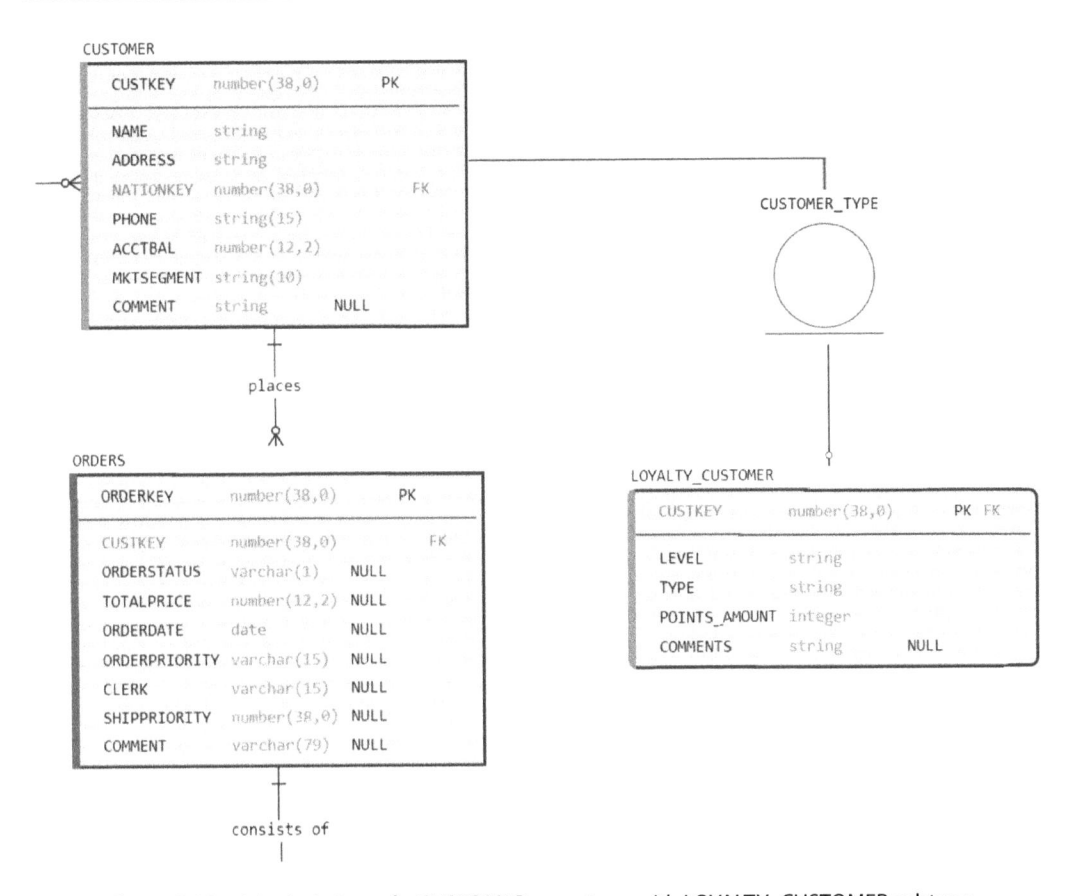

```
CUSTOMER
  CUSTKEY      number(38,0)      PK
  NAME         string
  ADDRESS      string
  NATIONKEY    number(38,0)      FK
  PHONE        string(15)
  ACCTBAL      number(12,2)
  MKTSEGMENT   string(10)
  COMMENT      string            NULL

                          CUSTOMER_TYPE

               places

ORDERS                                  LOYALTY_CUSTOMER
  ORDERKEY     number(38,0)      PK       CUSTKEY       number(38,0)     PK FK
  CUSTKEY      number(38,0)      FK       LEVEL         string
  ORDERSTATUS  varchar(1)   NULL          TYPE          string
  TOTALPRICE   number(12,2) NULL          POINTS_AMOUNT integer
  ORDERDATE    date         NULL          COMMENTS      string           NULL
  ORDERPRIORITY varchar(15) NULL
  CLERK        varchar(15)  NULL
  SHIPPRIORITY number(38,0) NULL
  COMMENT      varchar(79)  NULL

               consists of
```

Figure 8.10 – A logical view of a CUSTOMER supertype with LOYALTY_CUSTOMER subtype

Compared to *Figure 8.9*, *Figure 8.10* transmits the following business context:

- CUSTOMER is the parent/supertype entity whose attributes can be applied to its child/subtypes (defined by the discriminator symbol)
- The LOYALTY_CUSTOMER subtype is incomplete (single, as opposed to double, the line below the discriminator), meaning more subtypes may be added in the future
- The LOYALTY_CUSTOMER subtype is inclusive (the empty circle without an X mark), so a CUSTOMER can be a LOYALTY_CUSTOMER and other possible types that are yet to be defined

This completes the transition from a conceptual to a logical model. Let's review the completed model in the following diagram:

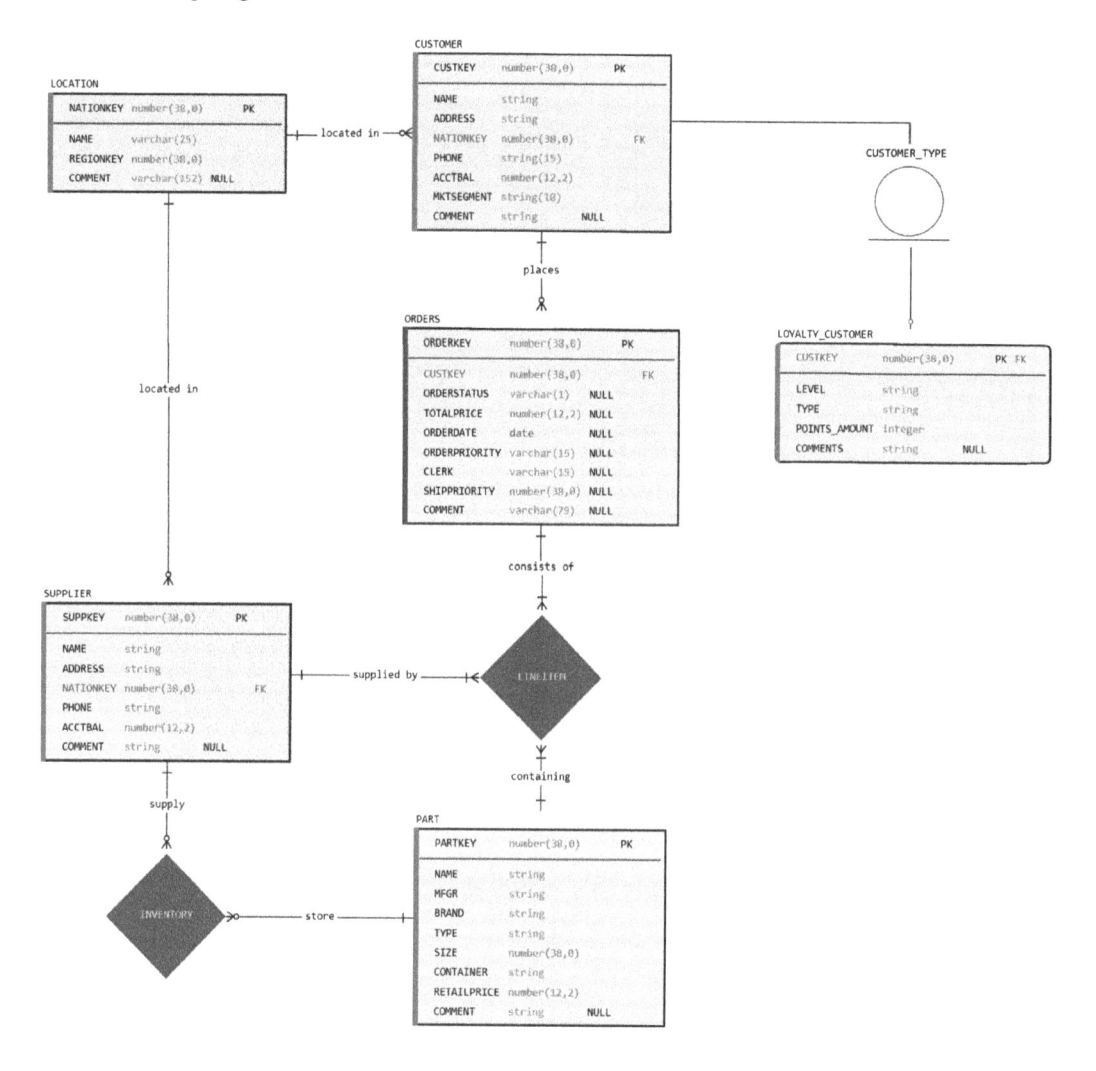

Figure 8.11 – A completed logical model

The conceptual model that we started with in *Figure 8.1* is a representation of the data requirements of our organization that is easy to understand and communicate to stakeholders. It does not focus on the specific implementation details of the database but rather on the overall structure and relationships between different data entities.

On the other hand, logical database modeling creates a detailed model of the (pending) database that adds structural details and expresses the existing entities and relationships in greater technical detail. The goal of logical modeling is to lay the groundwork for designing the actual database while capturing additional nuances that can not be represented using physical database objects.

## Summary

In this chapter, we continued the modeling journey by taking the conceptual design from the previous chapter and expanding it to logical by adding structural details and technical details that closely resemble the physical model we will create and deploy in later chapters.

Continuing to work with business experts from our organization, we identified the attributes that will be used to capture crucial business master data and transactions. We defined each business entity's identifiers, attributes and measures, and data types to do this.

Once attributes have been set in place, we reviewed the relationships between entities to understand the nuances of their associations to architect them in such a way as to fit the needs of the business and simplify their maintenance.

We started by identifying the M:M relationships. These relationships require an associative table to capture the interactions between the entities involved but are not considered entities themselves. Associative tables, therefore, do not have a business key but rely on the FKs of their related entities.

Next, we checked for weak entities that cannot be uniquely identified by their attributes alone. Depending on the business needs, weak entities may encumber the maintenance and analysis of the underlying entity, which can be split into separate, strong entities to overcome the problem.

Finally, we covered the concept of inheritance and how it manifests in database design through subtype and supertype relationships. Identifying subtypes and capturing their business context through a discriminator symbol helps set them apart from regular child tables.

The next step in the modeling journey is converting the logical model to a physical Snowflake database. However, before diving into the physical design, we will need to get comfortable with the concept of normalization and cover the best practices for structuring and maintaining physical objects in Snowflake, which we will do in the coming chapters.

# 9
# Database Normalization

Previous chapters have explored the method of capturing the real-world business workings of an organization and modeling them using visual semantics. The resulting model and accompanying diagrams make it easy for the domain and data teams to reach a consensus about the business's fundamental entities and the interactions between them. However, as the modeling process approaches the physical stage, we should understand that many ways exist to structure the data at the database level. The process of dividing the data into smaller, modularized segments is known as normalization. In this chapter, we will understand how it works and the advantages and disadvantages that go along with it.

Normalization is not a binary classification but a spectrum of ever-increasing rules a design must satisfy to achieve a stated level. While normalization contains the root word *normal*, along with the obvious positive connotations, more normalization does not necessarily imply a *better* design. As we will see in this chapter, greater levels of normalization impose more rigor on the database's structure—reducing data anomalies at the cost of increased maintenance and analytical complexity.

This chapter will explore normalization through its various levels to understand the rules, advantages, and trade-offs. After a thorough overview, we will focus on the most common types of normalization and understand the aspects that make them popular choices for database design. This chapter aims to provide a complete overview of normalization, its benefits, and its costs to allow users to find the right fit for the task at hand.

This chapter will cover the following main topics:

- Understanding normalization on a spectrum
- The pros and cons of normalization
- How much is too much? Finding the sweet spot
- Reviewing the data anomalies that normalization protects from
- Taking an in-depth look at normalization from the first to the sixth normal form

# An overview of database normalization

Database **normalization** is the process of organizing a database in a way that reduces redundancy and dependency within its tables. This is achieved by breaking a large table into smaller ones and linking them through foreign key relationships. Doing so leads to fewer data inconsistencies and improved data integrity. A normalized database results in a modular design that is easy to scale and modify.

Normalization occurs through escalating stages of formal rules called **normal forms**, ranging from the **first normal form (1NF)** to the **sixth normal form (6NF)**—although the first through third are most commonly used and are sufficient for most use cases.

Each normal form builds on the requirements of its predecessor and adds additional criteria that every database table must satisfy. A normal form is considered satisfied when every table in the database meets the criteria laid out for it (and, by extension, its predecessors).

Neglecting normalization rules may result in erroneous self-contradicting data that is difficult to manage. The following screenshot shows a table that violates nearly every consistency principle there is:

| Album | Artist | Artist Country | Label | Genre | Length | Format | Price | Certified Sales | RIAA Certification | RIAA Cert. ID |
|---|---|---|---|---|---|---|---|---|---|---|
| Aquemini | OutKast | USA | LaF | Progressive Rap, Soul, G-funk | 74:47 | CD | 10.99 | 2,000,000 | 2× Platinum | 2 |
| Aquemini | OutKast | America | LaFace | Progressive Rap, Soul, G-funk | 74:47 | CD | 9.99 | 2,000,000 | 3× Platinum | 2 |

Figure 9.1 – An example of data that does not follow any normalization rules

How many data issues could you spot in just two rows?

- No unique identifier makes knowing what a single row represents difficult
- Multiple values stored in the `Genre` column hinder the analysis
- The two rows appear to be duplicated but there is no way to tell without a primary key
- *USA* and *America*—two values describe the same entity
- Duplicate data entry in the `Label` column results in misspelled values
- The `Price` value is different between the two records, but there is no way to know which is correct
- The RIAA Certification value is a function of `Certified Sales`, so *3x Platinum* with *2,000,000* copies sold is impossible
- `RIAA Certification` is at odds with `RIAA Cert. ID`
- Adding a new `Format` value would require duplicating all `Album` values
- If the store in question wants to stop selling the *CD* format, deleting both rows would also remove album information

Normalization helps prevent data anomalies such as the preceding ones through schema design and database rules. As more normalization is applied, the possibility of anomalous information drops while the overall number of tables grows. Data quality safeguards obtained through normalization are offset by the complexity of querying information across multiple tables instead of having it in a single source.

Before we review the progression of normal forms, we need to better understand the data anomalies from which they help protect.

## Data anomalies

Bad data comes in many flavors. From misspellings to improper encoding, some data quality issues can not be avoided. However, denormalized designs make it possible to walk headlong into several well-known and preventable blunders.

To understand how normalization prevents data anomalies, we need to unpack the dual dangers it mitigates: redundancy and dependency:

- **Redundancy**: Repeated data, whether within one or across multiple tables. When data values are duplicated, synchronizing everything through DML operations becomes harder.
- **Dependency**: When the value of one attribute depends on the value of another. Dependencies can be **functional** (such as a person's age attribute depending on their name) or **multivalued** (such as name, age, and hobby stored in a single table would make it impossible to delete a hobby without deleting all the people who practice it).

With these dangers in mind, let's review the kinds of data anomalies that have the potential to creep into a denormalized database design.

### Update anomaly

An **update anomaly** results from a partial update of redundant information. For example, when information is duplicated over multiple records or tables, it becomes possible to update some but not all occurrences, resulting in conflicting or contradictory instances.

In the following example, the birth year, an attribute of the `Pirate` dimension, is included in the `Pirate Prizes` fact table. The birth year detail provides extra context for consumers of the fact table but results in duplicate data and opens the door to an update anomaly, as displayed in *Figure 9.2*:

**Pirate Prizes**

| Pirate Name | Born | Captured |
|---|---|---|
| Francis Drake | 1540 | Cacafuego |
| Francis Drake | 1680 | Nuestra Señora del Rosario |
| Henry Every | 1659 | Charles II |
| Henry Every | 1659 | Ganj-i-Sawai |

Figure 9.2 – Update anomaly

Because the birth year value is repeated instead of stored once as an attribute of the pirate entity, anomalous, contradicting records can occur. However, that is not the only anomaly that can result from placing details from various dimensions in a single table.

## Insertion anomaly

An **insertion anomaly** occurs when it is difficult or impossible to insert new data into the database consistently and accurately. When too many details of varying granularity are bunched into a single table, inserting information that does not simultaneously tick all the boxes becomes difficult.

In the following example, pirates and ships are stored in the same table, and both values are mandated through NOT NULL constraints. Here, *Anne Bonny* presents a challenge since she hung around *Calico Jack* and never captained a ship of her own:

**Pirates and their ships**

| Pirate Id | Name | Born | Ship |
|---|---|---|---|
| 1 | Francis Drake | 1540 | Golden Hind |
| 2 | Blackbeard | 1680 | Queen Anne's Revenge |
| 3 | Calico Jack | 1682 | Kingston |

| 4 | Anne Bonny | 1697 |   | No ship

Figure 9.3 – Insertion anomaly

In this example, the table constraints make it impossible to insert a pirate's information without specifying a ship. This dependency does not just encumber insertions, it affects deletions as well.

## Deletion anomaly

A **deletion anomaly** occurs when deleting data from the database results in the unintended loss of related information. Like an insertion anomaly, a deletion anomaly results from too many dimensions being bunched into one table (such as `Pirate Id` and `Ship`, from the previous example).

*Calico Jack* never could hold on to a ship for very long. The *Kingston* was repossessed (with cargo intact) less than two months after being taken.

However, as we can see in *Figure 9.4*, deleting Kingston from our table also means wiping away all mention of Calico Jack:

Pirates and their ships

| Pirate Id | Name | Born | Ship |
|---|---|---|---|
| 1 | Francis Drake | 1540 | Golden Hind |
| 2 | Blackbeard | 1680 | Queen Anne's Revenge |
| 3 | Calico Jack | 1682 | ~~Kingston~~ |

Figure 9.4 – Deletion anomaly

One thing all these anomalies have in common is that they are self-evident. However, some anomalies only reveal themselves through business knowledge.

## Domain anomaly

A **domain anomaly** occurs when a database fails to incorporate business rules into its design, thereby making it possible to create values that violate them. This anomaly is harder to catch because it requires functional knowledge of the data in question.

The following example shows a list of `Pirate` attributes:

Pirates

| Name | Born | Held Letter of Marque | Designation |
|---|---|---|---|
| Francis Drake | 1540 | Y | Privateer |
| Henry Every | 1659 | N | Pirate |
| Blackbeard | 1680 | N | Privateer |
| Calico Jack | 1682 | N | Pirate |

Figure 9.5 – Domain anomaly

Those unaware of the distinction between pirate and privateer (the latter performs piracy on behalf of a sovereign who authorizes the activity through a *letter of marque*) may miss the discrepancy in Blackbeard's record (he was as *piratey* as pirates come).

Normalization can prevent data anomalies by subdividing tables to reduce dependency and redundancy and encoding business rules into the design. In the following sections, we will follow the application of normal forms to see how this is achieved.

## Database normalization through examples

Normalization was first proposed by Edgar F. Codd, the inventor of the relational model for database management. Codd introduced normalization in 1NF form and later extended it to 2NF and 3NF. Later, Codd, working with Raymond F. Boyce, developed **Boyce-Codd Normal Form** (**BCNF**) also called **3.5NF**.

As database theory continues to develop, subsequent normal forms have been proposed up to 6NF, following the progression from least to most restrictive. While it is important to understand normalization in all its forms, it is also essential to recognize that typical business scenarios do not require going past 3NF.

To understand how normal forms organize a database and prevent data anomalies, we will run through an exercise of taking a wholly denormalized dataset and running it through the normalization rules required to satisfy each form. The exercises that follow use examples of data from the music industry. But, unlike the wide world of music, the examples assume that an album name is unique and that no two artists can have identically named albums.

With this in mind, let's begin cleaning up the messy data from *Figure 9.1* by converting it to 1NF.

### 1NF

1NF is satisfied when the following are in place:

- Every record is unique
- Every cell contains a single value

Ensuring unique records is one of the fundamental requirements of a relational database design. Working with the premise that Album is a unique identifier, we begin by eliminating the duplicate second row and assigning a primary key constraint on the Album column.

Next, we must ensure that every cell contains single (atomic) values. Storing multivalued data within a single cell presents a challenge for data analysis looking for meaningful insights. For example, without atomic values, calculations such as the Genre count or checking for the existence of a specific Genre value require parsing the contents of each cell before they can be analyzed.

In our example, multiple values are present in the Genre column:

| Genre |
|---|
| Progressive Rap, Soul, G-funk |

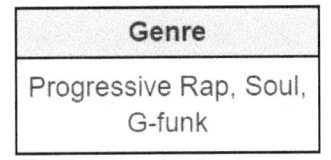

Figure 9.6 – Multivalued data

Pivoting these values into individual rows and creating a separate dimension for Genres satisfies 1NF. The resulting design allows efficient analysis of Genres without violating the Album table's primary key or duplicating its attributes:

Album

| Album | Artist | Artist Country | Label | Length | Format | Price | Certified Sales | RIAA Certification | RIAA Cert. ID |
|---|---|---|---|---|---|---|---|---|---|
| Aquemini | OutKast | America | LaFace | 74:47 | CD | 10.99 | 2,000,000 | 2× Platinum | 4 |

Album Genres

| Album | Genre |
|---|---|
| Aquemini | Progressive Rap |
| Aquemini | Soul |
| Aquemini | G-funk |

Figure 9.7 – A design that satisfies 1NF

Now that we have unique identifiers and no multivalued data, let's move on to the second normal form.

## 2NF

2NF is satisfied when the following are in place:

- 1NF rules are satisfied
- Every non-candidate-key attribute must depend on the whole candidate key (no partial dependencies)

Let's unpack that. A **candidate key** is a unique identifier that can not be further simplified and remain unique. The following example shows an instance of a partial dependency:

Artist Grammys by Year

| Artist | Year | Genre | Nominated | Won |
|---|---|---|---|---|
| Metallica | 2009 | Metal | 4 | 2 |
| Jay Z | 2009 | Rap | 6 | 1 |
| Lady Antebellum | 2009 | Country | 2 | 0 |

Figure 9.8 – An example of a partial dependency

While `Artist`, `Year`, and `Genre` together identify a unique record, only `Artist` and `Year` are required (this is the candidate key). The number of Grammys nominated and won depends entirely on the candidate key (`Artist` and `Year`) and would not make sense if all or part of the key were missing. However, `Genre` depends on `Artist` only (not `Year`)—forming a partial dependency and violating 2NF.

In our original example, the `Album` and `Format` columns form the candidate key in the following table. However, nearly all the attributes besides `Price` (such as `Artist` and `Length`) depend only on `Album`. That is to say, they partially depend on the candidate key and do not satisfy 2NF:

**Album**

| Album | Artist | Artist Country | Label | Length | Format | Price | Certified Sales | RIAA Certification | RIAA Cert. ID |
|---|---|---|---|---|---|---|---|---|---|
| Aquemini | OutKast | America | LaFace | 74:47 | CD | 10.99 | 2,000,000 | 2× Platinum | 4 |
| Aquemini | OutKast | America | LaFace | 74:47 | Vinyl | 24.99 | 2,000,000 | 2× Platinum | 4 |
| Birth of the Cool | Miles Davis | America | Capitol Records | 35:29 | CD | 7.99 | 280,000 | | |

Figure 9.9 – A table with partial dependencies

The present design requires us to duplicate all `Album` attributes for every available `Format`. In 2NF, we can achieve a much cleaner design by decomposing the preceding table into two separate tables with no partial dependencies. Every attribute now depends entirely on the complete candidate key (`Album` and `Album` + `Format`, respectively):

**Album**

| Album | Artist | Artist Country | Label | Length | Certified Sales | RIAA Certification | RIAA Cert. ID |
|---|---|---|---|---|---|---|---|
| Aquemini | OutKast | America | LaFace | 74:47 | 2,000,000 | 2× Platinum | 4 |
| Birth of the Cool | Miles Davis | America | Capitol Records | 35:29 | 280,000 | None | 1 |

**Album Formats**

| Album | Format | Price |
|---|---|---|
| Aquemini | CD | 10.99 |
| Aquemini | Vinyl | 24.99 |
| Birth of the Cool | CD | 7.99 |

Figure 9.10 – A design that satisfies 2NF

Now that every attribute in our tables depends on a candidate key, let's see what's required to satisfy the third normal form.

# 3NF

3NF is satisfied when the following are in place:

- 2NF rules are satisfied
- There are no transitive functional dependencies

What is the transitive world?

A **transitive functional dependency** (**TFD**) is formed when a non-primary key column depends on another non-primary column—for example, `Label Country`, which depends on `Label`. TFDs are a problem because they allow update anomalies, such as those in the following table, to occur:

**Album**

| Album | Artist | Artist Country | Label | Label Country | Length | Certified Sales | RIAA Certification | RIAA Cert. ID |
|---|---|---|---|---|---|---|---|---|
| Aquemini | OutKast | America | LaFace | USA | 74:47 | 2,000,000 | 2× Platinum | 4 |
| Birth of the Cool | Miles Davis | America | Capitol Records | USA | 35:29 | 280,000 | None | 1 |
| Hello Nasty | Beastie Boys | America | Capitol Records | Uzbekistan | 67:28 | 3,000,000 | 3× Platinum | 5 |

Figure 9.11 – An update anomaly due to a transitive dependency

To get around this issue, we must resolve all the TFDs by creating separate dimension tables for each of them, where all the attributes depend entirely on the complete primary key. The resulting schema satisfies 3NF:

**Album**

| Album | Artist | Release Year | Length | Certified Sales | RIAA Certification |
|---|---|---|---|---|---|
| Aquemini | OutKast | 1998 | 74:47 | 2,000,000 | 2× Platinum |
| Birth of the Cool | Miles Davis | 1957 | 35:29 | 280,000 | None |
| Hello Nasty | Beastie Boys | 1998 | 67:28 | 3,000,000 | 3× Platinum |

**Label**

| Label | Label Country |
|---|---|
| LaFace | USA |
| Capitol Records | USA |

**Album Price**

| Album | Format | Price |
|---|---|---|
| Aquemini | CD | 10.99 |
| Aquemini | Vinyl | 24.99 |
| Birth of the Cool | CD | 10.99 |
| Hello Nasty | Digital | 8.99 |

**RIAA Cert. Requirements**

| RIAA Cert. Req. ID | Minimum Sales | Name |
|---|---|---|
| 1 | 0 | None |
| 2 | 500,000 | Gold |
| 3 | 1,000,000 | Platinum |
| 4 | 2,000,000 | 2× Platinum |
| 5 | 3,000,000 | 3× Platinum |

**Artist**

| Artist | Artist Country |
|---|---|
| OutKast | America |
| Miles Davis | America |
| Beastie Boys | America |

Figure 9.12 – A design that satisfies 3NF

> **A mnemonic for remembering the first three normal forms**
>
> In court, sworn testimony is often accompanied by a commitment, to tell the truth, the whole truth, and nothing but the truth. In database design, normalization rules stipulate that records should depend on the key (1NF), the whole key (2NF), and nothing but the key (3NF).

We have removed TFDs from our design, but before moving on to the fourth normal form, let's examine a slightly more restrictive version of 3NF.

## BCNF

BCNF (also referred to as 3.5NF) is satisfied when the following are in place:

- 3NF rules are satisfied
- Every non-trivial functional dependency is itself a key

142   Database Normalization

In 1974, Raymond Boyce and Edgar Codd got together to invent a stricter version of 3NF to address additional potential anomalies. They aimed to reduce redundancy while having the structure reflect the underlying business rules. Before going into detail, it should be said that it is rare to encounter scenarios that satisfy 3NF but not BCNF. To invent such a scenario, let us abandon music for a moment and look at restaurants.

Take the following table of dining reservations from Nuovo Vesuvio, Artie Bucco's upscale Italian eatery:

### Today's Diners

| Table | Time | Reservation Type |
|---|---|---|
| 1 | 6:30 | walk-in |
| 2 | 7:00 | phone |
| 2 | 8:00 | phone |
| 3 | 6:30 | phone |
| 3 | 8:00 | walk-in |
| 4 | 11:30 | Tony Soprano |

Figure 9.13 – A 3NF-compliant table with hidden business logic

Although the table is in 3NF and free from data anomalies today, the design fails to reflect or enforce some important business restrictions. Namely, table 2 is available only to those who have phoned to reserve in advance, table 1 is for *walk-ins* only, and, most importantly, table 4 is exclusively reserved for Artie's childhood chum, *Tony Soprano*.

To satisfy Boyce, Codd, (and Soprano), a `Reservation Types` table must be created to maintain the set of allowable possibilities (including the unlikely event of Tony calling ahead to reserve table 4—never witnessed but allowed). The resulting layout would be as follows:

### Today's Diners

| Table | Time | Res. Type Key |
|---|---|---|
| 1 | 6:30 | A |
| 2 | 7:00 | B |
| 2 | 8:00 | B |
| 3 | 6:30 | C |
| 3 | 8:00 | D |
| 4 | 11:30 | E |
| 1 | 8:00 | A |

### Reservation Types

| Res. Type Key | Table | Called Ahead? | Is Tony Soprano? | Reservation Type Name |
|---|---|---|---|---|
| A | 1 | N | N | walk-in |
| B | 2 | Y | N | phone |
| C | 3 | Y | N | phone |
| D | 3 | N | N | walk-in |
| E | 4 | N | Y | Tony Soprano |
| F | 4 | Y | Y | Tony Soprano |

Figure 9.14 – A design that satisfies BCNF (and Soprano)

Nuovo Vesuvio, understandably, follows stringent rules about reservations that vary from table to table. But what if every table accepted every known reservation method? Could the existing design be improved to reduce redundancy? Ronald Fagin certainly thinks so—it's why he created the fourth normal form.

## 4NF

The **fourth normal form** (**4NF**) is satisfied when the following are in place:

- BCNF rules are satisfied
- Every non-trivial functional and multivalued functional dependency begins with a superkey

Recall that a **superkey** is a combination of columns that uniquely identifies a row (but, unlike a candidate key, it can also include extra columns). A **multivalued dependency** is a relationship between two or more attributes in a database, where the value of one attribute depends on the values of multiple other attributes. To understand this in practice, observe the following table, which shows album inventory by format across three stores:

**Store Album Formats**

| Store | Album | Format | Price |
|---|---|---|---|
| High Fidelity | Aquemini | Vinyl | 26.99 |
| High Fidelity | Birth of the Cool | Vinyl | 26.99 |
| High Fidelity | Hello Nasty | Vinyl | 26.99 |
| Empire Records | Aquemini | CD | 10.99 |
| Empire Records | Birth of the Cool | CD | 10.99 |
| Empire Records | Hello Nasty | CD | 10.99 |
| Empire Records | Aquemini | Vinyl | 24.99 |
| Empire Records | Birth of the Cool | Vinyl | 24.99 |
| Empire Records | Hello Nasty | Vinyl | 24.99 |
| e-music.com | Aquemini | Digital | 8.99 |
| e-music.com | Birth of the Cool | Digital | 8.99 |
| e-music.com | Hello Nasty | Digital | 8.99 |

Figure 9.15 – A table with multivalue dependencies

*High Fidelity* and *e-music.com* only sell one format (*vinyl* and *digital*, respectively), while *Empire Records* sells all albums on *CD* and *vinyl*. Storing everything in a single table means that `Album` depends on `Format` and `Store`, which are not superkeys. Separating the information into two tables removes the multivalued dependency and satisfies 4NF:

## Store Albums

| Store | Album |
|---|---|
| High Fidelity | Aquemini |
| High Fidelity | Birth of the Cool |
| High Fidelity | Hello Nasty |
| Empire Records | Aquemini |
| Empire Records | Birth of the Cool |
| Empire Records | Hello Nasty |
| e-music.com | Aquemini |
| e-music.com | Birth of the Cool |
| e-music.com | Hello Nasty |

## Store Formats

| Store | Format | Price |
|---|---|---|
| High Fidelity | Vinyl | 26.99 |
| Empire Records | Vinyl | 24.99 |
| Empire Records | CD | 10.99 |
| e-music.com | Digital | 8.99 |

Figure 9.16 – A design that satisfies 4NF

However, this is only true if the rules in the `Store Formats` table hold. If any store could sell any format, the table in *Figure 9.14*, which satisfies BCNF (and Soprano), would also satisfy 4NF. As business knowledge is required to determine 4NF, no systematic heuristics can guarantee it. The same holds true for the fifth normal form, as we will now discover.

## 5NF

The **fifth normal form** (**5NF**) is satisfied when the following is in place:

- 4NF rules are satisfied
- Tables can not be decomposed further without loss of data

After removing the functional and multivalued dependencies, the only way to reduce further is by analyzing the data as a function of existing business rules. Let us look at the following table, which shows albums in their available formats:

## Album Formats

| Album | Format |
|---|---|
| Aquemini | CD |
| Aquemini | Vinyl |
| Aquemini | Digital |
| Birth of the Cool | Digital |
| Hello Nasty | CD |
| Hello Nasty | Digital |

Figure 9.17 – Table of albums and available formats

Decomposing the table further will yield tables (seen in the subsequent diagram) that can not be joined to recreate the data in *Figure 9.17*:

**Albums**

| Album |
| --- |
| Aquemini |
| Birth of the Cool |
| Hello Nasty |

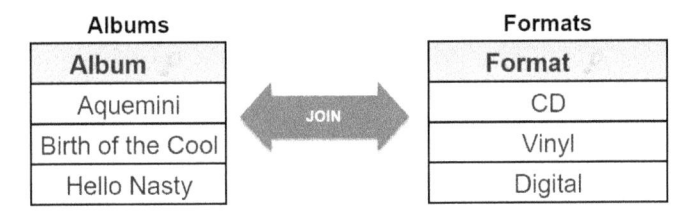

JOIN

**Formats**

| Format |
| --- |
| CD |
| Vinyl |
| Digital |

Figure 9.18 – A join between unique albums and unique formats

Attempting to join the smaller tables produces a Cartesian product with every combination of possible values, thereby losing the original detail.

Cartesian Product

| Album | Format |
| --- | --- |
| Aquemini | CD |
| Aquemini | CD |
| Aquemini | CD |
| Birth of the Cool | Vinyl |
| Birth of the Cool | Vinyl |
| Birth of the Cool | Vinyl |
| Hello Nasty | Digital |
| Hello Nasty | Digital |
| Hello Nasty | Digital |

!=

Orginal Table

| Album | Format |
| --- | --- |
| Aquemini | CD |
| Aquemini | Vinyl |
| Aquemini | Digital |
| Birth of the Cool | Digital |
| Hello Nasty | CD |
| Hello Nasty | Digital |

Figure 9.19 – A Cartesian product between decomposed tables results in data loss

5NF is not commonly used in practice, as it is difficult to achieve and unnecessary for most databases. Rarely do tables that satisfy 5NF not satisfy 4NF (and, by extension, BCNF).

However, even 5NF fails to guard against domain anomalies, which are common enough to consider avoiding.

## DKNF

The **domain-key normal form (DKNF)** is satisfied when the following are in place:

- 5NF rules are satisfied
- Domain constraints do not exist in any table

Various examples throughout this chapter have included an album's `RIAA Certification` and `Certified Sales`. In the music industry, RIAA certifications are assigned based on the number of albums sold: 500k units for *Gold*, then 1M increments for *Platinum*, *2x Platinum*, until reaching *Diamond* at 1B copies. This dynamic can be seen in the following table:

Album

| Album | Artist | Release Year | Length | Certified Sales | RIAA Certification |
|---|---|---|---|---|---|
| Aquemini | OutKast | 1998 | 74:47 | 2,000,000 | 2× Platinum |
| Birth of the Cool | Miles Davis | 1957 | 35:29 | 280,000 | None |
| Hello Nasty | Beastie Boys | 1998 | 67:28 | 3,000,000 | 3× Platinum |

Figure 9.20 – A design that satisfies 5NF but not DKNF

`Certified Sales` and `RIAA Certification` are both attributes that depend on the Album's primary key, but there is an implicit domain constraint between them as record sales dictate the RIAA status.

As we can see in the following table, it is subject to domain anomalies that may result in nonsensical data, which nevertheless conforms to 5NF:

Albums

| Album | Artist | Release Year | Length | Certified Sales | RIAA Certification |
|---|---|---|---|---|---|
| Aquemini | OutKast | 1998 | 74:47 | 2,000,000 | 2× Platinum |
| Birth of the Cool | Miles Davis | 1957 | 35:29 | 280,000 | 100× Platinum |
| Hello Nasty | Beastie Boys | 1998 | 67:28 | 3,878,000 | 3× Platinum |

Figure 9.21 – A domain anomaly occurs despite 5NF

To avoid the possibility of a domain anomaly, `RIAA Certification` must be separated into another table, with clearly defined bounds for each certification. This way, the correct certification can be derived logically from the album's `Certified Sales` column:

Albums

| Album | Artist | Release Year | Length | Certified Sales |
|---|---|---|---|---|
| Aquemini | OutKast | 1998 | 74:47 | 2,000,000 |
| Birth of the Cool | Miles Davis | 1957 | 35:29 | 280,000 |
| Hello Nasty | Beastie Boys | 1998 | 67:28 | 3,878,000 |

RIAA Cert. Requirements

| RIAA Cert. Req. ID | Minimum Sales | Maximum Sales | Name |
|---|---|---|---|
| 1 | 0 | 499,999 | None |
| 2 | 500,000 | 999,999 | Gold |
| 3 | 1,000,000 | 1,999,999 | Platinum |
| 4 | 2,000,000 | 2,999,999 | 2× Platinum |
| 5 | 3,000,000 | 3,999,999 | 3× Platinum |
| ... | ... | ... | ... |
| 12 | 10,000,000 | 9,999,999,999 | Diamond |

Figure 9.22 – A design that satisfies DKNF

Now it's time to get extreme. The final form we will cover is still under debate in the modeling community and is only practicable in rare cases. However, it is not without merit.

## 6NF

6NF is satisfied when the following are in place:

- 5NF rules are satisfied
- Every table contains a primary key and, at most, one attribute

6NF takes reducing dependencies to an extreme by making them a physical impossibility. In 6NF, tables are allowed no more than one attribute per table. The following example shows a table in 5NF consisting of a primary key and four attributes. Notice that the last record has no value for `Price`:

Albums

| Album | Artist | Release Year | Length | Price |
|---|---|---|---|---|
| Aquemini | OutKast | 1998 | 74:47 | 10.99 |
| Birth of the Cool | Miles Davis | 1957 | 35:29 | 24.99 |
| Hello Nasty | Beastie Boys | 1998 | 67:28 | |

Figure 9.23 – A design that satisfies 5NF but not 6NF

To satisfy 6NF, this table must be split into five smaller tables. Notice how the resulting tables conform to the original primary key column (`Album`), but the `Album Price` table has fewer records due to *Hello Nasty* missing that attribute:

**Albums**

| Album |
|---|
| Aquemini |
| Birth of the Cool |
| Hello Nasty |

**Album Artist**

| Album | Artist |
|---|---|
| Aquemini | OutKast |
| Birth of the Cool | Miles Davis |
| Hello Nasty | Beastie Boys |

**Album Release Year**

| Album | Release Year |
|---|---|
| Aquemini | 1998 |
| Birth of the Cool | 1957 |
| Hello Nasty | 1998 |

**Album Length**

| Album | Length |
|---|---|
| Aquemini | 74:47 |
| Birth of the Cool | 35:29 |
| Hello Nasty | 67:28 |

**Album Price**

| Album | Price |
|---|---|
| Aquemini | 10.99 |
| Birth of the Cool | 24.99 |

Figure 9.24 – A design that satisfies DKNF

The proliferation of tables under 6NF (and the effort required to query and maintain them) makes it impractical for most business purposes. 6NF has gained some notoriety through ensemble modeling frameworks such as Anchor Modeling, which falls outside the scope of this book. However, it is worth mentioning the database features that Anchor Modeling depends on, both of which are supported in Snowflake (and covered in more detail in later chapters).

With the many tables that 6NF requires, joins become exceedingly difficult to write. However, query performance can be significantly increased in 6NF through features such as join elimination compared to larger denormalized tables. With join elimination, the database optimizer can intelligently avoid performing certain joins if attributes from the related tables are not explicitly requested in the query. (More on join elimination in *Chapter 12, Putting Transformational Modeling into Practice*.)

Multi-table insert is another Snowflake feature with broad applications in many modeling scenarios, particularly in Data Vault (covered in *Chapter 17, Scaling Data Models through Modern Technique*) and Anchor Modeling. In *Figure 9.24*, we created five tables that share the same primary key. Snowflake's multi-table insert feature would allow us to load all five in a single load operation and even include conditional logic dictating which tables should be updated and when.

Let us summarize what we have learned after seeing the gradual tightening of database rules from 1NF to 6NF.

# Data models on a spectrum of normalization

The prior sections demonstrate how, as we move up the normal form scale, redundancy and the potential for data anomalies decrease while raising the number of tables and associated complexity. With this in mind, we can visualize where various data modeling patterns fall on the normal form spectrum to help understand their suitability in design scenarios. While the dimensional modeling process was discussed in *Chapter 7, Putting Conceptual Modeling into Practice*, the associated schema patterns (star and snowflake) are explained in further detail in *Chapter 17, Scaling Data Models through Modern Techniques*, along with Data Vault (where they are often implemented at the information mart layer). However, visualizing them in the context of normal forms will help lay the groundwork for later understanding their design. Also, bear in mind that the following assertions speak to general tendencies, not hard-set rules.

The following image displays the various modeling patterns and methodologies mentioned throughout this book on the normalization spectrum:

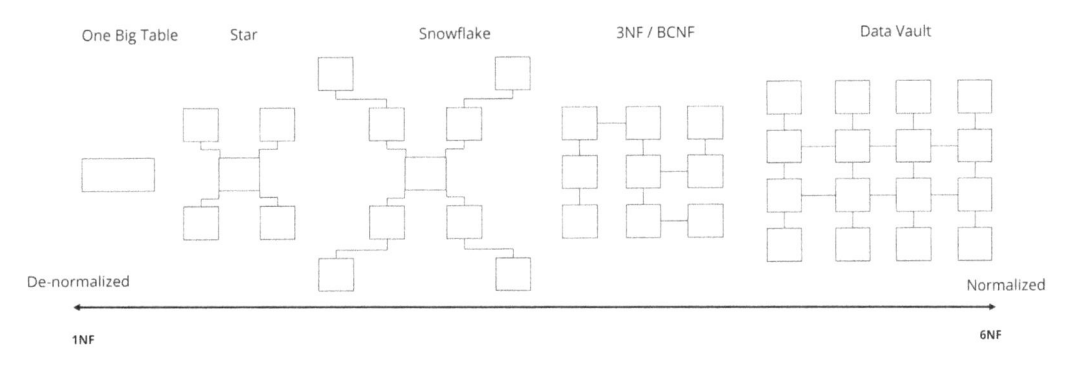

Figure 9.25 – Common data models arranged on the normalization spectrum

Arguably, 1NF (*the key*) is the minimum requirement for working with relational data. For its ease of understanding, 1NF is often seen in the **One Big Table (OBT)** approach, where facts and dimension attributes are all stored in a single table. While they are difficult to maintain, OBTs are dead-simple to query (i.e., no joins required). Business users are comfortable with OBTs, provided they don't get too big (by size or number of columns) to where usability begins to degrade.

Star and snowflake schemas are patterns often seen when following Kimball's dimensional approach and are good candidates for the data platform's analytical self-service or reporting layers. In both models, the central fact table is typically normalized to 3NF. In the star schema, dimension tables are connected directly to the fact table and denormalized to 2NF—a good trade-off between maintenance and ease of use. In the snowflake schema approach, dimension tables are generally normalized to 3NF, forming a hierarchy and trading on analytical complexity in exchange for easier maintenance with less redundancy.

At the far end of the normalization spectrum are Data Vault models. While Data Vault does not satisfy 6NF in the strict sense, it does incorporate many of its principles in its design.

Now that we have seen how various modeling patterns line up on the normalization spectrum let's review what we have learned.

## Summary

Through various examples in this chapter, we saw how the process of normalization organizes a database in a way that reduces redundancy and dependency within its tables.

Dependency and redundancy in database tables increase the likelihood of data anomalies, which come in many forms. Update anomalies occur due to redundancy, which makes it possible to update some, but not all, of the associated records. Physical (as opposed to logical) dependencies are the root cause of insertion and deletion anomalies. When too many details of varying granularity are bunched into a single table, inserting or deleting records that do not match all the criteria becomes difficult. The domain anomaly is the hardest to spot because it requires functional knowledge of the data in question.

Database normalization can be applied through escalating stages of formal rules called normal forms, ranging from 1NF to 6NF to avoid such anomalies. The most commonly used normal forms are the first through third, which are sufficient for most databases. The mnemonic, *the key, the whole key, and nothing but the key* aids in recalling the considerations for each of the first three forms.

Through practical examples that took data from a completely denormalized format and transformed it through each normal form, a common theme emerged—with each normal form, the possibility for data anomalies decreased while the number of tables grew, encumbering maintenance and analysis.

The examples in this chapter demonstrate that more normalization does not imply a better design—it simply imposes stricter rules on the database. Having seen the specific data issues that each of the normal forms addresses, applying their principles broadly or selectively will help modelers achieve an optimal design with the right balance of rigor and usability.

In the next chapter, rigor and usability will take center stage as we review database naming conventions and organization. Coupled with the insights from this chapter, we will then be ready to tackle the physical model.

# 10
# Database Naming and Structure

In previous chapters, we took a database design through the necessary steps to transform it into a logical model. While a logical model is database-independent, it is close enough to a physical design that it can easily be adapted and deployed to any database. However, before tackling the Snowflake-specific properties of the data model—which will be covered in the following chapter—we should get acquainted with naming conventions and database organization best practices that govern all database designs.

Naming conventions are the guiding principles with which database objects are constructed. Consistent naming standards reduce uncertainty for developers and help business users orient themselves within a database and find the required data assets. Beyond object naming, this chapter will also cover the structure of the database itself, organizing it into logical groupings by schema, which improves usability. Finally, we will look at database environments and replication to ensure reporting data is isolated from volatile development changes.

A theme that quickly emerges in every section of this chapter is the focus on consistency. Rather than advocating for the *right* way to name or structure a database, it's important to be flexible and adjust standards to organizational and project needs—then stick to those decisions. The main topics that will be covered in this chapter are as follows:

- Choosing a case standard that works best with Snowflake and maximizes cache reusability
- Object naming for tables and relationships for enhanced usability
- Styling and usage considerations to consider at design time
- Organizing a database through standard and managed schemas
- Structuring a database for OLAP and OLTP use cases
- Separating database environments for reporting, testing, and development

## Naming conventions

Before creating the physical model, naming conventions that govern its design need to be established. Following consistent naming conventions improves understanding, reduces errors, facilitates collaboration, and generally makes it easier to work with your database. While there are many (often conflicting) theories and standards on the right convention to follow, the most important thing is to choose one that is easy to understand and to use it consistently throughout your database.

However, there are some general best practices to keep in mind when naming objects in Snowflake. After all, object names are like the API to your data model and should be regarded as a contract between the modeler and the data consumers. Once an object is created, downstream systems, users, and processes will reference it by name, forming dependencies and increasing the cost of future changes.

This section will cover some of the most crucial considerations in database naming. Instead of presenting naming conventions by object type, this section will be organized by importance, starting with those rules that are strongly advised to those merely suggested. Whatever you decide, choose a standard that best aligns with your organization and stick to it.

With that, let's look at the critical considerations.

### Case

Internally, Snowflake stores all objects in uppercase unless enclosed in double quotes. For SQL queries, Snowflake's parser treats anything not enclosed in double quotes as uppercase to match storage. In practice, this means all of the following object names are compiled identically:

- `my_table`
- `MY_TABLE`
- `mY_TabLE`
- `"MY_TABLE"`

Object names in double quotes are case-sensitive and may include spaces. Therefore, any query that references an object in double quotes must precisely match the name (i.e., `"mY TabLE"` != `MY_TABLE`) to return the expected result. To avoid having to enclose every object and column in double quotes, it is advised to avoid them and use snake case instead. In snake case, spaces are replaced with underscores (_), and every word, including the first letter, is written in lowercase (e.g., `my_table`).

While object names may be case-insensitive, the results cache is not. Observe the following example where the same query is executed consecutively using various casing formats:

```
--upper
SELECT O_ORDERKEY, O_TOTALPRICE FROM ORDERS;
--snake
select o_orderkey, o_totalprice from orders;
--mixed
SELECT o_orderkey, o_totalprice FROM orders;
```

While all three queries will return the same result, none will leverage the results cache (and will consume credits) because of the difference in case. Whatever convention you settle on, ensure that the entire team is aligned on the chosen standard and stays consistent in object naming and keyword capitalization.

With case standards in place, let's look at object naming.

## Object naming

This section will focus on the naming conventions for the objects used most frequently in modeling and data analysis. Because users of the database and downstream tools will reference these objects for reporting and analytics, a consistent naming convention will save time for everyone by ensuring that required data assets are discoverable and self-explanatory.

### Tables

Plural or singular for table naming? The database community can't agree. Proponents of plural (i.e., `customers` instead of `customer`) argue that a table is a collection of many singular customer records and should therefore be named in the plural. The singular camp counters that pluralization often introduces unnecessary confusion. How to pluralize the person entity, for example, *persons* or *people*?

E.F. Codd's relational model—the basis for relational databases—is consistent with first-order predicate logic. Tuples become rows, and relations become tables, all referred to in the singular. Another advantage of singular names is that they transfer cleanly from conceptual modeling, where business entities tend to be thought of in the singular form (e.g., `customer`, `product`, `country`).

At least that is the academic opinion. To see what the data community does in practice, I conducted a LinkedIn poll to take the pulse of table naming standards in 2023 (`https://www.linkedin.com/posts/serge-cloud-connected_table-naming-for-databases-just-taking-the-activity-7021854119141257216-mm_2/`):

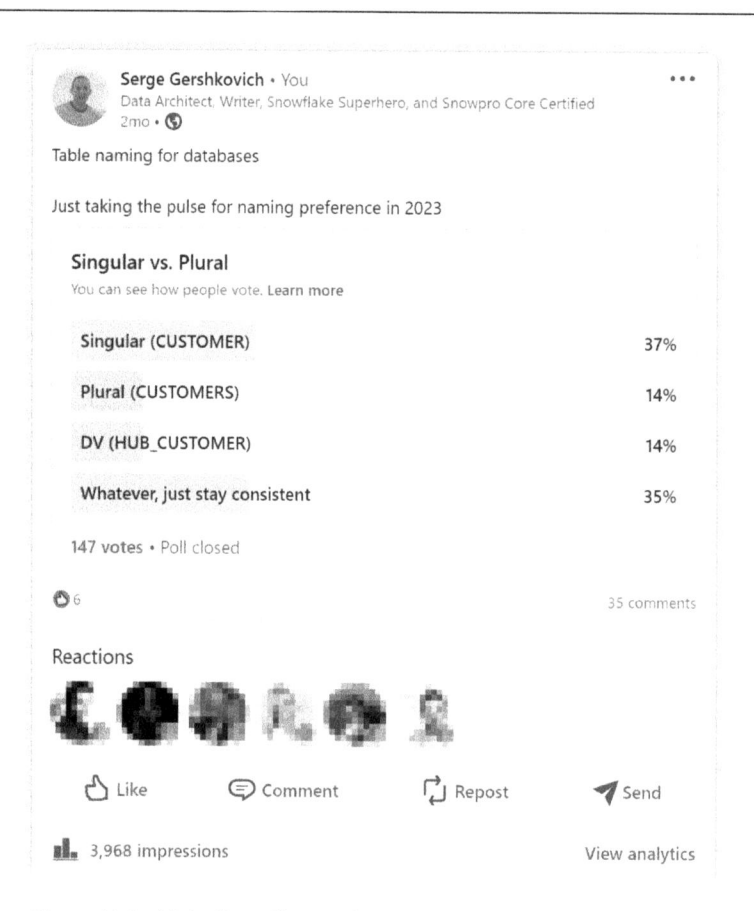

Figure 10.1 – LinkedIn poll - singular or plural for database table names

If you are still undecided, go with singular for table names—but more importantly, be consistent.

With table names covered, how about their identifiers?

## Primary key columns

Unlike tables, there is not much debate on naming their unique identifiers. Primary key columns should be named in singular format, following the table's name, as in `<singularTableName>_id`. Whether your table name is singular or plural (i.e., `person` or `people`), the unique identifier should be named `person_id`.

A generically named `ID` column for all tables is discouraged because it leads to confusion and ambiguity in downstream transformations. But what about additional unique identifiers such as surrogate and business keys?

As long as `primary_id` is present, include additional unique columns following a convention consistent throughout the database, which may include alternate ID suffixes such as `_skey` or `_BKEY`.

## Foreign key constraints

Because relationship names are not supported in physical models, a descriptive and consistent naming for foreign keys becomes the best alternative. Take an example that features relationship names between entities:

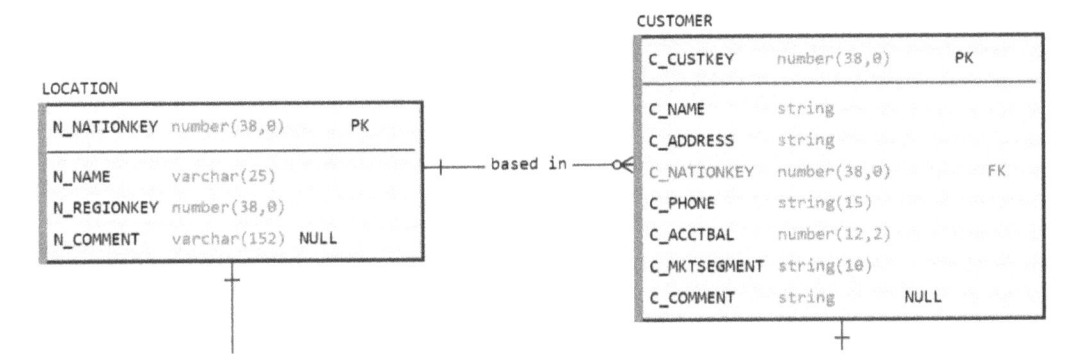

Figure 10.2 – A logical model with relationship names and data types

The example describes a many-to-many relationship where a CUSTOMER is *based in* a LOCATION. Although a physical model does not allow descriptions for foreign key constraints, naming conventions can be used to retain this information. Using a naming pattern of FK_<Child_Table>_<Relationship_Name>_<Parent_Table> (and PK_<Table_Name> for primary keys) results in a physical model that preserves the relationship details:

```
CREATE TABLE CUSTOMER
(
    CUSTOMER_ID number (38,0) NOT NULL,
    NAME varchar NOT NULL,
    ADDRESS varchar NOT NULL,
    LOCATION_ID number (38,0) NOT NULL,
    PHONE varchar NOT NULL,
    ACCOUNT_BALANCE number (12,2) NOT NULL,
    MARKET_SEGMENT varchar NOT NULL,
    COMMENT varchar,

    CONSTRAINT PK_CUSTOMER PRIMARY KEY ( CUSTOMER_ID ),
    CONSTRAINT FK_CUSTOMER_BASED_IN_LOCATION FOREIGN KEY ( LOCATION_ID
) REFERENCES LOCATION ( LOCATION_ID )
)
COMMENT = 'Registered customers';
```

While these are the most important considerations from a modeling perspective, there are a few more that should be considered.

## Suggested conventions

Effective and consistent naming for tables and relationships is of utmost importance when designing a physical model. The following suggestions should also be considered for clarity and adaptability in column and object names:

- Ensure consistent column names through conformed dimensions. **Conformed dimensions** are columns whose domain contents and naming do not change when used across multiple tables. As data moves across the data warehouse layers, ensure that column names are descriptive enough in the base layer that they do not need to be renamed for clarity or conflict in downstream tables (i.e., that the `ID` column does not become `CUSTOMER_ID` then `MAIN_CLIENT_CODE` as it moves from source to reporting layers).

- Avoid abbreviations in table and column names. Even if you think you will remember what the abbreviation stands for (you will not), the other users in the system will have a harder time interpreting it. Does `CUST_REF` imply *customer reference*, *custodial refund*, or *custom refrigeration*?

- Except for the unique identifier, avoid prefixing columns with the table name or initial (e.g., `C_NAME` in `CUSTOMER` table). This naming style guarantees having to rename the columns upstream and makes lineage tracking difficult. The benefit of this naming convention (unambiguous reference when writing queries) can be achieved by using table aliases (`C.NAME`) or qualifying with the complete table name (`CUSTOMER.NAME`).

- Avoid naming data sources using their object types (e.g., views as `<entity>_V` or materialized views as `<entity>_MV`). Depending on cost and performance considerations, the object type of data sources may change over time and referring to a static `<entity>` will prevent errors in the objects that reference it. Instead, use suffixes to identify special-use tables such as historical (`_hist`), control (`_ctrl`), and staging (`_stg`).

The naming suggestions discussed previously are:

- **Case**: Use unquoted snake case (lowercase with an underscore word separator)
- **Table names**: Singular
- **Primary key (columns)**: `<singular_table_name>_id`
- **Primary key (constraint)**: `pk_<table_name>`
- **Foreign key (constraint)**: `fk_<child_table>_<relationship_name>_<parent_table>`
- **Column names**: Be descriptive, stay consistent across tables, and avoid abbreviations
- **Object suffixes**: Avoid adding suffixes such as _v and _mv to denote object type

Most importantly, remember that these are general guidelines and that you should adapt them to existing company standards and use cases, which may vary from one project or database to another. In short, you can be flexible between databases if you are consistent within databases.

Now, let's cover the structure and logical organization within a database.

## Organizing a Snowflake database

The data objects stored by Snowflake—optimized and compressed in an internal columnar format—are not directly visible nor accessible by customers; they are only accessible through SQL query operations. The customer only manages the logical grouping of database objects into schemas and databases. As described in *Chapter 3, Mastering Snowflake's Architecture*, in Snowflake cloud architecture, data is shared virtually without needing to be physically replicated. Therefore, unlike traditional database platforms, the database structure in Snowflake is less concerned with the colocation of physical data and more with the logical grouping of objects—allowing for simple discovery and fine-tuning of access controls.

What does this look like in practice?

### Organization of databases and schemas

All Snowflake objects are assigned to a schema upon creation and form a logical hierarchy from object to schema to database. This tiered grouping affords several benefits when organizing a database, including organization, access management, and replication.

The apparent advantage of database/schema tiering is organization. Two-layer classification allows Snowflake users to group objects meaningfully and granularly according to project needs. This logical grouping makes it easy for users to find the tables they are looking for or separate the working layers of a warehouse (as described later in the chapter).

Data sharing and replication also benefit from having a well-organized database with schema grouping. The ability to clone objects individually or at schema and database level allows users to efficiently replicate datasets for testing and debugging. Sharing data beyond the account is possible, but only at the database level.

Another advantage of grouping objects into schemas and databases is its fine-grain access control. Assigning grants and ownership at the object, schema, or database levels affords Snowflake users great flexibility in managing and fine-tuning access controls to secure data access.

Managing access control within a schema can be handled in one of two ways.

### *Managed schemas*

In addition to traditional role-based access control, Snowflake provides an additional method for managing object access known as **managed schemas**, which delegate privilege management to the schema owner.

In regular schemas, the owner of an object (i.e., the role with the `OWNERSHIP` privilege on the object) can grant further privileges to other roles. In managed schemas, the schema owner manages all privilege grants on objects in the schema.

To create a managed schema, add the `WITH MANAGED ACCESS` parameter to the `CREATE SCHEMA` command like so:

```
create schema my_schema with managed access;
```

In managed schemas, developers can make changes and create new objects; however, only the schema owner can grant privileges to them. This approach is ideal for security-conscious organizations because it allows developers to work unhampered within a schema while delegating access management to a supervisory role.

## OLTP versus OLAP database structures

Suggestions for structuring a database will depend heavily on the application or use case that the database is designed for. **Online transaction processing** (OLTP) or transactional systems typically rely on centralized structures, while **online analytical processing** (OLAP) or data warehouses segment their architecture into layers.

As Snowflake has just begun a concerted push into the OLTP space in 2022 with Hybrid Unistore tables, such use cases have had limited applications. However, the unifying theme in such systems is that the database assets are centralized in a single main schema due to their relational dependencies. Because transactions affect multiple related tables, the logical grouping would not benefit usability and would only hamper usage.

However, in OLAP use cases—which make up the majority of Snowflake implementations—properly structuring the database will have a noticeable impact on usability. While there is no one-size-fits-all suggestion, the following schema divisions should be considered, starting with the landing area where data enters the warehouse.

### Source layer

All data warehouses should contain a source or raw layer where data is loaded in its original, unaltered state from source systems. Any renaming or transformation should be done downstream in subsequent warehouse layers to prevent having to reload in case of an adjustment in logic or business requirement.

Depending on the amount of data sources the warehouse contains and the number of tables in each, it may even make sense to dedicate an entire database to source data and separate source systems by schema. When source systems are separated by schema, tables can retain their original names. However, when tables from various sources share the same schema, adding a source system prefix to the table name is recommended to identify and separate the sources like so:

- `salesforce_account`
- `oracle_account`

Although column names and their contents should not be modified at this stage, standardized metadata fields may be added as long as this is done consistently for all tables in the schema. Such fields may include the following:

- **Load identifier**: This unique load identifier can be used to remove data from a particular load if data corruption or other data quality issues are discovered. A common technique is using the source system's extract date/time to generate a unique value.
- **Load date/time**: This is a timestamp that indicates when the data was loaded into the data warehouse. If loading or data quality issues occur, this field may differ from the extract date/time of the source system.
- **Source filename**: Because data in Snowflake must be loaded from external file storage, recording the filename will help facilitate traceability and debugging.
- **Loaded by**: When using various integration tools, recording the tool responsible for a given load will help point users to the location of logs, or the interface to retry failed loads is helpful.
- **Load type**: If the loading pattern or method varies, it may help identify the load types, such as daily, scheduled, or ad hoc.

A consistent naming pattern should be used to help distinguish data warehouse metadata fields from source fields (which may include similar metadata fields of their own). Common use cases include prefixing columns with a keyword or underscore as follows:

- `etl_load_id`
- `__load_id`

As a rule, access to the source schema should be limited to the central data or engineering team. Because the data has not yet been cleansed or conformed, business users will struggle to obtain meaningful results. However, if the data science team has sufficient business knowledge, they may benefit from direct access to the data in the source schema and glean meaningful insights without depending on the involvement of the warehouse team.

Once data is landed in the source layer, it's time to clean it up for downstream consumption, and having a designated schema where this takes place is ideal.

### *Staging layer*

The staging or working schema is intended as temporary storage for transformed source data as it makes its way downstream through the data warehouse. The tables in this schema are used for data loading and transformations and should be off-limits to users and reporting tools.

The advantages of grouping temporary tables in their own schema are as follows:

- It cleanly segregates provisional data from trusted data
- It avoids having to prefix tables to make the distinction (i.e., `stg_table_name`)
- It allows schema-level default settings for like data retention and transient table types

Once the data has been cleaned up, conformed, and enhanced through the application of business rules and formulas, it can be shared with the rest of the organization through the approaches described in the following sections.

## *Normalized self-service analytics*

A trusted and governed mid-level schema with clean normalized data can be a powerful tool for self-service and analytics. In organizations with high data literacy among analysts and business users (i.e., users capable of joining tables without help from the **business intelligence** (**BI**) team or ChatGPT), a schema that contains normalized (typically to **third normal form** (**3NF**)) and conformed dimensions (attributes from multiple source systems unified in individual dimension tables), can accelerate self-service reporting and analysis by removing the bottleneck from the warehousing team.

There is no standard for naming this schema, but common variants include `core`, `self_service`, and `analytics`. Because the data assets in this schema are meant to be analyzed and combined ad-hoc by everyone in the organization, due diligence must be applied to naming, documentation, auditing, stewardship, and governance. Therefore, participation from domain experts and data governance teams is encouraged.

The alternative (or add-on) to a lightly curated self-service schema is a strictly governed and denormalized reporting schema built for plug-and-play consumption.

## *Denormalized reporting analytics*

Even in organizations with high degrees of data literacy among analysts and business users, some analyses are too complex or too important to be done individually and must be centralized in a governed reporting schema.

Data sources in this schema—typically named reporting or analytics—are owned and maintained by the data team, who takes responsibility for their accuracy and reliability. Tables in the reporting schema tend to be denormalized (usually to **second normal form** (**2NF**)) because the emphasis is placed on having curated metrics and attributes in a single table to facilitate reporting.

Although the data warehouse team is responsible for building the reporting schema and keeping its contents up-to-date, the governance team typically plays a vital role in establishing and enforcing business rules and ensuring that naming and concepts are used consistently throughout the organization (i.e., if a *customer* is defined as someone having made a purchase in the last 12 months, then the definition is applied consistently to every table that includes a customer reference).

This completes the overview of the common schemas maintained by the warehouse and engineering teams. However, in larger organizations, business departments may have their own analytics teams and manage their own data sources.

## *Departmental data*

By lowering the technical and operational barrier to entry to using a data platform, Snowflake has opened the door for business teams to take advantage of robust analytical capabilities without having to depend on the (typically) overburdened warehouse team.

At a minimum, a department should have its own database to load and manage the data sources that its team depends on. While some handholding by the data team may be required initially to get started, a well-trained business department will quickly become self-sufficient.

Once this happens, sharing and incorporating trusted data assets from a departmental database into the self-service or reporting schemas mentioned previously will become feasible. Because the data already exists within the same Snowflake account, it can be shared instantly with the rest of the company without duplication or the integration tools required to do so.

Departmental databases can be thought of as miniature data warehouses unto themselves. Therefore, they will often include schemas separating source, stage, and reporting layers and separate schemas for sandbox, development, and testing.

However, unlike a departmental database, a data warehouse should be replicated and maintained across multiple environments to separate trusted data from that being developed.

## Database environments

Now that we have covered the layers within the database of a data warehouse, we should address the separation of its development environments. Once more, this is not meant to be a comprehensive guide on database environment segregation, merely a best-practice outline that the users should follow and possibly augment with specialized automation tools.

Separate database environments ensure that developers can make changes and test new projects without any risk of impacting existing data sources that the organization relies on. There should be at least three environments: **development** (**dev**), testing, and **production** (**prod**)—some organizations separate testing into various stages such as **quality assurance** (**QA**) and **user acceptance testing** (**UAT**). The purpose of each is summarized here:

- Prod: Governed, secured, and (near) up-to-date data used to drive company reports and analytics
- Test: A close copy of production where changes are validated before being applied to production
- Dev: A sandbox environment where developers are free to make changes and experiment

All environments should aim to be synchronized as closely as possible but vary in the degree to which productive standards are applied to them—from most restrictive in prod to least restrictive in dev.

The following are some of the criteria that should be observed and applied according to company needs and data volumes:

- **Access control**: This is listed above all other considerations for good reason. The critical concern in managing product data and ensuring trust and correctness is controlling who has access to consume (users and reporting tools) and make changes (ideally, no one). In a prod setting, human users should not be allowed to make changes or perform **data manipulation language** (**DML**) operations by hand. All such activities should be orchestrated by tools that handle deployment and execution. This ensures that processes are automated and auditable and require little or no human intervention.
- **Data freshness**: The prod environment should have the most up-to-date information required for operational decision-making. A prod snapshot from a given date may be sufficient in a test environment. Dev may benefit from a reduced sample size (for performance) and dummy data (for security).
- **Data volume and exactness**: For maximum precision in dev and testing environments, the underlying data should match that of prod. However, this would require additional maintenance and may hamper performance for simple changes that do not require a complete dataset. The ideal balance should be struck depending on data size and the type of testing that takes place in each environment.
- **Warehouse size**: Although the warehouse is independent of the database contents, testing and development should be done under similar conditions as those used in the prod environment. For example, even if development and testing are successfully performed with a medium warehouse, performance may prove unacceptable to prod business users who are limited to an extra-small warehouse.

The following diagram illustrates these principles on a spectrum across the database environments:

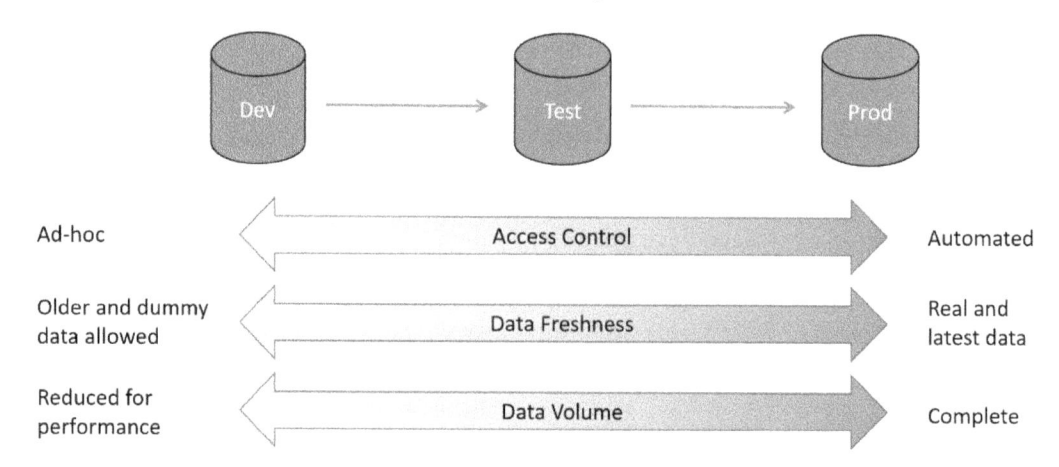

Figure 10.3 – Database environments governing principles

With this in mind, let's review what we have covered in this chapter.

## Summary

In this chapter, we saw how naming standards and an organized structure make the database easier to use and facilitate maintenance. But every organization is different and must choose the standard that best suits their needs and aligns with existing conventions.

Internally, Snowflake stores object names as uppercase, and its query compiler converts all unquoted names accordingly. It is recommended to use snake case for naming and stick to an established pattern to maximize the results cache utilization and to avoid enclosing every column and table name in double quotes.

For a clean transition between logical and physical models, singular table names are encouraged. The same applies to columns, which should be named consistently across the entire database. Using descriptive naming patterns for foreign keys allows users to preserve logical relationship names within the physical model.

After object naming, the attention turns to database organization through logical schema groupings. Snowflake allows for a two-tier hierarchy (database and schema) to maintain data access and replication across databases.

Following the warehouse data flow, the first step is the source or raw schema, where tables from source systems are replicated by the engineering team exactly as they appear. Following the source schema, preliminary table cleanup and renaming are performed in the staging schema—which is kept off-limits to users and reporting sources.

Once data has been renamed and formatted, it makes its way to the analytical schemas, where it is consumed by users and reporting tools. A normalized self-service schema is encouraged for organizations with knowledgeable and tech-savvy business users, as it lets business users derive analytical insights without depending on the data team. A denormalized reporting schema is used for governed reporting sources and more complex analyses. For larger enterprises, business teams may also have their own Snowflake databases, which function like miniature warehouses and can be integrated with the previously-mentioned reporting schemas.

Lastly, different database environments should be used to ensure data quality and separate works in progress from officially validated and governed data. From the least restrictive dev to the production-like test to the securely regulated prod, database environments should follow a spectrum of increasing access control and data quality.

To summarize even further, database administration comes down to two main factors:

- Keep it simple
- Keep it consistent

After covering the essentials of database governance and structure, the next chapter will take our data model from the logical phase to a physical Snowflake architecture.

# 11
# Putting Physical Modeling into Practice

The modern data warehouse is a fast-paced environment. Multi-source and near-real-time data in Snowflake streams and transforms at the speed that scalable virtual hardware will allow. With potentially limitless computing resources available at trivially low prices, there emerges a tendency to undervalue planning in favor of post hoc adjustment. When this happens, platform and maintenance costs spiral, and suspicion is cast on the platform instead of the data model (or lack thereof).

So tempting is Snowflake's promise of near-zero maintenance and effortless scalability that many take it as an excuse to perform adequate data modeling before diving in. The Snowflake data platform does indeed live up to expectations (and beyond) when the underlying data landscape is built on a pre-planned data model.

Compared to other data platforms, Snowflake handles much of the database administration on the user's behalf. However, as this chapter will demonstrate, some considerations still fall to the database architects to ensure desired levels of performance and scalability while keeping costs in check. The physical model will not only serve to deploy pre-existing conceptual designs but also helps in auditing existing databases.

This chapter will explore these concepts in detail through the following main topics:

- Factors to consider for establishing physical properties
- Translating conceptual modeling elements to physical equivalents
- Creating the relational foundation for transformations and analytics
- Ensuring error-free deployment of a physical model to Snowflake
- Generating a diagram for an existing database

## Technical requirements

The **data definition language** (DDL) for the completed physical model created through the exercises in this chapter is available to download and use from the following Git repository: https://github.com/PacktPublishing/Data-Modeling-with-Snowflake/tree/main/ch11. You will arrive at the same result by following the steps in this chapter or by using the code provided. The physical model will be used as the foundation for transformational examples in later chapters.

## Considerations before starting the implementation

When transitioning from a conceptual or logical design, where entities, attributes, relationships, and additional context have already been defined, there appears to be little to do at first glance when moving to a physical model. However, the specifics of Snowflake's unique cloud architecture (discussed in *Chapters 3* and *4*), from its variable-spend pricing to time-travel data retention, leave several factors to consider before embarking on physical design. We'll cover these factors in the following sections.

### Performance

Query performance in Snowflake is heavily dependent on the clustering depth of the micro-partitions, which, in turn, are influenced by the natural sort order of the data inserted. Apart from Hybrid Unistore tables, which allow users to enable indexes, there are few performance tuning options left to the user besides sorting data before inserting and clustering. If the data volume in a given table is expected to reach the terabyte range, Snowflake recommends defining a clustering key, which can be declared on one or more table columns or expressions.

Where data is meant for downstream consumption, the expected query patterns should be evaluated for performance and memory consumption against the intended warehouse size. If aggregations and complex calculations are required, Snowflake materialized views (single-table) or manual materialization via CTAS (multi-table) should be considered. These materializations will improve query performance compared to standard views by pre-aggregating and pre-joining data.

Of course, in a cloud platform, performance always comes at a price.

### Cost

The bulk of the cloud database costs will be incurred by query processing and data transformation, which will be the focus of subsequent chapters. However, data storage costs are directly associated with a physical design and should be considered at this stage before they accumulate unwittingly.

As discussed in *Chapter 4, Mastering Snowflake Objects*, Snowflake tables offer a configurable data retention period to allow time travel. Not all tables benefit from extended time travel periods; some may forgo it altogether, so be sure to set transient and data retention properties as and where needed (table, schema, or database level).

Some data may not require a database table at all. Recall that Snowflake can reference data in external storage, such as **Simple Storage Service** (**S3**), both in the internal and public clouds. If no **data manipulation language** (DML) is required, external tables provide a fully workable option without incurring storage costs. When DML is required for slow-changing datasets such as those used in data lakes, Snowflake is now offering support for external tables in Apache Iceberg format (in private preview as of this writing but expected in 2023).

## Data quality and integrity

While there is no guarantee of data quality for data coming into the warehouse, the physical data model should enforce critical business rules and preserve relational metadata. The importance of relational constraints is the central theme of this book but NOT NULL and UNIQUE constraints, default column values, and proper typing of columns are equally important when designing the physical model.

It is worth repeating that NOT NULL is the only constraint enforced by Snowflake. To ensure data integrity, user-enforced logic pre- or post-load should be considered. With the recent (November 2022) announcement of join elimination, the RELY property for relational constraints plays an important role in query performance and cost reduction. The use cases and implementation of the RELY property will be covered in detail in the following chapter on transformational modeling, but the foundation must be set in the physical model.

The next point to consider is data protection.

## Data security

The physical database model should include security measures to protect the data from unauthorized access and to meet compliance regulations. Snowflake's access controls, roles, and object ownership fall outside the scope of this book, but model-related features are mentioned here for reference, along with links to further reading. Bear in mind that the following features are only offered in Snowflake's Enterprise Edition or higher:

- **Column-level security**: Allows the application of a masking policy to a column within a table or view and is available through internal functions or external tokenization (https://docs.snowflake.com/en/user-guide/security-column.html).

- **Row-level security**: Allows the application of a row access policy to a table or view to determine which rows are visible in the query result for a given role (https://docs.snowflake.com/en/user-guide/security-row.html).

- **Object Tagging**: Allows data tracking for compliance, discovery, protection, and resource usage. Tags can be assigned to higher-level objects such as schemas and tables and inherited by their children (tables and columns, respectively) (https://docs.snowflake.com/en/user-guide/object-tagging.html).

- **Tag-based masking policies**: Allows protecting column data by assigning a masking policy to a tag and then setting the tag on a database object or the Snowflake account (https://docs.snowflake.com/en/user-guide/tag-based-masking-policies.html).
- **Data classification**: Auto-detects and categorizes (using tags) potentially personal or sensitive data to support compliance and privacy regulations (https://docs.snowflake.com/en/user-guide/governance-classify.html).

For all these data governance features, a visual data model becomes vital to their maintenance, management, and tracking. While Snowflake provides metadata on their application in the Account and Information schemas and through internal functions, a navigable diagram of the physical database beats tabular text results for usability and understanding.

For a complete overview of Snowflake access controls, refer to the documentation (https://docs.snowflake.com/en/user-guide/security-access-control-overview.html).

Having covered four primary considerations before embarking on a physical design, it's worth mentioning two that, while an integral part of traditional database design, are now handled by Snowflake architecture.

## Non-considerations

Snowflake's cloud-native architecture delivers on the promise of *near-zero maintenance* by removing two critical factors from database design, as follows:

- **Backup and recovery**: Using the CLONE command, Snowflake users can instantly create zero-copy snapshots of tables, schemas, or databases. This command can be combined with previously discussed time-travel features to give users even more flexibility to take a snapshot retroactively (see *Chapter 3, Mastering Snowflake's Architecture* for more details).
- **Scalability**: For storage, there is no (practical) limit on the size of individual tables or entire databases. For compute, virtual warehouses are independent of the database model and can be resized instantaneously.

With this in mind, let's continue the modeling journey toward physical design.

# Expanding from logical to physical modeling

At this stage in the modeling journey—preparing to transform a logical model into a physical one—the use of a modeling tool will make a marked difference in the effort required to generate the final DDL. While this exercise can be done using anything from a sheet of paper to Excel, using a data modeling tool to accelerate the process is encouraged. (See the *Technical requirements* section of *Chapter 1, Unlocking the Power of Modeling* for a link to a free trial of SqlDBM—the only cloud-based tool that supports Snowflake and offers a free tier.)

Picking up from the finished logical model from *Chapter 8, Putting Logical Modeling into Practice*, let's begin the physical transformation.

## Physicalizing the logical objects

Logical models contain all the information needed to transform them into a physical design, but they are not one-to-one equivalent regarding the number of elements. Besides the direct translations, such as entities to tables and relationships to constraints, some elements, such as subtypes, may not have a physical counterpart.

Working from the completed logical design from *Chapter 8, Putting Logical Modeling into Practice*, where many-to-many relationships have already been resolved, we are left to consider the subtype/supertype relationship between LOYALTY_CUSTOMER and CUSTOMER:

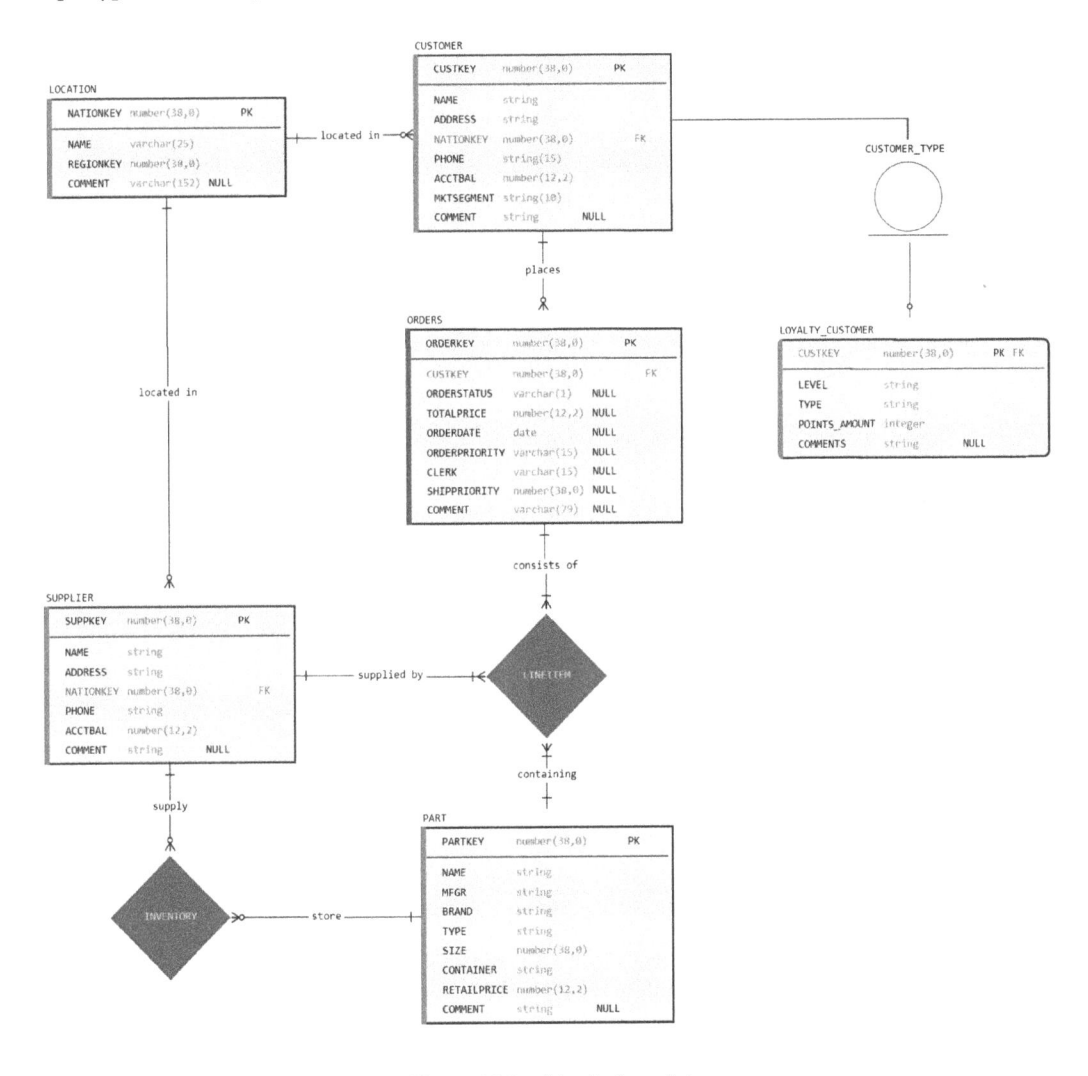

Figure 11.1 – A logical model

170　Putting Physical Modeling into Practice

Recall that subtypes represent inheritance between entity classes. Before defining the physical structure, inheritance rules should be decided.

Chihuahuas and mastiffs, despite obvious size differences, share many common properties of the dog class. Likewise, logical subtype properties are mutually compatible with the supertype (both CUSTOMER and LOYALTY_CUSTOMER have a CUSTOMER_ID). When deciding on a physical design, business requirements and query patterns will dictate whether the two should remain separate tables or fuse into one, and by what means if so.

Perhaps our organization has an entire marketing department dedicated to working with loyalty customers and frequently maintains attributes that are exclusive to them. In that case, a standalone LOYALTY_CUSTOMER table makes sense from a maintenance standpoint. If the organization were only concerned with keeping tabs on the percentage of loyalty customers relative to the total, a single CUSTOMER table containing loyalty attributes would be preferable.

There are several options when deciding the physical representation of subtypes based on the business requirements. Recall the scenario of superhero subtypes from *Chapter 2, An Introduction to the Four Modeling Types*:

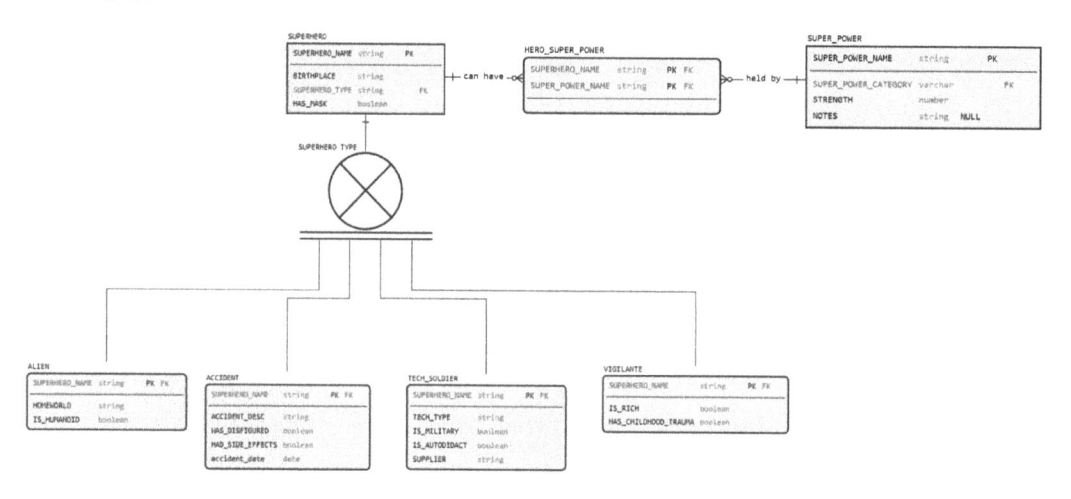

Figure 11.2 – A logical subtype/supertype relationship

Converting this arrangement to a physical model can happen in one of the following ways:

- **Maintain logical**: Keep all five tables and existing attributes as defined in the logical model.
- **Inherit from supertype**: Keep all five tables and duplicate supertype attributes (such as BIRTHPLACE and HAS_MASK) to the subtypes. This results in denormalized supertypes that are easier to query but harder to maintain.

- **Rollup**: Keep only the supertype (SUPERHERO) by inheriting the attributes from the four subtypes.
- **Rolldown**: Keep only the four subtypes by inheriting the supertype's properties (such as BIRTHPLACE and HAS_MASK).

For this exercise, we will choose the first option and maintain the logical definition, which results in two physical tables (CUSTOMER and LOYALTY_CUSTOMER).

Now that all the tables are known, it's time to adjust their physical properties.

## Defining the tables

It is time to unify the lessons of previous chapters and put them into practice. This is the point in the design process where decisions about naming, such as case, plurality, prefixes, and suffixes, must be finalized.

### Naming

This example will follow standard modeling best practices, reiterating the caveat that every organization must choose what works best and aligns with any existing standards. The conversion yields the following changes from the logical model:

- **Case and table naming**: Convert to singular snake case (ORDERS to sales_order)
- **Unique identifiers**: Name unique identifiers consistently <table_name>_id (P_PARTKEY to part_id)
- **Remove prefixes and suffixes**: Applies to table and column names (P_NAME to name)
- **Remove abbreviations**: Make columns unambiguous (P_MFGR to manufacturer)
- **Add units to amounts**: Make amounts unambiguous by adding units (C_ACCTBAL to account_balance_usd and L_DISCOUNT to discount_percent)

With naming in place, it's time to determine the table properties for the entities in our model.

### Table properties

Considering storage costs, backup requirements, data sensitivity, and performance, table properties should be set according to business needs. Suppose our example will be used to manage daily operations at the historic *AdventureWorks* company. In this case, we should opt for standard (non-transient) tables that offer a fail-safe and an adjustable retention period.

If 2 weeks of fail-safe is required for our data, we can set that default at the schema level to be used by all tables unless otherwise specified. Because this is an operational schema, access should be tightly controlled by the owner, so we opt for managed access.

The database and schema declaration would look something like this:

```
create database adventureworks;

create schema operations
    WITH MANAGED ACCESS
    DATA_RETENTION_TIME_IN_DAYS = 14;
```

Although performance and data volume are a concern, Snowflake does not recommend clustering or re-partitioning before baseline usage metrics are established. We require two pieces of information before clustering: current query and DML performance and query and loading patterns.

After table properties, column data types are configured. Recall that Snowflake accepts common data-type synonyms such as `string` and `integer` and automatically translates them to their equivalents (`varchar` and `number`, respectively).

The final element that remains is table constraints.

### *Declaring constraints*

Physical constraints translate directly from the logical model to help ensure data integrity and usability. Although `NOT NULL` is the only constraint enforced by Snowflake, `PK`, `FK`, and `UNIQUE` (AK or **alternate key**) constraints provide valuable relational context and aid in query performance when used with the `RELY` property.

The Snowflake query engine uses the `RELY` constraint property to eliminate unnecessary joins. A deep dive into its use cases and implementation will follow in the next chapter, so this discussion will focus only on its declaration. It should be noted that there is no monetary or performance cost to using the `RELY` property in tables that don't violate uniqueness constraints. For nearly all use cases, setting the `RELY` property is recommended.

Following the previous chapter's naming suggestions for relational constraints, we now declare the `PK`, `FK`, and `AK` constraints for our tables. To provide an example of an alternate key, we declare one on the `NAME` column of the `LOCATION` table. To retain relationship names, remember to include them in the foreign key, as discussed previously. In summary, the following conventions are suggested:

- **PK naming**: Include table name (`pk_supplier` for `supplier` table)
- **FK naming**: Include child table, logical relationship name, and parent (`fk_sales_order_placed_by_customer`)
- **AK naming**: Include table name and qualifier as multiple alternate keys can be declared (`ak_location_name` for the alternate key name in the location table)

> **Alternate keys as a foreign key reference**
>
> Foreign key relationships can reference alternate keys (`UNIQUE`) as well as primary keys. This fact is often overlooked in database modeling but opens many more possibilities when establishing relations between tables. In cases where a surrogate key is declared primary, users can still reference the business key as a foreign key if declared as an alternate key.

The resulting physical model is now complete, and can be seen in the following diagram:

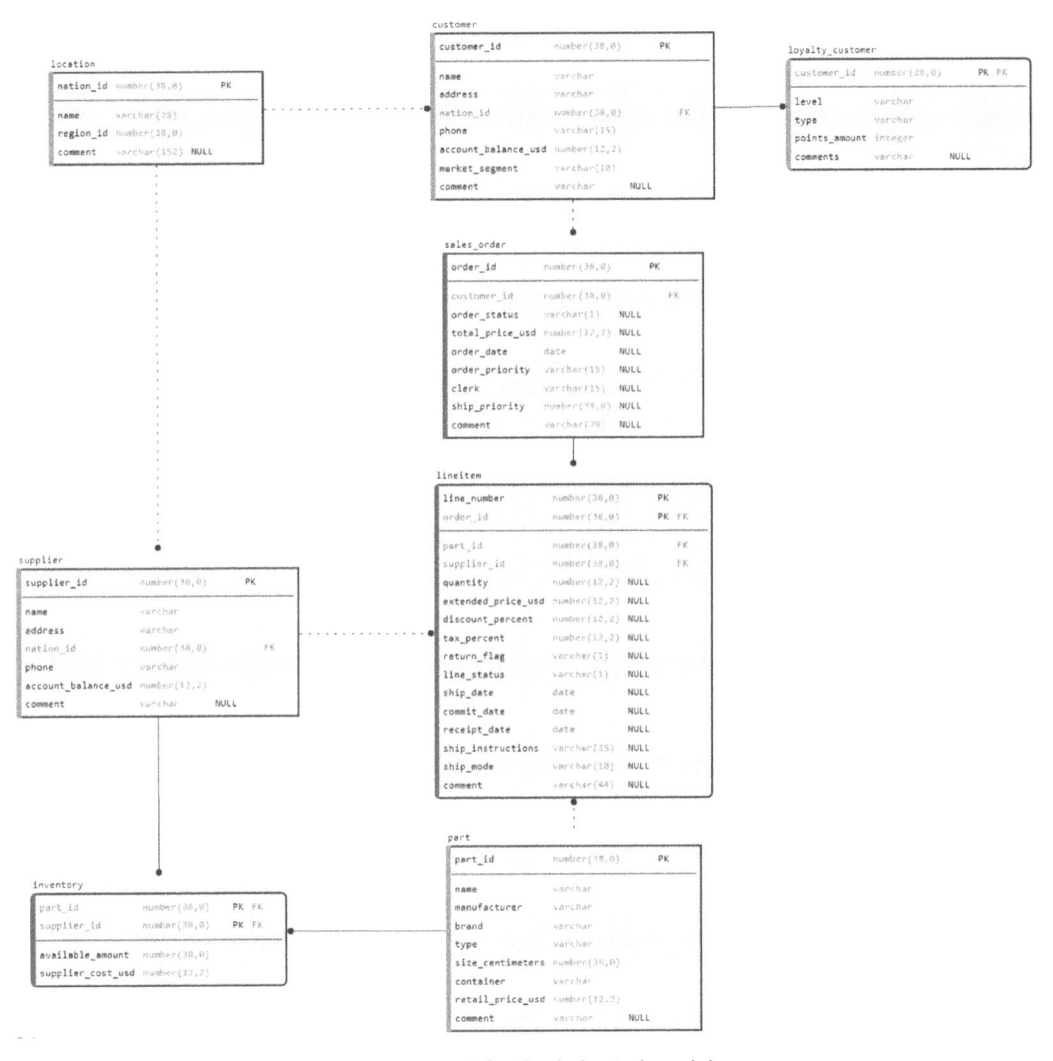

Figure 11.3 – A finished physical model

With all the parameters configured, the physical model is ready to be deployed.

## Deploying a physical model

At this point, all the tables, relationships, and properties have been defined and are ready to be deployed to Snowflake. If you use a modeling tool, all the DDL will be generated behind the scenes as adjustments are made to the diagram through a process called **forward engineering**. While it's not strictly necessary to use a modeling tool to forward engineer, doing so will make it easier to make adjustments and generate valid, neatly formatted SQL for your data model.

For those following the exercise, the forward-engineered DDL from this exercise is available in a shared Git repository mentioned at the start of this chapter.

With the DDL in hand, pay attention to the database and schema context in the Snowflake UI. Creating a database or schema will automatically set the context for a given session. To switch to an existing database or schema, use the context menu in the UI or the USE <object> <object name> SQL expression. Here's an example of this:

```
use database adventureworks;
```

```
use schema operations;
```

Now, run the DDL you've generated or use the example provided.

The physical model has been deployed to the database. But what happens if you want to visualize an existing database schema? Can modeling be used in reverse to help navigate unfamiliar databases?

## Creating an ERD from a physical model

As we just demonstrated through the forward engineering deployment process, a physical database model is a one-to-one representation of its relational diagram. This implies that the process of generating a diagram can be run in reverse—from Snowflake DDL to a modeling tool—a process known as **reverse engineering**. Again, it's not strictly necessary to use a dedicated modeling tool—many SQL IDEs such as Visual Studio Code and DBeaver can generate **Entity-Relationship Diagrams** (**ERDs**)—doing so will offer greater flexibility in organizing, navigating, and making adjustments to your model.

A similar diagram to the one created in the previous exercise can be generated by connecting to our deployed model through a SQL IDE:

# Creating an ERD from a physical model  175

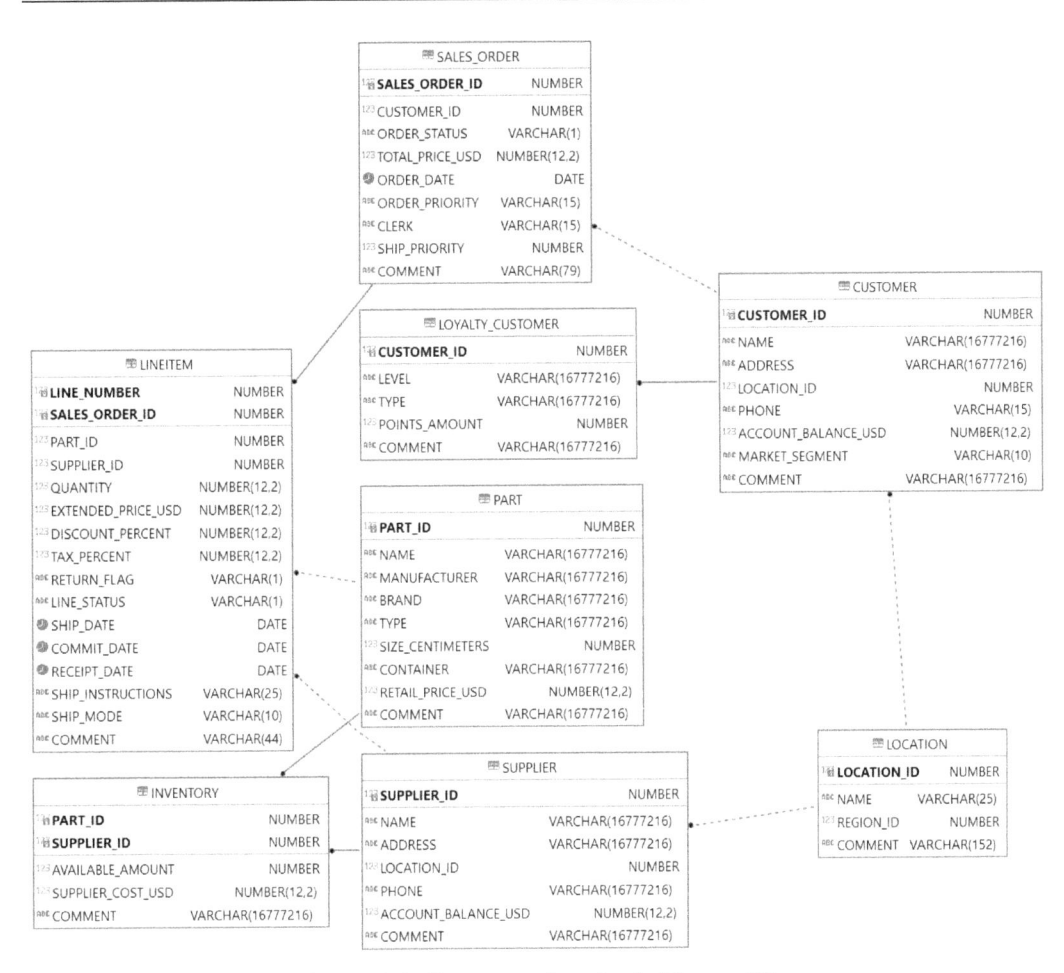

*Figure 11.4 – Reverse engineering in DBeaver IDE*

What is evident in this exercise is often overlooked in database designs—the fact that a neat, related, documented ERD is quickly rendered through reverse engineering only when due diligence has been done to properly model its details. While some IDEs can render an ERD from a physical database, they do not have the editing capabilities of a modeling tool. Without following proper modeling guidelines, any generated ERD will be lacking in practical value.

## Summary

The exercises in this chapter demonstrate what is required to transform a logical model into a deployable, physical design. However, before such transformation occurs, each project's use case should be carefully considered. As there is no one-size-fits-all guideline for Snowflake databases, decisions must be made considering performance, cost, data integrity, security, and usability. However, unlike traditional databases, long-standing issues such as backup, recovery, and scalability are handled by Snowflake features and architecture.

Once the physical properties have been decided, users create physical equivalents of all logical objects, including many-to-many and subtype/supertype relationships, yielding a final set of physical tables. Following this, naming standards, database objects, columns, and their relationships are declared before deploying the resulting model.

Deployable Snowflake DDL code is produced from an ERD through a process called forward engineering. As the physical model and its diagram are one-to-one equivalents, the deployment process is straightforward and can be run just as easily in reverse.

Generating ERDs from existing Snowflake databases can be done through reverse engineering, a process supported by modeling tools and many SQL IDEs. However, as the database structure and its physical diagram are equivalent, reverse engineering cannot miraculously create usable diagrams if proper modeling has not occurred—garbage in, garbage out.

The next chapter will demonstrate just how valuable a good physical model can be as we begin to transform the data using Snowflake queries.

# Part 3: Solving Real-World Problems with Transformational Modeling

This part focuses on advanced transformational modeling techniques and covers the theory and practice of putting them into action in Snowflake. First, we explore slowly changing dimensions—critical for maintaining historical data accuracy and ensuring consistency across different versions of data. Then, we learn how to model facts for rapid analysis, including best practices for optimizing query performance. We then explore semi-structured data formats and hierarchies, which are becoming increasingly prevalent and which Snowflake is so adept at handling. This part also covers the basics of Data Vault methodology for building agile, scalable, and auditable architectures, as well as Data Mesh, which is becoming an increasingly popular approach to managing data domains at scale across large organizations. Finally, you will experiment hands-on with fun and effective SQL recipes that couldn't be included in the rest of the chapters.

This part has the following chapters:

- *Chapter 12, Putting Transformational Modeling into Practice*
- *Chapter 13, Modeling Slowly Changing Dimensions*
- *Chapter 14, Modeling Facts for Rapid Analysis*
- *Chapter 15, Modeling Semi-Structured Data*
- *Chapter 16, Modeling Hierarchies*
- *Chapter 17, Scaling Data Models through Modern Techniques*
- *Chapter 18, Appendix*

# 12
# Putting Transformational Modeling into Practice

In the preceding chapters, we went from gathering requirements with business teams to creating and deploying a physical data model to Snowflake, which aligns with our organization's operations. Now it is time to leverage Snowflake's powerful query processing engine and its full-featured library of functions and data manipulation features to creatively transform data to answer business questions.

While physical modeling creates objects by defining the structure, transformational modeling uses logic—*selecting* existing data and creating a new object from the query result. However, query processing in Snowflake comes at the cost of compute credits. This chapter will cover the best practices for writing efficient queries in Snowflake to help control costs and increase performance.

As we build transformational models, we will also learn how to monitor their performance and detect issues using the Snowflake query profile. Most importantly, we will see how the structural foundation of relational modeling helps us create transformations faster and drives down warehouse costs through join elimination and other features.

This chapter will cover the following topics related to transformational modeling:

- Separating logic from objects to improve the database design
- Using the physical model to drive transformational design
- Performance gains through join elimination
- Joins and set operators available in Snowflake
- Monitoring Snowflake queries to identify common issues
- Building a transformational model from a business requirement

## Technical requirements

The examples and exercises in this chapter require data to execute. The script used to load the model created in the previous chapter with sample data is `create_physical_model_w_data.sql`, and is included in the following GitHub repository: https://github.com/PacktPublishing/Data-Modeling-with-Snowflake/tree/main/ch12. The complete transformational model for the exercise at the end of the chapter is also included (`create_loyalty_customer.sql`), although readers are encouraged to recreate it from scratch.

## Separating the model from the object

The ability to instantly scale up warehouses gives Snowflake users easy control over query performance and duration. However, increased warehouse size comes at the price of compute credits. Even keeping the warehouse size constant, changes in data volume and query patterns can cause performant and cost-effective data sources to degrade. To mitigate performance degradation, a view may need to be materialized as a table, or a table may need to become a materialized view.

However, even when converting from a view to a table, the transformational logic stays constant. While traditional modeling advice advocates differentiating views and other objects through suffixes (e.g., CUSTOMER_V), Snowflake users are encouraged to avoid such conventions. Orienting object names to their contents (e.g., CUSTOMER, DIM_DATE) rather than their object type allows modelers to easily pivot between them without breaking downstream dependencies.

## Shaping transformations through relationships

The exercises in previous chapters devoted much attention to relational constraints and how they help ensure data integrity, consistency, and quality while making data management easier. Exactly how much easier will be the recurring theme of this chapter.

Even simple business questions, such as *What is the customer and location name for the customer with identifier 775699?*, require us to refer to the relational model to find the tables in which these attributes are stored and the foreign key columns that can be used to join them.

Figure 12.1 – Foreign key constraint between location and customer tables

Using the information from the physical model, we can construct a query to obtain customer and location names for customer 775699 as follows:

```
SELECT c.name AS customer_name , l.name AS location_name FROM customer c
JOIN location l ON c.location_id = l.location_id
WHERE customer_id = 775699;
```

And we obtain the result we are interested in:

```
CUSTOMER_NAME      |LOCATION_NAME|
-------------------+-------------+
Customer#000775699|ROMANIA       |
```

> **Using descriptive aliases**
>
> The examples in this book use a single-letter alias style. This is intended to maximize readability on a printed page but is not recommended as a general practice. Recommended alias guidelines are covered later in this chapter.

Paying attention to constraints also allows users to avoid **join explosions**—queries that return more rows than expected. Join explosions distort query results by returning duplicate values and multiplying the amount values returned by the query. However, join explosions are even more insidious at scale because they can multiply the number of records returned by a query by several orders of magnitude— severely impacting performance and needlessly burning through warehouse credits.

Blindly trying to obtain a customer name from the SALES_ORDER table can have unexpected consequences. As the relational diagram indicates, a customer may place multiple orders; therefore, CUSTOMER_ID is not unique in the SALES_ORDER table.

## 182 Putting Transformational Modeling into Practice

**customer**

| customer_id | number(38,0) | PK |
|---|---|---|
| name | varchar | |
| address | varchar | |
| location_id | number(38,0) | FK |
| phone | varchar(15) | |
| account_balance_usd | number(12,2) | |
| market_segment | varchar(10) | |
| comment | varchar | NULL |

**sales_order**

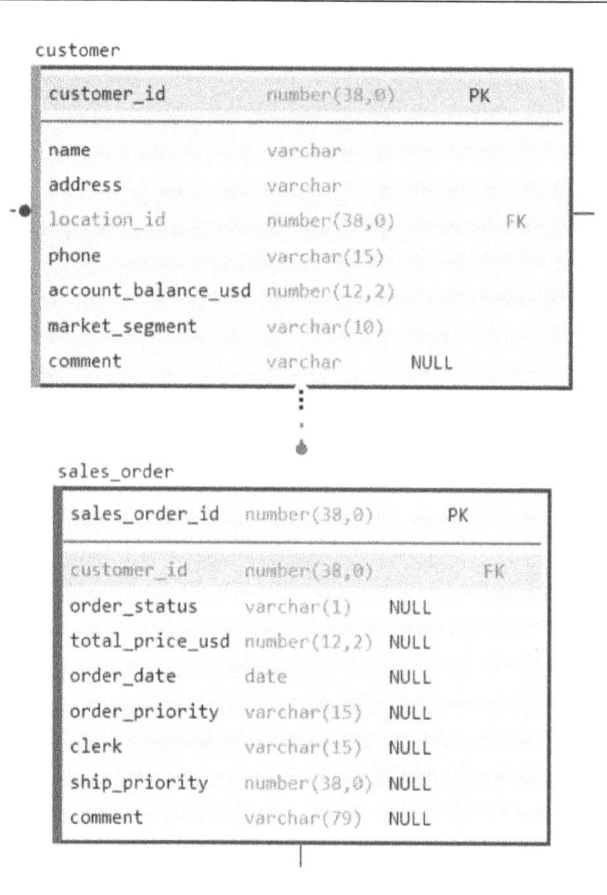

| sales_order_id | number(38,0) | PK |
|---|---|---|
| customer_id | number(38,0) | FK |
| order_status | varchar(1) | NULL |
| total_price_usd | number(12,2) | NULL |
| order_date | date | NULL |
| order_priority | varchar(15) | NULL |
| clerk | varchar(15) | NULL |
| ship_priority | number(38,0) | NULL |
| comment | varchar(79) | NULL |

Figure 12.2 – Foreign key constraint between customer and sales_order tables

Attempting to join CUSTOMER to SALES_ORDER to obtain the customer name would not be as straightforward as in the previous example, although the resulting query would look similar:

```
SELECT c.name AS customer_name FROM sales_order AS so
JOIN customer AS c ON c.customer_id = so.customer_id
WHERE so.customer_id = 775699;
```

However, the query returns multiple records in place of a single name (one per order made by customer 775699):

```
CUSTOMER_NAME      |
-------------------+
Customer#000775699|
Customer#000775699|
Customer#000775699|
Customer#000775699|
Customer#000775699|
Customer#000775699|
```

```
Customer#000775699|
Customer#000775699|
Customer#000775699|
Customer#000775699|
Customer#000775699|
```

The constraints in a relational model accelerate analytics by informing users how to link data from multiple data sources to answer business questions and avoid unpleasant surprises. But constraints can play an even more important role in query performance by eliminating certain joins altogether.

## Join elimination using constraints

In the previous chapter, we set the `RELY` property on our constraints to pave the way for the performance gains we will now explore. Snowflake uses the `RELY` property to perform **join elimination**—avoiding unnecessary or redundant joins in queries. Depending on table size, joins can be memory-intensive, so avoiding them when possible can significantly improve performance and save compute credits.

Even if a join is specified in the query, but no columns from the joined table are selected as part of the result, the `RELY` property will tell the Snowflake query engine to avoid performing the join.

If we modify the previous query—joining `CUSTOMER` and `LOCATION` tables—but only request information from `CUSTOMER`, the `RELY` property will help us avoid the unnecessary join operation.

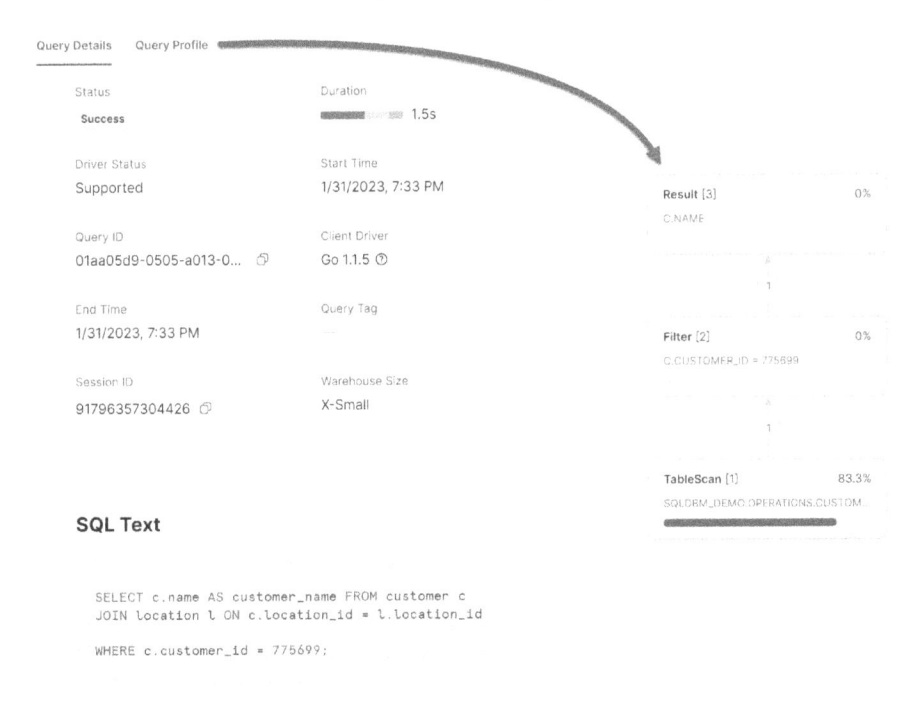

Figure 12.3 – A query with join elimination

A look at the query profile (which we will explore later in this chapter) confirms that only the CUSTOMER table was referenced as part of the query operation—saving us an extra table scan and join.

Here is the same query, pointing at the equivalent tables in the SNOWFLAKE_SAMPLE_DATA database that do not use the RELY property.

Figure 12.4 – A query without join elimination

Notice that without RELY, Snowflake scans both CUSTOMER and NATION tables. While join elimination can significantly improve query performance in some cases, there are times when it may present unintended consequences.

## When to use RELY for join elimination

Star and snowflake schemas (discussed in detail in *Chapter 17, Scaling Data Models through Modern Techniques*) are popular modeling choices and offer great opportunities for improving query performance through join elimination. In these scenarios, a central fact table is joined to several dimension tables, which add descriptive attributes. Enabling the RELY property on the constraints between the fact table and dimensions allows us to encapsulate all the join conditions and business logic in a multidimensional view and make it available to all users, regardless of the dimensions each is interested in. When a query references the view, Snowflake will only perform the join on the dimensions explicitly requested.

## When to be careful using RELY

Not all joins that reference columns from only one table are redundant. Inner joins return matching records between two tables and are often used as a filter instead of returning values from two tables. Often, master data exists as a subset of itself (e.g., `VIP_CUSTOMERS` as a subset of `CUSTOMERS`). In such cases, the constraints, if set, are semi-reliable—the primary key contains valid and unique values, but not all of them. Happily, the Snowflake optimizer is smart enough to detect and handle such scenarios when the `RELY` property is set on the primary key and alternate key constraints.

In the following example, a `MAIN_REGION` table is created as a subset of `REGION`. A duly titled `LOCATION_BAD_FK` table references `REGION_MAIN` as its foreign key as seen in the following image:

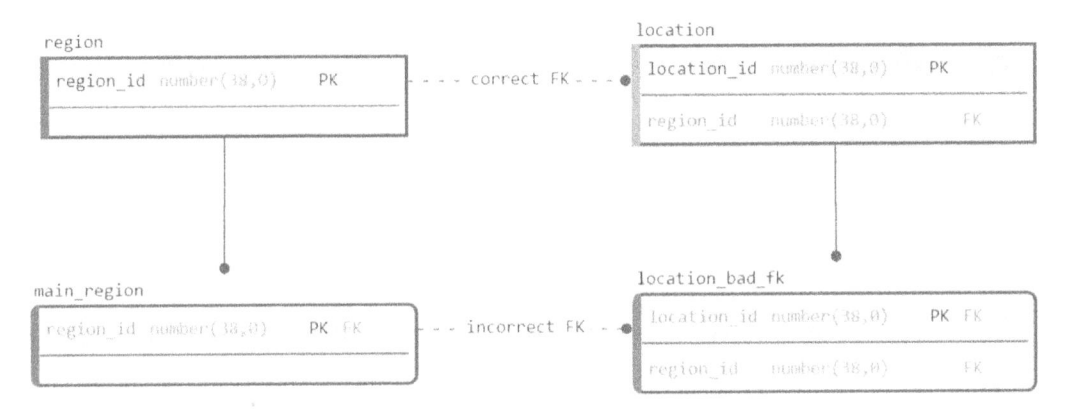

Figure 12.5 – A table using an incomplete subset of data as its foreign key

Without an explicit foreign key constraint, join elimination is handled correctly for redundant joins and non-redundant `INNER` filter joins.

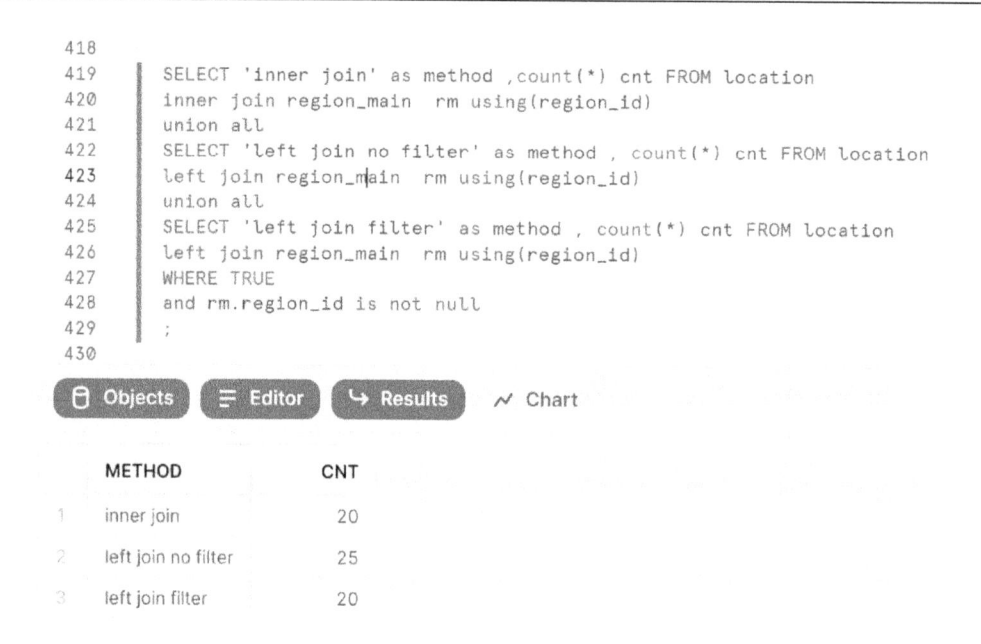

```sql
418
419      SELECT 'inner join' as method ,count(*) cnt FROM location
420      inner join region_main  rm using(region_id)
421      union all
422      SELECT 'left join no filter' as method , count(*) cnt FROM location
423      left join region_main  rm using(region_id)
424      union all
425      SELECT 'left join filter' as method , count(*) cnt FROM location
426      left join region_main  rm using(region_id)
427      WHERE TRUE
428      and rm.region_id is not null
429      ;
430
```

| METHOD | CNT |
|---|---|
| 1  inner join | 20 |
| 2  left join no filter | 25 |
| 3  left join filter | 20 |

Figure 12.6 – Join elimination handled correctly on primary key and alternate key constraints

It's only when we create an incorrect foreign key relationship between the duly titled LOCATION_BAD_FK and REGION_MAIN that we can trick the optimizer into giving us an incorrect result. To perform the experiment yourself, refer to the accompanying code in the file named join_elimination.sql in the repository for this chapter.

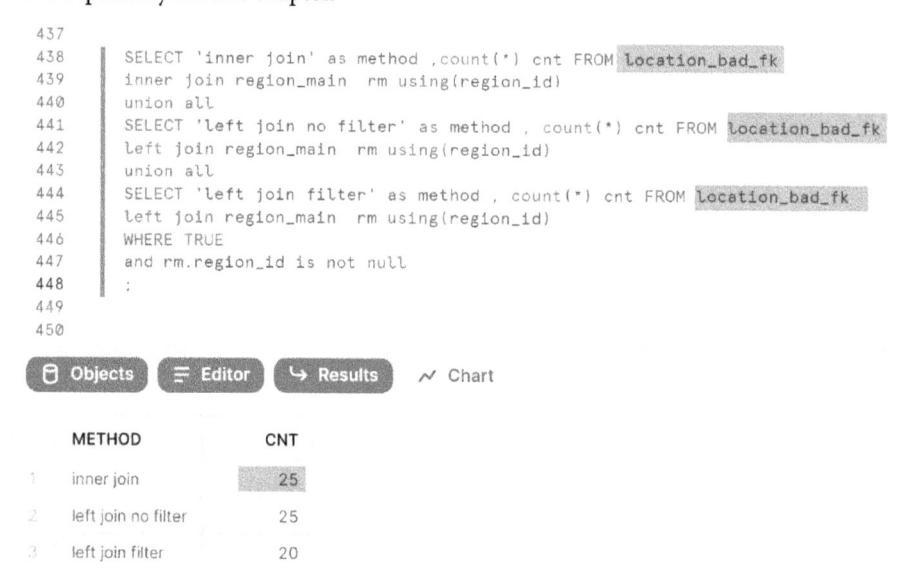

```sql
437
438      SELECT 'inner join' as method ,count(*) cnt FROM location_bad_fk
439      inner join region_main  rm using(region_id)
440      union all
441      SELECT 'left join no filter' as method , count(*) cnt FROM location_bad_fk
442      left join region_main  rm using(region_id)
443      union all
444      SELECT 'left join filter' as method , count(*) cnt FROM location_bad_fk
445      left join region_main  rm using(region_id)
446      WHERE TRUE
447      and rm.region_id is not null
448      ;
449
450
```

| METHOD | CNT |
|---|---|
| 1  inner join | 25 |
| 2  left join no filter | 25 |
| 3  left join filter | 20 |

Figure 12.7 – Join elimination handled incorrectly with a bad foreign key constraint

The takeaway is that the `RELY` property is an effortless and *nearly* risk-free way to optimize query performance on Snowflake views. (For more on join elimination and using it in multidimensional queries, refer to the extras section of the repository at `https://github.com/PacktPublishing/Data-Modeling-with-Snowflake/tree/main/extras/04_join_elimination`).

Now that we have begun to experiment with bringing together data from multiple tables, it would be a good time to review the complete list of joins and set operators that Snowflake offers to ensure that everyone is familiar with their usage.

## Joins and set operators

In a database, there are two ways to bring sources of data together: joins and set operators. A **join** combines rows from two or more tables based on related columns, and a **set operator**—such as `UNION`—combines the results of multiple `SELECT` statements. But, you can also use join on multiple `SELECT` statements.

An easier way to think about it is that joins combine data horizontally—across related rows—and set operators work vertically. The following example shows how identical records would look in a `JOIN` or `UNION` result.

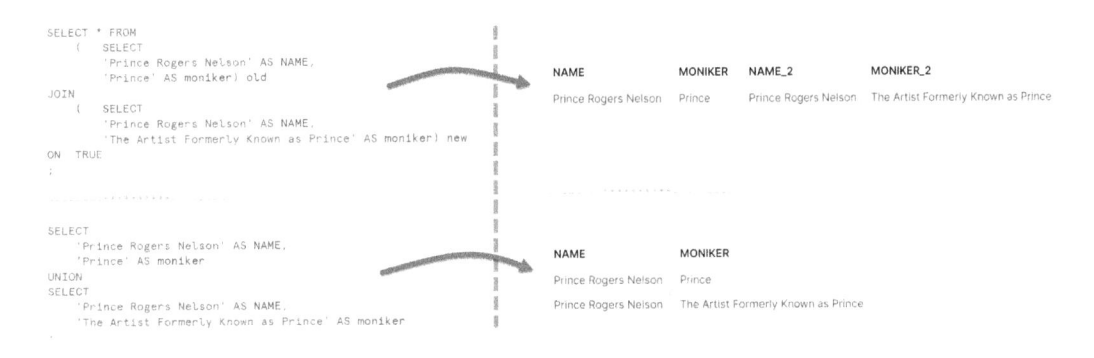

```
SELECT * FROM
    ( SELECT
        'Prince Rogers Nelson' AS NAME,
        'Prince' AS moniker) old
JOIN
    ( SELECT
        'Prince Rogers Nelson' AS NAME,
        'The Artist Formerly Known as Prince' AS moniker) new
ON TRUE
;
```

| NAME | MONIKER | NAME_2 | MONIKER_2 |
|---|---|---|---|
| Prince Rogers Nelson | Prince | Prince Rogers Nelson | The Artist Formerly Known as Prince |

```
SELECT
    'Prince Rogers Nelson' AS NAME,
    'Prince' AS moniker
UNION
SELECT
    'Prince Rogers Nelson' AS NAME,
    'The Artist Formerly Known as Prince' AS moniker
```

| NAME | MONIKER |
|---|---|
| Prince Rogers Nelson | Prince |
| Prince Rogers Nelson | The Artist Formerly Known as Prince |

Figure 12.8 – An example of a JOIN and a UNION operation

`JOIN` and `UNION` are just some of the tools at the developer's disposal. Let's review all the join and set operators that Snowflake provides and briefly cover some of their use cases.

The following diagram shows the join and set operators available in Snowflake.

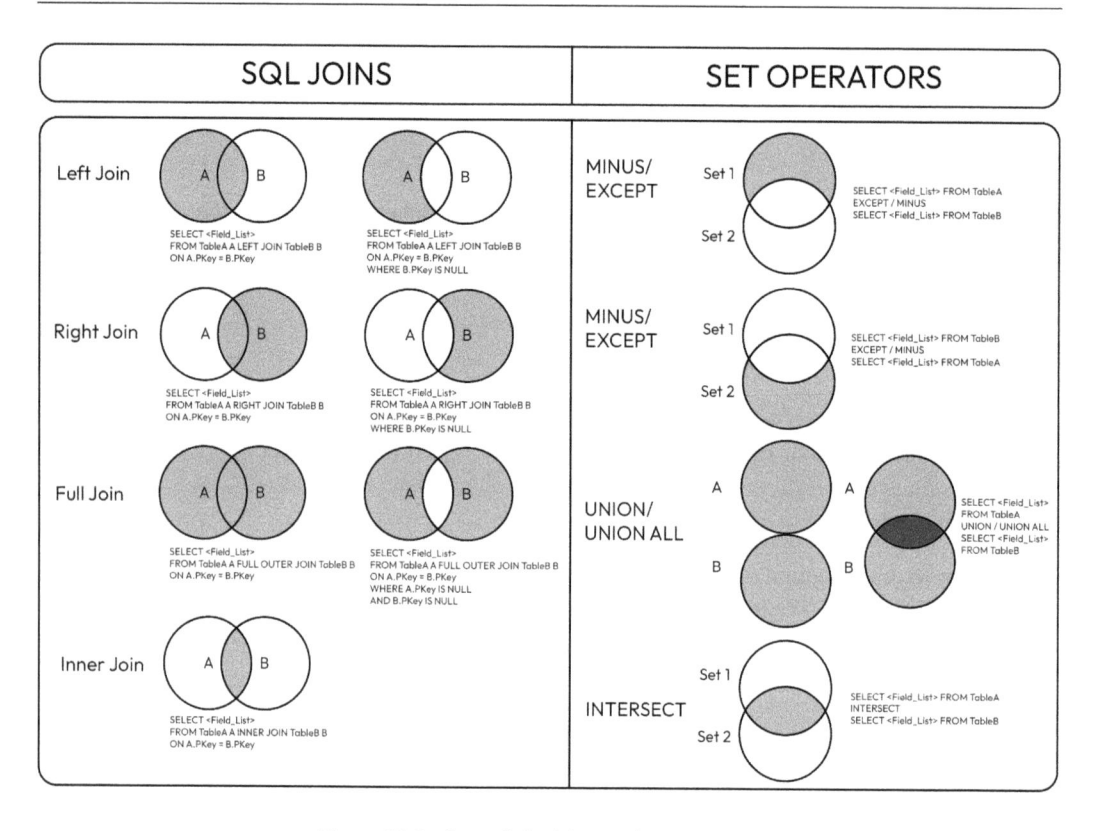

Figure 12.9 – Snowflake joins and set operators

Here's an overview of joins:

- `INNER JOIN` – Selects records that have matching values in both tables. By doing so, this join also acts as a filter. Unless data integrity is guaranteed, avoid using the inner join to add related attributes in a query. For example, selecting from a fact table and joining a related dimension to obtain descriptive attributes will cause certain fact records to disappear if no matching dimension records exist. The `INNER` keyword is optional but encouraged for readability.

- `LEFT JOIN` – Returns all records from the left table and the matched records from the right table, thereby avoiding the issue described with `INNER JOIN`.

- `RIGHT JOIN` – Returns all records from the right table and the matched records from the left table.

- `FULL JOIN` – Returns all records when there is a match in either the left or right table. The full join is helpful for data reconciliation and missing data analysis.

Set operators combine the result set of two or more `SELECT` statements as long as the following applies:

- Every `SELECT` statement has the same number of columns.
- The columns all have similar data types.
- The columns are in the same order.

Here's an overview of set operators:

- `UNION ALL` – Combines the result set of two or more `SELECT` statements without performing duplicate elimination. If a record exists in multiple sets, it will be included multiple times.
- `UNION` – Does the same as `UNION ALL` but performs duplicate elimination (using `DISTINCT`). Unless duplicate elimination is required, it is recommended to use `UNION ALL` to avoid the performance penalty of sorting `DISTINCT` records.
- `MINUS/EXCEPT` – Removes rows from one query's result set that appear in another query's result set, with duplicate elimination—often used in data validation and auditing (such as tracking changes in data over time).
- `INTERSECT` – Returns rows from one query's result set that also appear in another query's result set, with duplicate elimination—used in data reconciliation to ensure consistent data across all sources.

Before putting these into practice, let's review some of the performance and query-writing best practices that will help make our queries easier to read and maintain.

## Performance considerations and monitoring

Because the Snowflake services layer takes care of query tuning and optimization, writing efficient queries and following best practices should be the developer's only concern. To do this, Snowflake provides a visual query profile to break down query execution into constituent substeps and help identify potential issues. A sample query profile can be seen in the following screenshot:

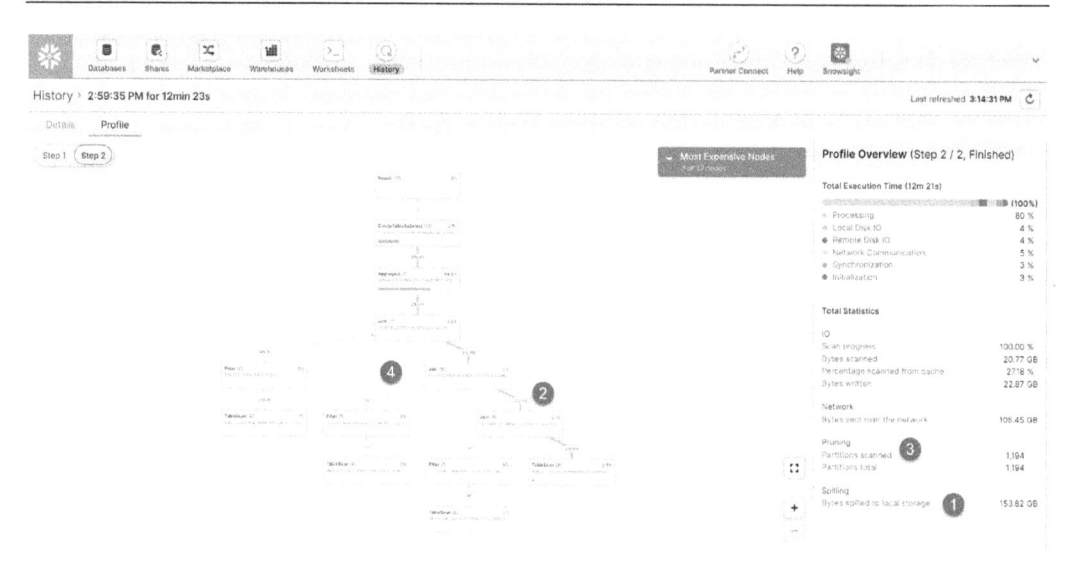

Figure 12.10 – Snowflake query profile

A good way to familiarize yourself with the query profile screen is by reviewing the kinds of query issues that it is designed to identify. The numbers in the query profile correspond to the topics listed in the following section.

## Common query problems

Most day-to-day query issues can be identified by paying attention to the information displayed in the query profile and following the query best practices described here:

- **Queuing** – When Snowflake determines that further queries in a data warehouse would lead to performance degradation, the query is queued and waits for the necessary system resources to become available. While a query queues, no profile information is visible.

    To mitigate queuing issues, users can scale out (add warehouses) or adjust the MAX_CONCURRENCY_LEVEL warehouse parameter to accommodate more processes (with less resource allocation for each) (https://docs.snowflake.com/en/sql-reference/parameters.html#max-concurrency-level).

- **Spilling** – [1] When a query cannot fit into warehouse memory, it begins **spilling** (writing) data to the local disk and then to network remote storage. Although it causes noticeable performance degradation, spilling is doubly pernicious because users incur credit costs for warehouse memory usage while getting the performance of writing to disk.

    If spilling occurs, review the query for potential issues and increase the warehouse size to give the operation more memory to work with. Another strategy is to split the query into multiple steps or process the data in smaller segments. This strategy is explained in the point on *Inefficient join order*.

- **Join explosion** – [2] When a join results in a **Cartesian product** (also known as a **cross join**), reviewing the row counts entering and exiting a join node will reveal the error. The number of records resulting from a join between two tables should be equal to or less than (in the case of INNER) the greater of the two.

  While record multiplication is desired in some cases, it usually results from an incorrect join condition. If the join condition matches the relational model, the tables should be checked for duplicate records.

- **Insufficient pruning** – [3] As described in *Chapter 5, Speaking Modeling through Snowflake Objects*, Snowflake clusters table data in micro-partitions and maintains metadata and statistics for data stored in each partition. Snowflake must read every partition if a query selects all records from a table. However, if a query filter is applied, it should ideally prune (avoid scanning) some partitions and improve performance. Review the number of partitions scanned versus the total partitions in every table scan node to determine whether the pruning result is adequate.

  To improve pruning, the general recommendation is to consider whether clustering can be improved. Review the examples in *Chapter 5, Speaking Modeling through Snowflake Objects* for more details on how to achieve better query pruning.

- **Inefficient join order** – [4] Snowflake does not support query hints, and the SQL query optimizer generally chooses the optimal join order for queries.

  However, if, on the rare occasion, you notice that joins are not being performed in the order of most to least restrictive, you can break the query up and enforce the desired order yourself. For example, consider the following query:

  ```
  SELECT a,b FROM x              --large fact table
      INNER JOIN y on x.c=y.c    --more restrictive join
      INNER JOIN z on x.d=z.d;   --less restrictive join
  ```

Reviewing the query profile, you see that tables Y and Z are being joined first, and the result is used to join table X. Knowing the data, you determine that there is a better way and rewrite the query, like so:

```
CREATE TEMPORARY TABLE temp_xy AS
    SELECT a,b,d FROM x              --large fact table
    INNER JOIN y on x.c=y.c;         --more restrictive join

SELECT a,b FROM temp_xy
    INNER JOIN z on temp_xy.d=z.d;   --less restrictive join
```

While the temporary table will only persist for the duration of the session, it still requires additional overhead to create. Snowflake provides a more efficient alternative that takes advantage of the results cache. This is achieved with the Snowflake functions LAST_QUERY_ID() and RESULT_SCAN, and casting to the table.

The previous example can be rewritten to use the query cache by making the following adjustments:

```
SELECT a,b,d FROM x              --large fact table
    INNER JOIN y on x.c=y.c;     --more restrictive join

SELECT a,b FROM TABLE(RESULT_SCAN(LAST_QUERY_ID())) rs_xy
    INNER JOIN z on rs_xy.d=z.d; --less restrictive join
```

When increasing warehouse size is impossible, the preceding technique can *fit* a query into available warehouse resources without spilling. In addition to the discussed methods, there are other suggestions to ensure clean, readable, and efficient queries.

## Additional query considerations

Besides the performance tips mentioned in the previous section, the following guidelines should also be considered to make your queries more readable and easier to test and maintain:

- **Use table aliases** – Aliases are a good way to make queries more readable and avoid naming collisions when joining tables. Table aliases can also make referencing columns from specific tables in the query easier. When choosing an alias, use the Goldilocks principle: not too long to type out but not too short that you forget what they mean—just right. As with the table naming advice in *Chapter 10, Database Naming and Structure*, the guiding principle is to pick a style and be consistent.

- **Use common table expressions (CTEs)** – CTEs can simplify reading and debugging complex queries by creating named subqueries using a `WITH` clause. This creates modular code blocks that can be separately debugged. As with all advice, exercise constraint and avoid excessive modularization, which can be as challenging to read as the spaghetti code it is meant to replace. More info on CTEs can be found here: `https://docs.snowflake.com/en/user-guide/queries-cte.html`.

- **Limit the rows returned** – When testing queries, row limits can reduce the number of records that need to be processed. The traditional way to do this is using the `LIMIT` keyword, but this suffers from two disadvantages: `LIMIT` works on the final query result (after all joins and calculations have been performed), and it returns rows in the order they were saved to Snowflake. If new data is written incrementally, `LIMIT` returns the same N (older) records every time. A better way is to use the `SAMPLE` function, which picks records randomly from the entire table, giving a much better representation of the data. It can also be customized to return different kinds of samples. More information on how to use and tune the `SAMPLE` command can be found here: `https://docs.snowflake.com/en/sql-reference/constructs/sample.html`. An example of limiting query results is shown here:

    ```
    --Good
    SELECT * FROM customer LIMIT 10;

    --Better
    SELECT * FROM customer SAMPLE (10 ROWS);
    ```

- **UNION without ALL** – Unless the added `DISTINCT` step is required to de-duplicate the result set, use `UNION ALL`.
- **Use EXPLAIN PLAN** – Generating a query plan requires users to run the query in question. However, you can check the execution plan of a query to see how Snowflake will execute it and check whether any issues need to be addressed. This option will not include statistics on rows returned or spilling but can be useful in validating the join order. The command to do this is `SYSTEM$EXPLAIN_PLAN_JSON`, and more info, including how to convert the output to a table or text, can be found in the documentation: (https://docs.snowflake.com/en/sql-reference/functions/explain_json.html).
- **Continuous monitoring** – Even performant queries can degrade over time as data volumes grow or data quality deteriorates. Consistent monitoring is essential to detect performance drift before it impacts warehouse costs.

The complete guide to using Snowflake's query profile can be found in the documentation: https://docs.snowflake.com/en/user-guide/ui-query-profile.html.

Let us put these techniques into practice by using them to create the final table in our operational schema.

## Putting transformational modeling into practice

In the last chapter, we deployed our sample physical model. Here, we will populate it with data and create a transformational model to satisfy a business requirement using the techniques and best practices covered in the preceding sections.

Transformational modeling requires data. The script to populate our operational schema with sample data can be found in the Git repository for this chapter. Please run the script titled `create_physical_model_w_data.sql` to recreate the physical model and load it with data from the `SNOWFLAKE_SAMPLE_DATA` database if you have not already done so.

After running the script, all the transactional tables in the schema will have been populated with data. However, the `LOYALTY_CUSTOMER` table is not transactional; it needs to be created through a transformational model. Just as the data model in the previous chapters took shape after getting to know the workings of our company by communicating with the business teams, transformational modeling works to satisfy business questions.

### Gathering the business requirements

Knowing the structure of the `LOYALTY_CUSTOMER` table from the physical model tells us little about what constitutes a loyal customer. By sitting down with domain experts from the marketing team, we can glean the business logic.

The marketing team confirms that there are two kinds of loyal customers: the top 400 based on order volume and 5 early supporters. They summarize the business logic in a formal request to define a table that recalculates the results every week. The requirements are as follows:

- The 5 early supporters, identified by `customer_id`, are 349642, 896215, 350965, 404707, and 509986. These are of type *early supporter*.
- The top 400 customers are calculated based on the sum of `total_price_usd` from `sales_order`. These are of type *top 400*.

  The loyalty level is calculated as follows:

  - Gold: early supporters and top 20 customers by `total_price_usd`
  - Silver: top 21-100 customers by `total_price_usd`
  - Bronze: top 101-400 customers by `total_price_usd`

- Customers in `location_id` 22 are not eligible for the program.
- Customers with a negative account balance are not eligible.
- The table should have a `points_amount` column, which the marketing team will maintain.

It appears that various tables need to be joined to complete this calculation. Before attempting to write the query, we should validate the join conditions in the physical model.

## Reviewing the relational model

Using the physical model, we can analyze the business requirements without relying on other team members. The information we need to get started can be seen in the following figure:

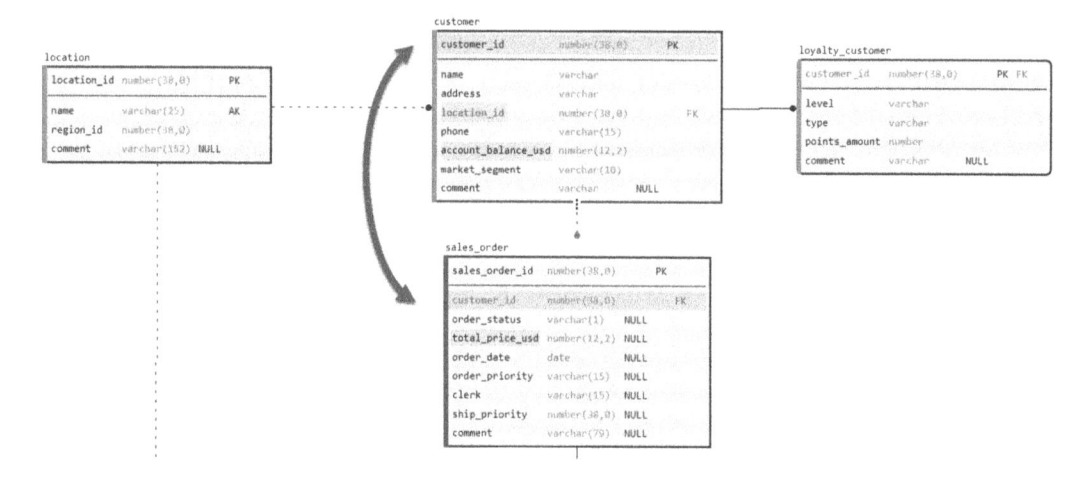

Figure 12.11 – Transformational analysis using the physical model

Reviewing the diagram, it seems that the information needed to determine a loyal customer is in a single table: SALES_ORDER. However, we need to join to CUSTOMER to exclude those who are ineligible, and the way to do so is through CUSTOMER_ID.

Having confirmed the details needed to create the transformational logic, we can write the necessary SQL.

## Building the transformational model

The SQL required to write the transformation in this example is straightforward and is included in this chapter's Git repository (`create_loyalty_customer.sql`) for reference. Instead of focusing on its exact implementation, it would be more beneficial to highlight the sections that relate to the principles mentioned in this chapter. The numbered sections in the following figure correspond to the numbered list that follows:

```
CREATE TABLE loyalty_customer
(
  customer_id    number(38,0) NOT NULL,
  level          varchar NOT NULL COMMENT 'loyalty points score',
  type           varchar NOT NULL COMMENT 'early supporter or frequent shopper',
  points_amount  number NOT NULL,
  comment        varchar COMMENT 'customer loyalty status calculated from sales order volume',

  CONSTRAINT pk_loyalty_customer PRIMARY KEY ( customer_id ) RELY,
  CONSTRAINT fk_loyalty_customer FOREIGN KEY ( customer_id ) REFERENCES customer ( customer_id ) RELY
)
COMMENT = 'client loyalty program with gold, silver, bronze status'
AS

WITH cust AS (
   ...

, business_logic AS (
    SELECT *

         , DENSE_RANK() OVER ( ORDER BY total_price_usd DESC ) AS cust_level

         , CASE
             WHEN  cust_level BETWEEN 1 AND 20 THEN 'Gold'
             WHEN  cust_level BETWEEN 21 AND 100 THEN 'Silver'
             WHEN  cust_level BETWEEN 101 AND 400 THEN 'Bronze'
             END AS loyalty_level

      FROM cust_ord
     WHERE TRUE
    QUALIFY cust_level <= 400
    ORDER BY cust_level ASC
)
   ...

, rename AS (

    SELECT
        customer_id
      , loyalty_level AS level
      , type
      , 0 AS points_amount  --will be updated by marketing team
      , '' AS comments
     FROM all_loyalty

)

SELECT *
  FROM rename
 WHERE true
;
```

Figure 12.12 – Areas of interest in the transformational model

Some of the techniques that have been implemented in this model include the following:

1. Although we are creating this table through transformational modeling, declaring relational constraints (primary keys and foreign keys) and updating the model remains equally important for usability. This example contains the constraints and the transformational logic in the same statement. Alternatively, constraints can be declared after the table has been created using an ALTER statement.
2. Breaking the logic into modular chunks using CTEs allows for cleaner code that is easier to read and debug. A developer could test the result of business_logic by simply calling it from the final SELECT statement.
3. Column renaming should be reserved until the end of the script. This allows developers to refer to source columns throughout the code and find all renaming in one standard place.
4. Modularizing sources, logic, and renaming simplify the final SELECT statement, allowing easy filtering and debugging.

After delivering the finished model, the marketing team decides—as business teams often do—that a weekly refresh is insufficient, and the data needs to be updated in real time. Without changing a single line of logic, we can change LOYALTY_CUSTOMER to be a view instead of a table by changing the first line of the CREATE statement:

```
CREATE VIEW loyalty_customer AS <existing logic>
```

By keeping the object name the same, downstream processes can continue to reference it without requiring updates.

Having created the transformational object and updated the relational model in the process, let's review the takeaways from this chapter.

## Summary

While a physical model reflects the company's business model, transformational models typically focus on addressing analytical business questions. Transformational models depend on existing data to perform their functions and, since data grows and changes over time, the object type used to represent the underlying logic may also change. By keeping object names constant, users can make adjustments and pivot between different database objects without breaking downstream processes.

The relationships established in the physical models can inform transformational designs as well as improving performance through join elimination by using the `RELY` property. Users can track performance to spot potential query issues using the query profile in the Snowflake UI. The query profile is a valuable tool for identifying performance issues such as exploding joins and inefficient pruning.

While transformational modeling is performed on top of the physical model, the two should always be kept in sync to provide database users with a complete overview of the system landscape. Keeping the relational model updated ensures that everyone in the organization can locate the data assets they need and identify where they fit in the overall model.

Having seen transformational modeling in action, the next chapter will put it to use in creating dimension entities and tracking their changes over time.

# 13
# Modeling Slowly Changing Dimensions

In *Chapter 7, Putting Conceptual Modeling into Practice*, we were introduced to database facts and dimensions. While facts capture the transactions of business operations, dimensions help give those transactions meaning by providing descriptive attributes, groupings, and other contextual details. Without careful curation and maintenance of dimension tables, databases would be like 1950s police dramas (just the facts, ma'am), lacking all color and making meaningful analysis impossible.

Dimensions shed light on the nature of entities in a data model, providing details such as a customer's billing address or a product's description. However, entity details are constantly in flux in the fast-paced business world—customers relocate, and products gain new features. A data warehouse must be able to keep up with the steady stream of changes and allow users to quickly pivot between the latest state of the world and a historical perspective.

This chapter will cover the various dimension types used to capture database entities' slowly (or quickly) changing details. Leveraging the unique Snowflake features discussed in previous chapters, we will learn to create and update historical dimension details in cost-effective ways that have never been possible in other databases.

This chapter will outline the common dimension types and their use cases and then provide the SQL recipes used to create and maintain them.

We will cover the following main topics:

- Historical tracking requirements in dimensional attributes
- The seven types of **slowly changing dimensions** (**SCDs**)
- The structure and use cases of each SCD type
- Unlocking performance gains through Snowflake-native features
- Handling multiple SCD types in a single table

- Keeping record counts in dimension tables in check using mini dimensions
- Creating multifunctional surrogate keys and comparisons with hashing
- Recipes for maintaining SCDs efficiently using Snowflake features

## Technical requirements

The scripts used to instantiate and load the examples in this chapter are available in the following GitHub repository: https://github.com/PacktPublishing/Data-Modeling-with-Snowflake/tree/main/ch13. While the key section of each script will be explained in the latter half of this chapter, please refer to the repository for the complete code used to maintain and schedule the loading of the objects discussed, as it is too long to reprint here.

## Dimensions overview

A dimension unifies (or conforms) similar attributes from one or various source systems into a single table under a common unique identifier known as a business key. A single surrogate key can also be used in place of multi-column business or primary keys. The unique key of a dimension table plays a critical role in identifying dimension records and allows the database team to track and maintain changes over time. A dimension table can be structured in predetermined ways to allow for different types of change tracking depending on the business requirement.

## SCD types

Attributes within a dimension have differing requirements for durability and change tracking. Some attributes are updated directly, while others require historical snapshots, yet others cannot change at all. This section will cover the types of SCDs, or update profiles, that a given attribute in a dimension can have.

It's important to note that the dimension type may not necessarily apply across all dimension attributes equally. Within the same dimension table, some attributes may be overwritten while others may not. By understanding SCD types and when to use them, database developers can implement the proper table structure and update techniques to satisfy the organization's reporting and analytics requirements.

### Example scenario

To explain the various SCD types, we will use a simplified CUSTOMER dimension as an example and track the change as it would appear under each configuration.

Suppose our fact table stores order details from customer *X*, made on the first of every month in 2022. Thanks to *X*'s patronage, their customer status went from **new** to **active** midway through the year. Not only do we want to track when the change occurred, but we want to tie the correct status to the recorded sales facts (that is, the customer is **active** today, but half their orders were made as status **new**).

The change in customer status is displayed here as it currently appears in the source system and data warehouse landing area:

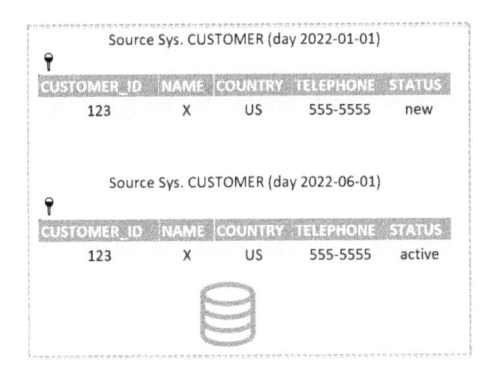

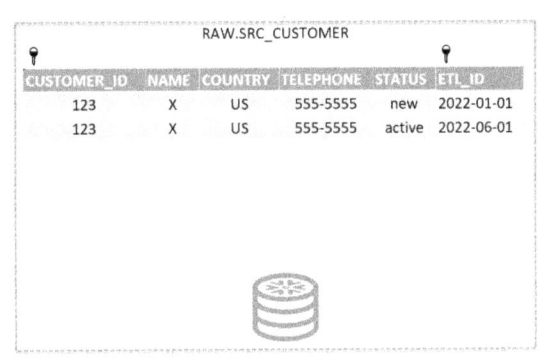

Figure 13.1 – A changed record in the source system and data warehouse raw schema

With this scenario in mind, let's explore the SCD types.

## Type 0 – maintain original

Ironically, the first SCD—Type 0—does not change. **Type 0** dimensions are intended for *durable* attributes that cannot change due to their business nature. Examples of Type 0 attributes include birth dates, calendar dates, and any attribute recorded at record creation that needs to be tracked as a baseline, such as original price, weight, or date of first login.

## Type 1 – overwrite

**Type 1** attributes do not require historical tracking and may be directly overwritten with an UPDATE statement. Sometimes, the latest attribute value is all that the business cares about. For example, our organization demands the latest customer status, and previous values are irrelevant. Maintaining a Type 1 dimension is relatively simple—for example, if the status changes, it is updated directly in the customer dimension, as illustrated here:

Figure 13.2 – new updated for STATUS change in Type 1 SCD

However, overwriting values is often not enough—a historical value must also be preserved.

## Type 2 – add a new row

For some attributes, an organization must register the latest value and maintain prior historical records. **Type 2** attributes generate a new row every time a change is recorded. Generating new rows for a given business key means that uniqueness is violated unless a time dimension (the effective date) is added to the primary key. The effective date of a Type 2 SCD not only separates historical values for a given business key but also allows those records to be tied to fact tables at a given point in time.

Maintaining a Type 2 SCD requires creating new rows when record changes are detected and additional metadata columns to track them. A single record in our example would generate the following change in a Type 2 table:

CUSTOMER

| CUSTOMER_ID | NAME | COUNTRY | TELEPHONE | STATUS | FROM_DATE | TO_DATE | HASH |
| --- | --- | --- | --- | --- | --- | --- | --- |
| 123 | X | US | 555-5555 | new | 2022-01-01 | 2022-05-31 | 4f1f37ea |
| 123 | X | US | 555-5555 | active | 2022-06-01 | 9999-12-31 | 0c680d79 |

Figure 13.3 – New row generated for a change in a Type 2 SCD

The following metadata fields make working with Type 2 attributes easier:

- **Validity intervals**: Because the business key is being duplicated with each change, another column must be added to the primary key to maintain uniqueness. Validity intervals (also named valid_from/to, start/end_date) provide the additional unique value for the primary key and timestamp when the change occurred, allowing facts to be linked with the correct point-in-time dimension value. The `TO_DATE` column also provides a flag for identifying the latest record using the standard surrogate high date of `9999-12-31`.

- **Hash**: Using a hashing function, such as `MD5`, provides a quick and standard way to identify when record changes occur. This concept is borrowed from Data Vault (discussed in *Chapter 17, Scaling Data Models through Modern Techniques*). When there are many Type 2 attributes in a table, instead of checking for changes one by one, hash all of them into a single column and compare them in a single go, as follows:

    - Create the hash field: `SELECT MD5 (Col1 || Col2 || ... || ColN) AS hash`
    - Compare the hash field: `IFF(hash_new = hash_old, 'same', 'changed')`

## Type 3 – add a new column

**Type 3** dimensions track changes by adding a new column to store the previous value when a change occurs. The original column is updated and not renamed to avoid breaking any existing downstream references. An effective date metadata column records the time of the change, allowing analytics processes to use the new or historical value based on their validity period.

An example of a status update in a Type 3 attribute is given here:

CUSTOMER

| CUSTOMER_ID | NAME | COUNTRY | TELEPHONE | STATUS | OLD_STATUS | EFFECTIVE_DATE |
|---|---|---|---|---|---|---|
| 123 | X | US | 555-5555 | active | new | 2022-06-01 |

Figure 13.4 – New row column created for a change in a Type 3 SCD

Although Type 3 is easier to maintain than Type 2, the limitation is storing multiple changes. While Type 2 attributes can change as often as needed, generating new rows each time, Type 3 can only show one change without creating additional columns—not a scalable design if regular changes occur.

## Type 4 – add a mini dimension

When SCDs become quickly changing dimensions—due to rapidly changing attributes—the number of records that Type 2 dimensions generate can cause performance issues. This is especially true with dimensions containing many records—as in millions of rows or more.

In a **Type 4** scenario, the solution is to split the frequently changing attributes into a separate **mini dimension**. To further curtail the number of records, the values in the mini dimension can be banded within business-agreed value ranges that provide a meaningful breakdown for analysis. The mini dimension has its own surrogate key and does not contain the main dimension foreign key—allowing both to retain a relatively low cardinality. However, to tie the main dimension to the mini, the mini dimension foreign key must be included in the fact table (as the main dimension appears at the time of the generated fact).

On a diagram, the arrangement of a Type 4 dimension would look like this:

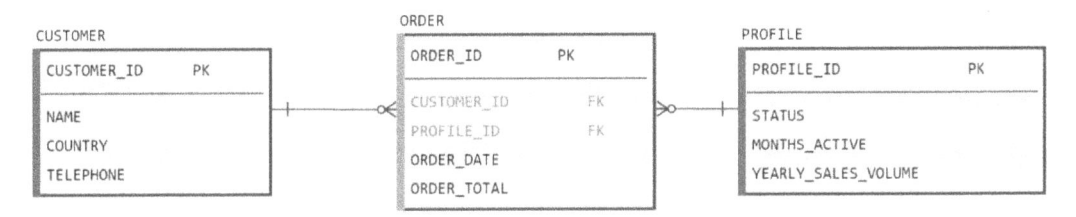

Figure 13.5 – A Type 4 SCD on a relational diagram

For our example, the business wants to track the length in months for how long a customer has been active, as well as their total yearly spend at the time of each sale. To avoid generating a record for each month and order placed, the business teams have agreed to group the MONTHS_ACTIVE attribute into two categories (less than or greater than 5 months) and band the sales volume into three groups. The mini dimension would need to contain every possible (or allowable by existing business rules) combination of groupings.

Our example would look like this (notice how the profile ID changes throughout the year as a function of the customer's attributes):

**CUSTOMER**

| CUSTOMER_ID | NAME | COUNTRY | TELEPHONE |
|---|---|---|---|
| 123 | X | US | 555-5555 |

**PROFILE**

| PROFILE_ID | STATUS | MONTHS_ACTIVE | YEARLY_SALES_VOLUME |
|---|---|---|---|
| 1 | new | 0-4 | <$10,000 |
| 2 | new | 0-4 | $10,001-100,000 |
| 3 | new | 0-4 | $100,001-999,999 |
| 4 | active | 5+ | <$10,000 |
| 5 | active | 5+ | $10,001-100,000 |
| 6 | active | 5+ | $100,001-999,999 |

**ORDER**

| ORDER_ID | CUSTOMER_ID FK (CUSTOMER) | PROFILE_ID FK (PROFILE) | ORDER_DATE | ORDER_TOTAL |
|---|---|---|---|---|
| 1 | 123 | 2 | 2020-01-01 | $ 16,668 |
| 2 | 123 | 2 | 2020-02-01 | $ 16,668 |
| 3 | 123 | 2 | 2020-03-01 | $ 16,668 |
| 4 | 123 | 2 | 2020-04-01 | $ 16,668 |
| 5 | 123 | 2 | 2020-05-01 | $ 16,668 |
| 6 | 123 | 3 | 2020-06-01 | $ 16,668 |
| 7 | 123 | 6 | 2020-07-01 | $ 16,668 |
| 8 | 123 | 6 | 2020-08-01 | $ 16,668 |

Figure 13.6 – Mini-dimension and foreign key in fact table in a Type 4 SCD

While this arrangement satisfies the reporting requirement, bridging dimension tables via a fact encumbers analysis on the dimension itself. To unify the main and mini dimensions into one, a Type 5 SCD is used.

### Type 5 – Type 4 mini dimension + Type 1

A **Type 5** SCD is an extension of the Type 4 mini-dimension technique—adding the mini-dimension key as a Type 1 attribute in the main dimension (hence the name, 4+1 = 5). This approach affords the performance gains of a Type 4 dimension by avoiding the explosive growth of rapidly changing Type 2 records and gives users a simple way to unify the main dimension with the mini dimension through a common join column.

On a diagram, the arrangement of a Type 5 dimension would look like this:

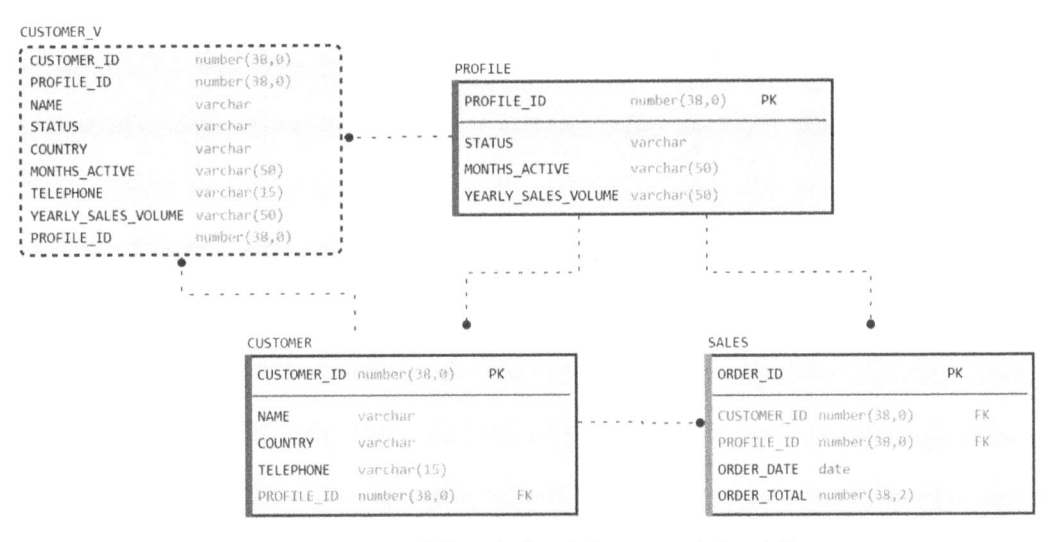

Figure 13.7 – A Type 5 SCD and related view on a relational diagram

Notice that to further simplify the user experience, a view is created over the main and mini dimensions to give the users a single entity to work with. Analysis of the fact table becomes more versatile by allowing users to join on one entity (the view) instead of the main and mini dimensions if historical values are not required.

The same scenario described in the section on Type 4 would look like this under Type 5:

Figure 13.8 – Mini-dimension and a related view in a Type 5 SCD

Unfortunately, Type 4, and by extension, Type 5, suffer from the inconvenience of calculating the mini-dimension value to include it as part of each fact. The performance implications involved in adding the mini-dimension foreign key to the fact table should outweigh the performance gain in reducing the number of dimension records through the use of the mini dimension.

## Type 6 – the Type 1,2,3 hybrid

A **Type 6** SCD is so named because it combines the techniques of Type 1, 2, and 3 (1+2+3 = 6) dimensions into one table. Based on business needs, users will demand different levels of historical values to achieve a balance of detail and flexibility in their analytics.

Suppose our customer *X* from previous examples began to relocate—moving headquarters to *Mexico* in *2023*, then to *Brazil* in *2024*. A Type 6 approach yields a dimension table that gives analysts every possible temporal attribute value in every snapshot: a Type 1 current value, a Type 2 effective dated value, and a Type 3 previous value.

To recap the status and country changes mentioned in this example, a snapshot of the source system over time is presented here:

Source Sys. CUSTOMER

| CUSTOMER_ID | NAME | COUNTRY | TELEPHONE | STATUS | |
|---|---|---|---|---|---|
| 123 | X | US | 555-5555 | new | in H1 2022 |
| 123 | X | US | 555-5555 | active | in H2 2022 |
| 123 | X | MX | 555-5555 | active | in 2023 |
| 123 | X | BR | 555-5555 | active | in 2024 |

Figure 13.9 – Source system showing changes for customer X

In a business scenario where the customer status needed Type 2 and the country was presented as Type 1, 2, and 3, the resulting table would look like this (the hash column is now calculated as a function of status and country):

CUSTOMER

| | | (T2) | (T1) | (T3) | | | | | |
|---|---|---|---|---|---|---|---|---|---|
| CUSTOMER_ID | NAME | COUNTRY | COUNTRY_CURRENT | COUNTRY_OLD | TELEPHONE | STATUS | FROM_DATE | TO_DATE | HASH |
| 123 | X | US | BR | US | 555-5555 | new | 2022-01-01 | 2022-05-31 | c0353bd3 |
| 123 | X | US | BR | US | 555-5555 | active | 2022-06-01 | 2022-12-31 | 6bbf42cb |
| 123 | X | MX | BR | US | 555-5555 | active | 2023-01-01 | 2023-12-31 | dc851de2 |
| 123 | X | BR | BR | MX | 555-5555 | active | 2024-01-01 | 9999-12-31 | 94402fe5 |

Figure 13.10 – Type 1, 2, and 3 columns combine in a Type 6 SCD

## Type 7 – complete as-at flexibility

Business users across all cultures and industries have a penchant for changing their minds. The Type 7 approach gives database modelers a way to deliver the needed historical attribute no matter the criteria or temporal reference point requested.

A Type 7 dimension (unimaginatively named as the number that follows 6) includes a natural key and a surrogate key in a Type 2 table structure and embeds both in the fact table.

> **A method for generating surrogate keys**
>
> An efficient—and data vault-inspired—way to generate a surrogate key for Type 2 records is to use an MD5 hash on the compound primary key (in this example, CUSTOMER_ID and FROM_DATE):
>
> ```
> SELECT MD5(customer_id || from_date) AS customer_skey
> ```

In a Type 7 configuration, a surrogate key is added to an otherwise Type 2 structure and is embedded in the fact (the latest SKEY as of the creation of each fact record). Based on the example scenario from the Type 6 section, the tables would look like this:

**CUSTOMER**

| CUSTOMER_ID (PK) | CUSTOMER_SKEY (AK) | NAME | COUNTRY | TELEPHONE | STATUS | FROM_DATE (PK) | TO_DATE | HASH |
|---|---|---|---|---|---|---|---|---|
| 123 | 4860a035 | X | US | 555-5555 | new | 2022-01-01 | 2022-05-31 | c0353bd3 |
| 123 | d0c90304 | X | US | 555-5555 | active | 2022-06-01 | 2022-12-31 | 6bbf42cb |
| 123 | ea5a543d | X | MX | 555-5555 | active | 2023-01-01 | 2023-12-31 | dc851de2 |
| 123 | 20c53233 | X | BR | 555-5555 | active | 2024-01-01 | 9999-12-31 | 94402fe5 |

**ORDER**
FK (CUSTOMER)

| ORDER_ID | CUSTOMER_ID | CUSTOMER_SKEY | ORDER_DATE | SHIPMENT_DATE | ORDER_TOTAL | LOAD_DATE |
|---|---|---|---|---|---|---|
| 1 | 123 | 4860a035 | 2022-01-01 | 2022-02-01 | $ 16,668 | 2022-01-02 |
| 2 | 123 | 4860a035 | 2022-02-01 | 2022-03-01 | $ 16,668 | 2022-02-02 |
| 3 | 123 | 4860a035 | 2022-03-01 | 2022-04-01 | $ 16,668 | 2022-03-02 |
| 4 | 123 | 4860a035 | 2022-04-01 | 2022-05-01 | $ 16,668 | 2022-04-02 |
| 5 | 123 | 4860a035 | 2022-05-01 | 2022-06-01 | $ 16,668 | 2022-05-02 |
| 6 | 123 | d0c90304 | 2022-06-01 | 2022-07-01 | $ 16,668 | 2022-06-02 |
| 7 | 123 | d0c90304 | 2022-07-01 | 2022-08-01 | $ 16,668 | 2022-07-02 |
| 8 | 123 | d0c90304 | 2022-08-01 | 2022-09-01 | $ 16,668 | 2022-08-02 |
| 9 | 123 | ea5a543d | 2023-08-01 | 2023-09-01 | $ 16,668 | 2023-08-02 |
| 10 | 123 | 20c53233 | 2024-08-01 | 2024-09-01 | $ 16,668 | 2024-08-02 |

Figure 13.11 – Type 7 SCD offers complete analytical flexibility

A Type 7 SCD allows business users to select the appropriate customer attributes based on the following criteria:

- The most recent or current information (that is, `TO_DATE = '9999-12-31'`)
- The primary effective date on the fact record (that is, `LOAD_DATE`)
- When the user changes their mind, any date associated with the fact record (that is, `ORDER_DATE` or `SHIPMENT_DATE`)

Here is how those queries might look:

```
--get current
SELECT < fact and attribute fields >
    FROM order o
    INNER JOIN customer c USING(customer_id)
    WHERE c.to_date = '9999-12-31'

--get dimension values as at the primary effective date on the fact record
SELECT < fact and attribute fields >
    FROM order o
    INNER JOIN customer c USING(customer_skey)

--get dimension values as-at any date on the fact record
--example will use SHIPMENT_DATE
SELECT < fact and attribute fields >
    FROM order o
    INNER JOIN customer c USING(customer_skey)
    AND o.shipment_date BETWEEN c.from_date AND c.to_date
```

Now that you have a general understanding of the different SCD types, let's recap before detailing the Snowflake recipes used to construct them.

## Overview of SCD types

The following screenshot summarizes the seven SCD types covered in the previous section, including their maintenance strategy and usage. While eight (including Type 0) SCDs may seem like a lot, most database designs rarely go beyond Type 3, as the first four SCD types strike an acceptable balance of performance, maintainability, and historical reporting needs:

| SCD Type | Strategy | Usage |
|---|---|---|
| 0 | No change | Durable attribute values that cannot change |
| 1 | Update / overwrite | No history, current attribute values only |
| 2 | Add new row | Change tracking by effective dated value range |
| 3 | Add new column | Last historical value available in the same row as current |
| 4 | Add mini dimension | Frequently changing attr. values reduced to banded ranges |
| 5 | 4+1 Add mini dimension and update | Type 4 functionality without relying on a fact table |
| 6 | 1+2+3 Add and update columns in type 2 | Handle multiple historical requirements in a single table |
| 7 | Add Surrogate key to fact and type 2 | Flexibility to handle any historical rollup on the fly |

Figure 13.12 – A comparison of SCD types

Now, let's see how to build SCDs with maximal efficiency using Snowflake-specific features.

## Recipes for maintaining SCDs in Snowflake

Understanding the structure of an SCD and being able to load it correctly are very different concepts. With a firm grasp of SCD types, we will now cook up the recipes for creating and maintaining them in Snowflake. Unlike generic SQL techniques you may have used in other databases, this book will take full advantage of the cost- and time-saving capabilities of Snowflake's core features, such as streams and zero-copy cloning.

### Setting the stage

To give readers complete autonomy to construct, experiment, and modify the upcoming exercises, we will first create a base table that will simulate the *day one* snapshot of the data warehouse raw/source schema. The base table will represent the initial *first* load of the source data into the data warehouse. Next, we construct a routine that simulates a daily load of new and changed records.

For consistency with the first half of this chapter, these examples will use the CUSTOMER table from the snowflake_sample_data.tpch_sf10 schema. Then, we create a simulated SRC_CUSTOMER table to represent the landing area of the data warehouse which, by default, will contain one quarter of the 1.5 million records of the sample CUSTOMER table. Finally, we construct a task, LOAD_SRC_CUSTOMER, which will randomly load 1,000 records into the SRC_CUSTOMER table (approximately 80% new, 10% modifications, and 10% existing unchanged records). The column that will receive changes in this example is account_balance_usd. The parameters for the number of records loaded can be changed directly in the code.

Let's recap the setup here:

| Object | Type | Purpose | Recod Count |
|---|---|---|---|
| source_system_customer | table | full data set for loading | 1,500,000 |
| src_customer | table | simulates DWH landing area | 375000 |
| load_src_customer | task | simulates daily changes | 1000 |

Figure 13.13 – Summary of the initial setup for creating SCD examples

To get started, instantiate a new schema for running these examples, then create the three base objects as indicated in the accompanying code. The file containing the examples is `create_snowflake_scd.sql`. We will also clone SRC_CUSTOMER to create a backup for resetting and rerunning the examples:

```
CREATE OR REPLACE SCHEMA ch13_dims;
CREATE OR REPLACE TABLE source_system_customer ... ;
CREATE OR REPLACE TABLE src_customer ... ;
CREATE OR REPLACE TASK load_src_customer ... ;
CREATE OR REPLACE TABLE src_customer_bak CLONE src_customer;
```

This script results in the following objects being created (the backup is not pictured):

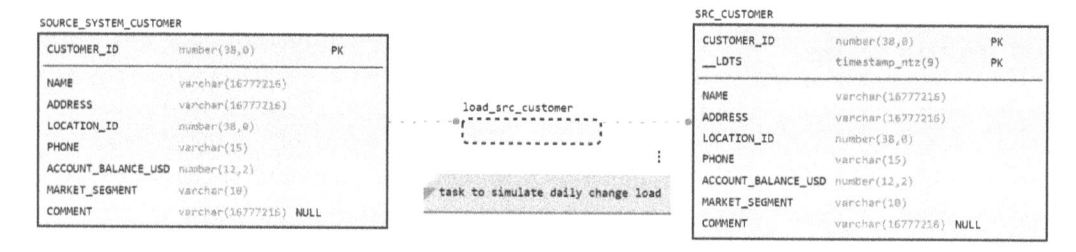

Figure 13.14 – Diagram of the initial setup for creating SCD examples

With the base objects in place, let's begin with a Type 1 SCD.

## Type 1 – merge

The Type 1 table will have a similar structure to SRC_CUSTOMER. It will even include the metadata load date column, __LDTS. However, unlike SRC_CUSTOMER, which captures changes by load date, the Type 1 table will only have one unique record for each entity in the dimension. For this reason, __LDTS cannot be part of the primary key but will be included as metadata to let users know the latest effective date of the record they are seeing.

Another field included in the Type 1 table is the DIFF_HASH column. Although the changes in our example only occur in one column, ACCOUNT_BALANCE_USD, using a DIFF_HASH field can make equality comparisons faster, cleaner, and easier.

Create and populate the Type 1 table with the initial base load from `SRC_CUSTOMER` by running the following statement:

```
CREATE OR REPLACE TABLE dim_customer_t1... ;
```

This results in the following table structure:

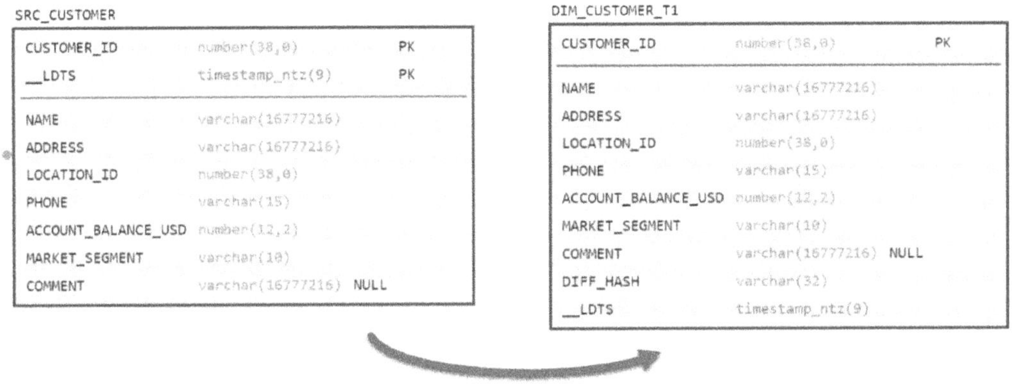

Figure 13.15 – A Type 1 table structure next to the source table it's loaded from

Now, prime the `SRC_CUSTOMER` table by calling the load task:

```
execute task load_src_customer ;
```

Now, we are ready to perform the update. Updating Type 1 attributes requires a MERGE statement—which inserts new records or updates changes. The key sections of the MERGE statement are highlighted here:

```
MERGE INTO dim_customer_t1 dc
    USING ( < SELECT latest snapshot from source > ) sc
    ON dc.customer_id = sc.customer_id --unique identifier
    WHEN NOT MATCHED --new records, insert
    THEN INSERT VALUES ( < source columns >)
    WHEN MATCHED --record exists
    AND dc.diff_hash != sc.diff_hash -only update if changes exist
    THEN UPDATE SET < target columns > = < source columns >
```

A `MERGE` statement is a relatively expensive database operation since it involves a join, a compare, and writing to disk in the form of inserts or updates. To ensure we are not comparing records that have already been processed, include a filter that only looks at source records that have not yet been processed (latest __LDTS). In a typical data warehouse scenario, this logic can be encapsulated in a view for ease of maintenance. In this example, the logic has been embedded into the merge for ease of understanding:

```
MERGE INTO dim_customer_t1 dc
    USING (SELECT *, MD5(account_balance_usd) AS diff_hash
```

```
          FROM src_customer  WHERE __ldts =
     (SELECT MAX(__ldts) FROM src_customer) ) sc
```

Run the MERGE statement and observe the impact on the dimension table:

```
MERGE INTO dim_customer_t1;
```

As expected, of the 1,000 records loaded, approximately three-quarters were new records, and 10% were changes:

Figure 13.16 – A MERGE statement for maintaining a Type 1 SCD

Feel free to experiment by running additional loads and varying the number of records to see the impact on performance. When you're ready, move on to Type 2.

## Type 2 – Type 1-like performance using streams

Type 2 tables are more performance-intensive than Type 1 because they contain historical changes and, over time, can grow to many times the size of the source table. However, in this section, we will explore a technique that uses Snowflake streams to achieve Type 1-like performance in a Type 2 load. If you are unfamiliar with streams and the meta columns they contain, please revisit *Chapter 4, Mastering Snowflake Objects,* before proceeding with the example.

Since we will be using the same base tables to perform a Type 2 load, remember to reset SRC_CUSTOMER to the original 375,000 rows by cloning it from the backup, like so:

```
CREATE OR REPLACE TABLE src_customer CLONE src_customer_bak;
```

Now, create and instantiate the Type 2 table by running the following statement:

```
CREATE OR REPLACE TABLE dim_customer_t2;
```

Recall that this table contains metadata columns to track the validity of changed records over time. The granularity of these validity intervals (for example, monthly, daily, and millisecond) will depend on the data's load frequency and reporting requirement. Although Snowflake can maintain microsecond splits using the `TIMESTAMP` data type, most reporting scenarios would not benefit from such near-real-time changes. Although daily changes (using the `DATE` data type) are the most commonly used, this example will use `TIMESTAMP` data types to allow users to run back-to-back loads on the same day.

The Type 2 table will look like this:

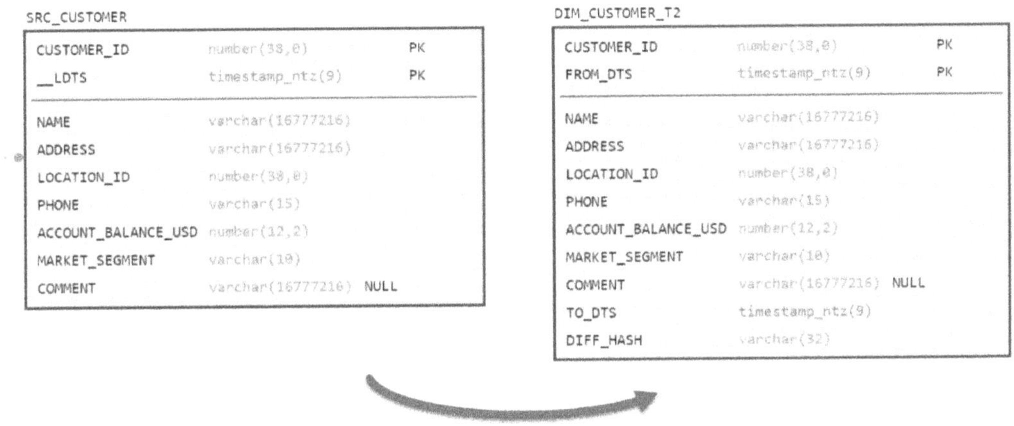

| SRC_CUSTOMER | | | | DIM_CUSTOMER_T2 | | |
|---|---|---|---|---|---|---|
| CUSTOMER_ID | number(38,0) | PK | | CUSTOMER_ID | number(38,0) | PK |
| __LDTS | timestamp_ntz(9) | PK | | FROM_DTS | timestamp_ntz(9) | PK |
| NAME | varchar(16777216) | | | NAME | varchar(16777216) | |
| ADDRESS | varchar(16777216) | | | ADDRESS | varchar(16777216) | |
| LOCATION_ID | number(38,0) | | | LOCATION_ID | number(38,0) | |
| PHONE | varchar(15) | | | PHONE | varchar(15) | |
| ACCOUNT_BALANCE_USD | number(12,2) | | | ACCOUNT_BALANCE_USD | number(12,2) | |
| MARKET_SEGMENT | varchar(10) | | | MARKET_SEGMENT | varchar(10) | |
| COMMENT | varchar(16777216) NULL | | | COMMENT | varchar(16777216) NULL | |
| | | | | TO_DTS | timestamp_ntz(9) | |
| | | | | DIFF_HASH | varchar(32) | |

Figure 13.17 – The structure of a Type 2 SCD

Note that only the `FROM` date column is required for the Type 2 primary key. In ensuring the data quality in a Type 2 setup, it is essential that for each `BKEY`, `FROM` dates are always unique, and `FROM` and `TO` intervals never overlap.

Now, instantiate the stream for the Type 2 table and kick off a simulated source load to prepare for the `MERGE` statement:

```
CREATE OR REPLACE STREAM strm_dim_customer_t2 ON TABLE dim_customer_t2;
EXECUTE TASK load_src_customer;
```

Updating a Type 2 table is done in two steps. First, we run a `MERGE` statement and update the changes like in a Type 1 load:

```
MERGE INTO dim_customer_t2 dc;
```

Notice here that the results and performance are identical to the Type 1 load so far:

```
201     MERGE INTO dim_customer_t2 dc
202     --get only latest records from src_customer. In a real-world scenario,
203     --create a view to get the latest records to make the logic leaner
```

| number of rows inserted | number of rows updated |
|---|---|
| 751 | 73 |

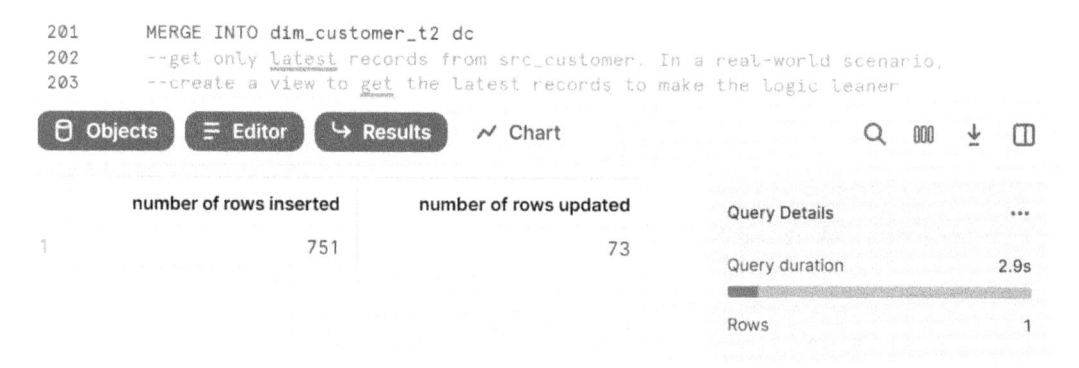

Query duration: 2.9s
Rows: 1

Figure 13.18 – Step 1 of a Type 2 load is identical to Type 1 in Figure 13.16

We have overwritten the current records with the latest values just like in a Type 1 load. Now comes the hard part: figuring out which *original* records were changed so that we can insert the before image and apply the correct FROM and TO dates. Luckily, thanks to the previously created stream, this can be done without lookups or window functions. The stream already contains the before-and-after images!

A sample record from the previous merge operation is displayed next. Bear in mind that under the hood, Snowflake is insert-only—it doesn't delete or update the records directly. Because of this, we can easily see the before image exactly as it appeared before the change:

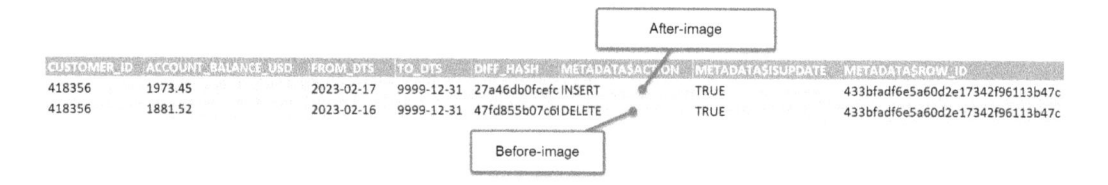

| CUSTOMER_ID | ACCOUNT_BALANCE_USD | FROM_DTS | TO_DTS | DIFF_HASH | METADATA$ACTION | METADATA$ISUPDATE | METADATA$ROW_ID |
|---|---|---|---|---|---|---|---|
| 418356 | 1973.45 | 2023-02-17 | 9999-12-31 | 27a46db0fcefc | INSERT | TRUE | 433bfadf6e5a60d2e17342f96113b47c |
| 418356 | 1881.52 | 2023-02-16 | 9999-12-31 | 47fd855b07c6l | DELETE | TRUE | 433bfadf6e5a60d2e17342f96113b47c |

Figure 13.19 – An updated record creates before-and-after images in a stream

Knowing this, we can insert the before images of all the changed records into the table in a single operation—without performance-intensive joins or updates:

```
INSERT INTO dim_customer_t2
    SELECT < stream columns > FROM strm_dim_customer_t2
    WHERE metadata$action = 'DELETE'
```

After the insert, notice that the number of rows inserted matches the rows updated in the previous step.

> **40% performance gain**
>
> The alternative to using streams for a Type 2 load is to use a temporary table. This approach, although still requiring two steps, involves slightly more logic and suffers from the performance penalty of writing to two separate tables. However, to demonstrate the effectiveness of the streams technique, a comparison with a dbt snapshot (snapshots are dbt's version of a Type 2 SCD) is included in the accompanying code. On the standard load (using 1,000 records) the performance of both methods was identical. However, when the record limit was removed and the full 1.5 million rows were processed, the streams technique was 40% faster. The dbt-generated DML and the results are included in the repository for this chapter.

To simplify the daily loading activity of a Type 2 table, the two-step loading process can be strung together as a series of sequential tasks that can be kicked off with a single command. The instructions for doing so are provided in the accompanying code.

Repeat the load operation using tasks, and when you are ready to move on to the Type 3 SCD, reset the SRC_CUSTOMER table to baseline and continue.

## Type 3 – one-time update

Creating a Type 3 attribute, relatively speaking, is a simple and inexpensive operation. The process involves altering the table to add an empty column and an update to set it equal to a base column. After that, keeping the Type 3 table up to date is identical to the method used in Type 1.

First, add the Type 3 column and set it to the baseline, like so:

```
ALTER TABLE dim_customer_t3 ADD COLUMN original_account_balance_usd
number(12,2);

UPDATE dim_customer_t3
    SET original_account_balance_usd = account_balance_usd;
```

With every insert, set the original column equal to the base column, and avoid updating it going forward. You can see the complete process in the accompanying code.

Having completed the exercise for a Type 3 dimension, we will wrap up the demonstration. As we saw in the first half of this chapter, the remaining SCDs either combine the techniques used in Types 1, 2, and 3 or rely on straightforward modeling practices that rely on basic DML commands.

## Summary

Due to the constantly changing nature of master data in the source system, the data warehouse must serve two critical functions to allow business users to pivot between current and historical attribute values in their reporting. These functions consist of capturing source system changes in a landing area and creating SCDs that meet the organization's reporting needs. Because master data plays such a key part in organizational analytics—often being tracked and scrutinized independently of fact records—learning to construct the required SCD structures and load them efficiently is a fundamental task for any data warehouse team.

In this chapter, we reviewed eight different SCD structures for meeting various analytical needs: from durable Type 0 attributes that never change to dynamic Type 7 configurations that can handle any requirement. Although many variations exist—even within SCD types—Types 1-3 are the most often used as they strike an acceptable balance between maintainability, performance, and reporting requirements.

Using the recipes provided in the accompanying SQL examples, this chapter explored the best practices for constructing SCDs by leveraging Snowflake-specific features such as streams, cloning, and hashing. As demonstrated, using native features such as streams can result in significant cost and performance savings compared to plain SQL methods.

Having understood dimensions, the following chapter will use the same approach to explore facts. Using best practices and Snowflake-only features, we will cover widely used techniques to keep fact tables up to date and enable change tracking and time-based rollups.

# 14
# Modeling Facts for Rapid Analysis

Fact tables are used to store the quantitative measurements of business operations or events such as sales, employee headcounts, or website traffic. Because they contain the official record of business transactions, fact tables are a prime target for operational analytics. Fact tables aggregate metrics such as sales totals and active users, as well as historical trends (deltas), such as the margin impact of daily returns or same-day bookings before cancelations.

Because business needs vary by industry and sector, various fact table models exist to fit these different demands. Facts such as product sales and returns are erratic, while others, such as manufacturing or fulfillment, follow a predictable pattern. The fact tables supporting such processes must anticipate not only the nature of the data they aim to capture but also the organization's analytical needs to allow for efficient reporting.

This chapter will cover the various fact table models and the industry use cases to which they are best suited. Most importantly, we will look at several Snowflake-driven patterns that can tackle some of the most common design challenges associated with fact tables in a cost-effective and low-maintenance manner.

In this chapter, we will cover the following main topics:

- Getting to know various fact table types
- Understanding the various types of measures or facts
- Reverse balance, the world's most versatile transactional fact table
- Recovering lost (physically deleted) facts
- Working with facts over points and ranges of time
- Snowflake recipes for building, maintaining, and querying each of these fact tables efficiently

## Technical requirements

The scripts used to instantiate and load the examples in this chapter are available in the following GitHub repo: https://github.com/PacktPublishing/Data-Modeling-with-Snowflake/tree/main/ch14. While the key section of each script will be explained in the latter half of this chapter, please refer to the repo for the complete code used to maintain and schedule the loading of the objects discussed, as it is too long to reprint here.

## Fact table types

By capturing the daily operational transactions of an organization, fact tables tend to contain large amounts of records that are constantly growing. By analyzing the data in fact tables, analysts and business users glean insights into business performance and identify trends and patterns. Considering these demands, fact tables must be designed in such a way that balances data loading efficiency with analytical needs and query patterns.

After nearly 20 years and three editions, the definitive guide to designing fact tables remains *The Data Warehouse Toolkit*. In it, authors Ralph Kimball and Margy Ross expertly cover the fundamentals of dimensional modeling, fact table design, and related industry case studies. This chapter will not attempt to replicate the content to which Kimball and Ross have dedicated nearly a quarter of their book. Instead, we will focus on what *The Data Warehouse Toolkit* does not cover: database-specific transformations for managing and maintaining fact tables in Snowflake in cost-efficient and analytically versatile ways. However, before jumping into Snowflake-specific recipes, an overview of fact table types and their various metrics is required.

Nearly every organization has some common analytical needs, such as obtaining operational totals through aggregations across business and temporal dimensions. However, differences in dimension types, such as time, geography, or product category, will drive design decisions that facilitate user-defined requirements such as drilling down or across or comparing historical records. To meet these needs, five basic fact table types have been identified:

- **Transaction fact tables** – These fact tables store information about individual transactions, such as sales or bookings. They typically have the most detailed level of information and the largest number of rows. Most organizations will use this type of fact table as the baseline for granular analysis, summarized aggregates, and generating the other types of fact tables in this list.

- **Snapshot fact tables** – These fact tables store information about a specific point in time, such as inventory levels or customer metrics at the end of a given period. They are usually updated on a regular basis, such as daily, weekly, or monthly. Snapshot fact tables do not contain granular information such as individual order details. Instead, snapshot tables provide predictably occurring slices of operational data, which can easily be compared due to their identical granularity. Snowflake's materialized views should be considered a maintenance-free way of maintaining snapshot tables using a transaction fact table as a source.

- **Accumulating snapshot fact tables** – These fact tables are similar to snapshot fact tables, but they track the progress of a process with predictable steps over time. They typically have a fixed set of milestones that reflect the stages of a fixed business process (e.g., the customer journey through a call center from receipt to resolution). Unlike other fact table types, in which records are only inserted and not updated (except to correct errors), accumulating fact tables contain milestone, status, and corresponding change-tracking columns, which receive updates as the underlying record changes.

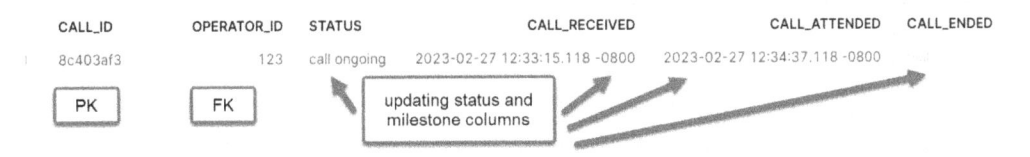

Figure 14.1 – A fact in progress in an accumulating snapshot table

- **Factless fact tables** – These fact tables do not contain any measures but are used to record events or transactions between dimensions, such as student enrollments in college courses.
- **Consolidated fact tables** – When separate but related facts share the same grain and need to be analyzed together, they are consolidated into a single fact table. Sales and sales forecasts are classic examples of consolidated facts that are analyzed side by side.

The choice of which type of fact table to use depends on the nature of the data being analyzed, the specific business requirements, and the performance and storage constraints of the **data warehouse** (**DWH**) platform. Just like **slowly changing dimension** (**SCD**) types, a DWH may combine the different fact table types to support various analytical needs.

Having seen the various types of fact table structures, we should familiarize ourselves with the different categories of measures they can contain. Understanding the kinds of measures will play an important role in creating the transformational logic required for maintaining them.

# Fact table measures

Numerical measures associated with a business transaction are called facts, and they fall into three basic categories:

- **Additive facts** – These are measures that can be summed across any dimension. Additive facts are the most common type of fact in a DWH, allowing for a wide variety of analytical calculations and insights. These values can be aggregated across any combination of dimensions, such as time, geography, or product. Examples of additive facts include sales revenue, profit, and quantity sold.

- **Semi-additive facts** – These are measures that can be summed across some dimensions but not all. These measures are usually numeric values that can only be aggregated across certain dimensions, such as customers or products. Examples of semi-additive facts include account balance and inventory levels, respectively. Semi-additive facts require special handling in data analysis to ensure that the aggregation is done correctly and does not spill over to non-compatible entity instances.

- **Non-additive facts** – These are measures that cannot be summed across any dimension. These measures are usually ratios, percentages, or other derived values that cannot be aggregated meaningfully. Examples of non-additive facts include the average price per unit or customer satisfaction score. Non-additive facts require special handling in data analysis and are typically used in more complex analytical calculations, such as forecasting or predictive modeling. In most cases, breaking non-additive facts into their fully additive components (e.g., the price and number of units instead of the average price per unit) is encouraged, as it gives users the flexibility to aggregate at any granularity and re-calculate the derived value.

Having understood the different types of fact tables and the measures they contain, we can look at the challenges involved in designing and maintaining fact tables, keeping in mind that where there's a challenge, there's a Snowflake feature to help overcome it.

## Getting the facts straight

The facts in a source system are recorded in real time and updated in case of adjustments. By definition, they are always current. A DWH has a much harder task because it needs to capture and report current facts and track historical changes. Suppose an order was adjusted from containing two items to one. The DWH must find a way to report that a change was made while avoiding the issue of double-counting (as the total quantity is now one, not three).

The task of historical tracking is made even more complicated when the facts are not point-in-time transactions but intervals such as advertising campaigns or employee hires and leavers. In such cases, tabulating the cost of a department can no longer be accomplished by simple aggregation because employees can come and go at various intervals.

Operating a business is messy and complex, and the data that it generates is no exception. Employees come and go, orders are returned, and in some cases, records in the source system may be physically deleted – leaving no artifact for the DWH to detect and reconcile.

In the following sections, we will address these age-old reporting challenges using versatile fact table designs incorporating unique Snowflake features to minimize the costs and required maintenance.

### The world's most versatile transactional fact table

When it comes to recording business transactions, capturing changes is often as important as their final states. For example, in online retail, being able to analyze the products that were removed from a shopping cart can yield valuable insight for understanding customer behavior and minimizing such actions in the future. However, tracking changes in a fact table presents a dual challenge: tying a changed record to its previous state and storing both without distorting the overall totals.

The following example shows a sales order placed on day one that suffers a change in the source system on day two and the resulting records that land in the DWH.

**Source System — ORDER**

| | ORDER_ID | PART_ID | QUANTITY | EXTENDED_PRICE_USD | DISCOUNT_PERCENT | RETURN_FLAG | ORDER_DATE |
|---|---|---|---|---|---|---|---|
| day 1 | ~~123~~ | ~~1~~ | ~~2~~ | ~~10.99~~ | ~~0.01~~ | ~~N~~ | ~~2020-01-01~~ |
| day 2 | 123 | 1 | 3 | 15.99 | 0.02 | N | 2020-01-01 |

**DWH landing — RAW.SRC_ORDER**

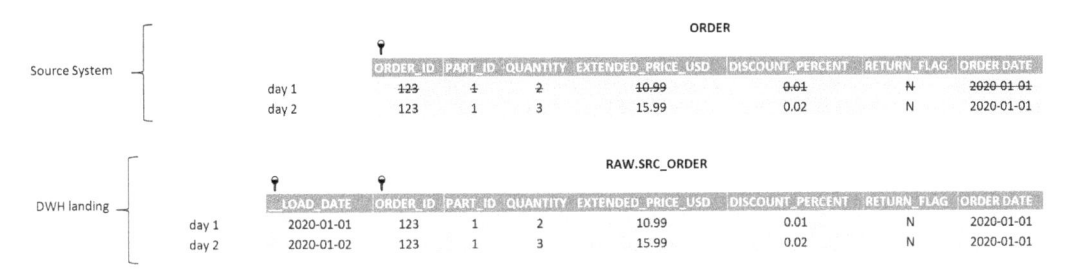

| | LOAD_DATE | ORDER_ID | PART_ID | QUANTITY | EXTENDED_PRICE_USD | DISCOUNT_PERCENT | RETURN_FLAG | ORDER_DATE |
|---|---|---|---|---|---|---|---|---|
| day 1 | 2020-01-01 | 123 | 1 | 2 | 10.99 | 0.01 | N | 2020-01-01 |
| day 2 | 2020-01-02 | 123 | 1 | 3 | 15.99 | 0.02 | N | 2020-01-01 |

Figure 14.2 – Facts in the source and DWH landing area

While the record in the source system is overwritten by the update, the DWH captures both versions. However, it is difficult to answer even simple business questions by looking at the RAW table. What is the total number of parts sold? (Three, not five.) How many parts were sold on day two? (One, not three.)

To help the business answer these (and many other) questions, we can use a fact table design known as reverse balance or mirror image. The reverse balance method yields a fact table that can answer virtually any business question using aggregation (the operation for which OLAP systems are optimized). As the name suggests, in a reverse balance structure, a change is performed by inserting not one but two records; one that contains the new values, and another that negates the original (the reverse balance). The result in our example would appear as follows, containing (from top to bottom) the original value, its reverse balance, and the updated value:

**DWH reporting — ORDER_REVERSE_BALANCE**

(additive measures) / (non-additive measure)

| | ASAT_DATE | IS_AFTERIMAGE | ORDER_ID | PART_ID | QUANTITY | EXTENDED_PRICE_USD | DISCOUNT_PERCENT | RETURN_FLAG | ORDER_DATE |
|---|---|---|---|---|---|---|---|---|---|
| day 1 | 2020-01-01 | TRUE | 123 | 1 | 2 | 10.99 | 0.01 | N | 2020-01-01 |
| day 2 | 2020-01-02 | FALSE | 123 | 1 | -2 | -10.99 | 0.01 | N | 2020-01-01 |
| | 2020-01-02 | TRUE | 123 | 1 | 3 | 15.99 | 0.02 | N | 2020-01-01 |

Figure 14.3 – A reverse balance fact table used for reporting

The reverse balance table resembles the raw table with a few key differences:

- The landing table load date becomes an as-at date, indicating when a given version of a fact is valid.

- A before/after-image indicator (IS_AFTERIMAGE, in this example) is added. The after-image flag distinguishes the reverse image (middle row) from the after-image (third row) and is therefore included in the primary key.

This approach makes it easy to answer the prior business questions:

```
--total number of parts sold
SELECT SUM(quantity) FROM lineitem_reverse_balance

-- parts sold on day two (delta)
SELECT SUM(quantity) FROM order_reverse_balance
    WHERE asat_date = '2020-01-02'
```

In addition, the as-at date makes it possible to observe historical facts as they appeared at that point in time. For example, what is the number of parts sold as is on day one versus day two?

```
-- parts sold on first of Jan as at day one
SELECT SUM(quantity) FROM order_reverse_balance
    WHERE order_date = '2020-01-01'
    AND asat_date= '2020-01-01'
    AND is_afterimage = TRUE

-- parts sold on first of Jan as at day two
SELECT SUM(quantity) FROM order_reverse_balance
    WHERE order_date = '2020-01-01'
    AND asat_date= '2020-01-02'
    AND is_afterimage = TRUE
```

Using this method, analysts can quickly aggregate and compare totals, deltas, point-in-time snapshots, and year-end totals as they appear today or at any point in the past. Later in this chapter, we will review an efficient technique for constructing and maintaining a reverse image fact table in Snowflake. The only thing we require is the updated record to be loaded in the landing area. Unfortunately, the data quality in some source systems is less than ideal and records are physically deleted instead of being canceled or corrected. Luckily, the DWH can look back in time and recover deleted records to align them with the source.

## The leading method for recovering deleted records

In a perfect world, records are never physically deleted in the source system. Instead, they should be nullified *logically* by marking them with a *deleted* flag and setting the measures to zero, but as we know, the world is not perfect, and records are occasionally removed. Deletions are not a grave problem in dimension tables because a quick aggregation from the landing area table can produce and identify the latest active and deleted entries:

```
SELECT < dimension PK >
, MAX(load_date) AS latest_load_date
, IFF(latest_load_date = current_date, false, true) AS is_deleted
    FROM src_dimension
    group by < dimension PK >
```

This is to say: in a full daily load, any records that don't exist but have been loaded previously must have been deleted.

Facts pose a greater challenge because they occur at a precise point in time and are typically too numerous to be loaded and compared using full loads. Instead, facts are typically loaded and processed as delta snapshots – containing only changes and updates that occurred since the previous load.

Whether using a reverse balance fact table or any alternative, the issue of orphaned records arises when the DWH is not informed of a deleted fact. In the following example, an order was placed for two parts on day one. On day two, the number of units for part one was increased to 20, but part 2 was (improperly) canceled by a physical deletion of the record.

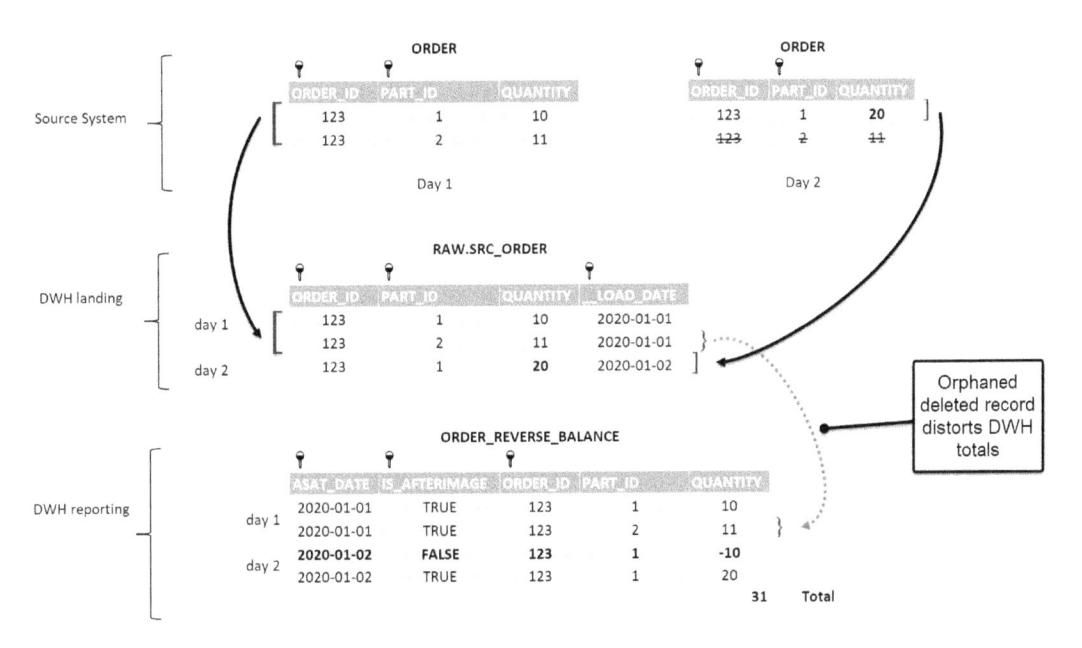

Figure 14.4 – A physical deletion in the source system

Physical deletion is a quick (and tempting) way to adjust data in the source system because there, it poses no risk to data accuracy (as of day two, the system correctly reflects the order for 20 units of part 1). However, the DWH is not informed of the change and is now out of sync with the official source of truth.

Unlike dimension entities, looking backward to detect and rectify deleted records in a DWH is a resource-intensive task that usually involves aggregates, temporary tables, window functions over large datasets, and comparisons. However, by turning the process on its head and looking forward, we can drastically reduce the processing resources necessary to identify and revert deleted changes.

The basic concept of the forward-leading-insertion method is to insert (and logically delete) the physically deleted record into the next load date in the raw/landing table. Let's say that an order is created on day one containing three parts. A part is subsequently deleted for days two and three. *Figure 14.5* illustrates the result of running the process on the DWH landing area table.

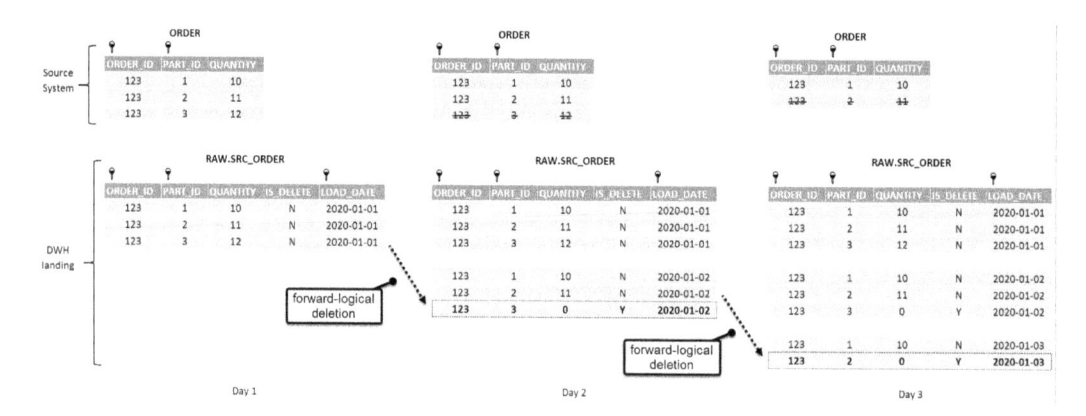

Figure 14.5 – Logically recreating deleted records in the DWH landing area

The logical deletion process aims to mark the physical deletion as it happened in a point-in-time snapshot. Therefore, the logically deleted record is inserted once and not passed down to future load dates, as can be seen with `PART_ID` 3 on day *two*.

In the second half of this chapter, we will write the script that will allow us to perform this operation for an entire fact table or restrict it to a single load date to economize DWH credits for a daily load. However, there is one more fact table scenario that we must learn to handle first: range-based facts.

For range-based facts such as employee active periods or promo campaigns, a single as-at date is insufficient, and a mix of intervals is required. Knowing how to construct a fact table to handle such records efficiently can save developers from writing some truly grisly analytical queries down the line.

## Type 2 slowly changing facts

While some business operations occur at a given moment, such as sales, others, such as contracts, endure for a length of time. Complex business data and factless fact tables often blur the line between facts and dimensions. Take, for example, the `EMPLOYEE` table, which may be used as a dimension when reporting store sales, but also as a fact when analyzing the **operational expenses** (**OPEX**) of a given department (e.g., a salary multiplied by the percentage of active service during a given period). In the latter scenario, analytics can be tricky.

For example, a start-up hires two employees at the start of 2020 – a contractor, Larry, due to leave in 4 months, and a full-time employee, Lisa. In June, as the lone active employee in the company, Lisa is given a raise. The source and DWH snapshots in January and June would look as follows:

## Getting the facts straight | 225

|  | EMPLOYEE | | | | | EMPLOYEE | | | | |
|---|---|---|---|---|---|---|---|---|---|---|
| Source System | EMPLOYEE_ID | Name | START_DATE | END_DATE | Salary | EMPLOYEE_ID | PRODUCT | START_DATE | END_DATE | Salary |
| | 123 | Larry | 2020-01-01 | 2020-03-31 | 50,000 | 123 | Larry | 2020-01-01 | 2020-03-31 | 50,000 |
| | 456 | Lisa | 2020-01-01 | 9999-12-31 | 50,000 | 456 | Lisa | 2020-01-01 | 9999-12-31 | ~~50,000~~ 100,000 |

|  | SRC_EMPLOYEE | | | | | | SRC_EMPLOYEE | | | | | |
|---|---|---|---|---|---|---|---|---|---|---|---|---|
| DWH landing | EMPLOYEE_ID | Name | START_DATE | END_DATE | Salary | LOAD_DATE | EMPLOYEE_ID | Name | START_DATE | END_DATE | Salary | LOAD_DATE |
| | 123 | Larry | 2020-01-01 | 2020-03-31 | 50,000 | 2020-01-01 | 123 | Larry | 2020-01-01 | 2020-03-31 | 50,000 | 2020-01-01 |
| | 456 | Lisa | 2020-01-01 | 9999-12-31 | 50,000 | 2020-01-01 | 456 | Lisa | 2020-01-01 | 9999-12-31 | 50,000 | 2020-01-01 |
| | | | | | | | 456 | Lisa | 2020-01-01 | 9999-12-31 | 100,000 | 2020-06-01 |

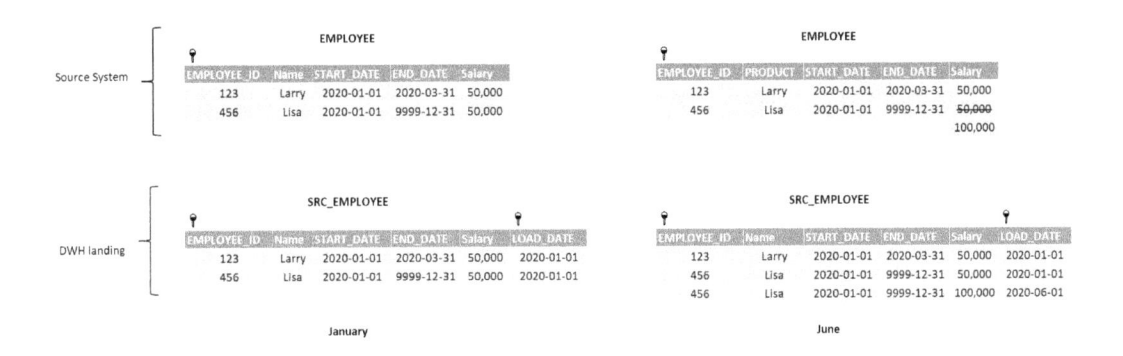

January / June

Figure 14.6 – Records with duration intervals in the source system and DWH landing area

With an eye toward tracking costs, the company's owners wish to know the exact OPEX costs of keeping the company running. They need a fact table allowing them to generate the figures as they appear in the following figure:

**Cumulated Employee Costs for 2020**

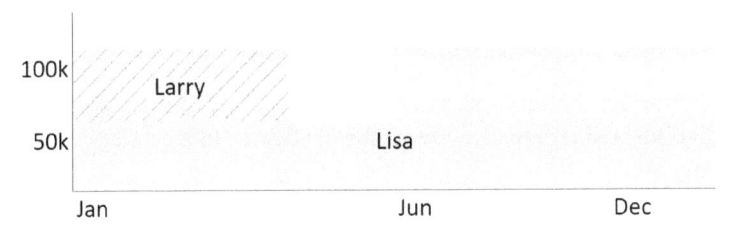

100k — Larry
50k — Lisa
Jan — Jun — Dec

Figure 14.7 – Cumulated Employee Costs for 2020

The solution is to use the Type 2 SCD structure covered in the previous chapter. Storing employee data in a Type 2 table allows you to query date intervals at a point in time and at any effective date or date range.

A Type 2 fact table for this example would contain the following data:

| SRC_EMPLOYEE | | | | | | | | |
|---|---|---|---|---|---|---|---|---|
| EMPLOYEE_ID | Name | START_DATE | END_DATE | Salary | FROM_DATE | TO_DATE | DIFF_HASH |
| 123 | Larry | 2020-01-01 | 2020-03-31 | 50,000 | 1900-01-01 | 9999-12-31 | sd9f87gr |
| 456 | Lisa | 2020-01-01 | 9999-12-31 | 50,000 | 1900-01-01 | 2020-05-31 | 9sbf89g6 |
| 456 | Lisa | 2020-01-01 | 9999-12-31 | 100,000 | 2020-06-01 | 9999-12-31 | h3ghm2vf |

Figure 14.8 – A Type 2 table for employee data

A surrogate low-date such as the one in the FROM_DATE column is often used, as it allows users to identify original/unmodified versions of a record. Otherwise, the creation date can be used instead. Having the data in this format allows us to write a query to answer the OPEX question without having to use window functions or compare records:

```
SELECT name
 , IFF (start_date > from_date, start_date, from_date) AS query_from_date
 , IFF (end_date < to_date, end_date, to_date) AS query_to_date
 , salary
     FROM employee
     WHERE TRUE
     AND start_date <= '2020-01-01'
     AND end_date >= '2020-12-31'
```

This simple example uses only one time band (employee start/end date) besides the meta from_date/to_date columns. However, in the real world, entities may contain multiple date ranges and sets of additive, semi-additive, and non-additive measures. For example, a contract may have the following date attributes – service start/end, creation, modification, signing, authorization, release, renewal, review, and many others – which the business teams may wish to interrogate. The Type 2 structure, as we will see in the practice section in this chapter, allows us to easily obtain counts, aggregates, and snapshots for any date range or measure required by the business.

Having seen the approaches that need to be taken to meet some of the most frequent fact table challenges, let us dive into and explore the code that will allow us to meet these with minimal effort and WH credit usage.

## Maintaining fact tables using Snowflake features

In this section, we will practice creating and maintaining the fact table techniques discussed previously using available Snowflake features. Like in previous chapters, we will load data from the snowflake_sample_data.tpch_sf10 schema, which will serve as the sample set. We will then simulate source system updates by randomly loading records from this sample.

The first two exercises will use data from the LINEITEM table. To continue, create a schema to house the exercises from this chapter and instantiate the source system table, as well as the DWH landing area.

Open the first file in this chapter's repository, ch_14.1_reverse_balance_fact.sql, and run the first three steps:

```
CREATE OR REPLACE SCHEMA ch14_facts;
CREATE OR REPLACE TABLE source_system_lineitem ...;
CREATE OR REPLACE TABLE src_lineitem ...;
```

These examples require `lineitem` orders to be loaded and processed in their entirety (containing all constituent line items for a given order). To accomplish this, order IDs are first selected at random from the sample set, and then all related line items are loaded:

```
WITH complete_orders AS (
    SELECT DISTINCT sales_order_id
    FROM source_system_lineitem SAMPLE (< N > rows)
)
SELECT < source columns > FROM source_system_lineitem src
    INNER JOIN complete_orders co ON     src.sales_order_id = co.sales_order_id
```

Let's begin by constructing the model for a reverse balance fact table and building a script to load it using a merge/insert strategy using Streams.

## Building a reverse balance fact table with Streams

While querying a reverse balance fact table is simple, traditional databases have often run into performance constraints when attempting to maintain one. This is due to the difficulty of isolating the previous version of a change (to create the reverse balance). This operation typically requires temporary tables and window functions to lag and compare the same business key across various load dates. However, using Snowflake Streams, we can generate the reverse balance by simply negating the additive measures in the before-image of an updated record – a massive performance improvement over the traditional method. This is a similar strategy to the one used in the previous chapter for Type 2 SCDs.

Let's continue with the exercise from the file (`ch_14.1_reverse_balance_fact.sql`) we started with.

After cloning `src_lineitem` as a backup for re-running the exercise, let's create the structure of the reverse balance table and populate it with an initial dataset (before any changes occur):

```
CREATE OR REPLACE TABLE lineitem_rb ...;
```

Note the characteristic columns that this type of table requires:

- **Load type** – An optional but useful metadata column that identifies the type of change in a record. The values in this column are user-defined to fit the nature of the data and the types of changes that occur. Our example uses values of *initial* and *update* to distinguish between newly created and updated records. The exercise on recovering deleted records will use this field to mark *deletion* records.

- **As-at date** – Although its value is equivalent to the load date, the term as-at paints a clear picture of the column's function – identifying the state of a fact at any point in time. Although facts are typically loaded daily, requiring a date type for this column, our example is meant to be run multiple times per day, so a timestamp is used instead.

- **Before/after-image flag** – This field is used to split out an update into the new version and its reverse balance. As such, it must be included in the primary key of the table (in addition to the as-at date and the business key).

With the reverse balance table created, create a Stream to handle the upcoming changes:

```
CREATE OR replace STREAM strm_lineitem_rb ON TABLE lineitem_rb;
```

Now, simulate a load from the source system, which will include new records, as well as updates to ones already loaded:

```
INSERT INTO src_lineitem ...;
```

Now, merge the newly loaded records into the reverse balance table using its primary key. Our example assumes only new and updated records and can't contain existing line items with no changes. If this were the case, use `diff_hash` to determine whether an existing record does indeed constitute a change:

```
MERGE INTO lineitem_rb rb ...;
```

The result of the merge will insert new orders and update existing orders, and it is the update that concerns us. Because we overwrote the original order values, we now have to insert the previous version, and its reverse balance. The process is illustrated in the following diagram:

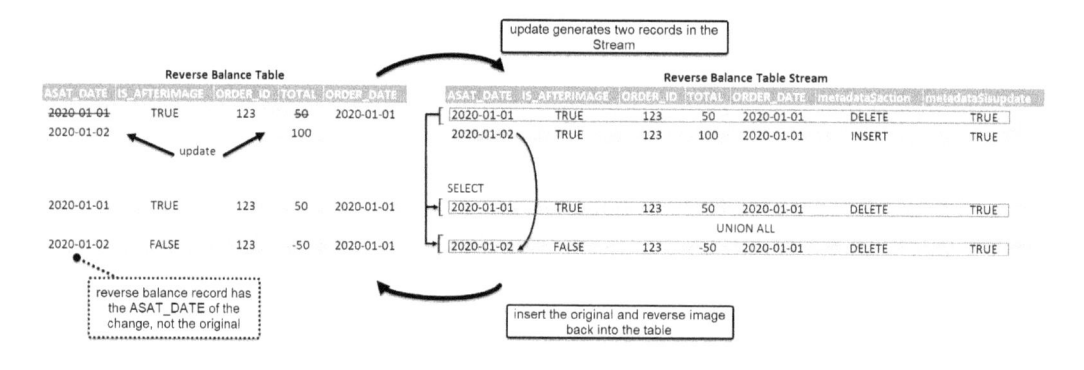

Figure 14.9 – A reverse balance is created from a Stream update action

As we need to generate two records (the original and reverse-balanced one) from a single record in the Stream, we can use a CTE to select the row once and insert it twice using `UNION ALL`. As demonstrated in *Figure 14.9*, the original record is inserted as it appears in the Stream, while the following modifications must be made to the reverse image:

- The as-at date is that of the latest record, not the original
- The before/after-image flag is marked as before
- Additive and semi-additive measures are multiplied by -1

When you run the insert from the Stream (`INSERT INTO lineitem_rb ... ;`), observe where these operations take place:

```
INSERT INTO lineitem_rb
    WITH before_records AS (
       SELECT *, asat_after FROM strm_lineitem_rb
       WHERE metadata$action = 'DELETE'
    )
--insert the original after image that we updated
--no changes required to column values
SELECT < stream fields > FROM   before_records
UNION ALL
--insert the before image as at after dts, but negate additive
measures
SELECT < stream fields >
, asat_after as ASAT_DTS --USE the asat OF the AFTER image
, FALSE as IS_AFTERIMAGE --because this IS the BEFORE image
, -1 * quantity
, -1 * extended_price_usd
, discount_percent --do NOT negate, non-additive measure
    FROM   before_records;
```

Now that the reverse balance table has been fully updated, select an *update* record to verify and inspect the result. A sample `lineitem` update should generate three records, as in the following screenshot:

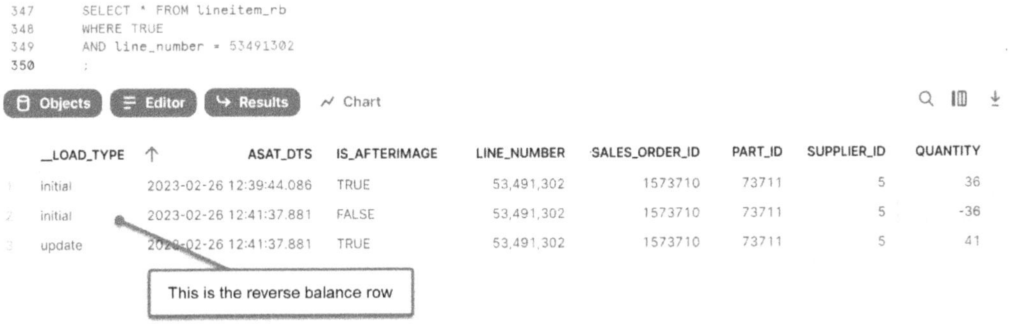
347 SELECT * FROM lineitem_rb
348 WHERE TRUE
349 AND line_number = 53491302
350 ;
Objects
Editor
Results
Chart
_LOAD_TYPE ASAT_DTS IS_AFTERIMAGE LINE_NUMBER SALES_ORDER_ID PART_ID SUPPLIER_ID QUANTITY
1 initial 2023-02-26 12:39:44.086 TRUE 53,491,302 1573710 73711 5 36
2 initial 2023-02-26 12:41:37.881 FALSE 53,491,302 1573710 73711 5 -36
3 update 02-26 12:41:37.881 TRUE 53,491,302 1573710 73711 5 41
This is the reverse balance row

Figure 14.10 – An update to a reverse balance record results in two new records

The reverse balance fact table is a powerful tool because it allows us to query the state of truth as it appeared on any date. For example, in sales or reservations, a registered transaction may still be canceled in the future, but the as-at date gives us a simple filter with which to travel back in time to observe historical records as they appear today, or at any point in the past. In the following example, we can query last year's bookings as they appear today (with cancelations) and as they appeared last year (before this year's cancelations):

```
--last year bookings with future cancelations
SELECT sum(sales)
    FROM bookings
    WHERE booking_date = <LAST_YEAR>
    AND asat_date <= <TODAY> --implicit

--last year bookings without future cancelations
SELECT sum(sales)
    FROM reservations
    WHERE booking_date = <LAST_YEAR>
    AND asat_date <= <LAST_YEAR>
```

Now that we have a working fact table, we will demonstrate how to detect and recover physically deleted records to set the correct balance in the landing area, so that the fact table perceives the event.

## Recovering deleted records with leading load dates

This exercise will build on the objects created in the reverse balance example. Open the `ch_14.2_deleted_records.sql` file from the repository to get started.

First, use the backups from the previous example to reset the source objects to their initial state:

```
CREATE OR REPLACE TABLE src_lineitem CLONE src_lineitem_bak;
CREATE OR REPLACE TABLE lineitem_rb CLONE lineitem_rb_bak;
CREATE OR replace STREAM strm_lineitem_rb ON TABLE lineitem_rb;
```

Now, we will simulate order updates that contain deleted records by filtering out line numbers ending in any number less than three. Run `INSERT INTO` for the source table:

```
INSERT INTO src_lineitem ...;
```

Now comes the task of detecting and recovering the deletions. Although this can be done as a single operation, this example has split the process out using temporary tables to allow for testing and debugging.

The first step is taking the orders in the current load and building a structure that contains the primary key of the parent object (`sales_order_id`) and the corresponding load dates and using the `LEAD` window function to obtain the next parent object load date. Build the temporary table using the following command and observe the result:

```
CREATE OR REPLACE TEMPORARY TABLE line_load_hist ...;
```

This generates a structure of today's order IDs with corresponding and leading load dates:

Maintaining fact tables using Snowflake features    231

| | Today's orders | Corresponding load date | LEAD to get the next load date |
|---|---|---|---|
| | SALES_ORDER_ID | _LDTS | NEXT_ORDER_LOAD_DT |
| 1 | 1958222 | 2023-02-26 12:39:44.086 | 2023-02-27 07:02:33.630 |
| 2 | 130962 | 2023-02-26 12:39:44.086 | 2023-02-27 07:02:33.630 |
| 3 | 154079 | 2023-02-26 12:39:44.086 | 2023-02-27 07:02:33.630 |
| 4 | 623246 | 2023-02-26 12:39:44.086 | 2023-02-27 07:02:33.630 |
| 5 | 1182475 | 2023-02-26 12:39:44.086 | 2023-02-27 07:02:33.630 |

Figure 14.11 – A temporary structure of parent primary keys and corresponding load dates

Knowing the current and leading load dates for the order IDs, we can now do the same for the associated line numbers. Run the temporary `line_deletions` table by running the following command:

```
CREATE OR REPLACE TEMPORARY TABLE line_deletions ...;
```

By inner-joining the line number with the previously created list of order IDs and load dates, we are able to dramatically reduce the number of records that needs to be processed using the LEAD window function. Having done so, deleted line items can be identified because they do not have a leading load date when we look forward. A sample deleted record would look like this:

| NEXT_ORDER_LOAD_DT | NEXT_LINE_LOAD_DT | ... | _LDTS | SALES_ORDER_ID | LINE_NUMBER | _LOAD_TYPE |
|---|---|---|---|---|---|---|
| 2023-02-27 07:02:33.630 | (null) | | 2023-02-26 12:39:44.086 | 1958222 | 3,676,900 | initial |

*If it existed previously, but not currently, it is a deleted record*

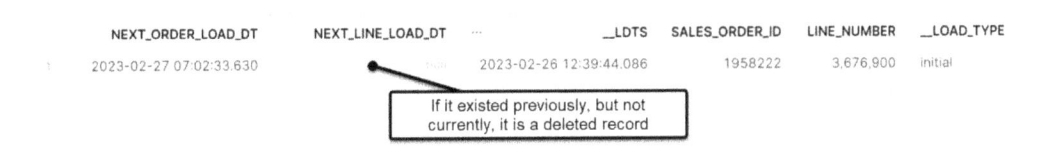

Figure 14.12 – A temporary structure of full primary keys and corresponding load dates

Now that we have identified the deleted records and when they were last loaded, we can insert from the source table, zeroing out the additive measures. Run the following statement to *logically* delete the missing records:

```
INSERT INTO src_lineitem...;
```

Observe that during this process, we zero out the additive measures and use the LEAD load date that we obtained for the missing record. Also, it is essential to create a flag that identifies a logically deleted record for the following reasons:

- We need to use it to avoid re-inserting logically deleted records in the future (as they won't exist in any subsequent load either)
- We need to have a way to reconcile with the source system if asked why there are more records in the DWH

## Modeling Facts for Rapid Analysis

This is all handled during `INSERT`, as seen here:

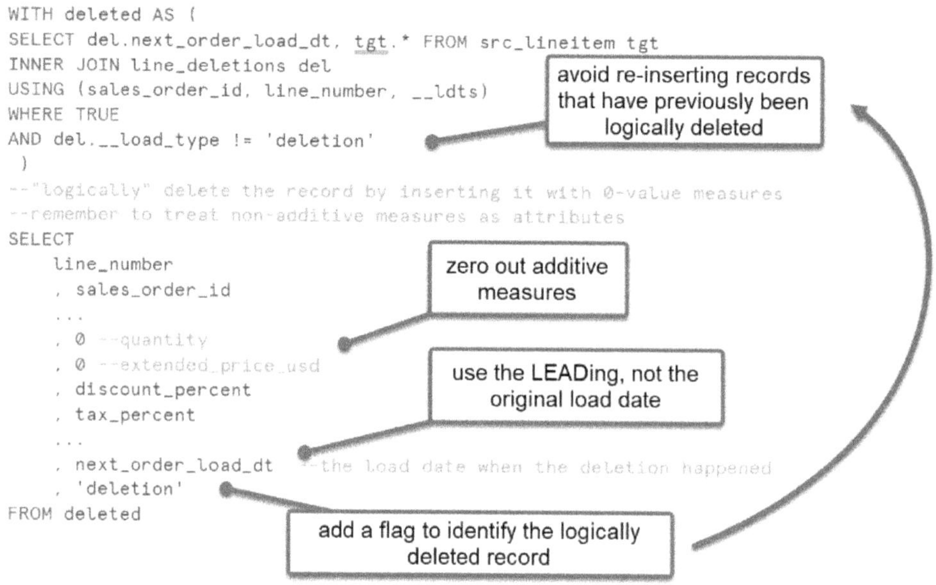

```
WITH deleted AS (
SELECT del.next_order_load_dt, tgt.* FROM src_lineitem tgt
INNER JOIN line_deletions del
USING (sales_order_id, line_number, __ldts)
WHERE TRUE
AND del.__load_type != 'deletion'
)
--"logically" delete the record by inserting it with 0-value measures
--remember to treat non-additive measures as attributes
SELECT
    line_number
    , sales_order_id
    ...
    , 0 --quantity
    , 0 --extended_price_usd
    , discount_percent
    , tax_percent
    ...
    , next_order_load_dt   --the load date when the deletion happened
    , 'deletion'
FROM deleted
```

Annotations:
- avoid re-inserting records that have previously been logically deleted
- zero out additive measures
- use the LEADing, not the original load date
- add a flag to identify the logically deleted record

Figure 14.13 – Inserting a logically deleted record

Now that the missing records have been re-inserted as logical deletions, we can observe the impact on the fact table by loading it as in the previous example. Note that although this example used a reverse balance fact table, logical deletions must be performed in the landing area to avoid distorting the totals regardless of the type of fact table used. Load the fact table by running the two commands discussed previously:

```
MERGE INTO lineitem_rb rb...;
INSERT INTO lineitem_rb...;
```

The fact table has now been updated to allow us to aggregate as-at totals correctly. A sample deletion would generate two records to net out the original as seen here:

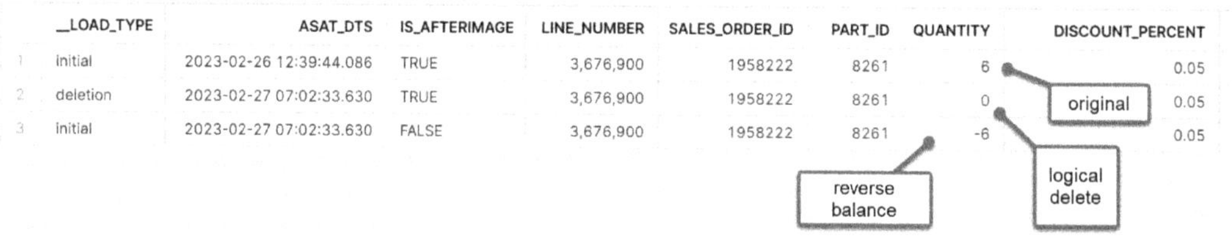

| | _LOAD_TYPE | ASAT_DTS | IS_AFTERIMAGE | LINE_NUMBER | SALES_ORDER_ID | PART_ID | QUANTITY | DISCOUNT_PERCENT |
|---|---|---|---|---|---|---|---|---|
| 1 | initial | 2023-02-26 12:39:44.086 | TRUE | 3,676,900 | 1958222 | 8261 | 6 | 0.05 |
| 2 | deletion | 2023-02-27 07:02:33.630 | TRUE | 3,676,900 | 1958222 | 8261 | 0 | 0.05 |
| 3 | initial | 2023-02-27 07:02:33.630 | FALSE | 3,676,900 | 1958222 | 8261 | -6 | 0.05 |

Annotations: reverse balance; original; logical delete

Figure 14.14 – A logically deleted record in the fact table

Adjust the example parameters to repeat the exercise to see how new records and deletions on top of already deleted line items impact the final fact table.

Having covered point-in-time fact tables and how to treat possible deletions, we will move on to an example that teaches us how to maintain and interrogate interval-based facts.

## Handling time intervals in a Type 2 fact table

In this exercise, we will experiment with employee data that simulates the daily operations of an active business: hiring/terminating employees, adjusting salaries, and balancing headcounts between fixed-term contractors and full-time employees. Open the `ch_14.3_type2_facts.sql` file from the chapter repo to get started.

As the sample data contains records from within the range 1992-1998, we will use a variable to set *today's* date to *1995-12-01* to allow us to load the historical data for *existing* employees, and also give us plenty of sample data for *future* changes:

```
SET today = '1995-12-01';
```

Now, instantiate the sample dataset for the simulated source system and the initial DWH landing area:

```
CREATE OR REPLACE TABLE source_system_employee...;
CREATE OR REPLACE TABLE src_employee...;
```

In creating the initial tables, we can use the `today` variable, just as we would use the `current_date()` function in a real-world scenario.

Next, we create the Type 2 fact table using the method described in the previous chapter:

```
CREATE OR REPLACE TABLE employee_t2 ...;
```

Note that we will use the surrogate low/high dates of `1900-01-01` and `9999-12-31` for the meta `from_date`/`to_date` fields, respectively.

With the Type 2 table created, we will increment the `today` variable by one and start to insert changes into the landing area: new hires, terminations, and promotions for some existing employees:

```
SET today = $today::date+1;
INSERT INTO src_employee...;
```

Unlike the reverse balance fact table, a Type 2 fact table does not discriminate between additive and non-additive measures – it updates all changes accordingly and creates a new effectively dated record.

Update the fact table with the latest records:

```
MERGE INTO employee_t2 tgt...;
INSERT INTO employee_t2...;
```

Now, increment the `today` variable and simulate several more days of changes to generate some meaningful data to query. Once several load dates have been added, we can begin to ask business questions about our organization's headcounts.

The surrogate high date will always return the latest version of a fact, so we can use it as a filter when asking questions about the current state of the company, such as *how many employees are currently active?*

```
--currently active employees
SELECT COUNT(*) cnt FROM employee_t2
    WHERE TRUE
    AND is_active
    AND to_date = '9999-12-31';    --currently
```

What about at a point in the past? Here, we must consider a range of dates: records with an effective date valid before the target date, and after. For example, a contractor with a start-to-end range of 1994-12-01 to 1995-12-31 should match the target date that we're interested in (1995-12-01):

```
--active employees on day 1995-12-01
SELECT COUNT(DISTINCT employee_id) cnt
    FROM employee_t2
    WHERE TRUE
    AND is_active
    AND from_date <= '1995-12-01'
    AND to_date >= '1995-12-01' ;
```

Instead of a point in time, the query can use a range as well, for example, to calculate (without double-counting changes) the number of active employees for the entire year of 1995:

```
--active employees in all of 1995
SELECT COUNT(DISTINCT employee_id) cnt FROM employee_t2
    WHERE TRUE
    AND is_active
    AND YEAR(from_date) <= 1995
    AND YEAR(to_date) >= 1995 ;
```

Using various time criteria, we can mix current and historical values to ask targeted questions such as *who was hired in Q1 1994 last year and was still active on the date of 1995-12-01?*

```
--active employees on day 1995-12-01
--who were hired in Q1 of 1994
SELECT COUNT(DISTINCT employee_id) cnt
```

```
    FROM employee_t2
    WHERE TRUE
    AND is_active
    AND hire_date BETWEEN '1994-01-01' AND '1994-03-31'
    AND from_date <= '1995-12-01'
    AND to_date >= '1995-12-01';
```

Yes, but now, only show me those who received a promotion. We can query this table, adding ever more complex criteria:

```
--active employees on day 1995-12-01
--who were hired in Q1 of 1994
--and received a promotion
WITH promotions AS (
    SELECT DISTINCT employee_id FROM employee_t2
    WHERE TRUE
    AND last_change = 'Promoted' )
    SELECT COUNT(DISTINCT employee_id) cnt
    FROM employee_t2
    INNER JOIN promotions USING (employee_id)
    WHERE TRUE
    AND is_active
    AND hire_date BETWEEN '1994-01-01' AND '1994-03-31'
    AND from_date <= '1995-12-01'
    AND to_date >= '1995-12-01';
```

Whether it's capturing distinct groupings by date – as seen in the following example – or aggregating totals over a range of dates, the Type 2 fact table can handle any range-based query that users throw at it:

```
--what are the total changes per day by change type
--since the first load ( excluding 1995-12-01)
SELECT from_date, last_change,  COUNT( employee_id) cnt
    FROM employee_t2
    WHERE TRUE
    AND from_date > '1995-12-01'
    AND to_date = '9999-12-31'   --currently
    GROUP BY 1,2
    ORDER BY 1,2;
```

The following screenshot shows the result of daily headcount movements since we started the exercise:

```
--what are the total changes per day by change type
--since the first load ( excluding 1995-12-01)
SELECT from_date, last_change, COUNT( employee_id) cnt
FROM employee_t2
WHERE TRUE
AND from_date > '1995-12-01'
AND to_date = '9999-12-31'  --currently
GROUP BY 1,2
ORDER BY 1,2;
```

| FROM_DATE | LAST_CHANGE | CNT |
|---|---|---|
| 1995-12-02 | Hire | 100 |
| 1995-12-02 | Leaver | 41 |
| 1995-12-02 | Promoted | 109 |
| 1995-12-03 | Hire | 100 |
| 1995-12-03 | Leaver | 40 |
| 1995-12-03 | Promoted | 110 |

Figure 14.14 – Querying a range of dates from a Type 2 fact table

When facts pivot around several different dates and date ranges, a Type 2 configuration is the ideal table structure to take advantage of the performance of aggregate functions for a columnar database such as Snowflake.

## Summary

In a DWH, fact tables present an additional challenge on top of merely capturing the latest values – they must also be able to capture and reconcile historical changes in a way that allows users to flexibly and cost-effectively query them to resolve business questions, because when it comes to operational analytics, analyzing changes, variations, and what didn't happen can be just as valuable as the current state of truth.

Various types of fact tables exist to help an organization meet these demanding analytical needs, such as transactional, snapshot, and accumulating snapshot fact tables, among others. These fact tables must differentiate between the various kinds of measures they store (e.g., additive, semi-additive, and non-additive) because each is treated differently when updating or recording changes.

To help data teams construct and maintain these tables in Snowflake, this chapter dissected some of the toughest challenges in maintaining fact tables in a DWH and came up with cost-effective recipes for learning to tackle the challenges using Snowflake-native features. Even if you don't encounter these exact scenarios in your work, the concepts and features demonstrated in these examples will surely provide a sound first-principles framework that can be applied to similar situations.

Having tackled the traditional elements of relational databases, such as facts and dimensions, we will focus on semi-structured data in the next chapter, to see how elegantly Snowflake allows users to handle it with table-like performance.

# 15
# Modeling Semi-Structured Data

So far, this book has focused on modeling structured data, the kind used in relational databases since the early 70s. However, with the rise of the internet, a different style of data became prevalent: semi-structured. Semi-structured data, such as website traffic and social media feeds, contain some organizational structure but do not conform to the formal structure of a relational database.

New file formats also emerged to support this new type of data, starting with the advent of **Extensible Markup Language (XML)** in the early 2000s, followed by **JavaScript Object Notation (JSON)**, and, with the rise of distributed computing, formats such as Avro, ORC, and Parquet. These formats offered a lightweight and flexible way to structure data, making them ideal for web-based and mobile app data.

The popularity of semi-structured data can be attributed to its flexibility, adaptability, and ability to handle data sources that do not fit neatly into traditional relational databases. As a modern cloud data platform, Snowflake is capable of natively ingesting semi-structured data, storing it efficiently, and accessing it using simple extensions to standard SQL.

However, to consumers of semi-structured data, the challenge of wrangling nested entities and establishing meaningful relationships remains. This chapter will explore the tools that Snowflake offers to make working with semi-structured data easy. Using these tools, we will learn how to analyze and deconstruct semi-structured data into a relational model that BI tools and traditional analytics can consume.

In this chapter, we will cover the following main topics:

- The benefits of semi-structured data
- How Snowflake makes working with semi-structured data easy
- The flexibility of schema-on-read
- Techniques for flattening semi-structured data into rows
- The benefits of transforming semi-structured data into a relational schema
- A rule-based method for transforming semi-structured data into relational data

# Technical requirements

The scripts used to instantiate and load the examples in this chapter are available in the following GitHub repo: https://github.com/PacktPublishing/Data-Modeling-with-Snowflake/tree/main/ch15. While key sections of this script will be highlighted in this chapter, please refer to the ch_15_semistruct.sql file for the complete code required to load, query, and transform semi-structured data, as it is too long to reprint here in full.

# The benefits of semi-structured data in Snowflake

Semi-structured data formats are popular due to their flexibility when working with dynamically varying information. Unlike relational schemas, in which a precise entity structure must be known and fixed ahead of time, semi-structured data is free to include or omit attributes as needed, as long as they are properly nested within corresponding parent objects.

Think of the contact list on your phone. It contains a list of people and their contact details but does not capture those details uniformly. For example, some contacts may contain multiple phone numbers while others have one. Some entries contain information such as an email address and street address, while others have only a number and a vague description in lieu of a name (seriously, who is *Green Vespa Laura Friend*, and who is Laura?).

To handle this type of data, Snowflake uses the VARIANT data type, which allows semi-structured data to be stored as a column in a relational table. As with all column types, Snowflake optimizes how VARIANT data is stored internally, ensuring better compression and faster access. Not only can semi-structured data sit next to relational data in the same table but users can also access it using basic extensions to standard SQL and achieve similar performance.

Another compelling reason to use the VARIANT data type for semi-structured data is its adaptability to change. If columns are added or removed from semi-structured data, there is no need to modify **ELT** (**extract, load, and transform**) pipelines. The VARIANT data type does not care whether the schema changes – even read operations won't fail for an attribute that no longer exists.

Let's load some semi-structured data to see these features in action.

## Getting hands-on with semi-structured data

Although we will query semi-structured JSON data as part of this exercise, its storage still conforms to modeling best practices such as naming and standard columns. In this example, we will use semi-structured data containing information about pirates – such as details about the crew, weapons, and their ship – all stored in a single `VARIANT` data type. With relational data, a row represents a single entity; in semi-structured data, a row is an entire file (although the file itself can contain single or countless entities). For this reason, metadata columns to mark individual loads and source filenames are stored alongside `VARIANT`.

```
pirate_json
__load_id      number IDENTITY      PK
__load_name    varchar
__load_dts     timestamp_ntz
v              variant
```

```
CREATE OR REPLACE TABLE pirate_json
(
    __load_id    number NOT NULL AUTOINCREMENT START 1 INCREMENT 1,
    __load_name  varchar NOT NULL,
    __load_dts   timestamp_ntz NOT NULL,
    v            variant NOT NULL,
    CONSTRAINT pirate_json___load_id PRIMARY KEY ( __load_id )
)
COMMENT = 'table w. a variant for pirate data, with meta ELT fields'
```

Figure 15.1 – A table with ELT meta columns and VARIANT for storing semi-structured data

This example uses `AUTOINCREMENT` (a.k.a. `IDENTITY`) as the default to generate a sequential unique ID for each load/record inserted.

In a real-world scenario, semi-structured data would be loaded into external stages and then to Snowflake tables using Snowpipe (streaming) or `COPY INTO` (bulk).

> **Note**
> Snowpipe instructions can be found on the Snowflake website: `https://docs.snowflake.com/en/user-guide/data-load-snowpipe-intro`.

However, in this example, we will learn how to create JSON data on the fly and work with that instead. But first, an overview of semi-structured data in a JSON file.

JSON files contain nested objects, which consist of name-value pairs (a.k.a key-value pairs) and have the following properties:

- Data is stored in name-value pairs
- Data is separated by commas
- Curly braces hold objects
- Square brackets hold arrays

- Object and array values may also be (nested) objects and arrays
- Values (including object and array values) can be one of the following data types:
    - An object
    - An array
    - A Boolean
    - A string
    - A number
    - NULL

The following figure shows a simple example of data in JSON format:

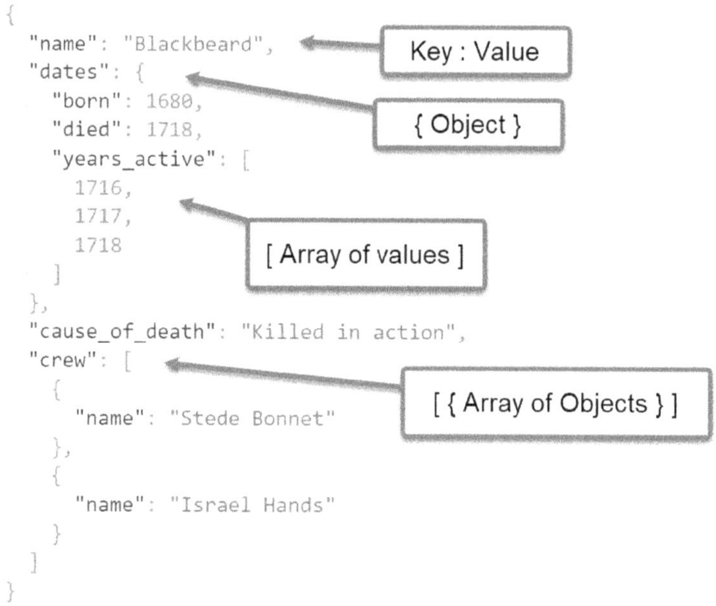

```
{
    "name": "Blackbeard",              ← Key : Value
    "dates": {
        "born": 1680,
        "died": 1718,                  ← { Object }
        "years_active": [
            1716,
            1717,
            1718
        ]                              ← [ Array of values ]
    },
    "cause_of_death": "Killed in action",
    "crew": [
        {
            "name": "Stede Bonnet"     ← [ { Array of Objects } ]
        },
        {
            "name": "Israel Hands"
        }
    ]
}
```

Figure 15.2 – Elements in semi-structured JSON data

For this exercise, we will use a slightly more advanced example:

```json
{
  "name": "Edward Teach",
  "nickname": "Blackbeard",
  "years_active": [
    1716,
    1717,
    1718
  ],
  "born": 1680,
  "died": 1718,
  "cause_of_death": "Killed in action",
  "crew": [
    {
      "name": "Stede Bonnet",
      "nickname": "Gentleman pirate",
      "weapons": [
        "blunderbuss"
      ],
      "years_active": [
        1717,
        1718
      ]
    },
    {
      "name": "Israel Hands",
      "nickname": null,
      "had_bird": true,
      "weapons": [
        "flintlock pistol",
        "cutlass",
        "boarding axe"
      ],
      "years_active": [
        1716,
        1717,
        1718
      ]
    }
  ],
  "ship": {
    "name": "Queen Anne's Revenge",
    "type": "Frigate",
    "original_name": "La Concorde",
    "year_captured": 1717
  }
}
```

Figure 15.3 – JSON data for this exercise

Load this data into the previously created table using the code provided:

```
INSERT INTO pirate_json...;
```

Now, we are ready to perform some analysis.

## Schema-on-read != schema-no-need

With the rising popularity of semi-structured data, schema-on-read also entered the lexicon of big data. **Schema-on-read** is the idea that, unlike in relational modeling, the schema definition for semi-structured data can be delayed until long after the data has been loaded into the data platform. Delaying this task means there are no bottlenecks within the ETL process for generating and ingesting semi-structured data. However, implicit in the design is that a knowable schema exists underneath the flexible semi-structured form.

In this section, we will learn how to query JSON data and infer details about its contents using SQL and Snowflake-native functions. Let's begin by extracting some basic attributes for our pirate:

```
SELECT * FROM pirate_json;
```

Although we can query a table containing semi-structured data in a VARIANT column, a simple SELECT * statement does not return meaningful results, as you can see in the following figure:

| | _LOAD_ID | _LOAD_NAME | _LOAD_DTS | V | ... |
|---|---|---|---|---|---|
| 1 | 1 | ad-hoc load | 2023-03-05 03:51:15.049 | { "born": 1680, "cause_of_death": "Killed in action", "crew": [ { "name": "St | |

Figure 15.4 – The result of standard SQL operators on semi-structured data

To access information stored inside VARIANT, Snowflake uses the colon operator (a period would have been ideal, but SQL claimed that). Using this method, let's find out what dreaded pirate we are dealing with. Recall that v is the name of the variant column in the pirate_json table:

```
SELECT v:name AS pirate_name_json
, v:name::STRING AS pirate_name_string
, v:nickname::STRING AS pirate_name_string
FROM pirate_json;
-------result--------
PIRATE_NAME_JSON|PIRATE_NAME_STRING|PIRATE_NAME_STRING|
----------------+------------------+------------------+
"Edward Teach"  |Edward Teach      |Blackbeard        |
```

Because Snowflake returns JSON data in quotes and often contains similar attribute names for nested objects, casting and aliasing the results is encouraged for readability. Now, let's move down a level and query a sub-column using a familiar dot notation:

```
SELECT v:name::STRING AS pirate_name
, v:ship.name:: STRING AS ship_name
FROM pirate_json;
-------result--------
```

```
PIRATE_NAME  |SHIP_NAME            |
------------+---------------------+
Edward Teach|Queen Anne's Revenge|
```

Remember the claim that semi-structured data is flexible enough to handle new and deleted attributes? Let's see what happens when we query a column that does not exist (spoiler alert, there's no error):

```
SELECT v:name::STRING AS pirate_name
, v:loc_buried_treasure::STRING AS pirate_treasure_location
FROM pirate_json;
-------result--------
PIRATE_NAME  |PIRATE_TREASURE_LOCATION|
------------+------------------------+
Edward Teach|                        |
```

Now, let's learn how to interrogate an array. As in other programming languages, arrays in Snowflake represent an indexed set of objects. Individual elements can be selected using familiar square-bracket notation, and common functions such as ARRAY_SIZE/CONTAINS/ADD are available. Let's get some information regarding Blackbeard's reign of terror:

```
SELECT v:name::STRING AS pirate_name
, v:years_active AS years_active
, v:years_active[0] AS active_from
, v:years_active[ARRAY_SIZE(v:years_active)-1] AS active_to
FROM pirate_json;
-------result--------
PIRATE_NAME  |YEARS_ACTIVE      |ACTIVE_FROM|ACTIVE_TO|
------------+------------------+-----------+---------+
Edward Teach|[1716, 1717, 1718]|1716       |1718     |
```

Now, let's learn how to dynamically handle multiple repeating values. Although arrays can be queried directly, their nested values remain in VARIANT format and are not treated as rows. Let's try and get to know two of Blackbeard's crew members:

```
--query multiple elements
SELECT v:name::STRING AS pirate_name
, v:crew::VARIANT AS pirate_crew
FROM pirate_json;
-------result--------
PIRATE_NAME  |PIRATE_CREW
------------+---------------------------------.......
Edward Teach|[   {     "name": "Stede Bonnet", .......
```

Unfortunately, the result is not user-readable. If we would like to pivot the elements of an array into intelligible rows, we must use two Snowflake features in conjunction: lateral and flatten.

- **Lateral join** – A LATERAL join behaves similarly to a loop in a correlated subquery and can reference columns from a table expression:

    ```
    SELECT ...
    FROM <left_hand_table_expression>, LATERAL (<inline_view>)
    ```

- **Flatten** – This is a table function that takes a VARIANT, OBJECT, or ARRAY column and produces a lateral view (i.e., an inline view that contains correlation referring to other tables that precede it in the FROM clause). More information on FLATTEN and its parameters can be found in the Snowflake documentation (https://docs.snowflake.com/en/sql-reference/functions/flatten). Please review this documentation and familiarize yourself with its list of output columns before continuing.

With these tools, let's transform those crew members into individual rows:

```
SELECT v:name::STRING AS pirate_name
, c.VALUE:name::STRING AS crew_name
, c.VALUE:nickname::STRING AS crew_nickname
FROM pirate_json, LATERAL FLATTEN(v:crew) c;
-------result--------
PIRATE_NAME  |CREW_NAME     |CREW_NICKNAME    |
-------------+--------------+-----------------+
Edward Teach|Stede Bonnet|Gentleman pirate|
Edward Teach|Israel Hands|                |
```

In this example, c is the output of the FLATTEN function, which is joined to the columns selected from the table. We use the dot operator to reference its VALUE property, which contains a VARIANT data type (where a colon is used to extract contents). (Note that NULL values are returned as empty strings.) Using the same technique, we can handle multiple nested arrays. For example, what weapons did each of Blackbeard's crew mates employ?

```
SELECT v:name::STRING AS pirate_name
, c.VALUE:name::STRING AS crew_name
, w.VALUE::STRING AS crew_weapons
FROM pirate_json, LATERAL FLATTEN(v:crew) c
,LATERAL FLATTEN(c.VALUE:weapons) w;
-------result--------
PIRATE_NAME  |CREW_NAME     |CREW_WEAPONS     |
-------------+--------------+-----------------+
Edward Teach|Stede Bonnet|blunderbuss     |
Edward Teach|Israel Hands|flintlock pistol|
Edward Teach|Israel Hands|cutlass         |
Edward Teach|Israel Hands|boarding axe    |
```

Remember that working with information inferred from a semi-structured schema is like running standard SQL on relational tables. For example, if we wish to know how many different weapons Israel Hands employed, we can turn to familiar SQL filters and aggregates:

```
SELECT COUNT(crew_weapons) AS num_weapons FROM (
SELECT c.VALUE:name::STRING AS crew_name
, w.VALUE::STRING AS crew_weapons
FROM pirate_json, LATERAL FLATTEN(v:crew) c
,LATERAL FLATTEN(c. VALUE:weapons) w
WHERE crew_name = 'Israel Hands' );
-------result--------
NUM_WEAPONS|
-----------+
          3|
```

> **Mind your Hands**
>
> If the name Israel Hands sounds familiar, it is the basis for the treacherous sidekick in Robert Louis Stevenson's novel *Treasure Island*, but Hands was indeed part of Blackbeard's crew and is remembered for having been shot by Teach during a game of cards, who then remarked that "*if [he] did not know and then kill one of them, they would forget who [he] was.*" Interestingly, the injury saved Hands from the gallows, as he was convalescent on shore when Blackbeard was captured. He died a few years later, a beggar on the streets of London.

As these examples demonstrate, Snowflake makes schema-on-read easy thanks to simple SQL extensions and the VARIANT data type, which is optimized for semi-structured data. However, inferring a schema and transforming semi-structured data into cleanly formatted rows and columns takes time. In more advanced cases, inferring schema-on-read requires input and guidance from the business users who specialize in it – just as in logical and conceptual modeling.

Remember that schema-on-read only delays the work of relational modeling, which must be done eventually to allow the organization to query it through traditional methods. The next section will examine a simple method for converting semi-structured data into a structured, relational schema.

# Converting semi-structured data into relational data

As we saw in the previous exercise, semi-structured data is flexible and can accommodate any amount of densely or sparsely nested elements. However, in nested objects, it can be inferred that lower-level elements are attributes of their immediate parents.

Observe the following simplified example of semi-structured data with three levels of nesting and use the indentation to count the depth.

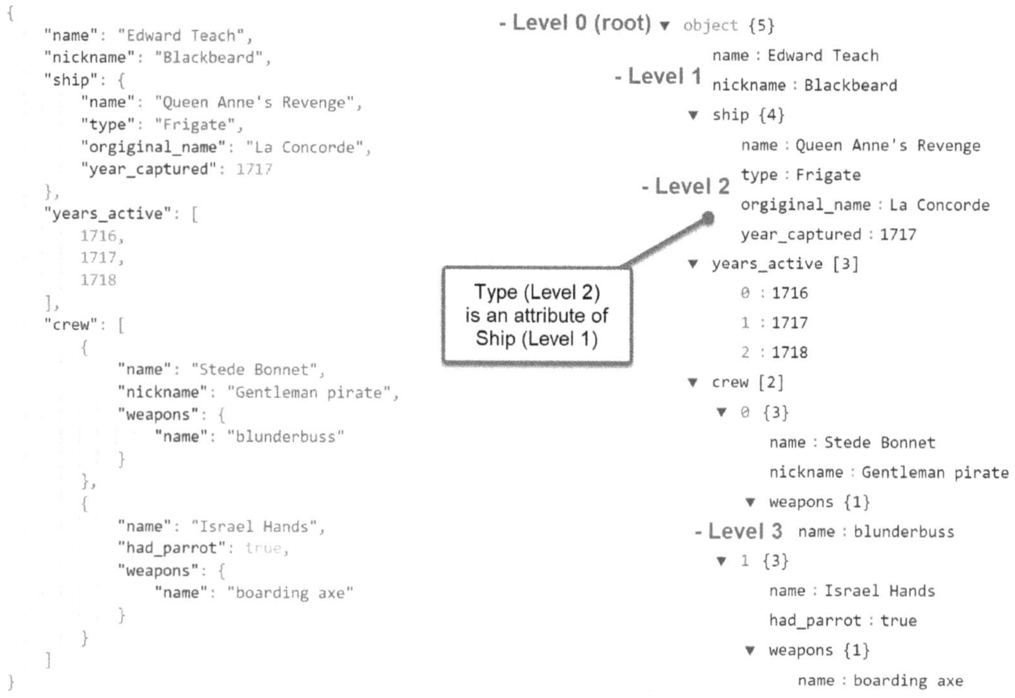

```
{
    "name": "Edward Teach",
    "nickname": "Blackbeard",
    "ship": {
        "name": "Queen Anne's Revenge",
        "type": "Frigate",
        "orginal_name": "La Concorde",
        "year_captured": 1717
    },
    "years_active": [
        1716,
        1717,
        1718
    ],
    "crew": [
        {
            "name": "Stede Bonnet",
            "nickname": "Gentleman pirate",
            "weapons": {
                "name": "blunderbuss"
            }
        },
        {
            "name": "Israel Hands",
            "had_parrot": true,
            "weapons": {
                "name": "boarding axe"
            }
        }
    ]
}
```

- Level 0 (root) ▼ object {5}
    name : Edward Teach
- Level 1  nickname : Blackbeard
  ▼ ship {4}
    name : Queen Anne's Revenge
- Level 2  type : Frigate
    orginal_name : La Concorde
    year_captured : 1717
  ▼ years_active [3]
    0 : 1716
    1 : 1717
    2 : 1718
  ▼ crew [2]
    ▼ 0 {3}
      name : Stede Bonnet
      nickname : Gentleman pirate
      ▼ weapons {1}
- Level 3  name : blunderbuss
    ▼ 1 {3}
      name : Israel Hands
      had_parrot : true
      ▼ weapons {1}
        name : boarding axe

*Type (Level 2) is an attribute of Ship (Level 1)*

Figure 15.5 – Observing the number of nested levels in a semi-structured object

Here, we can see that a *(ship) type*, of depth 2, is an attribute of `ship`, which is a level-one attribute of the root object. By this logic, if we follow the levels of a semi-structured object to its maximum depth N, those elements become attributes of an entity N-1. Then, N-1 entities become attributes of N-2, repeating recursively until arriving at the root.

In the current example, `boarding axe` and `blunderbuss` become instances in the weapon entity, which is an attribute of `crew` member, which is an attribute of `pirate`. However, there are several nuances to consider. Due to its dynamic nature, any object in a semi-structured file is free to vary and include whatever attributes or nested objects it needs. This means, unlike in structured data, looking at one instance of an entity, such as `crew` member, tells us nothing about the attributes of another. Notice how `Stede Bonnet` has a `nickname` attribute while `Israel Hands` has a Boolean parrot indicator. The only way to fully know all the levels and attributes of a semi-structured file is to scan it to the very end. Even then, there is no guarantee that new attributes won't appear tomorrow.

The good news is that the process of determining the depth of a semi-structured file can be automated through Snowflake functions. Using the `FLATTEN` function covered in the previous section, we can set the `RECURSIVE` parameter to automatically expand every element to its ultimate depth. The output of recursive flattening can be seen in the following figure:

```
671     SELECT f.*
672     FROM pirate_json p, LATERAL FLATTEN( v , RECURSIVE => TRUE ) f ;
673
```

| SEQ | KEY | PATH | INDEX | VALUE | THIS |
|---|---|---|---|---|---|
| 24 | 1 | name | name | null | "Edward Teach" | { "born": 1680, "cause_of_death": "Killed |
| 25 | 1 | nickname | nickname | null | "Blackbeard" | { "born": 1680, "cause_of_death": "Killed |
| 26 | 1 | ship | ship | null | { "name": "Queen Anne's Revenge", "orgigina | { "born": 1680, "cause_of_death": "Killed |
| 27 | 1 | name | ship.name | null | "Queen Anne's Revenge" | { "name": "Queen Anne's Revenge", "orgi |
| 28 | 1 | orgiginal_name | ship.orgiginal_name | null | "La Concorde" | { "name": "Queen Anne's Revenge", "orgi |
| 29 | 1 | type | ship.type | null | "Frigate" | { "name": "Queen Anne's Revenge", "orgi |
| 30 | 1 | year_captured | ship.year_captured | null | 1717 | { "name": "Queen Anne's Revenge", "orgi |
| 31 | 1 | years_active | years_active | null | [ 1716, 1717, 1718 ] | { "born": 1680, "cause_of_death": "Killed |
| 32 | 1 | null | years_active[0] | 0 | 1716 | [ 1716, 1717, 1718 ] |
| 33 | 1 | null | years_active[1] | 1 | 1717 | [ 1716, 1717, 1718 ] |

Figure 15.6 – Recursively flattening an entire JSON file

Notice that this output does not select from the VARIANT column v, but from the result of the lateral FLATTEN operation. Using the PATH column, we could calculate the depth by counting the number of dots and end-level array elements to give us a complete list of elements and their level in the semi-structured hierarchy.

```
675     SELECT ARRAY_SIZE(
676             STRTOK_TO_ARRAY (IFF (
677                     STARTSWITH( RIGHT(path,3), '['),
678                     LEFT(PATH ,LENGTH(path)-3) || '.'|| SUBSTR(path,LENGTH(PATH)-1,2),
679                     path), '.'
680                     )
681             ) AS depth
682     , f.key
683     , f.path
684     , f.value
685     FROM pirate_json p, LATERAL FLATTEN( v , RECURSIVE => TRUE ) f
686     ORDER BY 1 ASC ;
```

| DEPTH | KEY | PATH | VALUE |
|---|---|---|---|
| 6 | 1 | nickname | nickname | "Blackbeard" |
| 7 | 1 | name | name | "Edward Teach" |
| 8 | 1 | died | died | 1718 |
| 9 | 2 | null | years_active[2] | 1718 |
| 10 | 2 | null | years_active[1] | 1717 |
| 11 | 2 | null | years_active[0] | 1716 |
| 12 | 2 | year_captured | ship.year_captured | 1717 |
| 13 | 2 | type | ship.type | "Frigate" |

Figure 15.7 – All elements of a semi-structured file and their depth

Now that we have the structure, we can deconstruct the semi-structured data into normalized relational tables. Starting with the maximum depth (weapons at depth 3), we can create a dimension with metadata columns and a surrogate key (some elements, such as account numbers, contain natural keys, which can be used instead).

Start by creating a table for the `weapon` dimension. We will use a sequence to generate a surrogate key, but a hash or a natural key can be used instead:

```
CREATE OR REPLACE TABLE weapon
(
    weapon_id number(38,0) NOT NULL AUTOINCREMENT START 1 INCREMENT 1,
    name varchar NOT NULL,
    __load_name varchar NOT NULL,
    __load_dts timestamp_ntz NOT NULL,
    CONSTRAINT pk_weapon_weapon_id PRIMARY KEY ( weapon_id ),
    CONSTRAINT ak_weapon_name UNIQUE ( name )
)
COMMENT = 'weapons used by pirates';
```

Now, merge the `weapon` values from the JSON in the latest load and insert them if they don't already exist:

```
MERGE INTO weapon w...;
```

Have a look at the table contents:

```
SELECT weapon_id, name FROM weapon;
-------result--------
WEAPON_ID|NAME             |
---------+----------------+
        1|blunderbuss      |
        2|flintlock pistol|
        3|cutlass          |
        4|boarding axe     |
```

Now, repeat the process for the elements at depth 2. The `ship` dimension poses no challenge because it has no child relationships; however, some questions need to be answered before being able to model `crew` and `years_active`. Is a crew member a separate entity from a pirate captain or is it a subtype? Do `years_active` refer to how long a crew member has worked under the current captain or how long they have been active over their entire pirating career? Here, just as with modeling relational entities, only business experts can help determine the nuances of what the data represents and how it is used.

Let's suppose that our domain experts confirm that a crew member is a subtype of `pirate` and all attributes, including `years_active`, are shared as part of a single `pirate` dimension (this is the logical-to-physical rollup scenario described in *Chapter 11, Putting Physical Modeling into Practice*). As part of the pirate rollup, we must make sure to include an FK reference to itself to store the relationship between the crew and captain. First, we create the table structure:

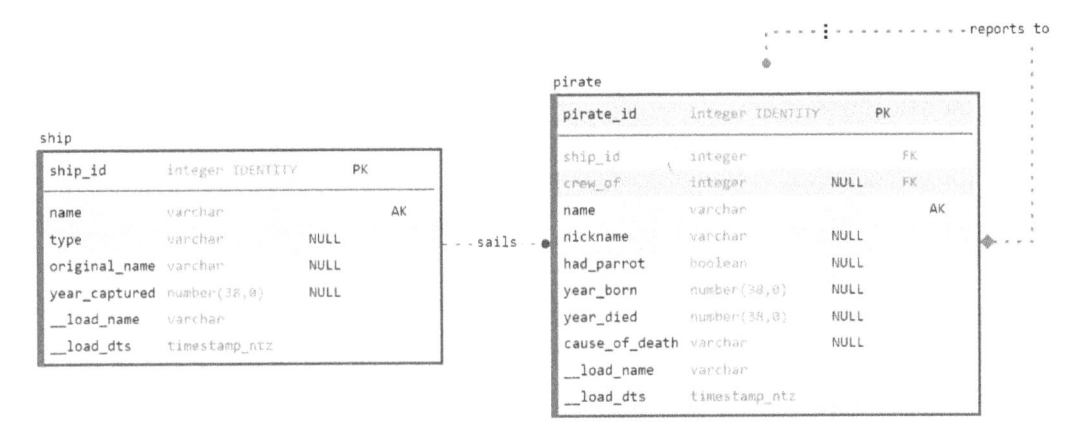

Figure 15.8 – A rollup of the crew into the supertype pirate dimension

As we have fused a level-2 entity with its supertype, we must load the data starting with the top-level dimension (as `crew` will need an existing `pirate_id` to report to). First, load the level-1 pirate entities (i.e., Blackbeard):

```
MERGE INTO pirate p USING (< select level 1 pirates>)...;
```

Once the top-level object has been loaded, we can load the crew details, referencing their captain's surrogate key in the `crew_of` column. Load the crew details and verify the result:

```
MERGE INTO pirate p USING ( < select level 2 crew > )...;
```

The output will look something like this:

| PIRATE_ID | SHIP_ID | CREW_OF | NAME | NICKNAME | HAD_PARROT | YEAR_BORN | YEAR_DIED | CAUSE_OF_DEATH |
|---|---|---|---|---|---|---|---|---|
| 1 | 1 | null | Edward Teach | Blackbeard | null | 1,680 | 1,718 | Killed in action |
| 2 | 1 | 1 | Stede Bonnet | Gentleman pirate | null | null | null | null |
| 3 | 1 | 1 | Israel Hands | null | TRUE | null | null | null |

Figure 15.9 – Converted semi-structured pirate attributes in 3NF

Look carefully and you will notice that one of the attributes, `years_active`, is missing from the table. Because this data is multi-valued, it cannot be included in the `pirate` dimension without violating 1NF. For this, we must create and load a separate `pirate_years_active` entity.

250　　Modeling Semi-Structured Data

The last missing attribute is pirate *weapons*. In this scenario, we have a many-to-many relationship between the `pirate` and `weapon` dimensions. As described in *Chapter 8, Putting Logical Modeling into Practice*, modeling many-to-many relationships requires an associative table in the physical layer. This table holds the PKs for the associated entities (i.e., pirate and weapon), as well as the metadata fields that tell us when a certain relationship was first loaded. With this, the relational model is complete, as seen in the following diagram:

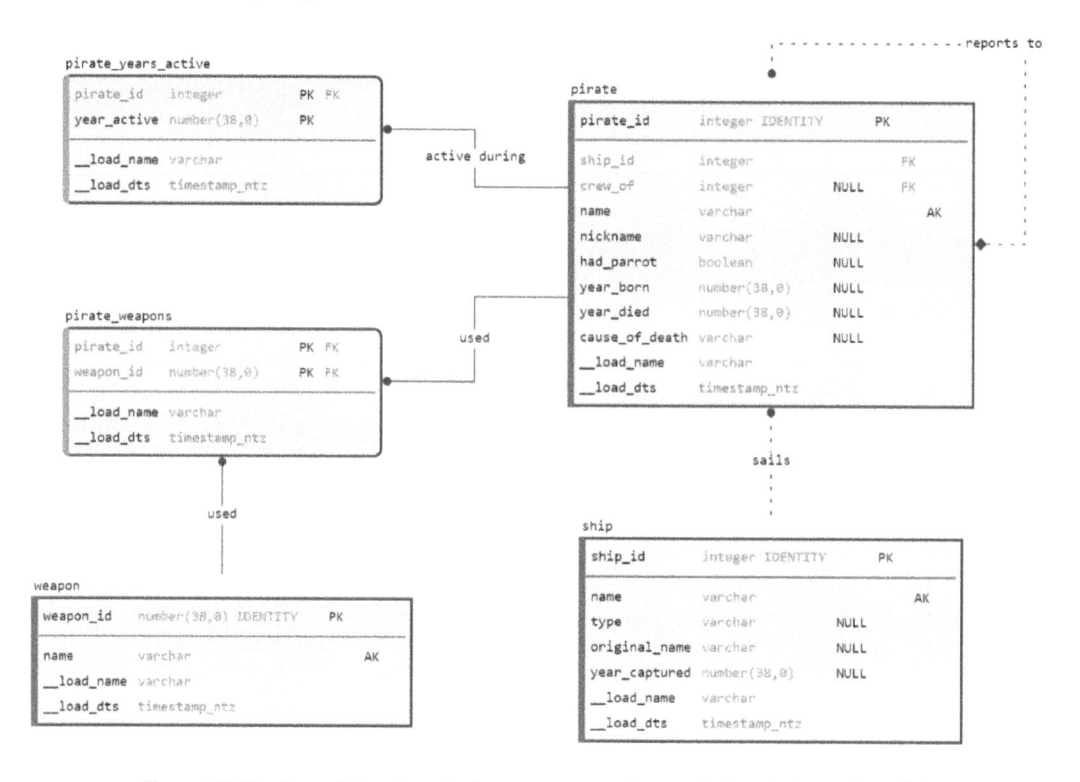

Figure 15.10 – A semi-structured schema converted to a relational physical model

Follow the steps in the accompanying code to load the `pirate_weapons` and `pirate_years_active` tables. Once loaded, we are free to analyze the data using traditional relational methods, for example:

```
SELECT p.NAME AS pirate_name
, nvl(p.nickname, 'none') AS nickname
, s.type AS ship_type
, nvl(w.NAME , 'none') AS weapon_name
FROM pirate p
INNER JOIN ship s USING (ship_id)
LEFT JOIN pirate_weapons pw USING (pirate_id)
LEFT JOIN weapon w USING (weapon_id) ;
```

```
-------result--------
PIRATE_NAME |NICKNAME         |SHIP_TYPE|WEAPON_NAME     |
------------+-----------------+---------+----------------+
Stede Bonnet|Gentleman pirate |Frigate  |blunderbuss     |
Israel Hands|none             |Frigate  |flintlock pistol|
Israel Hands|none             |Frigate  |cutlass         |
Israel Hands|none             |Frigate  |boarding axe    |
Edward Teach|Blackbeard       |Frigate  |none            |
```

This exercise demonstrates that although Snowflake features ease the technical burden of schema-on-read, the process is not trivial. The fact that Snowflake can easily handle semi-structured data does not guarantee that your organization will have the functional or technical capacity to make sense of it. However, by using a repeatable step-by-step process to transform semi-structured data into relational data, as we have done in this chapter, Snowflake users benefit from better organization and data consistency.

## Summary

With the rising popularity of web applications and IoT data, semi-structured data has gained prominence for its flexibility in creating and loading dynamically changing objects without affecting ELT pipelines. Semi-structured formats, such as JSON, can handle any amount of variable nested data, which doesn't need to conform to a pre-defined structure. Snowflake makes working with semi-structured formats easy thanks to its VARIANT data type – optimized for storage and analytical queries using easy-to-learn extensions to ANSI-standard SQL.

Querying a VARIANT data type provides the same performance as standard relational data types without needing to analyze the structure ahead of time – an approach known as schema-on-read. This means Snowflake users can work with semi-structured and relational data on the same platform using familiar SQL commands. However, although Snowflake gives users all the tools necessary for analyzing semi-structured data, schema-on-read only delays but does not eliminate the need for relational-style modeling.

Once the elements of semi-structured data have been understood, they can be converted into a relational schema by looking at element depth to determine its attributes and relationships. As with traditional modeling, engaging the business teams for their expertise will be required to create a normalized schema that meets an organization's analytical needs.

Having familiarized ourselves with Snowflake's semi-structured features, we can use many of the same techniques to handle another kind of variable structure: the hierarchy. In the next chapter, we will learn how to model various types of hierarchies using functions provided by Snowflake to make the job easier.

# 16
# Modeling Hierarchies

In the previous chapter, we learned about the methods and techniques for exploring semi-structured data in Snowflake. While not everyone works with operational web or app data such as JSON, there is another type of (semi-)structured data that exists across all organizations: hierarchies. Every company operates with hierarchical entities such as org levels (tiers of management and the reporting relationships between managers and employees) or calendar dimensions (rollups of days, months, fiscal periods, and years).

Whether formally maintained or naturally occurring, hierarchies are used within an organization to organize entities into meaningful groups and subgroups to facilitate rollups or drill-downs in data analysis. Besides aiding in the analysis of facts, hierarchies themselves can be examined to help organizations understand how they are structured, how they function, and how they can improve their performance by eliminating operational bottlenecks.

This chapter will cover the various ways hierarchical data is modeled in relational databases and Snowflake-specific techniques that enable its rapid analysis and conversion. Drawing upon the techniques covered in previous chapters, we will learn how to anticipate changes in hierarchical data and create models that allow for easy maintenance and impact analysis.

This chapter will cover the following main topics:

- Understanding hierarchies and how they are used in data warehouses
- Distinguishing between the various hierarchy types
- Modeling techniques for maintaining each type of hierarchy
- Snowflake features for traversing a recursive tree structure
- Handling changes in hierarchy dimensions

## Technical requirements

The scripts used to instantiate and load the examples in this chapter are available in the following GitHub repo: https://github.com/PacktPublishing/Data-Modeling-with-Snowflake/tree/main/ch16. While key sections of this script will be highlighted in this chapter, please refer to the ch_16_hierarchies.sql file for the complete code required to load, query, and transform semi-structured data, as it is too long to reprint here in full.

## Understanding and distinguishing between hierarchies

A **hierarchy** is a system in which people, objects, or concepts are organized into a tree-like structure, with each level representing a different category or grouping of data. In modeling, hierarchies can be thought of as a series of descending one-to-many relationships.

At the top of the hierarchy sits the root node, which contains child nodes. Each child node represents a subcategory of the data contained in the parent node and may, in turn, have its own child nodes. This arrangement of nodes and their relationships is often called a tree structure or diagram. If we were to proverbially chop down such a tree and observe it laterally, we would see the hierarchy in its relational form.

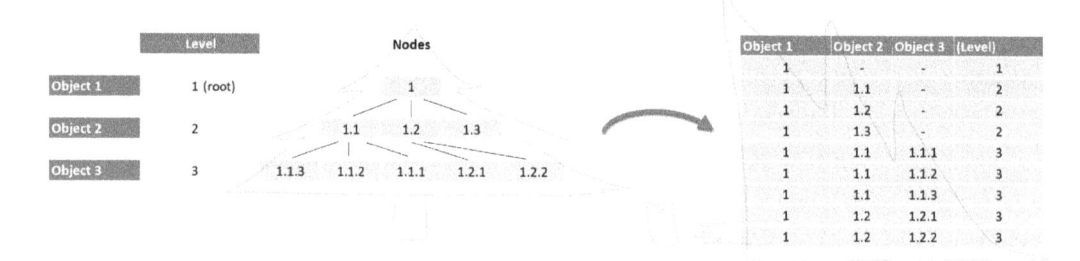

Figure 16.1 – A hierarchy seen in a tree (left) and relational format (right)

Hierarchies fall into three general categories depending on the variability in their levels. Let's look at each of these categories.

### A fixed-depth hierarchy

A **fixed-depth** hierarchy has a pre-defined and agreed-upon number of levels. Such a hierarchy is simple to model and analyze because it is just a relational table with individual attributes for each level. Take a calendar dimension as an example: the day attribute rolls up into a month, which rolls up into a year. It can be expressed as a simple table with three attributes, each corresponding to a separate level.

**Calendar**

| (pk) | Level 1 | Level 2 | Level 3 |
|---|---|---|---|
| Date | Year | Month | Day |
| 2020-01-01 | 2020 | 1 | 1 |
| 2020-01-02 | 2020 | 1 | 2 |
| ... | ... | ... | ... |
| 2022-12-31 | 2022 | 12 | 31 |

Figure 16.2 – An example of a fixed-depth hierarchy

In some cases, though, hierarchy levels are not completely fixed.

## A slightly ragged hierarchy

A **slightly ragged** (or slightly variable) hierarchy also has a fixed depth, but not all members occupy all the levels. Think of a region hierarchy that contains cities of various sizes. A city such as *New York* is big enough to be broken down into smaller zones for analysis, while its neighbor, *Jersey City*, is tiny, and further segmentation is not useful.

Because slightly ragged hierarchies have a fixed depth, they can be modeled using the previously discussed structure. The variable attribute levels can then be populated based on business rules, as seen in *Figure 16.3*.

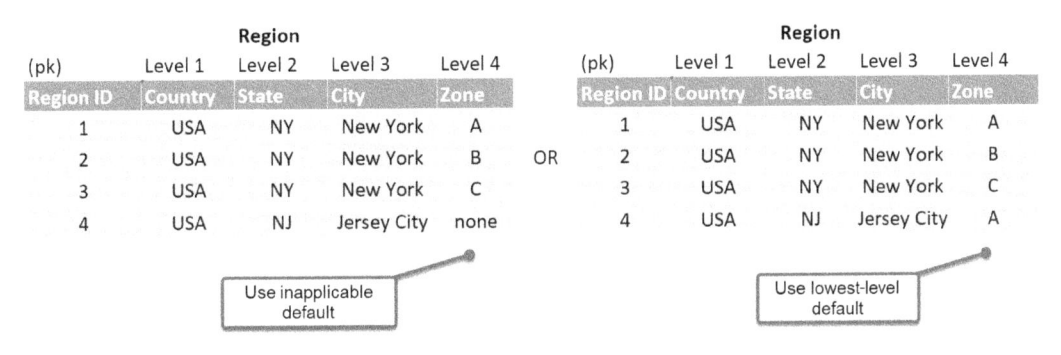

**Region**

| (pk) | Level 1 | Level 2 | Level 3 | Level 4 |
|---|---|---|---|---|
| Region ID | Country | State | City | Zone |
| 1 | USA | NY | New York | A |
| 2 | USA | NY | New York | B |
| 3 | USA | NY | New York | C |
| 4 | USA | NJ | Jersey City | none |

*Use inapplicable default*

OR

**Region**

| (pk) | Level 1 | Level 2 | Level 3 | Level 4 |
|---|---|---|---|---|
| Region ID | Country | State | City | Zone |
| 1 | USA | NY | New York | A |
| 2 | USA | NY | New York | B |
| 3 | USA | NY | New York | C |
| 4 | USA | NJ | Jersey City | A |

*Use lowest-level default*

Figure 16.3 – Examples of a slightly ragged hierarchy

The following business rules are commonly used for fitting slightly ragged hierarchies into a fixed depth:

- **Mark inapplicable values** – When a node does not have a value for a given level of the hierarchy, use a default value (e.g., *none* or *N/A*) to label it accordingly. This approach ensures that aggregates and analytical filters treat not applicable values differently from those that are labeled.
- **Use the lowest level** – When a node does not have a value for a given level of the hierarchy, label it with the lowest value of that level by default. This method allows all nodes in the hierarchy to be grouped under each level's corresponding rank.

Fixed and slightly ragged hierarchies can be analyzed using standard relational methods. However, there are hierarchies whose nodes can vary wildly in the number of levels and children, and a standard relational approach is no longer viable.

## A ragged hierarchy

A **ragged** (a.k.a. variable-depth, unbalanced, uneven) hierarchy contains levels or categories that do not have a uniform number of members. One that most people will recognize is an org hierarchy. In an org hierarchy, the highest level may have only one member (CEO), while the next level may have several vice presidents with their own direct reports, and the CEO's lone secretary.

Ragged hierarchies are difficult to analyze because they are of indeterminate depth and do not fit neatly into a relational structure. A ragged hierarchy does not have separate attributes corresponding to fixed levels but instead uses a self-referential PK/FK relationship to link parent and child nodes. While the parent/child relationship can be recorded in a single record, as seen in the following example of the relationship between an employee and a manager, analyzing such a hierarchy takes some effort.

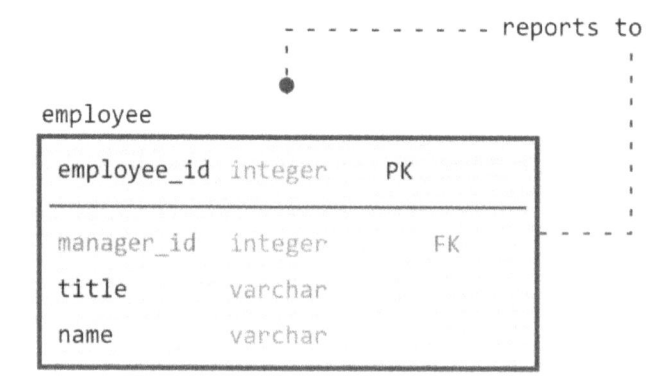

Figure 16.4 – A ragged hierarchy with a recursive relationship

Snowflake provides several nifty extensions to ANSI SQL that allow users to traverse a ragged hierarchy's recursive parent/child relationships at runtime. These same features can also aid in generating a flattened representation of the hierarchy, known as a bridge table. A **bridge table** contains a row for every possible path in the ragged hierarchy and, as a standalone dimension, allows for alternate versions using familiar SCD patterns. By removing `manager_id` from `employee` and moving it to the bridge table, both dimensions can change without impacting one another. Most importantly, the hierarchy can be analyzed or joined to corresponding entities using traditional relational methods. An example can be seen in the following figure:

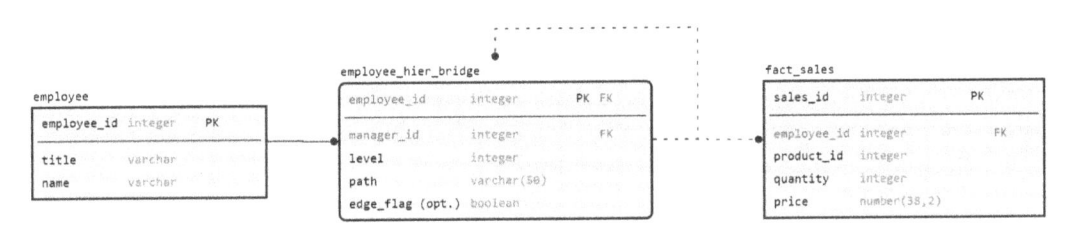

Figure 16.5 – A ragged hierarchy with a bridge table

A bridge table makes it easy to read the paths and levels of a ragged hierarchy. The model in this example also includes a column to identify **edges** (nodes without any children). An edge flag can simplify the queries required to answer questions such as *do all VPs have direct reports?*

The following is an example of a simple tree hierarchy and its representation as a bridge table (a denormalized version is provided for easier understanding):

**Employee Bridge**

| Employee Id | Manager Id | Level | Path | Edge Flag |
|---|---|---|---|---|
| 1 | - | 1 | 1 | N |
| 2 | 1 | 2 | 1 -> 2 | N |
| 3 | 1 | 2 | 1 -> 3 | N |
| 4 | 1 | 2 | 1 -> 4 | Y |
| 5 | 2 | 3 | 1 -> 2 -> 5 | Y |
| 6 | 3 | 3 | 1 -> 3 -> 6 | Y |

**Employee Bridge**

| Employee ID | Manager ID | Level | Title | Path | Edge Flag |
|---|---|---|---|---|---|
| 1 | - | 1 | President | President | N |
| 2 | 1 | 2 | Sales | President -> Sales | N |
| 3 | 1 | 2 | Marketing | President -> Marketing | N |
| 4 | 1 | 2 | Secretary | President -> Secretary | Y |
| 5 | 2 | 3 | Sales Agent | President -> Sales -> Sales Agent | Y |
| 6 | 3 | 3 | Marketing Agent | President -> Marketing -> Marketing Agent | Y |

Figure 16.6 – Sample data in a ragged hierarchy bridge table

Now that we are familiar with the types of hierarchies and their structure, let's learn how to handle changes and create a bridge table by traversing a recursive relationship.

## Maintaining hierarchies in Snowflake

As we have seen, a hierarchy is a grouping of classifications and relationships. It is an adjacent but separate dimension to the entity that it organizes. As a standalone dimension, hierarchies are subject to the same changes in business rules as any master data. However, before we attend to change-tracking, we must get comfortable traversing a ragged hierarchy's recursive relationships.

Once again, Snowflake has us covered with native features that allow us to easily map out the paths and levels of a ragged hierarchy.

### Recursively navigating a ragged hierarchy

You have been put in charge of the pirate frigate Queen Anne's Revenge. Its logbook shows all crew members, ranks, and direct reports. The details are listed as follows:

| PIRATE_ID | NAME | RANK | SUPERIOR_ID |
|---|---|---|---|
| 1 | Blackbeard | Captain | null |
| 2 | Calico Jack | First Mate | 1 |
| 3 | Anne Bonny | Second Mate | 1 |
| 4 | Mary Read | Navigator | 2 |
| 5 | Israel Hands | Boatswain | 2 |
| 6 | John Silver | Carpenter | 3 |
| 7 | Long John | Gunner | 3 |
| 8 | Billy Bones | Cook | 4 |
| 9 | Tom Morgan | Sailor | 5 |
| 10 | Harry Hawkins | Sailor | 5 |
| 11 | Black Dog | Sailor | 6 |
| 12 | Dick Johnson | Sailor | 6 |
| 13 | Roger Pew | Sailor | 7 |
| 14 | Dirk van der Heide | Sailor | 7 |
| 15 | Ned Low | Sailor | 9 |
| 16 | Edward England | Sailor | 9 |
| 17 | Stede Bonnet | Sailor | 10 |
| 18 | Charles Vane | Sailor | 10 |
| 19 | James Kidd | Sailor | 11 |
| 20 | William Kidd | Sailor | 11 |

PIRATE
| PIRATE_ID | number(38,0) | PK |
| NAME | varchar(50) | |
| RANK | varchar(50) | |
| SUPERIOR_ID | number(38,0) NULL | FK |

Figure 16.7 – A ragged hierarchy contained in the pirate dimension

As you review the records, you realize that this list makes it difficult to make sense of the complex web of the variable-depth relationships of the crew. To understand the ship's chain of command, you need a way to traverse the hierarchical tree structure. To accomplish this, Snowflake offers the `CONNECT BY` clause.

Maintaining hierarchies in Snowflake    259

The CONNECT BY clause follows a parent-child relationship between rows in a table. Each row has a parent identified by a foreign key in the same table. The CONNECT BY clause uses a recursive query approach to traverse this hierarchical structure. It starts with a root row (which can be specified using the START WITH predicate) and then recursively traverses the structure by finding all the children of the current row and repeating the process until it reaches the bottom of the tree.

Within the CONNECT BY clause, Snowflake uses a function called SYS_CONNECT_BY_PATH to generate the path. The output is a string column, which shows the path from the root row to each row in the tree. This column is a concatenated string of the values in the column that is used to establish the hierarchy.

Use the code provided in the repository for this chapter to load the pirate table and observe the parameters in the CONNECT BY statement that generate the pirate hierarchy in the following figure:

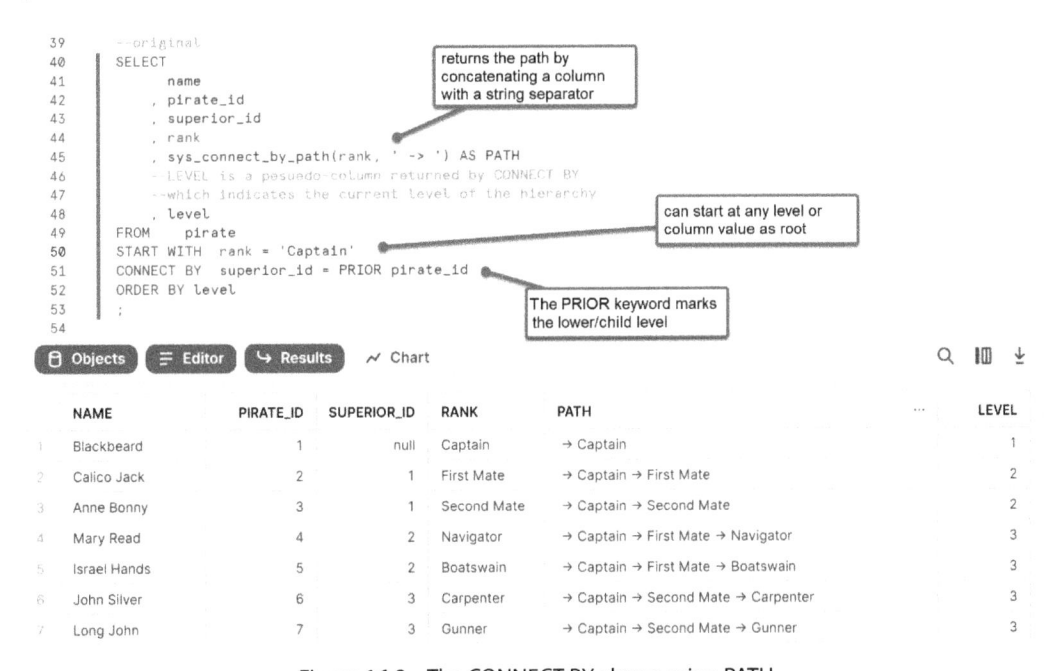

```
--original
SELECT
    name
    , pirate_id
    , superior_id
    , rank
    , sys_connect_by_path(rank, ' -> ') AS PATH
    --LEVEL is a pesuedo-column returned by CONNECT BY
    --which indicates the current level of the hierarchy
    , level
FROM    pirate
START WITH  rank = 'Captain'
CONNECT BY  superior_id = PRIOR pirate_id
ORDER BY level
;
```

- sys_connect_by_path: returns the path by concatenating a column with a string separator
- START WITH: can start at any level or column value as root
- The PRIOR keyword marks the lower/child level

| NAME | PIRATE_ID | SUPERIOR_ID | RANK | PATH | LEVEL |
|---|---|---|---|---|---|
| Blackbeard | 1 | null | Captain | → Captain | 1 |
| Calico Jack | 2 | 1 | First Mate | → Captain → First Mate | 2 |
| Anne Bonny | 3 | 1 | Second Mate | → Captain → Second Mate | 2 |
| Mary Read | 4 | 2 | Navigator | → Captain → First Mate → Navigator | 3 |
| Israel Hands | 5 | 2 | Boatswain | → Captain → First Mate → Boatswain | 3 |
| John Silver | 6 | 3 | Carpenter | → Captain → Second Mate → Carpenter | 3 |
| Long John | 7 | 3 | Gunner | → Captain → Second Mate → Gunner | 3 |

Figure 16.8 – The CONNECT BY clause using PATH

Using the CONNECT BY query result, we can easily determine how many levels and branches exist in the crew hierarchy. The pirate crew is as complex as any organization – containing five levels of depth and comprising two distinct branches (those of First Mate and Second Mate). If we wanted to label these branches to make future analysis easier, we could use the CONNECT_BY_ROOT function to return the top-level root node of the branch we are traversing.

## Modeling Hierarchies

```
59    SELECT
60         name
61       , pirate_id
62       , superior_id
63       , rank
64       , sys_connect_by_path(rank, ' -> ') AS PATH
65       , CONNECT_BY_ROOT rank AS crew_branch
66       , level + 1 AS level
67    FROM    pirate
68    START WITH  STRTOK(rank, ' ', 2) = 'Mate'
69    CONNECT BY  superior_id = PRIOR pirate_id
70
```

*CONNECT_BY_ROOT displays the root node of CONNECT BY*

*START WITH the First and Second mates as root nodes*

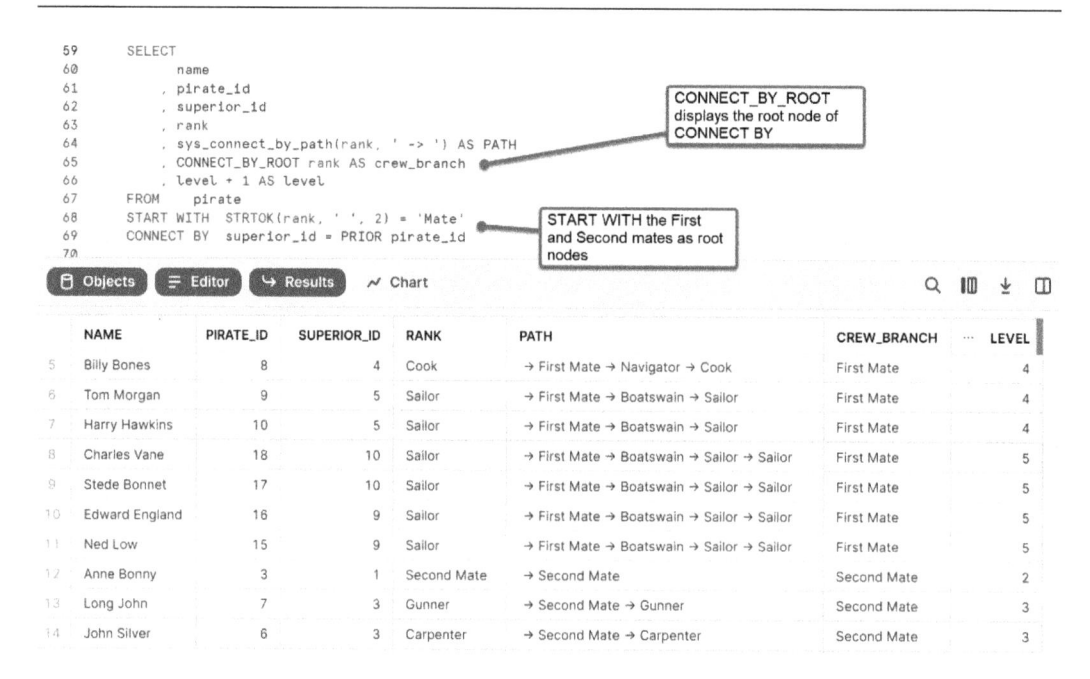

| | NAME | PIRATE_ID | SUPERIOR_ID | RANK | PATH | CREW_BRANCH | LEVEL |
|---|---|---|---|---|---|---|---|
| 5 | Billy Bones | 8 | 4 | Cook | → First Mate → Navigator → Cook | First Mate | 4 |
| 6 | Tom Morgan | 9 | 5 | Sailor | → First Mate → Boatswain → Sailor | First Mate | 4 |
| 7 | Harry Hawkins | 10 | 5 | Sailor | → First Mate → Boatswain → Sailor | First Mate | 4 |
| 8 | Charles Vane | 18 | 10 | Sailor | → First Mate → Boatswain → Sailor → Sailor | First Mate | 5 |
| 9 | Stede Bonnet | 17 | 10 | Sailor | → First Mate → Boatswain → Sailor → Sailor | First Mate | 5 |
| 10 | Edward England | 16 | 9 | Sailor | → First Mate → Boatswain → Sailor → Sailor | First Mate | 5 |
| 11 | Ned Low | 15 | 9 | Sailor | → First Mate → Boatswain → Sailor → Sailor | First Mate | 5 |
| 12 | Anne Bonny | 3 | 1 | Second Mate | → Second Mate | Second Mate | 2 |
| 13 | Long John | 7 | 3 | Gunner | → Second Mate → Gunner | Second Mate | 3 |
| 14 | John Silver | 6 | 3 | Carpenter | → Second Mate → Carpenter | Second Mate | 3 |

Figure 16.9 – Split the hierarchy into multiple root branches

Now that we have multiple branches, we can add an edge flag to identify members without direct reports. To do this, use `LEFT JOIN` for a distinct list of `SUPERIOR_ID` values (e.g., pirates with direct reports) from the query result we obtained previously. Any `NULL` value returned by the right table identifies an edge, as seen in the following figure:

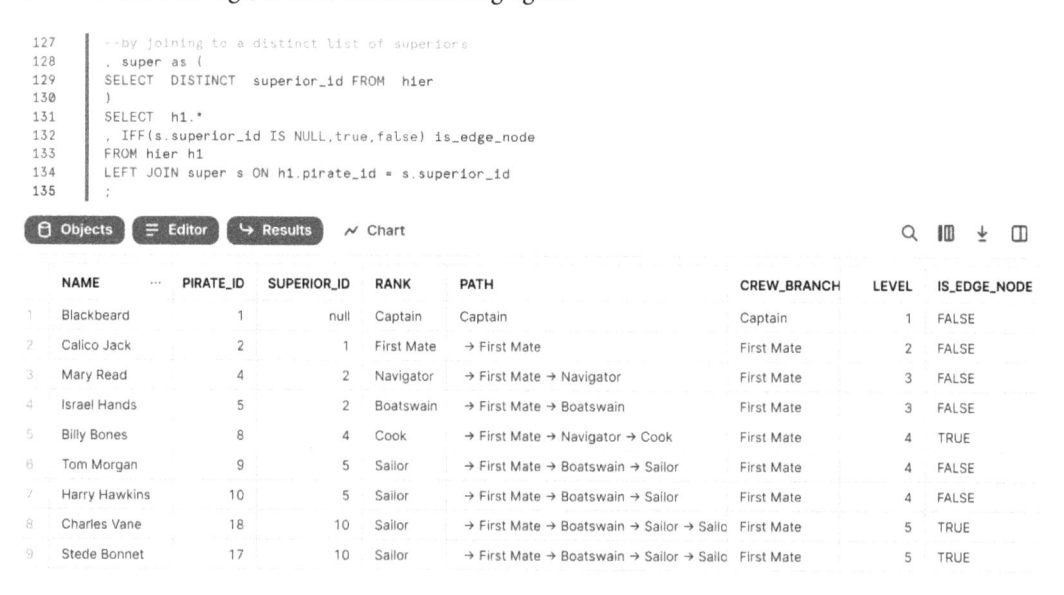

```
127    --by joining to a distinct list of superiors
128    , super as (
129    SELECT DISTINCT superior_id FROM hier
130    )
131    SELECT h1.*
132      , IFF(s.superior_id IS NULL,true,false) is_edge_node
133    FROM hier h1
134    LEFT JOIN super s ON h1.pirate_id = s.superior_id
135    ;
```

| | NAME | PIRATE_ID | SUPERIOR_ID | RANK | PATH | CREW_BRANCH | LEVEL | IS_EDGE_NODE |
|---|---|---|---|---|---|---|---|---|
| 1 | Blackbeard | 1 | null | Captain | Captain | Captain | 1 | FALSE |
| 2 | Calico Jack | 2 | 1 | First Mate | → First Mate | First Mate | 2 | FALSE |
| 3 | Mary Read | 4 | 2 | Navigator | → First Mate → Navigator | First Mate | 3 | FALSE |
| 4 | Israel Hands | 5 | 2 | Boatswain | → First Mate → Boatswain | First Mate | 3 | FALSE |
| 5 | Billy Bones | 8 | 4 | Cook | → First Mate → Navigator → Cook | First Mate | 4 | TRUE |
| 6 | Tom Morgan | 9 | 5 | Sailor | → First Mate → Boatswain → Sailor | First Mate | 4 | FALSE |
| 7 | Harry Hawkins | 10 | 5 | Sailor | → First Mate → Boatswain → Sailor | First Mate | 4 | FALSE |
| 8 | Charles Vane | 18 | 10 | Sailor | → First Mate → Boatswain → Sailor → Sailo | First Mate | 5 | TRUE |
| 9 | Stede Bonnet | 17 | 10 | Sailor | → First Mate → Boatswain → Sailor → Sailo | First Mate | 5 | TRUE |

Figure 16.10 – Add an indicator for edge nodes

Now that we have all the details needed for the bridge table, we can create it as a standalone dimension for future analysis and subsequent changes. Keeping the hierarchy separate from the source entity ensures that each can be maintained without impacting the other. Also, we can use familiar modeling techniques to track changes in hierarchies of any kind.

## Handling changes

A hierarchy can be updated and modified as a standalone dimension without impacting the underlying entities. Imagine if hierarchy details were stored alongside an already large Type-2 employee dimension – every title or manager change would generate a massive cascade of new records. Instead, we can use the SCD models covered in *Chapter 13, Modeling Slowly Changing Dimensions* to maintain changes to hierarchy dimensions efficiently and according to business needs.

Suppose that region groupings or pirate stations changed regularly. Our organization may be interested in the historical (or proposed) changes for planning and comparison purposes. The following are some of the common historical tracking scenarios that can occur and how to treat them:

- **History not required** – Use Type 1 SCD. If tracking historical changes to the hierarchy is not required, then a Type 1 strategy of *overwrite* is the simplest way to handle changes.

- **Compare last** – Use Type 3 SCD. When a change is made (or proposed) to an existing hierarchy, an organization may wish to compare the impact of the new grouping on the existing facts. For example, what if, in *Figure 16.3*, we grouped *New York City Zones A* and *B* but wanted to compare sales volumes to the previous classification? Adding a Type 3 `last value` column to the hierarchy dimension allows the business to analyze the before-and-after impact using the same join they would normally use to tie the fact to the hierarchy dimension.

- **Compare point-in-time** – Use Type 2 SCD. When historical versions of the hierarchy need to be tied back to the facts at various effective dates, the Type 2 model of *add new row* is used. This approach allows the hierarchy dimension to be joined to a fact table using any effective date to obtain the classification or assignment at a given moment. This allows organizations to answer questions such as *who did employee X report to last year versus currently?*

Now that we have familiarized ourselves with the types of hierarchies that exist in our organization and learned how to model and analyze them, let's review what we've learned.

## Summary

From how employees are organized to how customers or products are segmented, hierarchies exist in every organization. By learning how to model hierarchies as business dimensions, organizations can analyze and maintain them as they would any other entity. However, not all hierarchies behave the same way, and learning to understand their differences is the key to modeling them accordingly.

The biggest difference between hierarchies is the degree of variance between their members. Fixed and slightly ragged hierarchies have a set number of levels corresponding to their attributes' natural grouping. Ragged hierarchies, such as org levels, can vary in depth and the number of branches for each node. Because of their tree-like structure, ragged hierarchies present a challenge for relational databases that rely on a columnar structure.

Using native extensions to standard SQL, Snowflake allows users to easily perform complex operations, such as recursively traversing a tree structure and determining its branches and depth levels. The result can be stored in a separate dimension known as a bridge table, which allows the hierarchy to change independently of the associated entity. Once hierarchy details are separated into dimension tables, they can be historified according to business needs using the SCD techniques covered previously.

Now that we are familiar with the structures commonly found in a data warehouse and the tools that Snowflake provides to maintain them, we can discuss more advanced modeling patterns. In the next chapter, we will explore a popular data warehouse modeling methodology and discover the properties that make it one of the fastest-growing and scalable solutions to date.

# 17
# Scaling Data Models through Modern Techniques

After covering theory, architecture, terminology, methodology, and Snowflake-centered transformation strategies throughout the book, this chapter will build upon that foundational knowledge to address common data management challenges in large, complex environments. Specifically, this chapter will explore Data Vault 2.0 and Data Mesh methodologies—popular solutions that have emerged in response to some of the biggest challenges facing large organizations today. Despite their similar naming, Data Vault and Data Mesh attempt to tackle very different challenges, and are often used together.

Data Vault is a methodology that focuses on the efficient and flexible storage of data, with a primary focus on auditing and effortless scalability. It is made up of three pillars: modeling, methodology, and architecture. Its standardized, repeatable design patterns can be applied regardless of the complexity of the data or how many source systems are used.

Data Mesh exists for a very different purpose: to facilitate data discovery and sharing among distributed enterprise teams. Data Mesh is not a specific technology or tool, but rather a set of principles and best practices that can be applied to any architecture or platform. It emphasizes the importance of domain-driven design, self-service, federated data governance, and the use of data products and APIs to facilitate data discovery and sharing.

Data Mesh consists of principles and technical practices that enable effective communication and collaboration between domains. Many of these principles should be considered general best practices whether or not an organization decides to take up the Data Mesh banner wholeheartedly. As such, an overview of Data Mesh and the various modeling guidelines covered throughout this book will close out the final chapter as a general summary.

With this in mind, let's dive in and familiarize ourselves with Data Vault and how it can help organizations overcome some of the challenges associated with traditional data warehousing and analytics.

In this chapter, we're going to cover the following main topics:

- An introduction to Data Vault and its utility in modern data platforms
- Addressing the challenges of managing large, complex, and rapidly changing data environments with Data Vault
- The functional layers of the Data Vault architecture and core elements of the Raw Vault
- Efficiently loading Data Vault with multi-table inserts
- Modeling techniques for data marts
- An introduction to Data Mesh and managing data in large, complex organizations
- Reviewing Data Mesh and modeling best practices mentioned throughout the book

## Technical requirements

The scripts used to instantiate and load the examples in this chapter are available in the following GitHub repo: (https://github.com/PacktPublishing/Data-Modeling-with-Snowflake/tree/main/ch17). While key sections of this script will be highlighted in this chapter, please refer to the ch_17_data_vault.sql file for the complete code required for following the Data Vault exercise, as it is too long to reprint here in full.

## Demystifying Data Vault 2.0

**Data Vault** emerged in the early 2000s as a response to the extensibility limitations of warehouses built using 3NF and star schema (discussed later in the chapter) models. Data Vault overcame these limitations while retaining the strengths of 3NF and star schema architectures by using a methodology especially suited to meet the needs of large enterprises. Around 2013, Data Vault was expanded to accommodate the growing demand for distributed computing and NoSQL databases, giving rise to its current iteration, Data Vault 2.0.

Data Vault uses a pattern-based design methodology to build an auditable and extensible data warehouse. When most people refer to Data Vault, they are referring to the **Raw Vault**, which consists of Link, Hub, and Satellite tables. Atop the Raw Vault, sits the **Business Vault**—designed to be a business-centric layer that abstracts the technical complexities of the underlying data sources and uses constructs such as **Point-in-Time** (**PIT**) and **Bridge** tables. Data cleansing and additional business rules are performed in separate data mart—or information mart—layers based on department and organizational reporting requirements. The Business Vault and information mart layers are then exposed to end users for curated and self-service analytics.

Auditability is a major focus in Data Vault. Data warehouses are often more than just sources of historical data—as source systems are updated or decommissioned, a data warehouse becomes the system of record. Depending on where and how data is modified in a data warehouse, traceability to the source system may be permanently severed. To overcome this problem, Data Vault uses an insert-only strategy—no updates, no data cleansing, and no business rules in the base layers (this is handled downstream of the data marts and information delivery layers). As Data Vault practitioners often say: *Data Vault is a source of facts, not a source of truth* (since truth, in the data world, can vary based on whose business rules you follow).

> **Architectural alignment with Snowflake**
>
> Under the hood, Snowflake architecture is insert-only. Data stored in Snowflake micro partitions is never physically modified. Rather, modifications such as deletions or updates are performed logically, based on the record ID. This design makes Snowflake architecture an ideal fit for the insert-only methodology of Data Vault.

While the Data Vault methodology is simple to understand, it requires training and experience to execute correctly. This chapter will examine the core elements of the Raw Vault and highlight Snowflake-specific features that aid in efficient design and data loading. However, before undertaking a Data Vault implementation, consider obtaining a certification or enlisting the help of an expert to help decide whether and how Data Vault should be implemented in your organization.

Remember, Data Vault is scalable because it is source-system-agnostic and business-focused. To ensure the success of your Data Vault endeavor, start the same way as you would with any design: by understanding business semantics and building a conceptual business model as described in *Chapter 7, Putting Conceptual Modeling into Practice*. By doing so, you will preemptively address many of the design questions to come.

This exercise will use only one source system and a small subset of tables to demonstrate the core elements of the Raw Vault. The conceptual model in *Figure 17.1* will guide the design. Even though only one source system is used in this example, an accurate conceptual model will ensure that business entities and their relationships are modeled correctly (no matter where they are sourced from, referred to as *country* or *nation*, or identified by columns labeled *key* or *id*). If the business model is not well understood in advance, the Data Vault model will be built on a shaky foundation and fail to deliver the expected outcomes.

The conceptual business model and the physical source system model in this example consist of two dimension tables and a fact table, as shown here:

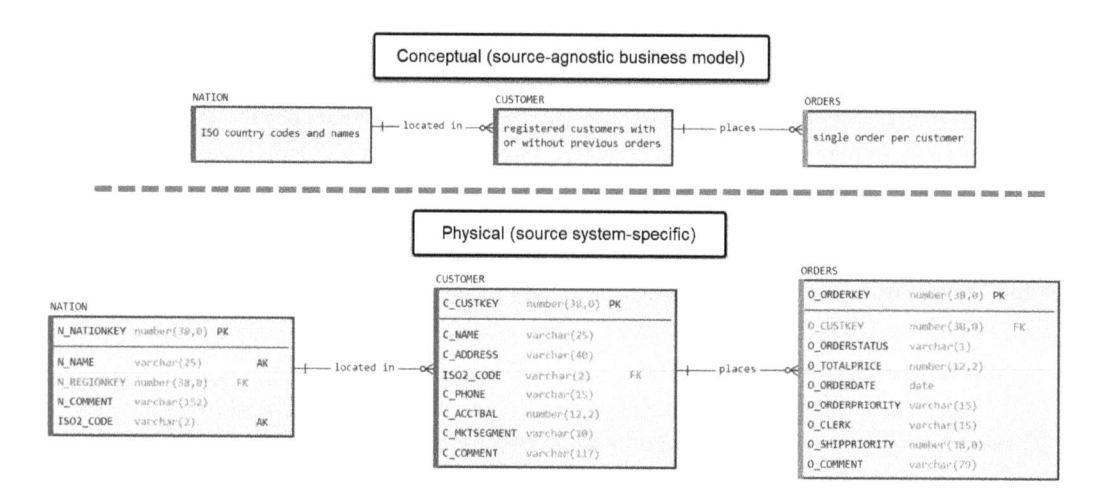

Figure 17.1 – ERD of the source system that serves as the base for the Data Vault exercise

For this exercise, we will again source data from Snowflake's TPCH sample data. Use the accompanying code to instantiate the environments and create the landing area tables and associated objects by running the code in the sections titled as follows:

- Setting up environments
- Setting up the landing area
- Simulating data loads from the source system

Starting with this foundation, let's get to know the core elements of the Raw Vault: links, hubs, and satellites.

## Building the Raw Vault

In this section, we will familiarize ourselves with the building blocks of the Data Vault by constructing a basic Raw Vault. Data Vault is a rule-based methodology and also highlights the importance of understanding general modeling standards like the ones covered throughout this book. Data Vault standards mandate the structure, transformation rules, and naming conventions. The latter can vary as long as it is consistent across the entire implementation and follows suggested guidelines (a list of suggested naming standards can be found on the Data Vault Alliance website: https://datavaultalliance.com/news/dv/dv-standards/data-vault-2-0-suggested-object-naming-conventions/).

To begin the exercise, we will create a landing area for the source tables we'll work with using the code provided in this chapter. Once the source data is loaded, we can begin modeling the core of the Data Vault design: hubs.

## Hubs

The first building block of Data Vault is the hubs. **Hubs** are a collection of business keys belonging to a business entity. In modeling terms, this would be a natural key—not a surrogate with no intrinsic meaning.

Take the LOCATION table as an example:

```
SELECT n_nationkey, iso2_code, n_name FROM src_nation LIMIT 5;
--
N_NATIONKEY|ISO2_CODE|N_NAME    |
-----------+---------+----------+
          0|AL       |ALGERIA   |
          1|AR       |ARGENTINA |
          2|BR       |BRAZIL    |
          3|CA       |CANADA    |
          4|EG       |EGYPT     |
```

N_NATIONKEY, the PK in the source system, is a surrogate key unrelated to any business concept. ISO2_CODE, which is also unique and contains meaningful values, is better suited to act as the hub key.

A hub table is a simple structure consisting of the following:

- **Hash key** – A calculated field consisting of a hash (e.g., SHA Binary or MD5) of the Business Key columns that serves as the PK for the hub. This technique has been used to generate unique IDs in previous chapters. This example will use the naming format <dv_object>_<entity_name>_hk (e.g., hub_customer_hk).

- **Business key column(s)** – Natural keys (not surrogates) that the business understands and commonly refers to. This can be a single or compound key and uses the same column names as the source table.

- **Load date** – The timestamp of when the record was first loaded into the Data Vault. This example will use the naming format load_dts.

- **Source system** – An identifier for the source system from where the data is being loaded. This identifier should be consistent across the entire Data Vault. This example will use the naming format rec_src.

- **Hub table naming convention** – Hub tables should follow a uniform naming convention that identifies them as hubs and points to the source business entity (not necessarily the table name). This example will use the naming format hub_<entity> (e.g., hub_customer).

> **A note on repeating keys and multiple source systems**
>
> Hubs, like all Raw Vault objects, record only the first instance and source system that introduced a business key to the Data Vault. Once a business key exists in the hub, subsequent loads, even those originating in other source systems, are not inserted or updated. By incorporating the timestamp into their PK, sats track historical changes to business attributes, but, like other Data Vault objects, only do so the first time a record enters the Data Vault.

An example of a hub based on the CUSTOMER source table would look as follows:

```
L1_RDV.HUB_CUSTOMER
MD5_HUB_CUSTOMER   varchar(32)            PK
C_CUSTKEY          number(38,0)
LOAD_DTS           timestamp_ntz(9)
REC_SRC            varchar(16777216)
```

Figure 17.2 – An example of a hub table structure

While a hub may be simple in nature, it can already answer business questions, such as counting the number of entity instances and the sources that provide data on each. Now, we will learn how to record transactions between entities using link tables.

### Links

Data Vault owes much of its versatility to its links. **Links** store the intersection of business keys, or the FKs, from related hubs. In this regard, links can be thought of as fact tables without facts or attributes—they contain nothing but business keys and must be connected to two or more hubs.

A link structure resembles that of a hub in its simplicity. It contains the following:

- **A link PK** – A calculated field consisting of a hash of the Business Key columns. This example will use the naming format `<dv_object>_<entity_names>_hk` (e.g., `lnk_customer_order_hk`).
- **Associated hub PKs** – The hashed PK columns used in the associated hubs, declared here as FKs.
- **Load date** – The timestamp of when the record was first loaded into the Data Vault.
- **Source system** – An identifier for the source system from where the data is being loaded.
- **Link table naming convention** – Link tables should follow a uniform naming convention that identifies them as such. This example will use the naming format `<dv_object>_<entity_names>` (e.g., `lnk_customer_order`).

Just like hubs, links record only the first instance of a relationship loaded into the Data Vault. An example of a link between CUSTOMER and ORDER entities would look as follows:

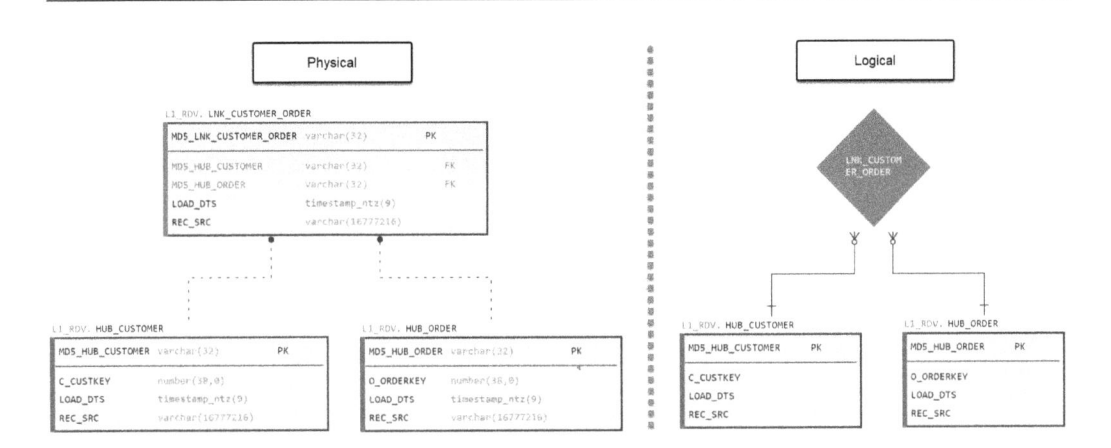

Figure 17.3 – An example of a link table structure

Notice that, logically, a link is identical to an M:M associative table. Even though CUSTOMER happens to have a one-to-many (optional) relationship with ORDER, links are designed with flexibility in mind and can store relationships of any cardinality with no changes required. If business rules changed to allow joint orders from multiple customers, the Data Vault could continue loading without changing its structure or ETL processes.

Now that we have a way to store entity business keys and interactions between them, we can learn how to record attributes and their changes using satellites.

## Satellites

**Satellites** (**sats**) store the attributes in a Data Vault and provide change history. Sats function very much like Type-2 SCDs except, like all Data Vault tables, they are insert-only. Because sats can be split to accommodate scenarios such as multiple source systems, rate of change, and security, it is a good practice to include the scenario abbreviation in the sat table name (in this basic example, we use a single source system called *system 1*).

A sat has the following structure:

- **A hub PK column** – A sat uses the associated hub or link PK column (name and value) as its PK (e.g., hub_customer_hk).
- **Load date** – The timestamp of when each set of attribute values was first loaded into the Data Vault.
- **Hash Diff** – A hash of all attribute values to allow for easy comparison of changes on new loads. This technique was used in *Chapter 13, Modeling Slowly Changing Dimensions* (SCDs) for its convenience, as it is much faster to compare one column than write out comparisons for every attribute in the table. Due to the name, beginners often mistake this column as a diff between multiple records, but it is only the concatenation of the attributes in one—the diff occurs (or doesn't) when two hash diffs are compared.

- **Source system** – An identifier for the source system from where the data is being loaded. This value may not match that of the hub (e.g., if the business key was first loaded from Sys A but later modified in Sys B).
- **Non-PK source attribute columns** – All the non-PK columns that did not make it into the hub (or link) are included in the sat.
- **Sat table naming convention** – Sat tables should follow a uniform naming convention that identifies them as sats and points to the source business entity (not necessarily the table name). This example will use the naming format `sat_<src system>_<entity>` (e.g., `sat_sys1_customer`).

Sats use a two-part PK consisting of the associated hub key and load date. On every load, the records are compared using the business key and hash diff. When changes are detected, the new records are inserted and given a timestamp (this implies that Data Vault is real-time compatible).

An example of a sat based on the `CUSTOMER` source table would look as follows:

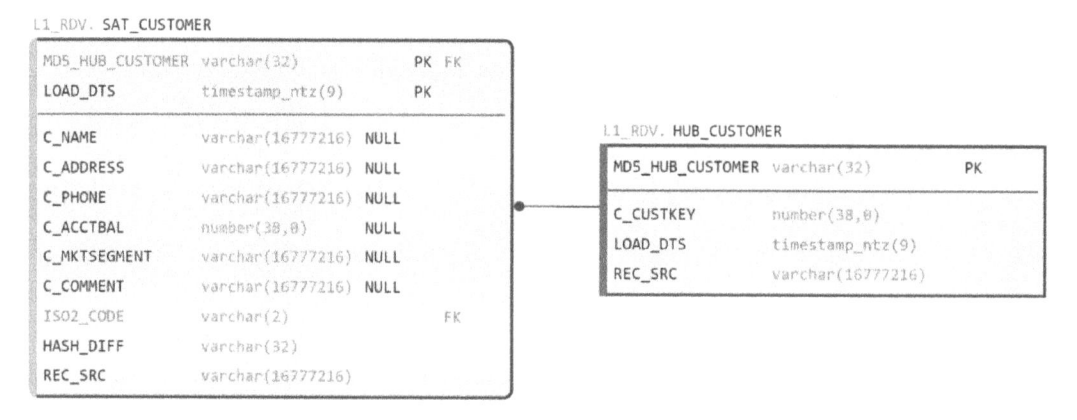

Figure 17.4 – An example of a satellite table structure

Every column that didn't make it into the hub or link ends up as an attribute in the sat. Although hubs, links, and sats comprise the Raw Vault's core, an additional object type can also be found at this level.

### Reference tables

**Reference (ref)** tables store descriptive data about information in satellites or other Data Vault objects but do not warrant a business key. Common examples of ref tables include date dimensions (with month, year, and quarter attributes) or descriptive information about the source systems in the `REC_SRC` field. Rather than creating a link table for every satellite with a date dimension, you can use a reference table for direct joins instead. While Data Vault rules prohibit sat-to-sat joins, a sat may reference a ref table through an FK.

In this example, the NATION table contains ISO 3166 values that are not source system-dependent. Instead of decomposing NATION into a hub and sat and *link*-ing it to CUSTOMER, a ref table can instead be used. This gives us the completed Data Vault structure based on the original three source tables we started with:

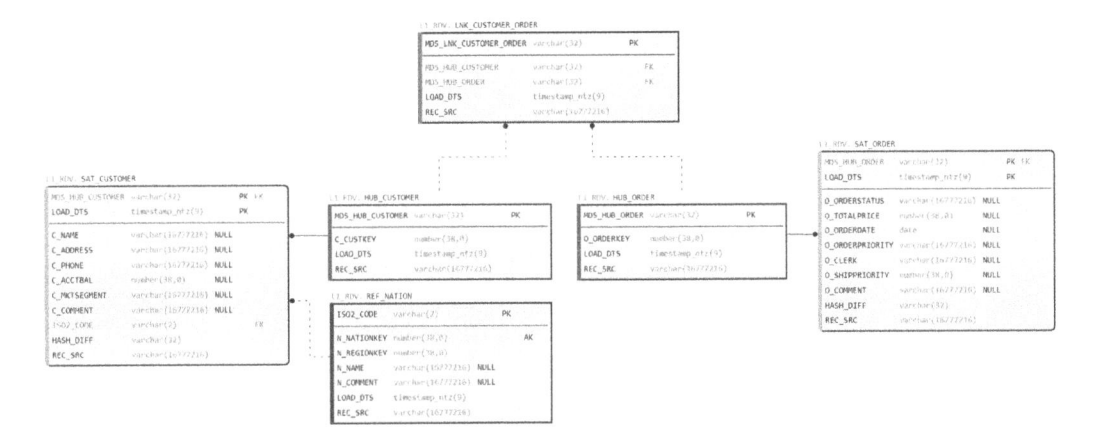

Figure 17.5 – A completed data vault structure

With the structure in place, all that remains is to create an efficient pipeline to load records into the vault.

## Loading with multi-table inserts

Although the loads in a Data Vault are insert-only, they are not trivial—validations for new records and CDC checks must be performed to keep the data consistent. As we saw with the ORDER table, which generated three objects (hub, link, sat) in the Raw Vault, the challenge of loading multiple objects from a single source also exists. Snowflake provides a **multi-table insert** operator to allow users to perform such an operation efficiently.

In its basic (unconditional) form, the multi-table insert loads data from a single subquery into a list of target tables:

```
INSERT ALL
    INTO t1
    INTO t1 (c1, c2, c3) VALUES (n2, n1, DEFAULT)
    INTO t2 (c1, c2, c3)
    INTO t2 VALUES (n3, n2, n1)
SELECT n1, n2, n3 from src;
```

However, in Data Vault, we must define conditions that only insert records (business keys, transactions, and attributes) when the Data Vault *sees* them for the first time. For this, we will use the conditional multi-table insert. Besides the WHEN condition, the multi-table insert allows users to specify an operator that determines whether all WHEN clauses are executed for a record or only the first that evaluates to TRUE:

```
-- Conditional multi-table insert
INSERT [ OVERWRITE ] { FIRST | ALL }
    { WHEN <condition> THEN intoClause [ ... ] }
    [ ... ]
    [ ELSE intoClause ]
<subquery>
```

> **Pull over to the side of the load**
>
> Outside of the Data Vault framework, the multi-table insert is a tool that can aid in tactical data quality enforcement. When the type of data anomaly is known in advance (e.g., out of range or not permitted values), the multi-table insert can divert anomalous records to a staging table for review while allowing the rest of the load to proceed as planned to the intended target.

Before writing the multi-table insert, we define the outbound views that contain all the source fields and Data Vault required columns to simplify downstream loads. The view is constructed over the stream object created in the previous exercise because it allows us to identify new records without added logic. To follow along with the accompanying code, execute the scripts in the sections titled as follows:

- Creating views for loading the Raw Vault
- Setting up the Raw Vault

The outbound view for the ORDER table would look as follows:

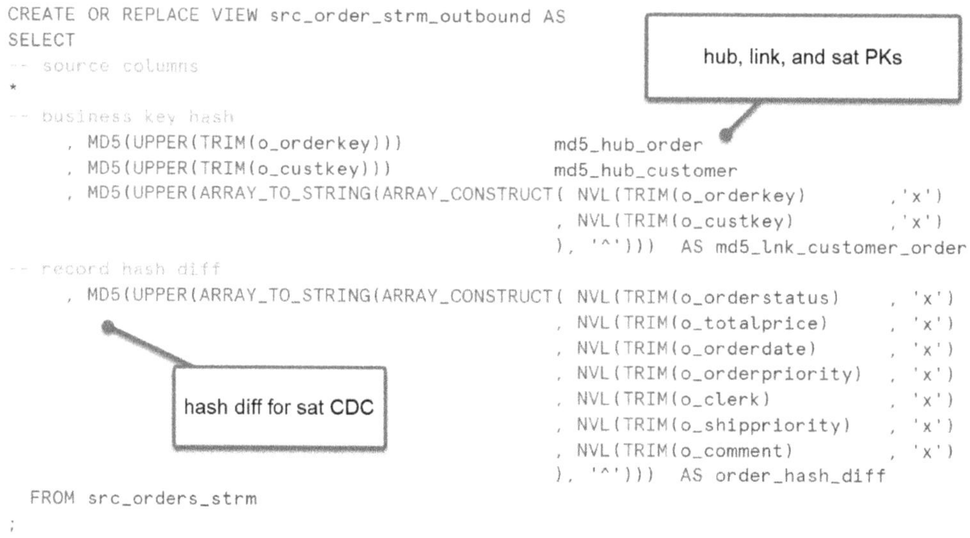

```
CREATE OR REPLACE VIEW src_order_strm_outbound AS
SELECT
    -- source columns
    *
    -- business key hash
    , MD5(UPPER(TRIM(o_orderkey)))                          md5_hub_order
    , MD5(UPPER(TRIM(o_custkey)))                           md5_hub_customer
    , MD5(UPPER(ARRAY_TO_STRING(ARRAY_CONSTRUCT( NVL(TRIM(o_orderkey)) ,'x')
                                              , NVL(TRIM(o_custkey))  ,'x')
                                              ), '^')))   AS md5_lnk_customer_order
    -- record hash diff
    , MD5(UPPER(ARRAY_TO_STRING(ARRAY_CONSTRUCT( NVL(TRIM(o_orderstatus))    , 'x')
                                              , NVL(TRIM(o_totalprice))      , 'x')
                                              , NVL(TRIM(o_orderdate))       , 'x')
                                              , NVL(TRIM(o_orderpriority))   , 'x')
                                              , NVL(TRIM(o_clerk))           , 'x')
                                              , NVL(TRIM(o_shippriority))    , 'x')
                                              , NVL(TRIM(o_comment))         , 'x')
                                              ), '^')))   AS order_hash_diff
FROM src_orders_strm
;
```

(hub, link, and sat PKs)

(hash diff for sat CDC)

Figure 17.6 – A view with all required columns for the outbound loads

Using these views, which contain all the columns needed to load the Raw Vault objects, we can configure the multi-table insert statement—allowing us to take a single subquery that selects from the source table and load the associated links, hubs, and satellites in parallel. The multi-table insert would have the following structure:

```
INSERT ALL
-- condition to check if BKEY exists in the hub
WHEN (SELECT COUNT(1) FROM hub_customer tgt WHERE tgt.hub_customer_hk
= src_hub_customer_hk) = 0
-- if it's a new BKEY, insert into the hub table
THEN INTO hub_customer
( < hub columns> )
VALUES
( < hub columns> )
-- condition to check if BKEY exists in the sat
WHEN (SELECT COUNT(1) FROM sat_sys1_customer tgt WHERE tgt.hub_
customer_hk = src_hub_customer_hk
-- and only insert if changes based on
-- hash diff are detected
AND tgt.hash_diff = src_customer_hash_diff) = 0
-- if it's a new BKEY, or changes to attribute values
-- are detected, insert into the hub table
THEN INTO sat_sys1_customer
( < sat columns> )
VALUES
( < sat columns> )
-- subquery
SELECT < columns AS src_columns> --aliased source columns
FROM l0_src.src_customer_strm_outbound src;
```

Complete (and optionally repeat) the Raw Vault load by running the script in the section titled *Loading the Raw Vault using multi-table insert*.

Each simulated load will process 1,000 customer records and approximately ten times as many related order records. Due to the new-records-only insert nature of Data Vault, repeating the same batch of customer records into the landing area tables will result in no records being loaded into the Vault.

Now that we are familiar with the Raw Vault and the fundamentals and applications of the Data Vault methodology in conjunction with relevant Snowflake features, it is worth spending some time on the modeling patterns often used in information marts (or data marts, as they are called outside of Data Vault) to serve as a springboard for architecting the reporting layer.

## Modeling the data marts

This section will explore the Star and Snowflake schemas—popular options for architecting user-facing self-service schemas and data marts due to their efficiency and ease of understanding. Both approaches are designed to optimize the performance of data analysis by organizing data into a structure that makes it easy to query and analyze. But first, a quick overview of what a data mart is.

> **Data mart versus data warehouse**
>
> A data warehouse and a data mart are repositories for storing and managing data, but they differ in scope, purpose, and design. A **data warehouse** is a large, centralized repository of integrated data used to support decision-making and analysis across an entire organization. Data warehouses are optimized for complex queries and often use Kimball's dimensional modeling technique or Inmon's 3NF approach (described in his book *Building the Data Warehouse*). On the other hand, a **data mart** is a subset of a data warehouse designed to serve a specific department or function within an organization. Data marts are typically designed using a star or snowflake schema model.

With this in mind, let's get to know the first of these two architectures: the star schema.

## Star schema

A **star schema** is a database architecture that consists of a central fact table surrounded by several dimension tables radiating out in a star-like pattern. The fact table contains the measures (e.g., sales or revenue), while the dimension tables represent the attributes (e.g., time, geography, and product).

A star schema is highly denormalized, making it efficient for querying large datasets and allowing for fast aggregations and drill-downs. The advantage of a star schema is that it is simple to understand and easy to query. The downside, as with any denormalized design, is that integrity issues and data anomalies can occur. While the star schema may be simple to create, it becomes difficult to maintain as the schema grows due to redundancy concerns, and the inability to create entity hierarchies or many-to-many relationships. Such concerns are addressed by the snowflake schema approach.

## Snowflake schema

A **snowflake schema** is a variation of the star schema where the dimension tables are further normalized into sub-dimension tables. For example, a product dimension might be split into product, product category, and product sub-category dimensions—forming a hierarchy.

In a snowflake schema, the dimension tables are connected through a series of one-to-many relationships, creating a snowflake-like pattern. While this approach increases data normalization, it makes writing queries more complex and harder to understand than a star schema. The snowflake schema is generally considered less performant than a star because of the number of joins required to query it. However, that may not be true once Snowflake's performance enhancements, such as join elimination through RELY (*Chapter 12, Putting Transformational Modeling into Practice*), are considered.

The following table summarizes the differences between the star and snowflake schemas, highlighting their respective benefits in **bold**:

Comparison of star and snowflake schemas

| Star | Snowflake |
| --- | --- |
| **Simple and easy to understand** | More complicated than a star |
| Denormalized—increasing redundancy and anomaly risk | **More normalized with less possibility of anomalies** |
| Less flexible and harder to scale | **More flexible and scalable than a star** |
| **Easier to write and understand queries** | More complex queries due to number of joins required |
| Faster performance due to fewer joins | Faster performance if leveraging join elimination |
| Efficient for querying large datasets | Better suited for analysis of individual dimensions |
| Can be difficult to handle dimensions with many attributes | **Better suited for handling dimensions with many attributes** |

Figure 17.7 – A comparison of star and snowflake modeling approaches

Choosing between a star and snowflake schema will ultimately depend on the organization's specific needs and goals. A star schema is simpler and more efficient for querying large datasets but may not be as flexible for complex table relationships. A snowflake schema offers greater data normalization and flexibility but at the cost of increased complexity. As a modeler, it's important to understand these differences and choose the appropriate approach for each data mart.

When organizations become large enough to warrant multiple data marts, or even warehouses, coordinating them without creating data siloes becomes challenging. In the last few years, a new data management framework, Data Mesh, has emerged to facilitate sharing and collaboration among organizational data domains.

## Discovering Data Mesh

**Data Mesh** (**DM**) is an approach to organizing and managing data in large, complex organizations, introduced in 2019 by Zhamak Dehghani, a thought leader in the field of data architecture.

The DM approach advocates for decentralized data ownership and governance, with data treated as a product owned and managed by the teams using it. This contrasts with the traditional centralized (or, as Zhamak calls it, *monolithic*) approach to data management, where a single team or department is responsible for all data-related activities.

In a DM architecture, data is organized into self-contained domains, each responsible for its own data curation and sharing. These domains are often organized around business capabilities or processes and are staffed by cross-functional teams that include technical and business experts.

DM consists of four principles that aim to enable effective communication and collaboration between domains: domain-driven design, self-service, and data product thinking. These practices help ensure that each domain can operate independently while still being able to share data and insights with other domains as needed.

The four principles of DM are as follows:

- **Domain-oriented decentralized data ownership** – In DM, data is owned by the domain that produces it, and the domain is responsible for making it available to the rest of the organization. This means that each domain has the autonomy to choose its technology stack, data models, and data storage.
- **Data as a product** – Data is treated as a product designed and built for consumption by other teams. Data is managed with the same rigor and discipline as software products, focusing on delivering customer value.
- **Self-serve data infrastructure as a platform** – DM promotes the idea of building self-serve data infrastructure that provides a set of core data services that different domains can consume. This helps reduce the complexity of data integration and allows domains to focus on their core competencies.
- **Federated governance** – DM recognizes that governance is important for ensuring data quality, compliance, and security. However, instead of centralized governance, DM promotes federated governance, where each domain has the autonomy to govern its own data while adhering to organization-wide standards and policies.

While DM attempts to tackle the biggest data challenges that enterprises face, it has also been criticized for its complexity and the skillset required to execute it correctly because, when mismanaged, the decentralization of DM can lead to a proliferation of data siloes—the very thing it intends to mitigate. But, on the face of it, DM is a collection of best practices that are hard to argue with. Best of all, DM guidelines are perfectly aligned and reinforced by Snowflake architecture and innate functionality. As a fitting end to this book, we will close with a rundown of best practices for DM and the broader modeling context.

## Start with the business

A successful data model must accurately reflect the business model. As the understanding of business rules and processes does not sit with the data team, attempting to build any system without the guidance and express approval of business teams is folly. In larger organizations with multiple business lines, identifying domain boundaries is key to segmenting the modeling task into smaller independent chunks.

Depending on the depth and breadth of the organizational hierarchy, a segmented data model can be separated logically into schemas, databases, or even Snowflake accounts. Snowflake sharing and securitization features are then used to establish appropriate access rights for anyone within the organization.

## Adopt governance guidelines

Governance must be woven throughout the development process to ensure end-to-end consistency. Define a development workflow that starts with modeling (iterated through all its stages) and provides the appropriate levels of checks and approvals throughout. Ensure that naming conventions are clearly defined and enforced at every stage of the process.

Be sure that all the work within a team, from the model to the transformational logic, is versioned and source controlled. Most people are familiar with code repositories such as Git and should also be aware that modern modeling tools allow for version control and parallel development of the same kind. Version control allows teams to compare and recover prior states of their modeling structure or transformational logic.

Once checked into a repository and validated, physical deployments must also be accompanied by the requisite documentation and metadata collateral to ensure usability by others in the organization, including other departments. Such materials include ER diagrams, table and column-level descriptions, and table constraints. Following these guidelines will accelerate self-service and data discovery.

## Emphasize data quality

Data quality is driven by the design of the systems that generate it, and good design starts with an accurate model. When the model and the business it supports are in alignment, anomalous data, such as values that fall outside the accepted bounds or violate established cardinality, will be less likely to occur. However, if the data is inconsistent by nature, integrity checks must be built as far upstream in the loading process as possible. Some anomalies, such as null values, can be caught by Snowflake table constraints. However, integrity checks on FKs, PKs, and AKs must be performed manually during loading. As Data Vault rightly suggests, truth is subjective, while facts are not. Transitive business rules (e.g., active customers) may change over time or vary by department, but a customer entity remains a cornerstone of the business model. Pushing transitive business rules downstream to mutable reporting layers while keeping data in its original form at the lower levels will ensure the model can handle changes or re-interpretations of business rules without requiring an integral redesign.

One of the pillars of DM and a best practice that all data teams stand to benefit from is the concept of data as a product. This simple change of perspective helps domain and centralized data teams embrace data quality holistically and take responsibility for the data they generate or maintain.

## Encourage a culture of data sharing

Whether facilitating sharing or reviewing data assets within or across teams, data sharing is the foundation of Snowflake's cloud architecture—allowing organizations to convene on a single source of truth without moving or copying data through cloning and time travel. The documentation and governance guidelines mentioned previously will enable everyone in the organization to use and interpret the data assets in a straightforward manner.

The same principles of sharing and collaboration that Snowflake has baked into its architecture also apply to the data modeling assets. Data modeling is an essential tool for engineering and deploying to a physical database, but its utility extends much further when shared with the broader organization. Once a data model is deployed and operational, the diagrams, definitions, and functional details must be made available to the organization through a collaborative interface that keeps everyone aligned and allows for iterative enhancement. Modern modeling solutions provide the previously mentioned features and integrations with other tools in the BI stack.

After understanding the core concepts of Data Vault modeling and the foundational best practices of DM methodology, let's review what we have learned.

## Summary

Data Vault 2.0 is designed to address the challenges of managing large, complex, and rapidly changing data environments. It is a hybrid approach that combines elements of 3NF and star schema and uses a standardized, repeatable design pattern that can be applied to any dataset, regardless of size or complexity.

Data Vault design begins by defining the business model and constructing the base layer, known as the Raw Vault. The Raw Vault contains the following elements:

- Hubs – natural keys that identify business entities
- Links – store the interactions between business entities
- Satellites – store the descriptions and attributes of business entities
- Reference tables – include descriptive information and metadata

On top of the Raw Vault, a Business Vault is constructed to meet changing business needs and requirements without disrupting the overall data architecture. Next, domain-oriented information marts are built to meet organizational reporting demands.

All of these features working in unison provide agility, scalability, change history, and full auditability/traceability, given any number of source systems while absorbing source and business rule changes without requiring redesign. Whether on top of Data Vault or other data warehouse architectures, reporting and self-service layers are often modeled using star and snowflake schema designs. A star schema consists of a central fact table connected to multiple dimension tables, while a snowflake schema expands on this by further normalizing the dimension tables to reduce redundancy. Business users prefer these architectures over fully normalized schemas because they are more intuitive and easier to query. Some organizations are large enough to contain a mix of modeling architectures and data platforms.

When an organization is large enough to warrant multiple data domains, the Data Mesh framework, introduced in 2019, has been instrumental in establishing best practice guidelines to ensure cross-domain data access and self-service. By pushing the responsibility of data stewardship to the domain teams and treating data as a product, data assets are held to standards similar to those of software products.

Whether embracing Data Mesh in full or applying its most effective practices to an existing data platform, establishing and solidifying standards and governance rules will ensure data quality, usability, and easy maintenance of the data models you produce. Starting with the business model and ensuring a conceptual alignment between functional and data teams provides a solid foundation for building the technical solution. Governance guidelines and standards must then be set in place to ensure a ubiquitous language is understood by everyone in the organization in the technical and semantic domains. A data model built with business domain consensus will provide a scalable foundation that ensures data quality and consistency. However, treating data as a product is the responsibility of every data domain, not just the central BI team. When multiple data domains exist within an organization, a mix of architectures and data platforms will pose a barrier to effective sharing. To overcome this, teams must leverage the native sharing features of the Snowflake Data Cloud and other tools that comprise their BI stack to equip everyone with the technical means and functional documents to discover and consume cross-domain information.

No matter the platform or the methodology, an accurate and accessible data model is the key to simplifying and making sense of complex systems. I hope the information in this book will serve as a reliable map for navigating the increasing complexity of our data terrain.

# 18
# Appendix

Wouldn't it be fitting if a book on modeling was itself modeled after something? Well, it has been! This book follows a spiral model, starting from a high-level overview of modeling and rising in winding loops, revisiting its core elements in ever-greater depth and complexity. This may seem like an unorthodox approach, but I believe that the difficulty of the technical *how* is alleviated by the understanding of the conceptual *why*. As such, I made it a point not to presuppose any modeling knowledge beyond a basic understanding of SQL and to never lean on a term or concept before formally introducing it.

Following a helical structure while writing this text allowed me to carve out a clear path from the theoretical to the technical and kept me from drifting into areas that were not core to the central theme. Inevitably, some exercises had to be excluded because they did not cleanly fit within the framework of the chapters. Rather than leave them on the proverbial cutting room floor, I have decided to include them as extras in the associated GitHub repository of this book.

While the book must be finalized for printing, I plan to continue adding interesting examples to the extras folder of the repo. The following is a summary of the types of content that can already be found there.

## Technical requirements

The scripts used to instantiate and load the examples in this chapter are available in the following GitHub repo: `https://github.com/PacktPublishing/Data-Modeling-with-Snowflake/tree/main/extras`.

## The exceptional time traveler

What changed? This a question that's been asked since the first **data manipulation language** (DML) operations were performed on a database. While Snowflake's built-in table change tracking and streams can help answer this question, they are not enabled on tables by default. However, even in Snowflake's Standard edition, all tables have a default time travel data retention period of one day.

The time travel feature can be combined with the `EXCEPT` set operator to isolate and compare any changes made. The exercise uses a randomly generated filter when selecting which records to update to make things interesting. The only way to solve the mystery is to use Snowflake's exceptional time-traveling powers.

The exercise is explained in the file titled `01_exceptional_time_travel.sql`.

## The secret column type Snowflake refuses to document

Snowflake's co-founders and chief architects, Benoit Dageville and Thierry Cruanes, spent many years working at Oracle. In fact, Oracle's influence can be seen in many of the SQL constructs and functions that Snowflake supports. One such example is the concept of the virtual column.

Virtual columns straddle the line between physical and transformational modeling—between table and view. Virtual columns look like normal table columns, but their values are derived rather than stored on disc. They are an efficient way to embed simple business rules and transformational logic in a table without the overhead of maintaining views and incurring storage costs. Virtual columns can be defined through constants or transformational expressions such as the `DEFAULT` column operator. Strangely, they are not mentioned in the `CREATE TABLE` documentation at the time of writing (https://docs.snowflake.com/en/sql-reference/sql/create-table). However, references to Snowflake users taking advantage of them can be found in the community forums as far back as 2018 (https://community.snowflake.com/s/question/0D50Z00008ixGQKSA2/does-snowflake-supports-computed-columns-in-a-table-while-creating-table).

For an overview of the advantages of using virtual/computed columns in tables and how they differ from column defaults, see the example in the file titled `02_secret_virtual_columns.sql`.

## Read the functional manual (RTFM)

Snowflake's technical documentation is among the clearest and most informative I have ever encountered (virtual columns aside). Paying attention to the usage notes and best practices or simply scrolling down the list of available functions helped me elevate my SQL game and discover new features when I first started, and it continues to pay dividends. One such discovery came—putting aside pride—while reading the usage notes for `ORDER BY` (https://docs.snowflake.com/en/sql-reference/constructs/order-by). There, I learned about the `NULLS FIRST` and `NULLS LAST` keywords and how they override the default ordering of `NULL` when arranging in `ASC` or `DESC`. It's a feature that has come in handy many times since. Most importantly, it serves as a reminder to check the documentation periodically to help spot new features and functionality.

See the example in the file titled `03_order_by_nulls.sql`.

## Summary

If you have made it this far, thank you. Truly. Writing this book could not have been possible without input from my peers throughout the data community and their thought-provoking modeling questions and suggestions. I hope this book and its further reading materials have given you a solid base from which to expand your modeling practice in Snowflake and beyond. If you have any questions, nifty tricks to include in the extras section, or just want to say *hi*, find me on LinkedIn (`https://www.linkedin.com/in/serge-cloud-connected/`).

Here's to taking modeling from a *lost art* to an *essential skill* in the world of data together.

# Index

## A

**accumulating snapshot fact tables** 219
**additive facts** 219
**alternate keys (AKs)**
  as unique constraints 80
**associative entity** 123
**atomic grain** 110
**attributes** 22
  adding 121
**attributes, as columns** 70
  semi-structured data, storing 72
  Snowflake data types 71
**auditability** 265

## B

**Boyce-Codd Normal Form (BCNF)** 138, 141, 142
**bridge table** 256, 264
**Business Event Analysis and Modeling (BEAM) method** 106
**business intelligence (BI)** 31
  tools 85
**business key** 78, 200
**Business Vault** 264
**bus matrix**
  visualizing, in conceptual model 112, 113

## C

**cache**
  metadata cache 44
  query results cache 44
  services layer 44
  storage layer 45
  using 43
  warehouse cache 45
**candidate key** 139
**capital expenditure (CapEx)** 36
**cardinality** 22
**Cartesian product** 191
**change data capture (CDC)** 53
**change tracking** 59, 60
**clustering** 67
  automatic clustering 69, 70
**clustering key** 70
  benefits 70
**column-level security**
  reference link 167

common table expressions (CTEs)  192
composite  74
compound key  74
compute layer, Snowflake architecture  40
conceptual model
    business process, defining  109, 110
    bus matrix, visualizing in  112, 113
    dimensions, determining  110, 111
    facts, identifying  111, 112
    four-step DM method  107-109
    grain, determining  110
conceptual modeling  21-23, 106, 120
    entity  21
    entity-relationship (ER) modeling  23, 24
conformed attributes  115
conformed dimensions  115, 156
consolidated fact tables  219
constraints  73
    used, for performing join
        elimination  183, 184
costs
    compute costs  43
    considering  42
    service costs  43
    storage costs  42
CREATE TABLE AS SELECT
    (CTAS) tables  29
CREATE TABLE documentation
    reference link  282
crow's foot notation  95, 96

## D

data anomalies  135
    deletion anomaly  137
    domain anomaly  137, 138
    insertion anomaly  136
    update anomaly  135, 136

database environments  161
    criteria  162
    development (dev)  161
    governing principles  162
    production (prod)  161
database modeling
    benefits  7-9
database normalization  134, 135, 138
data classification
    reference link  168
data definition language (DDL)  28, 166
data manipulation language (DML)  167
    operations  64, 281
data marts
    modeling  273
    snowflake schema  274, 275
    star schema  274
Data Mesh (DM)  263, 275
    best practices  276-278
    principles  276
data modeling  18, 90
data models
    on normalization spectrum  149
Data Vault  107, 263-265
    multi-table inserts, loading with  271-273
Data Vault 2.0  264
data warehouse (DWH)  10, 219, 220, 274
Decision Support Systems (DSS)  10
deletion anomaly  137
dependency  135
development (dev) environment  161
dimensional modeling  106
    record, setting on  106
dimensions
    overview  200
    SCD types  200
domain anomaly  137, 138
domain-key normal form (DKNF)  146

# E

edges  257
ELT (extract, load, and transform)  238
enforcement  73
entities  21, 94
entity, as tables  64
   clustering  67-69
   data storage  64-67
entity granularity  22
entity instances  21
Entity-Relationship Diagrams (ERDs)  9, 91, 109, 174,
   creating, from physical model  174, 175
   in Chen notation  90, 91
   versus relational model (RM)  92, 93
exceptional time traveler  281, 282
Extract Transform Load (ETL)  13

# F

factless fact tables  219
facts  109, 111
fact table, measures
   additive facts  219
   non-additive facts  220
   semi-additive facts  220
fact tables  109, 217
   deleted records, recovering with load dates  230-233
   maintaining, with Snowflake features  226, 227
   method, for recovering deleted records  222-224
fact tables, types
   accumulating snapshot fact tables  219
   consolidated fact tables  219
   factless fact tables  219
   snapshot fact tables  218
   transaction fact tables  218
Fail-safe  49
fifth normal form (5NF)  144, 145
file formats  49
   CSV  49
   JSON  49
   Parquet  49
first normal form (1NF)  134, 138, 139
fixed-depth hierarchy  254
flatten join  244
foreign keys (FK)  173
   benefits  84
   BI tool functionality, automating  85
   data model, visualizing  84
   joins, informing  84
   referential integrity, enforcing  85, 86
   relationships  81-83
foreign keys (FKs)  115
forward engineering  174
fourth normal form (4NF)  143, 144

# G

grain  110

# H

hashing function  202
hierarchy  254
   fixed-depth hierarchy  254
   ragged hierarchy  256, 257
   slightly ragged hierarchy  255
hierarchy maintenance  258
   changes, handling  261
   common historical tracking scenarios  261
   ragged hierarchy, navigating  258-261

**hubs** 267
**hub table**
   business key column(s) 267
   example 268
   hash key 267
   load date 267
   naming convention 267
   source system 267
**hybrid transactional and analytical processing (HTAP)** 52
**Hybrid Unistore tables** 11, 41, 52, 53

# I

**IDEF1X notation** 97
**identifier** 74
   as primary keys 74
**Information Engineering (IE)** 19
**inheritance** 128
**insertion anomaly** 136
**integrated development environments (IDEs)** 28

# J

**join** 187
   FULL JOIN 188
   INNER JOIN 188
   LEFT JOIN 188
   RIGHT JOIN 188
**join elimination**
   performing, with constraints 183, 184
   RELY, usage criteria 185-187
   RELY, using 184, 185
**join explosions** 181
**junction entity** 123

# L

**lateral join** 244
**links** 268
   associated hub PKs 268
   link PK 268
   load date 268
   source system 268
   structure 268
   table naming convention 268
**logical modeling** 25, 120
   attributes, adding 120, 121
   expanding, to physical modeling 168
   many-to-many relationships 26, 27
   relationships, cementing 122, 123
**logical objects**
   physicalizing 169-171

# M

**Management Information Systems (MIS)** 10
**mandatory columns**
   as NOT NULL constraints 86, 87
**many-to-many (M:M) relationship** 93, 98, 99, 123-125
**materialized views** 56, 57
**MERGE statement** 211
**metadata cache** 44
**micro-partitions** 64, 65
**model**
   separating, from object 180
**modeling**
   analytical modeling scenarios 10, 11
   in analytical systems 13, 14
   in operational systems 12
   operational modeling scenarios 10, 11
   principles 20

purpose 4, 5
relational modeling 11
transformational modeling 11
**modeling, in reverse 113**
business processes, proposing 117
business processes, validating 117
dimensions, identifying 114
facts, identifying 114
relationships, establishing 115, 116
**modeling notation examples 20**
**modeling toolkit**
leveraging 5-7
natural language semantics 6
technical semantics 6
visual semantics 6, 7
**modeling types 18**
conceptual modeling 21
logical modeling 25
physical modeling 28
transformational modeling 31
ubiquitous modeling 18
**multi-table insert 148**
**multivalued dependency 143**

# N

**naming conventions 152**
casing 152
considerations 152
object naming 153
suggested conventions 156
**non-additive facts 220**
**normal forms 134**
Boyce-Codd Normal Form (BCNF) 141, 142
domain-key normal form (DKNF) 146
fifth normal form (5NF) 144, 145
first normal form (1NF) 138, 139

fourth normal form (4NF) 143, 144
second normal form (2NF) 139, 140
sixth normal form (6NF) 147, 148
third normal form (3NF) 140
**normalization 133**
**normalization spectrum**
data models, arranging on 149

# O

**object naming 153**
foreign key constraints 155
primary key columns 154
tables 153
**object tagging**
reference link 167
**offset storage technique 57**
**OLAP use cases 158**
**OLTP, versus OLAP database structures**
denormalized reporting analytics 160
departmental data 161
normalized self-service analytics 160
source layer 158, 159
staging layer 159, 160
**One Big Table (OBT) approach 149**
**Online Analytical Processing (OLAP) 10, 31**
**Online Transaction Processing (OLTP) 10, 31, 41**
**operational expenses (OPEX) 224**
**optionality 22**

# P

**performance**
considerations 189
monitoring 189
**permanent tables 51**

**physical model**
   deploying 174
   Entity-Relationship Diagrams
      (ERDs), creating 174, 175
**physical modeling 28, 29**
   logical modeling, expanding from 168
   superhero database 29, 30
   views 29
**physical tables 50, 51**
   defining 171
   Hybrid Unistore tables 52, 53
   naming 171
   permanent tables 51
   table constraints 172, 173
   table properties 171
   table types summary 53
   temporary tables 52
   transient tables 51
**Point-in-Time (PIT) table 264**
**primary key (PK) 115**
**primary keys 74**
   benefits 75
   business key 78
   duplicate values, avoiding 76
   granularity, determining 75
   join results, ensuring 76
   specifying 77
   surrogate key 78
   taxonomy 77
**production (prod) environment 161**

# Q

**quality assurance (QA) 161**
**query best practices, query profile**
   inefficient join order 191
   insufficient pruning 191
   join explosion 191
   queuing 190
   spilling 190
**query profile 190**
   query cache, using 192
   query considerations 192
**query results cache 44**

# R

**ragged hierarchy 256, 257**
**Raw Vault 264**
   building 266
   hubs 267
   links 268
   reference (ref) tables 270
   satellites 269, 270
**redundancy 135**
**reference (ref) tables 270**
**referential integrity 85**
**relational data**
   semi-structured data, converting to 245-251
**Relational Database Management**
   **System (RDBMS) 6**
**relational modeling**
   history 90, 91
**relational model (RM) 90**
   versus entity-relationship
      diagram (ERD) 92, 93
**relationship granularity 22**
**relationships 22**
   depicting 95
   transformations, shaping through 180-182
**relationships, logical modeling**
   cementing 122, 123
   inheritance 128-130
   many-to-many relationships 123-125
   weak entity 126-128

Index    291

**RELY**
  usage criteria  185-187
  used, for join elimination  184
**reverse balance fact table**
  building, with Snowflake Streams  227-229
**reverse balance table**
  differences  221
  versatile transactional fact table  220-222
**reverse engineering**  28, 114, 174
**row-level security**
  reference link  167

## S

**SAMPLE command**
  reference link  192
**satellites (sats)**  269
  hash diff  269
  hub PK column  269
  load date  269
  non-PK source attribute columns  270
  source system  270
  table naming convention  270
**schema-on-read**  7, 242-245
**second normal form (2NF)**  139, 140
**secret column type**  282
**semi-additive facts**  220
**semi-structured data**
  benefits  238
  converting, into relational data  245-251
  working with  239-241
**sequence**  78-80
**services layer, Snowflake architecture**  40
**set operator**  187
  INTERSECT  189
  MINUS/EXCEPT  189
  UNION  189
  UNION ALL  189

**shared-disk architecture**  37
**shared-nothing architecture**  37, 38
  Snowflake's solution  38
**Simple Storage Service (S3)**  167
**sixth normal form (6NF)**  134, 147, 148
**slightly ragged hierarchy**  255
  inapplicable values, marking  255
  lowest level, using  255
**slowly changing dimensions (SCDs)**  58, 219
  base table, setting  209, 210
  maintaining, in Snowflake  209
  Type 1-like performance in Type 2, achieving
    with Snowflake streams  212-214
  Type 1 table  210-212
  Type 3 tables update, maintaining  215
  types  200
**slowly changing dimensions (SCDs), types**
  overview  208
  scenario, example  200
  Type 0  201
  Type 1  201
  Type 2  202
  Type 3  202
  Type 4  203
  Type 5  204, 205
  Type 6  206
  Type 7  207, 208
**snapshot fact tables**  218
**Snowflake access controls**
  reference link  168
**Snowflake architecture**  39
  compute layer  40
  services layer  40
  storage layer  40
**Snowflake cloud architecture**
  considerations  166
  cost  166
  data quality and integrity  167

data security  167
  non-considerations  168
  performance  166
**Snowflake database**
  environments  161, 162
  managed schemas, organizing  157
  OLTP, versus OLAP database structures  158
  organizing  157
  schemas, organizing  157
**Snowflake Data Cloud  36**
**Snowflake Enterprise Edition**
  column-level security  167
  data classification  168
  object tagging  167
  row-level security  167
  tag-based masking policies  168
**Snowflake features  40**
  Hybrid Unistore tables  41
  semi-structured data  42
  structured data  42
  Time Travel  41
  unstructured data  42
  used, for maintaining fact tables  226, 227
  zero-copy cloning  41
**snowflake schema  274, 275**
**Snowflake Streams**
  used, for building reverse balance
      fact table  227-229
**Snowflake views  55**
  caching  55
  security  56
**Snowpipe instructions**
  reference link  239
**Social Security number (SSN)  12**
**software as a service (SaaS) model  36**
**stage metadata tables  54**
  directory tables  54
  external tables  54

**stages  47, 48**
  external stage  48
  internal stage  48
**star schema  274**
**storage layer, Snowflake architecture  40**
**streams  57**
  append/insert-only  58
  combining, with tasks  62
  loading from  58
  standard  58
**strong entity  94**
**subtypes  98**
  representing  99, 100
**suggested conventions  156**
**superkey  143**
**supertypes  128**
  representing  100
**surrogate key  78**
**synchronized modeling**
  benefit  101

# T

**table aliases  192**
**tables  49, 50**
  physical tables  50, 51
  stage metadata tables  54
**table types summary  53**
**tag-based masking policies**
  reference link  168
**tasks  60**
  combining, with streams  62
  creating  61
**technical documentation  282**
**temporary tables  51, 52**
**third normal form (3NF)  140**
**Time Travel  49**

# Index

traditional architectures  36
   shared-disk architecture  37
   shared-nothing architecture  37, 38
transaction fact tables  218
transformational modeling  30, 31
   best practices  193
   business requirements  193, 194
   relational model, reviewing  194, 195
   transformational model, building  195, 196
transformations
   shaping, through relationships  180-182
transient tables  51
transitive functional dependency (TFD)  141
Type 2 fact table
   time intervals, handling  233-236
Type-2 slowly changing dimensions (SCD)  107
Type 2 table
   facts, modifying  224-226

## U

ubiquitous modeling  18-20
Unified Modeling Language (UML)  19
update anomaly  135, 136
user acceptance testing (UAT)  161

## V

validity intervals  202
visual modeling conventions  93, 94
   conceptual context, adding to Snowflake architecture  98
   entities, depicting  94
   relationships, depicting  95

## W

warehouse cache  45
warehouses  40
weak entities  94, 126-128

# ‹packt›

packtpub.com

Subscribe to our online digital library for full access to over 7,000 books and videos, as well as industry leading tools to help you plan your personal development and advance your career. For more information, please visit our website.

## Why subscribe?

- Spend less time learning and more time coding with practical eBooks and Videos from over 4,000 industry professionals
- Improve your learning with Skill Plans built especially for you
- Get a free eBook or video every month
- Fully searchable for easy access to vital information
- Copy and paste, print, and bookmark content

Did you know that Packt offers eBook versions of every book published, with PDF and ePub files available? You can upgrade to the eBook version at packtpub.com and as a print book customer, you are entitled to a discount on the eBook copy. Get in touch with us at customercare@packtpub.com for more details.

At www.packtpub.com, you can also read a collection of free technical articles, sign up for a range of free newsletters, and receive exclusive discounts and offers on Packt books and eBooks.

# Other Books You May Enjoy

If you enjoyed this book, you may be interested in these other books by Packt:

**Data Modeling with Tableau**

Kirk Munroe

ISBN: 978-1-80324-802-8

- Showcase Tableau published data sources and embedded connections
- Apply Ask Data in data cataloging and natural language query
- Understand the features of Tableau Prep Builder with the help of hands-on exercises
- Model data with Tableau Desktop using examples
- Formulate a governed data strategy using Tableau Server and Tableau Cloud
- Optimize data models for Ask and Explain Data

## SQL Query Design Patterns and Best Practices

Steve Hughes, Dennis Neer, Dr. Ram Babu Singh, Shabbir H. Mala, Leslie Andrews, Chi Zhang

ISBN: 978-1-83763-328-9

- Build efficient queries by reducing the data being returned
- Manipulate your data and format it for easier consumption
- Form common table expressions and window functions to solve complex business issues
- Understand the impact of SQL security on your results
- Understand and use query plans to optimize your queries
- Understand the impact of indexes on your query performance and design
- Work with data lake data and JSON in SQL queries
- Organize your queries using Jupyter notebooks

## Packt is searching for authors like you

If you're interested in becoming an author for Packt, please visit `authors.packtpub.com` and apply today. We have worked with thousands of developers and tech professionals, just like you, to help them share their insight with the global tech community. You can make a general application, apply for a specific hot topic that we are recruiting an author for, or submit your own idea.

## Share Your Thoughts

Now you've finished *Data Modeling with Snowflake*, we'd love to hear your thoughts! Scan the QR code below to go straight to the Amazon review page for this book and share your feedback or leave a review on the site that you purchased it from.

`https://packt.link/r/1-837-63445-9`

Your review is important to us and the tech community and will help us make sure we're delivering excellent quality content.

# Download a free PDF copy of this book

Thanks for purchasing this book!

Do you like to read on the go but are unable to carry your print books everywhere? Is your eBook purchase not compatible with the device of your choice?

Don't worry, now with every Packt book you get a DRM-free PDF version of that book at no cost.

Read anywhere, any place, on any device. Search, copy, and paste code from your favorite technical books directly into your application.

The perks don't stop there, you can get exclusive access to discounts, newsletters, and great free content in your inbox daily

Follow these simple steps to get the benefits:

1. Scan the QR code or visit the link below

   https://packt.link/free-ebook/9781837634453

2. Submit your proof of purchase
3. That's it! We'll send your free PDF and other benefits to your email directly

Milton Keynes UK
Ingram Content Group UK Ltd.
UKHW051811230424
441624UK00057B/828